Foreign Direct Investment and Human Development

This book presents original research that examines the growth of international investment agreements as a means to attract foreign direct investment (FDI) and considers how this affects the ability of capital-importing countries to pursue their development goals. The hope of countries signing such treaties is that foreign capital will accelerate transfers of technologies, create employment, and benefit the local economy through various types of linkages. But do international investment agreements in fact succeed in attracting foreign direct investment? And if so, are the sovereignty costs involved worth paying? In particular, are these costs such that they risk undermining the very purpose of attracting investors, which is to promote human development in the host country? This book uses both economic and legal analysis to answer these questions that have become central to discussions on the impact of economic globalization on human rights and human development. It explains the dangers of developing countries being tempted to 'signal' their willingness to attract investors by providing far-reaching protections to investors' rights that would annul, or at least seriously diminish, the benefits they have a right to expect from the arrival of FDI. It examines a variety of tools that could be used, by capital-exporting countries and by capital-importing countries alike, to ensure that FDI works for development, and that international investment agreements contribute to that end.

This uniquely interdisciplinary study, located at the intersection of development economics, international investment law, and international human rights is written in accessible language, and should attract the attention of anyone who cares about the role of private investment in supporting the efforts of poor countries to climb up the development ladder.

Olivier De Schutter has been the UN Special Rapporteur on the right to food since May 2008. He is a Professor at the Catholic University of Louvain and at the College of Europe (Natolin). He is also a Member of the Global Law School Faculty at New York University and is Visiting Professor at Columbia University.

Johan Swinnen is Professor of Development Economics, KU Leuven and the Director of LICOS-Center for Institutions and Economic Performance, KU Leuven. He was Lead Economist at the World Bank in 2003 and 2004 and Economic Advisor to the European Commission, DG-Economic and Financial Affairs, from 1998 to 2001.

Jan Wouters holds the Jean Monnet Chair Ad Personam on EU and Global Governance at the KU Leuven, where he is Professor of International Law and International Organizations. He is the Director of the Leuven Centre for Global Governance Studies – Institute for International Law, University of Leuven, and chair of the Flemish Foreign Affairs Council.

"This interdisciplinary volume is a rare and laudable effort to increase our understanding of the complex interface between international investment law and economic development. It will be of great interest to anyone who seeks a better understanding of this important subject."

Karl P. Sauvant, Founding Executive Director of the Vale Columbia Center on Sustainable International Investment, Former Director, UNCTAD's Investment Division, and Founder and former Lead Author of UNCTAD's *World Investment Report*.

"This work, edited by an eminent economist and two leading international lawyers, contains pioneering studies on the economic, legal and policy conflicts behind inflexible investment protection through investment treaties and the consequent loss of regulatory power in the state to advance human development. The interplay between economics and law on these issues is thoroughly analyzed in the studies. The policy prescriptions advanced from the results of these studies indicate innovative means of shaping the law so that it achieves investment protection without sacrificing the law's essential function of promoting human rights and other values such as the protection of local communities. This neatly structured collection will set new standards for research in the international law on foreign investment which must avoid fragmentation and accommodate the areas of international law that promote human development."

M Sornarajah, CJ Koh Professor of Law at the National University of Singapore. Sornarajah is the author of *The International Law on Foreign Investment* (Cambridge, 3rd edn, 2010).

"This book brilliantly illuminates the complex relationship between foreign direct investment and human development. The volume shifts the debate away from increasing FDI to the tools home and host states can use to maximize the positive impacts of FDI. This innovative and interdisciplinary study of international investment agreements should be on the bookshelf of anyone interested in cutting-edge international investment law, economics and policy."

Andrew Newcombe, Associate Professor at the Faculty of Law, University of Victoria, editor of *Sustainable Development and World Investment Law*. Newcombe is the co-author of *Law and Practice of Investment Treaties: Standards of Treatment* (Kluwer, 2009) and co-editor of *Sustainable Development in World Investment Law* (Kluwer, 2011); founder and administrator of the international treaty arbitration website (italaw.com) (everyone working on international investment law knows and uses this website).

Foreign Direct Investment and Human Development

The law and economics of international investment agreements

Edited by
Olivier De Schutter, Johan Swinnen
and Jan Wouters

LONDON AND NEW YORK

First published 2013
by Routledge
2 Park Square, Milton Park, Abingdon, Oxon OX14 4RN

Simultaneously published in the USA and Canada
by Routledge
711 Third Avenue, New York, NY 10017

Routledge is an imprint of the Taylor & Francis Group, an informa business

British Library Cataloguing in Publication Data
A catalogue record for this book is available from the British Library

Library of Congress Cataloging in Publication Data
Foreign direct investment and human development : the law and
economics of international investment agreements / edited by Olivier
De Schutter, Johan F. Swinnen and Jan Wouters.
   p. cm.
ISBN 978-0-415-53547-2 (hardback)—ISBN 978-0-415-53548-9
(pbk.)—ISBN 978-0-203-07688-0 (e-book)   1. Investments,
Foreign—Law and legislation.   2. Law and economic
development.   3. Investments, Foreign (International
law)   4. Investments, Foreign—Economic aspects.   I. Schutter,
Olivier de. II. Swinnen, Johan F. M., 1962–   III. Wouters, Jan.
K3830.F67 2013
332.67'3—dc23   2012024082

ISBN: 978-0-415-53547-2 (hbk)
ISBN: 978-0-415-53548-9 (pbk)
ISBN: 978-0-203-07688-0 (ebk)

Typeset in Garamond
by RefineCatch Limited, Bungay, Suffolk

Printed and bound in the United States of America by Publishers Graphics,
LLC on sustainably sourced paper.

Contents

Illustrations

Figures

Tables

viii *Illustrations*

Contributors

Liesbeth Colen is a researcher at the LICOS-Center for Institutions and Economic Performance, KU Leuven, in Belgium. Her research focuses on the effects of globalization for developing countries, including such topics as foreign investments, food standards, changing gender roles and poverty dynamics.

Philip De Man is an FWO Aspirant with the Research Foundation – Flanders, associated with the Leuven Centre for Global Governance Studies of the University of Leuven, Belgium. His research interests include international space law, telecommunications law, the law of armed conflicts and international criminal law. He is currently preparing a PhD on the use of natural resources in outer space.

Olivier De Schutter, a professor at the University of Louvain (UCL), Belgium, and visiting professor at Columbia University, is the United Nations Special Rapporteur on the right to food. He has published widely on economic and social rights in the context of economic globalization, and on the relationship between human rights and governance.

Sanderijn Duquet is a doctoral researcher at the Leuven Centre for Global Governance Studies and the Institute for International Law (KU Leuven), Belgium. She is a research fellow of the Policy Research Centre for International Policy, International Entrepreneurship and Development Cooperation for the Flemish Government.

Andrea Guariso is a researcher at the LICOS-Center for Institutions and Economic Performance, KU Leuven, currently visiting IIES (Stockholm University). He graduated in Economics and Social Sciences at Bocconi University (Italy). His research interests are development economics and political economics.

Nicolas Hachez (LLM, NYU '07) is project manager and research fellow at the Leuven Centre for Global Governance Studies. His research interests and publications cover international investment law, business and human rights, and the study of global private regulation. Prior to joining the

Centre, he was an attorney at the Brussels office of an international law firm, where he practised EU law and international investment law.

Miet Maertens is assistant professor at the Department of Earth and Environmental Sciences, KU Leuven, Belgium. She holds a PhD from the Georg-August University in Goettingen, Germany. Her research focuses on food supply chains and sustainable agricultural development in developing regions. She has published on the implications of food supply chain innovations, agricultural technology adoption and sustainable land management.

Matthias Sant'Ana holds a law degree from the University of Brasilia, Brazil and master's degrees in International and European Law (DES, DEA), and in human rights law (DES) from the Université Catholique de Louvain, Belgium, and is currently preparing his doctoral dissertation at the Centre for the Philosophy of Law of the same university. He previously worked for the Inter-American Commission on Human Rights (Washington DC) and the Marangopoulos Foundation for Human Rights (Athens, Greece).

Johan Swinnen, currently Professor of Development Economics, KU Leuven and the Director of the LICOS-Center for Institutions and Economic Performance, KU Leuven, was Lead Economist at the World Bank in 2003 and 2004 and Economic Advisor to the European Commission, DG-Economic and Financial Affairs, from 1998 to 2001. He has published widely in the areas of agricultural economics and has been focusing in particular on investment in the agricultural sector, on food chains and on standards in the agrifood system.

Jan Wouters holds the Jean Monnet Chair Ad Personam on EU and Global Governance at the KU Leuven in Belgium, where he is Professor of International Law and International Organizations and Director of the Leuven Centre for Global Governance Studies – Institute for International Law, University of Leuven. He has written widely on a broad range of topics in the areas of international trade and investment law, EU law and public international law.

1 Introduction

Foreign direct investment and human development[1]

Olivier De Schutter, Johan Swinnen and Jan Wouters

1.1 Introduction

It is a widely held view that a positive relationship exists between the arrival of foreign direct investment (FDI) and development, and that attracting foreign capital is essential to developing countries in order to finance their growth and to improve their access to technologies. This consensus view is expressed, for instance, by the Partnership for Growth and Development adopted in 1996 at the Ninth United Nations Conference on Trade and Development,[2] which states that

> foreign direct investment can play a key role in the economic growth and development process. . . . FDI is now considered to be an instrument through which economies are being integrated at the level of production into the globalizing world economy by bringing a package of assets, including capital, technology, managerial capacities and skills, and access to foreign markets. It also stimulates technological capacity-building for production, innovation and entrepreneurship within the larger domestic economy through catalysing backward and forward linkages

However, beyond that general language, a number of questions remain. Perhaps the most widely studied of these concerns the relationship between the nature of the foreign investment considered and the impacts on development.[3] On the side of the investor, FDI may be undertaken in order to gain access to natural resources or other strategic assets, such as research and development capabilities; in order to reach new consumer markets; or in order to exploit locational

---

1 The authors thank Liesbeth Colen and Nicolas Hachez for useful comments on an earlier version of the chapter.
2 UN doc. No. TD/378.
3 See in particular B. Sharma and A. Gani, 'The Effects of Foreign Direct Investment on Human Development', *Global Economy Journal* 4(2), 2004, Article 9; P. Nunnenkamp, 'To What Extent Can Foreign Direct Investment Help Achieve International Development Goals?' *The World Economy* 27(5), 2004, 657–677.

comparative advantage.[4] The investment can take the form of greenfield investment, thus contributing directly to capital formation and enhancing local productive capacity, or simply lead to a transfer of ownership by mergers and acquisitions of local firms by foreign investors. Both the improved access to global markets (due to the trade effects of FDI) and the linkages with the local economy (upstream and downstream from the investment itself) may diverge widely depending on which of these objectives of FDI is primarily pursued by the investor and which form, in turn, the investment strategy takes. Host countries' ability to capture the benefits from increased FDI depends on various factors, such as their general level of technological development, on existing macro-economic conditions, as well as on their absorptive capacity. In Chapter 3 of this volume, Colen et al. note, for instance, that developed economies generally benefit from the presence of foreign companies through the spillover effects of such presence to other companies, or through increased supply of products and increased demand for inputs and employment. At the same time, competing domestic firms may be hurt by increased competition. While FDI can contribute importantly to growth and poverty reduction in developing countries, it is important to acknowledge the complexity of the relationship between FDI and development when attracting foreign investors. Certain types of FDI create jobs for the poorest, yet other types of investment may require a minimum level of technology or education in order to learn from foreign companies, engage in their networks and take up the employment they provide.

1.2 The focus of this volume

In this volume, we pose another set of questions, which relate to the different tools that countries may rely on in order to attract FDI. Particularly throughout the 1990s, one important strategy relied on by countries lacking capital or seeking to improve their access to technology by attracting investors has been to conclude international investment agreements (IIAs).[5] These agreements may be bilateral or multilateral, and they can cover investment only or, as in the earlier 'Friendship, Commerce and Navigation' agreements, be part of broader trade or cooperation agreements. Although they differ in these respects, however, investment agreements present a striking similarity across regions and negotiation fora. Such treaties usually include provisions relating to the

---

4 For further explanations of these different motivations, see in this volume Chapter 3, section 3.2.4; and Chapter 4, section 4.2.3.

5 While the first bilateral investment treaty was concluded between Pakistan and Germany in 1959, the growth in BITs was especially remarkable during the 1980s and 1990s. In 1979 there were 179 BITs. The figure grew to 2,807 in 2010, see UNCTAD, 'Non-Equity Modes of Production and Development – World Investment Report 2011', 2011, p. 100. For a detailed discussion of the growth of investment treaties in this volume, see Chapter 4, section 4.4.

scope and definition of foreign investment; admission and establishment; national treatment in the post-establishment phase (a guarantee of non-discrimination against the investor of the other party established in one party); the most favoured nation clause (ensuring that the investor of the other party will benefit from the same treatment as any other foreign investor); fair and equitable treatment, including a protection from expropriation; guarantees of free transfers of funds and repatriation of capitals and profits; and dispute-settlement provisions (State–State and State–investor).

But how successful was such a strategy? Did it serve, indeed, to attract investment, if such was the primary aim of concluding investment agreements?[6] And even if the strategy did succeed in that respect, how can we assess the 'sovereignty costs', or the loss of 'policy space',[7] associated with the conclusion of IIAs? If countries compete for the arrival of foreign investment and if the conclusion of such agreements is one tool they rely on to gain an advantage over potential competitors, does this entail the risk that the concessions they make will go too far, for example by renouncing the possibility of imposing performance requirements on the investor (though this could arguably strengthen the linkages with the host economy), by guaranteeing a freeze in the regulatory framework applicable to the investment, or by authorizing transfer pricing between the local subsidiary and the foreign-based parent, thereby reducing the fiscal revenues that could be gained from the arrival of the foreign investor? By concluding an investment agreement, a country signals its intention to respect the rights of investors and to create a legal and policy framework that will provide the kind of stability they usually expect. But could it be that, while it may be understandable for each country considered individually to seek to conclude IIAs with a view to attracting investors, the

6 On this question, see Jeswald W. Salacuse and Nicholas P. Sullivan, 'Do BITs Really Work?: An Evaluation of Bilateral Investment Treaties and Their Grand Bargain', *Harvard International Law Journal* 46, 2005, 67; and Jason Webb Jackee, 'Do Bilateral Investment Treaties Promote Foreign Direct Investment? Some Hints from Alternative Evidence', *Virginia Journal of International Law* 51, 2011, 397. See also United Nations Conference on Trade and Development, *The Role of International Investment Agreements in attracting Foreign Direct Investment to Developing Countries*, UN doc. UNCTAD/DIAE/IA/2009/5 (2009).

7 On this notion, see Jörg Mayer, 'Policy Space: What, For What, and Where?', 27 *Development Policy Review* 373–395, 2009 (originally presented as UNCTAD Discussion Paper No. 191, UN Doc. UNCTAD/OSG/DP/2008/6 (October 2008)). Mayer distinguishes '*de jure* sovereignty, which involves the formal authority of national policy-makers over policy instruments, and *de facto* control, which involves the ability of national policy-makers to effectively influence specific targets through the skilful use of policy instruments' and he defines national policy space as 'the combination of *de jure* policy sovereignty and *de facto* national policy autonomy' (at p. 376). This notion was pioneered by Richard N. Cooper, *The Economics of Interdependence: Economic Policy in the Atlantic Community*, New York: McGraw Hill for the Council on Foreign Relations, 1968. See also Mary Hallward-Driemeier, *Do Bilateral Investment Treaties Attract FDI? Only a bit . . . and they could bite*, World Bank Policy Research Paper WPS 3121, 2003, World Bank: Washington DC.

result is collectively sub-optimal, as the IIAs lose their 'signalling' function once they come to be generalized?[8]

We concentrate specifically on the relationship between the role of IIAs in attracting FDI, and the contribution of FDI to human development. Economic growth, which is usually associated with FDI inflows, has lost its privileged position in debates about development since the mid-1980s, when the traditional focus on the expansion of gross national product or gross domestic product per capita shifted to a greater preoccupation with non purely economic values, encapsulated in the notion of human development understood as the expansion of human freedoms.[9] One indicator of this shift was the adoption, in 1986, by the United Nations General Assembly, of the Declaration on the Right to Development, which defines development as a 'comprehensive economic, social, cultural and political process, which aims at the constant improvement of the well-being of the entire population and of all individuals on the basis of their active, free and meaningful participation in development and in the fair distribution of benefits resulting therefrom', and in which 'all human rights and fundamental freedoms can be fully realized'.[10] This shift was further confirmed by the introduction of the Human Development Index (HDI) by the United Nations Development Programme (UNDP) in 1990, which for the first time[11] provided a clear, and operational alternative to the measures of GNP or GDP per capita.[12] Considering cross-country data availability and pertinence, the UNDP selected three basic dimensions of development to be the main focus of its analysis of development: longevity, as a proxy for health; adult literacy, and later mean years of school enrolment, as proxies for education and learning; and per capita income, or 'command over resources needed for a decent living'. The HDI, an indicator combining these three components, relied on a multidimensional definition of development, and was seen as capable of bridging the gap between academia and practical policy-making.[13] The measure of HDI has evolved in many ways since it was first introduced more than twenty years ago.[14] But its main importance lies not in

---

8 See, following this line of argument, Andrew T. Guzman, 'Why LDCs Sign Treaties That Hurt Them: Explaining the Popularity of Bilateral Investment Treaties', 38 *Virginia Journal of International Law*, 1998, 639–688; Zachary Elkins, Andrew T. Guzman and Beth A. Simmons, 'Competing for Capital: The Diffusion of Bilateral Investment Treaties, 1960–2000', *International Organization* 60, 2006, 811–846.

9 Amartya K. Sen, *Development as Freedom*, 1999, New York: Alfred A. Knopf.

10 Declaration on the Right to Development, adopted by the UN General Assembly in Res. 41/128 of 4 December 1986 (A/RES/41/128), Preamble and Art. 1.

11 Prior to the HDI, both the 'basic needs' and the Physical Quality of Life Index (PQLI) approaches relied heavily on social indicators.

12 UNDP, *Human Development Report: Concept and Measurement of Human Development*, 1990, United Nations, New York.

13 Desmond McNeill, 'Human Development': 'The Power of the Idea', *Journal of Human Development*, vol. 8, No. 1, March 2007, pp. 5–22, at p. 13.

14 See O. De Schutter, Jan Wouters, Philip De Man, Nicolas Hachez and Matthias Sant'Ana, 'Foreign Direct Investment, Human Development, and Human Rights: Framing the Issues', *Human Rights and International Legal Discourse* 3(2), 2009, 137–176.

the precise methodology it recommends, but in the changed view of development that it signalled.

In recent years, doubts have been expressed with an increased frequency about the adequacy of a strategy relying on the conclusion of IIAs in order to attract foreign investors, in part because the ability of IIAs to bring about increased investment flows has been questioned, and in part because economic growth, the end of past development efforts, is now considered merely a means towards the broader and richer objective of human development. While the flows of FDI have increased significantly over the years, from 55 billion US dollars of yearly flows of FDI in 1980 to 1,306 billion US dollars in 2006,[15] the impacts of investment agreements committing host countries to guaranteeing certain forms of treatment to the foreign investor have also become more visible. The Outcome Document on the implementation of the Millennium Development Goals (MDGs) that the General Assembly adopted by consensus on 22 September 2010 notes in this regard:

> We recognize that the increasing interdependence of national economies in a globalizing world and the emergence of rules-based regimes for international economic relations have meant that the space for national economic policy, that is, the scope for domestic policies, especially in the areas of trade, investment and international development, is now often framed by international disciplines, commitments and global market considerations. It is for each Government to evaluate the trade-off between the benefits of accepting international rules and commitments and the constraints posed by the loss of policy space.[16]

The wording chosen by the Outcome Document is cautious, and sounds almost like a warning addressed to States. It is, at least, far removed from the much more optimistic mood of the 1990s. What has happened in the meantime? In part, this change of attitude may be attributable to the fact that the IIAs concluded in large numbers in the late 1980s and in the 1990s have not always fulfilled their promises. Instead, governments may have gradually come to the realization that the agreements were severely imbalanced in favour of investors' rights. Over the past ten years, treaty-based investor–State dispute-settlement cases have multiplied: by the end of 2011, there were 450 known disputes,[17] 220 of which had been concluded. Of this total, approximately 40 per cent were decided in favour of the State and approximately 30 per cent in favour of the

---

15 The steady increase of FDI flows was interrupted between 2001 and 2003, following the economic downturn during that period. This slowing down of FDI affected developed economies far more significantly than developing economies, however. For a more detailed discussion of these trends, see Chapter 3.

16 UNGA Res. A/65/L.1, 'Keeping the promise: united to achieve the Millennium Development Goals', para. 37.

17 In the absence of a public registry of claims in most arbitration fora, the total number of investor–State disputes under existing investment treaties may in fact be much higher.

investor, the remaining disputes being settled.[18] Altogether, 89 countries have been defendants in such claims, including 55 developing countries: the States facing the largest number of claims are Argentina (51 cases, mostly related to the privatization of the water services), Venezuela (25), Ecuador (23) and Mexico (19). Some of these claims relate to issues that raise important public interest concerns. In 2010 for instance, invoking the Australia–Hong Kong bilateral investment treaty (BIT), tobacco company Philip Morris filed a claim against Australia challenging measures that its government had adopted in order to protect public health and to discharge its obligations under the World Health Organization Framework Convention on Tobacco Control (FCTC).[19] A Swedish investor operating nuclear plants in Germany challenged the decision by that country to phase out its production of energy from nuclear power, following the Fukushima catastrophe in Japan. In addition, some provisions of investment treaties remain subject to widely diverging interpretations by arbitrators, creating the risk of a 'chilling effect' on the host State seeking to adopt certain regulations. That is the case, in particular, for the clause referring to the 'fair and equitable treatment' that should benefit the investor,[20] as well as to the significance of a necessity clause included in an investment treaty.[21]

18 For this estimate and the information contained in this paragraph, see United Nations Conference on Trade and Development, *IIA Issues Note – Latest Developments in Investor-State Dispute Settlement*, No. 1, April 2012.

19 For a similar claim filed by the same multinational group against Uruguay in March 2010, see *Philip Morris Brand Sàrl (Switzerland), Philip Morris Products S.A. (Switzerland) and Abal Hermanos S.A. (Uruguay) v Oriental Republic of Uruguay* (ICSID Case No. ARB/10/7).

20 See United Nations Conference on Trade and Development, *Fair and Equitable Treatment*, UNCTAD Series on Issues in International Investment Agreements II, UN doc. UNCTAD/DIAE/IA/2011/5, New York and Geneva, 2012. As recently as 2009, an author could note of the 'fair and equitable treatment' standard, that it 'does not have a consolidated and conventional core meaning as such nor is there a definition of the standard that can be applied easily. So far it is only settled that fair and equitable treatment constitutes a standard that is independent from national legal order and is not limited to restricting bad faith conduct of host States. Apart from this very minimal concept, however, its exact normative content is contested, hardly substantiated by State practice, and impossible to narrow down by traditional means of interpretive syllogism' (S. Schill, *The Multilateralization of International Investment Law*, 2009, Cambridge: Cambridge University Press, p. 263). See also on this notion K. Vandevelde, 'A Unified Theory of Fair and Equitable Treatment', *New York University Journal of International Law and Policy*, 43(1), 2010, 43–106.

21 For instance, in *El Paso v Argentina*, the defending State invoked Article XI of the Argentina–United States BIT, which includes a necessity clause, explaining that it had been forced by circumstances (an extreme financial and economic crisis) to resort to the measures that led to the complaint. The majority disagreed, noting the responsibility of the Argentine government in the management of its public debt (*El Paso Energy International Company v Argentina*, ICSID Case No. ARB/03/15, Award, 31 October 2011, para. 656); one arbitrator however, Ms Brigitte Stern, expressed her concern that the view of the majority was overestimating the ability of the State to control such factors that may have external causes or result from developments in the market that a Government does not control (para. 667). On the suitability of the arbitral model for settling investor–State

To a growing number of governments, the lesson from the past fifteen years is that there are real costs to the conclusion of IIAs, that may or may not be fully compensated by the expected gains. Doubts are expressed as to whether countries should bind themselves through IIAs, when they risk losing too much 'policy space' – in particular, the ability to adopt certain regulations in the public interest or to impose on the investors a more equitable share of the value created by the investment. Indeed, even where the arrival of FDI is beneficial for economic growth and poverty reduction of the host country in aggregate terms, the debate has devoted increasing attention to the opportunities and threats it may pose to the well-being and human rights of more vulnerable groups of the population. There is general agreement that poor countries require more, rather than less, FDI in order to support their development. But the question that now emerges is under which conditions FDI should be encouraged, towards which ends it should be channelled, and which regulatory framework should be imposed in order to ensure that it effectively contributes to human development. The question in the past was how to increase the attractiveness of one jurisdiction to foreign investors, and the conclusion of IIAs was seen as an obvious means towards that end. The question is now how to align the incentives in order to maximize the positive impacts of FDI while minimizing the potential negative impacts. Both the capital-receiving (host) country and the capital-exporting (home) country may have a role to play in this regard. It is the aim of this book to examine the nature of the challenge they face, and the tools that they can use to achieve this balance.

1.3 An overview

Our contribution to this debate is the outcome of a multi-year research project[22] that was conducted jointly by lawyers and economists, from the University of Louvain's Centre for Legal Philosophy (CPDR), and from the University of Leuven's Institute for International Law (IIL) and Centre for Institutions and Economic Performances (LICOS). We proceed in four steps. First, we provide a general description of how international investment agreements have evolved, which legal regime they establish between investors, States of origin, and host States, and whether the proliferation of IIAs, often with very similar provisions, are formative of customary international law. The following chapter (Chapter 2), by Jan Wouters, Sanderijn Duquet and Nicolas Hachez, provides this assessment. It documents, in particular, how both arbitral practice and the

---

disputes involving issues of general interest, see generally Nicolas Hachez and Jan Wouters, 'International Investment Dispute Settlement in the 21st Century: Does the Preservation of the Public Interest Require an Alternative to the Arbitral Model?', forthcoming in Freya Baetens (ed.), *Investment Law Within International Law: An Integrationist Perspective*, 2012, Cambridge: Cambridge University Press.

22 Funded by the Interuniversity Attraction Poles Programme, Belgian State, Belgian Science Policy – Project IAP VI/06 (2007–2011).

IIAs themselves, in the way they are formulated, have gradually rebalanced the respective rights and duties of the parties to such treaties. This contribution highlights the emerging 'new generation' of BITs which, the authors cautiously conclude, may thus be indicating a progressive convergence in the interests of home and host States. Documenting the evolution of the most important clauses in the new generation of BITs – the fair and equitable treatment, expropriation, most favoured nation and national treatment standards – this chapter analyses the extent to which this renovated approach perhaps moves us closer to consistent practice coupled with *opinio juris* – in other terms, to the formation of a new regime of customary international law. It is following this mapping of the state of development of international law that the following chapters address what are the impacts of FDI on human development, and how States and other actors could maximize the positive impacts while reducing the risks FDI may entail in the host country.

1.3.1 *The economic consequences of foreign direct investment*

The second section of the book examines the economic consequences of FDI. It is composed of three chapters. In chapter 3, Liesbeth Colen, Miet Maertens and Johan Swinnen review the theoretical arguments and the empirical evidence of the impact of FDI on developing countries' economic growth and overall development. Theoretical arguments predict FDI to enhance growth by bringing capital and knowledge to the host country, and by creating linkages with domestic firms. Empirically, it remains difficult to identify the causality in the relation between FDI and growth, but micro-level studies provide strong evidence that FDI enhances growth through horizontal and (mainly) vertical spillovers, as the technology and know-how imported by the investor flow into the host economy. Through its effect on growth, but also through more direct channels, FDI is likely to contribute to poverty reduction, although inequality might increase in the short run. The importance of these different effects, and the ability of host country policies to cushion the impacts of transition, are likely to depend on the type of FDI, the economic sector and the absorptive capacity of the host economy. With respect to non-economic indicators of human development – human rights, labour standards, gender, the environment – a number of cases of foreign investors abusing lax host-country regulations have gained wide public attention. However, it would be a mistake to generalize this as applicable to FDI as a whole. In fact, most studies find that FDI creates a 'climb to the top' rather than a 'race to the bottom'. The authors acknowledge that FDI is not a simple solution for enhancing growth. However, when the conditions are right, it can be an important engine for growth and human development.

Chapter 4 looks at the use of international investment agreements (IIAs) as a tool to attract FDI: written again from an economists' perspective, it asks whether such a tool works. Liesbeth Colen, Miet Maertens and Johan Swinnen examine the literature concerning the determinants of FDI flows to developing countries, and they provide a detailed discussion of the role of international investment treaties. They find that a very large number of empirical studies have analysed what determines the decision of whether and where to invest. Following the typology used by Dunning and UNCTAD,[23] they divide host country determinants of FDI into (i) the legal and policy framework, (ii) the economic determinants and (iii) business facilitation. The legal and policy framework includes the treatment guaranteed to foreign investors both under domestic legislation and under investment treaties. The general sequence is that once a minimum legal and policy framework is established, investors will enter the country if there are economic incentives to do so, and this may be further encouraged by measures intended to improve the business climate: it would appear that, while in certain respects a necessary condition for FDI inflows, a legal and policy framework open to FDI is not necessarily a sufficient condition where other determinants are not present. The borders between these various determinants are fluid, however. For instance, although part of the legal and policy framework, investment agreements may provide certain financial incentives, for instance fiscal advantages or the guarantee that the profits may be repatriated; and in the name of creating a friendly business climate, investment promotion agencies may lower entry costs or subsidize the foreign investor. In addition, the quality of institutions – effective measures to reduce corruption and to ensure the adequate delivery of public goods and the maintenance of infrastructure – plays an important role in the investment decision at all three levels. Nevertheless, this typology is useful in ranking the different considerations that guide the choice of the investor whether to enter a country or not.

The empirical studies examined in Chapter 4 find that the major determinants of FDI are economic factors such as market size and trade openness, as measured by exports and imports in relation to total GDP, with a greater emphasis on the latter determinant in recent years as a result of globalization and the development of global supply chains. However, these determinants may not be equally important all over the world. For example, in Sub-Saharan Africa increased trade openness did not spur FDI as much as it did in other regions. For other variables there is less consensus in the literature. In general, the studies find that economic factors and policies such as market size, skilled labour and trade policies are more important for the locational decision of foreign investment than the legal structure such as the protection of investors' rights and the ability to avoid double taxation through treaties. Therefore, the empirical literature confirms the suspicion towards investment treaties that was expressed

---

23 UNCTAD, 1998. *World Investment Report 1998: Trends and Determinants*, United Nations Publications, New York and Geneva; J.H. Dunning, 'Toward an Eclectic Theory of International Production: Some Empirical Tests', *Journal of International Business Studies* 11, 1980, 9–31; J.H. Dunning, 'Determinants of foreign direct investment: globalization induced changes and the role of FDI policies', World Investment Prospects, 2002, Economist Intelligence Unit, London.

earlier by some in the legal literature:[24] there is only weak evidence that the conclusion of IIAs has more than a marginal impact on FDI inflows, and where it does seem to have some effect it is mostly as a substitute for poor institutional quality, particularly in Sub-Saharan African countries[25] or in transition economies swiftly moving towards open-market policies.[26] While there exists a positive correlation between the conclusion of IIAs and the presence of FDI,[27] the direction of causality is often far from clear: historically, it has not been unusual for IIAs to be concluded in order to protect already established investors, sometimes at their very request, and some empirical studies suggest that the positive correlation is mostly explained by increased FDI flows accelerating FDI.[28]

Because FDI inflows can take a number of different forms that will contribute more or less significantly to human development in the host country, it matters considerably which type of investment is encouraged by the conclusion of IIAs. Chapter 5, by Liesbeth Colen and Andrea Guariso, presents original research that, for the first time, studies the potentially heterogeneous effect of IIAs on different sectors of FDI. They test the hypothesis that if BITs attract FDI by reducing the risk of expropriation, the effect on FDI is likely to be stronger for those sectors in which foreign investment involves large primary investment costs and is susceptible to expropriation. Indeed, they note, investors in these sectors may have a higher demand for investment protection and therefore react more to policy measures providing such protection. It is evident that BITs are well tailored to reassuring investors, particularly in the extractive industry sector and the sector of basic utilities provision such as water and electricity, because of the importance of sunk investments and the long lifetime of such investments, leading to what the authors call a 'time inconsistency' problem: while the country where the resources are located needs to attract investors who have the capital and technology[29] that allow them to exploit such resources,

---

24 See, notably, M. Sornarajah, 'State responsibility and bilateral investment treaties', *Journal of World Trade Law* 20, 1986, 79–98; and, more recently, Jackee, 'Do Bilateral Investment Treaties Promote Foreign Direct Investment?', op. cit.

25 However, institutional quality in general and the conclusion of IIAs are rather strongly correlated. This would suggest that, rather than a substitute for poor institutional quality, IIAs are part of a broader strengthening of the legal and policy framework that serves to reassure investors, with a stronger impact in a poorer institutional setting.

26 As illustrated in Chapter 5 of this volume by Colen and Guariso, who find a positive correlation between FDI inflows and the growth of BITs in twelve post-Soviet Union Central and Eastern European countries during the transition phase (1995 to 2009).

27 M. Busse, J. Königer and P. Nunnenkamp, 'FDI Promotion through Bilateral Investment Treaties: More than a Bit?' *Review of World Economics*, 146, 2010, 147–177.

28 E. Aisbett, 'Bilateral Investment Treaties and Foreign Direct Investment: Correlation versus causation', 2009, in K.P. Sauvant and L.E. Sachs (eds), *The Effect of Treaties on Foreign Direct Investment: Bilateral Investment Treaties, Double Taxation Treaties, and Investment Flows*, Oxford: Oxford University Press.

29 This refers to infrastructure technology, rather than managerial skills, which play a more important role in the services industry.

once the investments are made the host country government may be tempted to breach its promises and extract rents or expropriate property or funds, especially following a change in government. It is politically tempting for the host government to invoke sovereignty reasons (and, even more precisely, the permanent sovereignty of its people over natural resources) or the need to provide basic services such as water and electricity to its population at an affordable price, in order to justify nationalization measures or the forced negotiation of the terms of agreement with the foreign investors present. It is therefore unsurprising that some studies show that this sector is perhaps the most susceptible to expropriation, causing serious economic losses to the investor.[30]

The empirical study presented, which takes a sample of twelve countries in Central and Eastern Europe and the former Soviet Union following their transition to an open market economy,[31] appears to confirm that suspicion. Colen and Guariso find that FDI in the mining sector is especially attracted by new BITs. However, the specialization of countries into the exploitation of natural resources – particularly non-renewable natural resources – entails a number of challenges, related both to the ability of the country concerned to move beyond the export of raw materials and to revenue-sharing, or larger governance issues.[32] The results from this cross-country comparison therefore lead the authors to challenge the idea that BITs are a desirable policy tool to enhance development through increased foreign investments. Although one should be careful in deriving general conclusions from one study, the results suggest that BITs may be most effective at attracting investors precisely in those sectors that are the most controversial, and where the policy space for host governments requires most to be protected, particularly in their ability to impose certain performance requirements or certain types of revenue sharing. The authors conclude that their results suggest that BITs 'do not attract the most development-enhancing FDI', since investments in the mining sector 'often have limited linkages with the local economy, create little knowledge transfer and are likely to repatriate the majority of profits made'. At the same time, we cannot ignore the reality of the dilemmas that governments of resource-rich but capital-poor countries face: typically, large-scale extractive projects are those that require the technology and scale of investment that they do not possess domestically; and while host government agreements (HGAs),

---

30 C. Hajzler, 'Expropriation of Foreign Direct Investments: Sectoral Patterns from 1993 to 2006', *University of Otago Economic Discussion Papers* No. 1011, 2010.

31 One advantage of this choice is that the sub-set of countries concerned have entered into a large number of investment agreements since the early 1990s, with 800 BITs entering into force between 1990 and 2009: thus the study, while geographically and temporally confined, provides an exceptionally useful ground for empirical study on the impacts of such agreements on the type of FDI attracted.

32 On the 'resource curse', see in particular M. Humphreys, J. Sachs, and J. Stiglitz (eds), *Escaping the Resource Curse*, New York: Columbia University Press, 2007, and in this volume, Chapter 6, section 6.1.

directly concluded between the host country government and the individual investor for a particular investment project, may to a certain extent substitute for IIAs, the bargaining position of the host government is not necessarily stronger in the negotiation of such individualized, project-level HGAs.

1.3.2 The role of the capital-importing State in channelling foreign direct investment towards development ends

The final section of the book draws some lessons, from the perspective of the policy-maker, from the conclusions arrived at in the preceding chapters. It focuses on the negotiation and the regulation of FDI, asking how investment agreements should be negotiated and which measures should be adopted to preserve the necessary policy space for host countries. It is composed of four chapters. In chapter 6, Olivier De Schutter examines how institutions and procedures established at the national level could be improved in order to ensure that investment agreements work for the benefit of human development, as defined in this volume. It first recalls the framework set by international human rights law, and the duties this body of law imposes on all organs of the State – including the Executive, but also parliaments and courts – to ensure that investment agreements shall not displace human rights obligations or otherwise discourage the State from progressively implementing human rights. This presentation distinguishes between two levels of agreements, and it discusses the different initiatives that have recently sought to reconcile investment liberalization with obligations imposed under human rights law. First, bilateral or multilateral agreements may be concluded in order to attract investors, by guaranteeing the investors of other parties certain forms of protection, which either confirm existing customary international law or go beyond it: in this volume, these have been referred to, generically, as international investment agreements (IIAs). Guiding principles have been proposed in this regard to the United Nations Human Rights Council in March 2012, in order to ensure that the negotiation and conclusion of such treaties shall not undermine human rights, defining a methodology for human rights impact assessments of investment agreements.[33] In addition to IIAs however, project-level investment agreements may be concluded, particularly for larger-scale investment projects that have a long duration, between the individual investor and the host government. Such agreements are often called host government agreements (HGAs): they are internationalized contracts, rather than international treaties. On the issue of HGAs also, a set of Principles for Responsible Contracts to favour the integration of the management of human rights risks in the negotiations between governments and investors has recently

---

33 See 'Guiding Principles on Human Rights Impact Assessments of Trade and Investment Agreements, Report of the Special Rapporteur on the right to food: Addendum', UN doc. A/HRC/19/59/Add.5 (19 December 2011).

been presented to the Human Rights Council;[34] like the above-mentioned methodology on human rights impact assessments, the presentation of these Principles demonstrates the growing interest for bridging the areas of investment and human rights, in part in order to ensure that the race to attract investors will not result in the host State neglecting its duties to protect and fulfil the human rights of its population.

Chapter 6 addresses the dilemmas we face when we attempt to bridge these two areas of international law, and to ensure that States remain faithful to their human rights duties while negotiating investment agreements. It discusses in particular some of the difficulties involved in managing tradeoffs, in the typical case where the arrival of FDI creates both winners and losers. It explains why cost–benefit analysis is generally inappropriate to address the question of tradeoffs, and why a procedural approach may be more desirable, emphasizing participation and inclusive deliberative processes rather than top-down approaches of a more technocratic brand. However, even while it looks attractive in principle, a participatory approach to addressing the tensions between investment agreements and human rights also raises a number of questions, particularly as regards project-level agreements that take the form of HGAs between the investor and the host State. How, for instance, should we consider the relationship between a substantive approach to assessing the adequacy of a particular HGA in the context of specific investment projects, and a procedural approach emphasizing participation? A substantive approach is one in which whether or not an investment should take place is decided on the basis of its contribution to human development as measured from a pre-defined scale, based on indicators and methodologies that are set not by the communities affected themselves, but by experts or under a pre-defined regulatory framework, and in principle on a uniform basis rather than on a project-specific basis. A procedural approach, by contrast, gives more weight to the result of deliberative processes within the communities affected. On this point, the chapter concludes that each of these approaches presents weaknesses, and that only by combining the two approaches can we arrive at satisfactory results: it is only through this combination, it suggests, that the notion of 'free, prior and informed consent' of the communities affected by the investment project can become both meaningful and workable.[35]

34 Addendum to the Report of the Special Representative of the Secretary-General on the Issue of Human Rights and Transnational Corporations and Other Business Enterprises, J. Ruggie – 'Principles for Responsible Contracts: Integrating the Management of Human Rights Risks into State-Investor Contract Negotiations: Guidance for Negotiators', 25 May 2011, UN Doc. A/HRC/17/31/Add.3.
35 'Free, prior and informed consent' is the generally accepted standard of agreement to be given by indigenous peoples when affected by, notably, investment projects. This standard was affirmed in a number of international instruments of a declaratory as well as binding nature. See e.g. UN General Assembly, 'United Nations Declaration on the Rights of Indigenous Peoples', Resolution 61/295, 13 September 2007, UN Doc. No. A/61/L.67 and Add.1; ILO Convention No. 169 concerning Indigenous and Tribal Peoples in

Chapter 6 also examines another question that arises in the context of project-specific assessments, concerning the institutional division of labour between the central authorities and the local communities more directly affected by the investment project. It emphasizes the complementarity of the processes that take place at the national level (and which determine the investment policy of the country as a whole) and the processes that take place at the local level (involving the local communities directly affected by the arrival of investment). Decisions cannot be made centrally without ensuring that the rights of the local communities are fully respected, and these communities have a right to participate in the decision-making process, to seek and obtain information, and to have access to remedies against any decision affecting them. But it is argued at the same time that, for local processes to be effective – i.e., for the local communities directly affected by the investment project to be able to truly express their preferences – a framework for investment is required at the national level.

Such a framework is first of all required for the obvious reason that the rights of the local communities must be effectively protected in order for these communities to be in a position that allows them to exercise effective bargaining power in their discussions with the investor. But in addition, the choices made by one community cannot be analysed or understood in isolation from the choices made by the other communities in the same jurisdiction. This is the case because the benefits linked to the arrival of investment primarily accrue to the region where the investment is located, which gains disproportionately in comparison to the other regions. This results in a collective action problem: while it may be rational for each region acting in isolation to agree to conditions that are less demanding for the investor (as each region may fear that the investor will otherwise relocate in another region, which in turn would attract more resources thanks to the presence of the investor), it is collectively sub-optimal for all regions not to impose more demanding conditions on the investor, in particular in order to maximize the multiplier effects on the local economy. This highlights the importance of a framework for investment set at the national level, rather than only at the level of each constituent unit within States, in order to ensure that the benefits of investment are maximized and the potential risks or costs minimized. The objective of such a framework, it is argued, should not only be to ensure that each local community may effectively participate in determining the conditions under which the investment may

Independent Countries, agreed in Geneva on 27 June 1989, effective 5 September 1991 (see particularly Arts 6.2 (in general) and 16.2 (in the specific context of relocations)). On the concrete application of this standard by the European Investment Bank, see this volume, Chapter 9, section 9.4.2. An important debate has now been launched in the international community as to whether the criterion of 'free, prior and informed consent' should extend beyond indigenous peoples to all communities who depend for their livelihoods on access to natural resources: see O. De Schutter, 'The Green Rush: The Race for Farmland and the Rights of Land Users', *Harvard International Law Journal*, 52(2), 2011, 503–559, particularly pp. 535–537.

proceed insofar as it is affected; it should also be to ensure that not all the benefits are captured by the local community, but that other parts of the country may reap part of the benefits. Such a framework should be explicitly conceived as redistributive: it should promote a more inclusive national economy rather than the formation of 'clusters' of prosperity co-existing with islands of poverty and under-development, thus at the same time removing an incentive for different regions in the country to pursue beggar-thy-neighbour policies that, ultimately, are self-defeating for the population as a whole.

1.3.3 *The role of the capital-exporting State in controlling investment abroad*

The following chapters of the final part of the book move further in identifying the tools through which the current situation could be improved, in order to support the efforts of host countries seeking to channel FDI towards the ends most conducive to human development. It may be worth noting at this juncture that States have a duty under international law to protect human rights, even outside their national territory, to the extent that they can influence situations that may lead to human rights violations. That applies, in particular, to the home States of transnational corporations, which deploy activities in other States than their State of origin.[36] In Article 56 of the Charter of the United Nations, 'All Members pledge themselves to take joint and separate action in cooperation with the Organization . . .' to achieve purposes set out in Article 55 of the Charter. Such purposes include: 'universal respect for, and observance of, human rights and fundamental freedoms for all without distinction as to race, sex, language, or religion.'[37] The Universal Declaration of Human Rights, which provides an authoritative interpretation of the requirements of the United Nations Charter[38] but has also come to be recognized as expressing general principles of law as a source of international law,[39] sets out a duty of

---

36 See O. De Schutter, 'The responsibility of states', 2009, in S. Chesterman and A. Fisher (eds), *Public Security, Private Order: The Outsourcing of Public Services and its Limits*, Oxford: Oxford University Press, pp. 17–37.

37 Charter of the United Nations, 26 June 1945, 59 Stat. 1031, T.S. 993, 3 Bevans 1153, entered into force 24 Oct. 1945.

38 See the Proclamation of Teheran, Final Act of the International Conference on Human Rights, Teheran, 22 April to 13 May 1968, UN Doc. A/CONF. 32/41 at 3 (1968), where it was stated unanimously that the Declaration 'states a common understanding of the peoples of the world concerning the inalienable and inviolable rights of all members of the human family and constitutes an obligation for all members of the international community' (para. 2).

39 International Court of Justice, *United States Diplomatic and Consular Staff in Tehran (United States v Iran) (Merits)* (ICJ Reports 1980), at 42. See Horst Hannum, 'The Status of the Universal Declaration of Human Rights in National and International Law', 25 *Georgia Journal of International and Comparative Law* 25, 1995–1996, 287 at 351–352; Thomas Buergenthal, 'International Human Rights Law and Institutions: Accomplishments and Prospects', *Washington Law Review* 63, 1988, 1 at 9; Bruno Simma and Philip Alston,

international cooperation in Article 22. This provision states that everyone is entitled to realization, 'through national effort and international co-operation and in accordance with the organization and resources of each State, of the economic, social and cultural rights indispensable for his dignity and the free development of his personality'. These rules impose on States a duty to cooperate internationally for the fulfilment of human rights by using all the means at their disposal within the limits set by international law. They include a duty to regulate the conduct of private investors, where such conduct could result in human rights violations even though such violations would occur under the territorial jurisdiction of another State.[40]

The same extraterritorial duties of States apply with respect to the realization of the right to development. The 1986 Declaration on the Right to Development referred to above provides that States are required to create international conditions favourable to the realization of the right to development, have the duty to cooperate in order to achieve this right, and are required to act collectively to formulate development policies oriented to the fulfilment of this right.[41] In the Millennium Declaration the Heads of States and Governments recognized unanimously that 'in addition to our separate responsibilities to our individual societies, we have a collective responsibility to uphold the principles of human dignity, equality and equity at the global level'.[42]

The duty to support human rights beyond the State's national territory also finds support in general international law. Customary international law prohibits a State from allowing its territory to be used to cause damage on the territory of another State, a principle that is at the origin of the whole corpus of international environmental law.[43] The International Court of Justice referred

'The Sources of Human Rights Law: Custom, Jus Cogens, and General Principles', *Australian Yearbook of International Law* 12, 1988–9, 82–108 at 100–102; O. De Schutter, 'The status of human rights in international law', 2009, in Catarina Krause and Martin Scheinin (eds), *International Protection of Human Rights: A Textbook* , Abo Akademi University Institute for Human Rights, Turku: Abo, pp. 39–60.

40 O. De Schutter, *International Human Rights Law. Cases, Materials and Commentary*, 2010, Cambridge: Cambridge University Press, chapter 4.

41 Articles 3 and 4. The right to development has been repeatedly referred to in subsequent declarations adopted unanimously, for example the Millennium Declaration and the 1993 Vienna Declaration and Programme of Action of the 1993 World Conference on Human Rights. See further Margot E. Salomon, *Global Responsibility for Human Rights: World Poverty and the Development of International Law*, 2007, Oxford: Oxford University Press.

42 Millennium Declaration, UNGA Res 55/2 (8 September 2000), para. 2.

43 *Trail Smelter Case (United States v Canada)*, 3 RIAA 1905 (1941); see also the dissenting opinion of Judge Weeramantry to the Advisory Opinion of the International Court of Justice on the *Legality of threat or use of nuclear weapons* in which, referring to the principle that 'damage must not be caused to other nations', Judge Weeramantry considered that the claim by New Zealand that nuclear tests should be prohibited where this could risk having an impact on that country's population should be decided 'in the context of [this] deeply entrenched principle, grounded in common sense, case law, international conventions, and customary international law'.

to the principle in the advisory opinion it adopted on the issue of the Legality of the Threat or Use of Nuclear Weapons – where New Zealand was asserting that nuclear tests should be prohibited where this would create a risk for the country's population – and, in contentious proceedings, in the Gabčíkovo-Nagymaros Project case opposing Hungary to Slovakia: in these cases, the Court affirms that 'the existence of the general obligation of States to ensure that activities within their jurisdiction and control respect the environment of other States or of areas beyond national control is now part of the corpus of international law relating to the environment'.[44] The principle was again referred to by the Court in its judgment of 20 April 2010 delivered in the *Pulp Mills* case opposing Argentina to Uruguay.[45]

But the 'do no harm' principle goes beyond transboundary pollution, and it extends beyond a duty to abstain from causing harm: it implies a positive duty to control private actors operating abroad to ensure that human rights, including the right to development, are not violated by such actors.[46] Indeed, the general obligation to exercise influence on the conduct of non-State actors where such conduct might lead to human rights being violated outside the State's national territory has been emphasized by various United Nations human rights treaty bodies. The Committee on Economic, Social and Cultural Rights in particular affirms that States parties should 'prevent third parties from violating the right [protected under the International Covenant on Economic, Social and Cultural Rights] in other countries, if they are able to influence these third parties by way of legal or political means, in accordance with the Charter of the United Nations and applicable international law'.[47] Specifically in regard to corporations, the Committee on Economic, Social and Cultural Rights has further stated that 'States Parties should also take steps to prevent human rights contraventions abroad by corporations that have their main seat under their jurisdiction, without infringing the sovereignty or

44 *Legality of the Threat or Use of Nuclear Weapons, Advisory Opinion*, ICJ Reports 1996 (I), pp. 241–242, para. 29; *Gabčíkovo-Nagymaros Project (Hungary/Slovakia)*, Judgment, ICJ Reports 1997, p. 78

45 *Case concerning Pulp Mills on the River Uruguay (Argentina v Uruguay)*, Judgment, ICJ Reports 2010, para. 193.

46 See also N. Jägers, *Corporate Human Rights Obligations: in Search of Accountability*, 2002, Antwerp and New York: Intersentia, p. 172 (deriving from 'the general principle formulated in the *Corfu Channel* case – that a State has the obligation not knowingly to allow its territory to be used for acts contrary to the rights of other States – that home State responsibility can arise where the home State has not exercised due diligence in controlling parent companies that are effectively under its control').

47 See e.g. Committee on Economic, Social and Cultural Rights, General Comment No. 14 (2000): The right to the highest attainable standard of health (Article 12 of the International Covenant on Economic, Social and Cultural Rights), UN Doc. E/C.12/2000/4 (2000), para. 39; or Committee on Economic, Social and Cultural Rights, General Comment No. 15 (2002), The right to water (Arts 11 and 12 of the International Covenant on Economic, Social and Cultural Rights), UN Doc. E/C.12/2002/11 (26 November 2002), para. 31.

diminishing the obligations of host states under the Covenant.'[48] Similarly, the Committee on the Elimination of Racial Discrimination has called upon States to regulate the extraterritorial actions of third parties registered in their territory. For example, in 2007, it called upon Canada to 'take appropriate legislative or administrative measures to prevent acts of transnational corporations registered in Canada which negatively impact on the enjoyment of rights of indigenous peoples in territories outside Canada', recommending in particular that the State party 'explore ways to hold transnational corporations registered in Canada accountable'.[49]

Chapters 7, 8 and 9 examine various tools through which States may – and perhaps should, consistent with the obligations outlined above – incentivize investors to proceed so as to contribute positively to development in the host country. Three channels through which such influence may be exercised are examined in turn: they are export credit agencies and investment insurance agencies (Chapter 7); the negotiation of bilateral or multilateral frameworks for investment (Chapter 8); and development banks, using the European Investment Bank as an illustration (Chapter 9). While a more direct way to achieve similar results would perhaps consist in the home State of the investor regulating that investor's behaviour and providing victims of human rights violations committed by that investor with remedies in the courts of the home State, the use of extraterritorial regulation has been heavily contested, and occasionally denounced as an infringement on the sovereignty of the host State.[50] Moreover, extraterritorial regulation of private companies by the State of origin may be ineffective, either because of the ability for such companies to organize themselves into separate legal entities so as to create a 'veil' between the parent and the subsidiary, and thus to allow the parent company to escape any form of liability for the acts of the subsidiary, or more generally because, unless combined with the appropriate incentives, the addressees of such regulations will be tempted to use all means at their disposal to circumvent them. Thus, the editors of this volume deliberately chose to focus on tools that are not regulatory in the strict or direct sense, but that could be used in order

48 Committee on Economic, Social and Cultural Rights, 'Statement on the obligations of States Parties regarding the corporate sector and economic, social and cultural rights', UN Doc. E/C.12/2011/1 (20 May 2011), para. 5.

49 CERD/C/CAN/CO/18, paragraph 17 (Concluding Observations/Comments, 25 May 2007).

50 On this debate, see, *inter alia*, N. Jägers, *Corporate Human Rights Obligations: in Search of Accountability*, op. cit.; and O. De Schutter, 'Les affaires *Total* et *Unocal*: complicité et extraterritorialité en matière d'imposition aux entreprises d'obligations en matière de droits de l'homme', *Annuaire français de droit international* LII, 2006, pp. 55–101; and O. De Schutter, 'Rapport général – La responsabilité des Etats dans le contrôle des sociétés transnationales: vers une Convention internationale sur la lutte contre les atteintes aux droits de l'homme commises par les sociétés transnationales', 2010, in *La responsabilité des entreprises multinationales en matière de droits de l'homme*, Brussels: Bruylant-Némésis, pp. 19–100.

to align the incentives private investors have to behave in certain ways with the requirements of human development.[51]

In Chapter 7, Matthias Sant'Ana examines the impacts of export credit and investment insurance agencies (ECAs) on human development and human rights. These institutions provide investors and exporters with loans, insurance and guarantees against risks incurred in international trade and investment activities. Because their role is to complement private actors in the lending and insurance markets, they have been increasingly subject to international disciplines to avoid the risks of trade distortions. Sant'Ana notes, however, that, while often considered with suspicion because of their ability to support the national exporters at the expense of their competitors (and thus to provide a form of subsidization), these agencies also can act as watchdogs vis-à-vis the very actors they support, by imposing on them certain conditionalities or reporting requirements. In recent years, he notes, export credit agencies have increasingly been moving in this direction. Sant'Ana documents this shift from export credit agencies as a tool for hidden and distortive subsidization, to these agencies operating in order to make globalization more humane – although the two, it should be added immediately, are not necessarily incompatible. In doing so, he assesses the manner in which this evolution squares with the requirement, under international law, that States should cooperate to promote development, and that they should take appropriate measures to avoid negative human rights impacts of the activities they support abroad: his premise in this regard is that 'States are required to exercise influence on non-state actors by properly regulating multinational corporations operating from their territory [and] by conditioning public support to these enterprises to adequate standards of human rights due diligence.'[52] Besides proposing that additional standards be integrated in ECA lending and insurance practice, he suggests that establishing procedural requirements, such as impact assessments, can be particularly useful by moving the debate from resignation with uncertainty, towards a commitment to formulate expectations, perceptions of risk and mitigation policies publicly and prior to any intervention.

In Chapter 8, Philip De Man and Jan Wouters then assess the possibility of improving the framework of negotiations on IIAs, in particular from the viewpoint of developing and least-developed capital-importing countries. Again, the issue they address is grounded in the understanding that, in the

---

51 See, however, for a discussion of the potential of extraterritorial regulation, by the State of origin, of transnational corporations, O. De Schutter, 'Sovereignty-plus in the era of interdependence: Towards an international convention on combating human rights violations by transnational corporations', 2010, in P. Bekker, R. Dolzer and M. Waibel (eds), *Making Transnational Law Work in the Global Economy: Essays in Honour of Detlev Vagts*, Cambridge: Cambridge University Press, pp. 245–284.

52 See *Protect, Respect and Remedy: a Framework for Business and Human Rights*, Report of the Special Representative of the Secretary-General on the issue of human rights and transnational corporations and other business enterprises, John Ruggie, 7 April 2008 (UN Doc A/HRC/8/5), paras 56–64.

negotiation of investment agreements, States cannot ignore their human rights obligations, including their obligations towards the right to development: this is the position adopted by the Committee on Economic, Social and Cultural Rights,[53] the Sub-Commission on Promotion and Protection of Human Rights (to which the Advisory Committee of the Human Rights Council has now succeeded),[54] and special procedures of the Human Rights Council.[55]

The establishment of an international framework for FDI should support the full realization of human rights and human development. But how then to move towards such a framework in a context in which a web of bilateral investment treaties has already been concluded, largely pre-empting the establishment of a multilateral approach? De Man and Wouters analyse the viability of deliberations on a multilateral investment framework in order to mitigate the perverse effects of the negotiation dynamics at the bilateral level. They fully acknowledge the pre-existing situation of an elaborate regime of bilateral investment treaties between developed and developing countries, which mortgages the negotiation options of the latter at the multilateral level.

Taking into account what they call this 'duality of parallel negotiations', the authors make a number of suggestions. First, they propose that rules set at the

53 See e.g. Statement of the Committee on Economic, Social and Cultural Rights to the Third Ministerial Conference of the World Trade Organization, Seattle, 30 November – 3 December 1999 (E/C.12/1999/9); Committee on Economic, Social and Cultural Rights, General Comment No. 12 (1999), *The right to adequate food (Art. 11)*, E/C.12/1999/5, at paras 19 and 36 ('States parties should, in international agreements whenever relevant, ensure that the right to adequate food is given due attention'); Committee on Economic, Social and Cultural Rights, General Comment No. 14 (2000), *The right to the highest attainable standard of health (Article 12 of the International Covenant on Economic. Social and Cultural Rights)*, E/C.12/2000/4 (2000), para. 39 ('In relation to the conclusion of other international agreements, States parties should take steps to ensure that these instruments do not adversely impact upon the right to health'); Committee on Economic, Social and Cultural Rights, General Comment No. 15 (2002), *The right to water (Arts 11 and 12 of the International Covenant on Economic, Social and Cultural Rights)*, UN Doc. E/C.12/2002/11 (26 November 2002), paras 31 and 35–36 ('States parties should ensure that the right to water is given due attention in international agreements and, to that end, should consider the development of further legal instruments. With regard to the conclusion and implementation of other international and regional agreements, States parties should take steps to ensure that these instruments do not adversely impact upon the right to water. Agreements concerning trade liberalization should not curtail or inhibit a country's capacity to ensure the full realization of the right to water').
54 Sub-Commission on Promotion and Protection of Human Rights, Human Rights as the Primary Objective of Trade, Investment and Financial Policy, UN Doc. E/CN.4/Sub.2/RES/1998/12 (1998); Report of the Sub-Commission on its 50th Sess., UN ESCOR, 50th Sess., at 39, UN Doc. E/CN.4/Sub.2/1998/45 (1998).
55 J. Oloka-Onyango and Deepika Udagama, 'The Realization of Economic, Social and Cultural Rights: Globalization and Its Impact on the Full Enjoyment of Human Rights', UN ESCOR, 52nd Sess., UN Doc. E/CN.4/Sub.2/2000/13 (2000); Report of the Special Rapporteur on the Right to food to the 19th session of the Human Rights Council, O. De Schutter, Addendum: Guiding Principles on Human Rights Impact Assessments of Trade and Investment Agreements, UN Doc. A/HRC/19/59/Add.5 (19 December 2011).

multilateral level (building, ideally, on the General Agreement on Trade in Services (GATS), part of the World Trade Organization agreements) should focus more modestly on technical issues that support, rather than compete with, ongoing bilateral processes. These include improving the transparency of the domestic regulatory framework for investment in order to ensure that, provided adequate macro-economic conditions are present, investors will be encouraged to enter the country; building the capacity of developing country regulators and negotiators; and providing technical assistance in order to 'improve the general economic infrastructure of host countries as a durable means of ensuring that FDI flows take root in poor countries'. In other terms, a multilateral framework for investment may have to be more modest if it is to succeed, and to steer away from the more contentious issues of investment liberalization and the rights of investors, towards an essentially facilitative and supportive role. This may be a 'second best' solution, in that there still remains a risk that capital-receiving countries will compete for investment by using the tool of incentives that, ultimately, lead to a sub-optimal solution for all. But it may still encourage countries to improve their macro-economic fundamentals rather than to provide investment incentives that are essentially a means to attempt to compensate, from the point of view of the potential investor, a deficient economic climate.

Second, De Man and Wouters also note that, in order to overcome the current obstacles to further progress on the establishment of a multilateral framework for investment, the issue of investment liberalization (on which developed, capital-exporting countries insist) could be linked to issues that developing countries (primarily those who oppose further investment liberalization) care most about: an obvious candidate is the movement of labour. As they note, 'in light of the importance attached to the movement of personnel by India, the staunchest opponent to multilateral rules on FDI flows, the option of conducting parallel negotiations on both issues should thus be given considerable thought'.

Third, the authors consider that a new multilateral framework for investment could include attributing to the dispute-settlement procedures of the World Trade Organization a competence to adjudicate investment disputes that arise under existing investment treaties. This, they remark, could reduce the uncertainty resulting from the vagueness of provisions in bilateral investment treaties that are interpreted by arbitral tribunals with a variable composition and that do not result in the gradual formation of a consistent case law: providing greater predictability would be in the interest of investors and host countries alike. Of course, this would represent a significant shift from the existing situation, in which investor–State disputes coexist with State–State disputes. However, as they note, the inclusion of investor–State dispute resolution provisions in the Multilateral Agreement on Investment negotiated under the auspices of the OECD between 1995 and 1998, before the attempt was abandoned under the pressure of civil society, was one of the most contentious aspects of the enterprise, and one that was most fiercely opposed. In addition, as they note, 'excluding investors' standing in dispute-settlement proceedings against host countries is likely to be to the benefit of developing countries, which often struggle in finding the necessary resources to defend themselves properly against more potent multinational enterprises'.

Finally, in Chapter 9 Nicolas Hachez and Jan Wouters examine the role of multilateral lending institutions (MLIs) in supporting transborder investment, taking as their example the practice of the European Investment Bank (EIB) and how it relates to human rights and to social and environmental concerns. They assess, first, whether the substantive rules applicable to the EIB's activities ensure that the lending practices of the Bank contribute to human development. These rules are the applicable rules of the EU legal order and the voluntary human rights, social and environmental principles and standards which the EIB has identified for itself as a guide to its lending operations – starting with a set of environmental principles adopted in 1996 under pressure from civil society, and at present most visibly expressed in the EIB Statement of Environmental and Social Principles and Standards, most recently updated in 2009. Remarkably, these principles and standards, as well as the requirements of EU law applicable to intra-EU investment projects, are also made applicable by the EIB to operations conducted in third countries that benefit from its funding, although not without limitation: the position of the Bank is that

> for a variety of reasons, including institutional capacity, technological capability, availability of investment funds and consumer ability and willingness to pay, for a particular project the immediate achievement of EU requirements may not be practical and in some cases may not be desirable. When the case arises, it is incumbent on the promoter to provide an acceptable justification to the Bank for a deviation from EU standards, within the framework of the environmental and social principles and standards set out in the Statement. In such cases, provision should be made for a phased approach to higher standards.[56]

Having reviewed the rules and standards applicable to the lending policies of the EIB, the conclusion of the authors is critical: they note that while the volume of lending of the EIB is significant, largely exceeding that of comparable multilateral lending institutions, the substantive accountability standards seem 'off the mark compared to MLIs' best practices, this in several respects ranging from the clarity and comprehensiveness of the applicable standards, to their binding and operational character'. As regards, then, the procedural accountability principles of transparency, participation and remedies, they too are seen as falling short of what would be required, particularly since the EIB's operations are excluded from review by the Court of Justice of the European Union.

---

56 See European Investment Bank, 'The EIB Statement of Social and Environmental Standards and Practices', 2009, para. 40, p. 17.

1.4 Conclusion

The chapters collected in the second section of this volume examining the links between FDI inflows and the conclusion of IIAs led to some key conclusions. Economic growth and human development in general have benefited from the arrival of FDI. In addition, contrary to a widely held assumption – and while exceptions exist – investors do not seek to enter into jurisdictions that have 'lower' standards in areas such as labour rights, environmental safeguards, or respect for the rights and livelihoods of the local communities. Theirs is a quest for profitability: what matters is that they have a stable investment framework, a sound business climate, and that the key macro-economic conditions are right. And while low labour costs may be an advantage, especially in relatively labour-intensive industries, what really matters is the relationship between the levels of wages and the productivity of labour: therefore, low productivity, for instance because of poor levels of qualification, is routinely seen to offset the 'benefits' of repressed wages. There is, in that sense, no inevitability to the classic 'race to the bottom' scenario between countries seeking to attract investment by resorting to regulatory competition. On the contrary, the reputational brand that the investors seek to protect, and the diffusion by foreign investors of best practices in social and environmental areas, may help provoke a 'race to the top', facilitated by the inflow of foreign capital. For low-income countries that require capital inflows in order to finance their development, the challenge is how to make this happen. It is not simply to attract capital: it is to do so under the right conditions, which can maximize the benefits while minimizing the potential negative impacts.

Do IIAs help in doing so? The short answer is: not much. The FDI inflows are generally dependent on other variables, especially the size of the market in the host country or trade openness. And although a predictable and safe legal environment does matter to the investor, such predictability can be provided by other means: indeed, the more a country's traditional respect for the rule of law is established, the less it will have to resort to investment treaties that protect the rights of investors. Moreover, if IIAs make any difference, this seems to be especially the case in the extractive industry, where very large investments are made that are 'sunk' at the early stages of the project, and that are only profitable after a long period of time, leading the investment to be particularly susceptible to risk.

It would therefore be ill-advised for countries seeking to attract investment to do so by concluding investment agreements which would result in exempting the investor from having to comply with requirements linked to human rights, or to social and environmental considerations – a risk that is real, especially, in host government agreements, that relate to specific investment projects (generally large-scale development projects). Such incentives are no substitute for the establishment of an attractive macro-economic and business climate, and they may in fact be counter-productive even as regards the immediate aim of attracting investors (let alone as regards the more ambitious aim of human development) if, as a result of entering the country, the investor would be risking its reputation and subjecting itself to criticism because of the laxity of the standards applied. For this globalized world is also one in which information about poor practices of transnational actors travels fast.

In sum, there are strong incentives that should encourage capital-importing countries to take the measures required to channel FDI towards the right ends, and to establish the regulatory and policy frameworks to ensure that it works in favour of human development; and there are reasons to believe that it is in the best interest of the investors themselves not to seek to benefit from investing under lower standards. It does not follow, however, that the market should be left to take care of itself, or that there is no responsibility for capital-exporting countries to help create an international environment that facilitates the efforts of countries seeking to attract FDI. Governments are sometimes poorly equipped to act in the public interest of their populations, and to decide in accordance with long-term considerations. They may be corrupt, or influenced by narrowly defined interests. They may be myopic and discount the long-term costs of present actions if they can achieve immediate gains. And, perhaps most importantly in this context, they may entertain an unrealistic representation of the real motivations of the investors: they may believe that the investors will not enter the country unless strong concessions are made to them and unless their expectations of profits are fully immune from being reduced as a result of regulatory changes, when in fact what the investors most desire is to invest in conditions that are sound from the macro-economic point of view, and in which their reputation will not suffer – although if offered certain protections they will accept them. It is therefore entirely justified to seek to explore in the context of negotiating IIAs which mechanisms should be established in order to ensure that the arrival of FDI will not negatively affect the rights of the local population and limit the host country's ability to protect these rights, and will instead contribute positively to human development indicators in the country; and it is fitting for capital-exporting countries and for agencies such as export credit agencies or multilateral lending institutions to support this effort.

Far from limiting the sovereignty of the countries seeking to attract investment, these tools are used in order to strengthen the bargaining position of these countries: they are a way to support them in making the choices that should benefit their populations most, when these countries could otherwise be tempted to 'signal' their willingness to attract investors by providing far-reaching forms of protection that reduce their policy space, or to offer advantages that will annul, or at least seriously diminish, the benefits they have a right to expect from the arrival of FDI. That is the form that sovereignty takes in the era of globalization: in order to be exercised effectively, it must be shared – and unless it is supported by international cooperation, it will not be real.

2   International investment law

The perpetual search for consensus

Jan Wouters, Sanderijn Duquet and Nicolas Hachez

2.1 Introduction

The risks associated with engaging in foreign direct investment (FDI) are well documented. Foreign investors put themselves under the rule of a foreign government, which may treat them unfavourably. The creation of international standards for the protection of foreign investors has always been a prime political objective for capital-exporting countries. Capital-receiving countries, on the other hand, have always been wary of such protective frameworks as they wish to retain as much of their sovereign regulatory powers as possible. For example, capital-importing countries insist that they are allowed to expropriate ('nationalize') foreign investments if the economic activity involved seems best carried out by the State itself or by its nationals. At the same time, these countries recognize the necessity of upholding certain principles of treatment of aliens, so as not to scare out potential investors and important economic resources with the perspective of reckless conduct by the host government.

In early times, customary international law (CIL) seemed the natural vehicle for an international standard of treatment of foreign investment. Soon, though, the high degree of international consensus required to create and uphold custom started to evaporate, as the economic interests and political inclinations of capital-exporting and importing States increasingly diverged in the course of the twentieth century. In the face of this, States have turned to the treaty solution, most often through bilateral investment treaties (BITs), whereby two countries agree on certain terms governing the treatment of their investors in the other country. To date, more than 2,800 BITs have been concluded. As these share quite similar content, certain authors argue that such a network of bilateral agreements in fact has generated CIL. As will be argued in the present contribution, we doubt this affirmation. Rather, it is submitted that the evolution of the protective regime for investors enshrined in BITs reflects the conflicts of interests running through investment relations between capital-importing and exporting nations. Through bilateral frameworks, developed countries were able to impose on developing countries their view of a liberal and protective international investment framework, which the customary law process failed to achieve. Developing countries, on the other hand, desperately looking to attract the capital needed to foster their economic development, and wishing to build a competitive advantage vis-à-vis other countries, have accepted ever stronger terms in their bilateral treaty relations, to the extent that their regulatory sovereignty on matters such as employment, environmental preservation and taxation found itself severely curtailed. A new generation of investment treaties is now emerging, which attempt to re-equilibrate the scales between the legitimate desire to protect foreign investors against unreasonable interference by the host State and the latter's equally legitimate need for enough policy space to pass the regulations it considers necessary.[1]

This chapter aims at depicting the international legal regime of FDI and of its contemporary evolutions as well as at briefly introducing the challenges which this regime is currently encountering. The first section sketches the customary standard of treatment of foreign investors which governed the field at the beginning of the twentieth century, followed by an explanation of why the customary consensus broke down. The second section examines the worldwide development of a dense network of – mainly bilateral – investment treaties. The third section studies the impact of such treaty networks on the state of CIL in the field of investment. In a fourth section we analyse the problems posed by the overprotective framework for investors laid down in BITs, including the serious incursions on the capacity of host States to pursue development policies (the issue of 'policy space'). This last section also inquires into how a recent trend in investment treaty practice is seeking to rebalance the rights and obligations of host States and whether this is having an impact on general State practice in the field of investment.

2.2 Customary international law on foreign direct investment before the age of BITs

2.2.1 Early customary minimum standard of treatment of aliens

For centuries, nationals of a great number of States have settled in other countries, which has often involved investments in profitable activities, that is, spending financial resources in order to start, develop or take over an economic venture in another country. If such enterprises were often likely to yield considerable profits, they were also fraught with danger. The network of treaties containing provisions on the protection of investment, trade and foreign-held assets was limited in scope and lacked proper enforcement mechanisms.[2] Most

---

1 See, regarding the protection of the host State's right to pursue measures of general interest in international investment instruments, W. Ben Hamida, 'La prise en compte de l'intérêt général et des impératifs de développement dans le droit des investissements', *Journal du droit international*, 2008, 10.

2 K.J. Vandevelde, 'A Brief History of International Investment Agreements', *U.C. Davis J. Int'l L. & Pol'y* 12, 2005, 159; J. Wouters, Ph. De Man and L. Chanet, 'The Long and

notably, a foreign investor was never sure that his property or his profits would be protected to the same extent as in his own country against harmful interference either by the government of the host State or by other actors. If a foreign investor believed that his rights with regard to his investment had been breached, he could always resort to the courts of the host State or, failing satisfactory outcomes, to his home State for diplomatic protection.[3] Even so, the question arose as to what rules should be applied to guarantee his protection against harm in the host State. Up until the early twentieth century, it was said that a national of a foreign country was entitled to the same protection of his rights as the nationals of the country he had settled in, as applied by the national courts. However, such protection had to meet certain 'international standards of treatment', which the foreigner's home State could try to enforce by way of diplomatic protection if the national judicial system of the host State failed to ensure respect thereof.[4]

The international consensus on those principles was quite solid until the beginning of the twentieth century (see *infra*, next subsection), and was even called 'axiomatic' by the arbitral tribunal deciding on a dispute between the United States and Norway on the compensation to be paid to the Norwegian owners of ships which were requisitioned by the US as part of the war effort during World War I.[5] This widespread consensus is even more clearly evidenced in a speech by the Nobel Prize winner Elihu Root, commenting in 1910 on the standard of treatment to be extended to aliens in a foreign country:

> The rule of obligation is perfectly distinct and settled. Each country is bound to give the nationals of another country in its territory the benefit of the same laws, the same administration, the same protection, and the same redress for injury which it gives to its own citizens, and neither more nor less: provided the protection which the country gives to its own citizens conforms to the established standard of civilization.
>
> There is a standard of justice, very simple, very fundamental, and of such general acceptance by all civilized countries as to form a part of the international law of the world. The condition upon which any country is entitled to measure the justice due from it to an alien by the justice which it accords to its own citizens is that its system of law and administration

Winding Road of International Investment Agreements', *Human Rights & Int'l Legal Disc.* 3, 2009, 265.

3 S. P. Subedi, *International Investment Law: Reconciling Policy and Principle*, Oxford: Hart Publishing, 2008, p. 12.

4 Vandevelde, op. cit., p. 160. Diplomatic protection still has a concrete function in investment dispute resolution: the 2006 French Model BIT, for example, expresses a preference to solve investment disputes via diplomatic channels. See Art. 10(1) French Model BIT (2006): 'Disputes relating to the interpretation or application of this Agreement shall be settled, if possible, by diplomatic channels.'

5 See A. Lowenfeld, *International Economic Law*, New York: Oxford University Press, 2008, 2nd edn, p. 474.

shall conform to this general standard. If any country's system of law and administration does not conform to that standard, although the people of the country may be content or compelled to live under it, no other country can be compelled to accept it as furnishing a satisfactory measure of treatment to its citizens.[6]

[. . .]

[I]n all nations the wisdom and sound policy of equal protection and impartial justice to the alien is steadily gaining acceptance in the remotest parts and throughout even the least instructed communities.[7]

2.2.2 Challenges to the early customary standard

Soon, however, the consensus described above was shattered as certain countries (most notably Mexico and the newly born USSR) started to nationalize and expropriate large segments of alien property in attempts to pursue policies inspired by socialist or communist doctrines.

In Mexico, large tracts of land notably owned by US citizens were expropriated as early as 1910, mainly in order to implement an agrarian reform which involved the redistribution of land to the peasants cultivating it.[8] As compensation claims dragged on, a famous exchange took place between Cordell Hull, then US Secretary of State, and the Mexican Ministry of Foreign Affairs. In this oft-quoted diplomatic correspondence, which extended over several years starting in 1938, two conceptions of the protection of aliens' property in foreign territories were opposed. Secretary Hull contended that, in cases of expropriation, it was a 'self-evident fact' that international law obliged the expropriating State to pay 'prompt, adequate and effective compensation' to the foreign investor, on the basis of 'applicable precedents and recognized authorities on international law'.[9] This view of the obligations of States in case of expropriation became known as the 'Hull formula', in which 'prompt' means, if not immediate, at least speedy compensation, 'adequate' refers to an appropriate valuation of the expropriated property coming close to its full or fair market value,[10] and 'effective' designates a form of payment effectively

---

6 E. Root, 'The Basis of Protection to Citizens Residing Abroad', *Am. J. Int'l L.* 4., 1910, 521–2.

7 Ibid., p. 528.

8 Lowenfeld, *International Economic Law*, op. cit., pp. 471–3; Wouters, De Man and Chanet, op. cit., p. 265.

9 Secr. Cordell Hull to Mexico, 22 Aug. 1938, quoted by Lowenfeld, *International Economic Law*, op. cit., pp. 478–9.

10 A landmark case of the Permanent Court of International Justice providing support for this view is the 1928 Factory at Chorzów case, which states: 'The essential principle contained in the actual notion of an illegal act – a principle which seems to be established by international practice and in particular by the decisions of international tribunals – is that reparation must, as far as possible, wipe out all the consequences of the illegal act and re-establish the situation which would, in all probability, have existed if that act had

usable by the recipient, in order to avoid payments being made, for example, in a non-convertible foreign currency.[11]

The Mexican position in turn relied on what was called the 'Calvo doctrine', named after the Argentinian scholar Carlos Calvo, and denied that State practice had ever evolved along the lines of the Hull formula. The Calvo doctrine stated in substance that, in cases of expropriation, international law did not impose any particular obligation on a State towards aliens, except that of non-discrimination. Therefore, aliens were to be subject to the same law as nationals, and could not rely on any international standard of treatment. They had to litigate their case before national courts exclusively, and could not rely on the protection of their own State or of foreign courts in the process.[12] Although they agreed on an overall settlement for the compensation, Mexico and the United States never found common ground on the contents of the law as a result of this diplomatic exchange.

The Soviet view on issues regarding the protection of alien property was influenced by communist ideology, which rejects the idea of private property. Accordingly, it claims that States have no international obligation with regard to aliens' property, and that a nation's right to nationalize property is a corollary of its right to self-determination.[13] The socialist view that the best path to economic development lays in State regulation of the economy rather than in the free market encouraged newly decolonized States fearing neo-colonialism to limit foreign control over their means of production via expropriations.[14]

2.2.3 UN declarations regarding rules on foreign investment

None of the three positions outlined above could ever gain sufficient significance to be considered as an expression of CIL. Disagreement grew to such an extent that the US Federal Supreme Court, in its famous *Sabbatino* judgment, involving US nationals expropriated by the Cuban government, stated in 1964 that '[t]here are few if any issues in international law today on which opinion seems to be so divided as the limitations on a State's power to expropriate the property of aliens.'[15] In light of these divisions, the UN General Assembly (UNGA), after years of debate in different organs and commissions, attempted to formulate, through a series of resolutions, consensual rules on foreign investment, and in particular on investment in the exploitation of natural resources. It must be recalled here that UNGA resolutions such as the ones

not been committed.' See PCIJ, *Case Concerning the Factory at Chorzów (Merits)*, 13 September 1928, PCIJ Series A – No. 17, p. 47.
11 On the Hull formula, see O. Schachter, 'Compensation for Expropriation', *Am. J. Int'l L.* 78, 1984, 121.
12 A. Lowenfeld, *International Private Investment*, Newark: Matthew Bender, 1982, p. 151.
13 Ibid.
14 Vandevelde, op. cit., pp. 164–7.
15 US Supreme Court, *Banco Nacional de Cuba v Sabbatino*, *U.S. Reports*, Vol. 376, 1964, p. 398, at 428.

discussed below have a declaratory character and have no legally binding effect. However, they can reflect the state of CIL on certain issues or contribute to the emergence of new CIL.[16]

2.2.3.1 The 1962 Declaration on Permanent Sovereignty over Natural Resources: a hint of custom?

In 1962, the UNGA adopted a resolution entitled 'Declaration on Permanent Sovereignty over Natural Resources'.[17] The Declaration affirms the 'inalienable right of all States freely to dispose of their natural wealth and resources in accordance with their national interests'.[18] With regard to the issue of the protection of foreign investors, it states that

> [n]ationalization, expropriation or requisitioning shall be based on grounds or reasons of public utility, security or the national interest which are recognized as overriding purely individual or private interests, both domestic and foreign. In such cases the owner *shall be paid appropriate compensation*, in accordance with the rules in force in the State taking such measures in the exercise of its sovereignty and *in accordance with international law*. In any case where the question of compensation gives rise to a controversy, the national jurisdiction of the State taking such measures shall be exhausted. However, upon agreement by sovereign States and other parties concerned, settlement of the dispute should be made through arbitration or international adjudication.[19]

The question of the standard of compensation was the subject of much debate, whereby the United States pushed for a formulation requiring prompt, adequate and effective compensation. However, the UNGA could only agree on 'appropriate' compensation, which is rather vague.[20] This being said, the reference that the matter is ultimately to be governed by international law seems clear. The Declaration was widely adopted, including

---

16 The International Court of Justice has treated General Assembly resolutions as evidence of *opinio juris*, not as State practice nor a declaration of CIL in itself. See *Case Concerning Military and Paramilitary Activities in and Against Nicaragua (Nicaragua v United States of America)*, Judgment, *ICJ Reports 1986*, paras 184 and 188 and *Legality of the Threat or Use of Nuclear Weapons, Advisory Opinion, ICJ Reports 1996*, para. 73.

17 UN General Assembly (UNGA), 'Permanent Sovereignty over Natural Resources', 14 December 1962, Resolution No. 1803 (XVII).

18 Ibid., fourth recital.

19 Ibid, para. 4, emphasis added.

20 The United States made a statement in this regard that it was confident that 'appropriate' meant 'prompt, adequate and effective'. See Lowenfeld, *International Economic Law*, op. cit., pp. 486–7.

by western countries,[21] but the eastern bloc abstained. This Resolution is probably the closest the international community ever got to a consensus on the contents of contemporary CIL on the protection of foreign investment.

2.2.3.2 Subsequent resolutions and uncertainty

Any hope for the persistence of such consensus was short-lived, though. From 1966, the 'appropriate' standard of treatment, as well as the reference to international law and diplomatic protection, were progressively watered down in two subsequent resolutions on the same topic.[22] This happened under the pressure of the growing number of developing countries joining the UN, who organized themselves as the Group of 77 (G77). These subsequent resolutions, which failed to gain the vote of the western countries, did away with the appropriateness requirement, only referred to 'possible compensation', and deleted any reference to international law altogether.[23]

In May 1974, the General Assembly expressly stated in the Declaration for the Establishment of a New International Economic Order (NIEO) that States dispose of the 'full permanent sovereignty of every State over its natural resources and all economic activities', including 'the right of nationalization or transfer of ownership to its nationals'.[24] Compensation *should* be paid, taking into account domestic law, but is not considered obligatory under international law.

Later that year the UNGA also adopted the 'Charter of Economic Rights and Duties of States'. It states that each State has the right

> [t]o regulate and exercise authority over foreign investment within its national jurisdiction in accordance with its law and regulations and in conformity with its national objectives and priorities. No State shall be compelled to grant preferential treatment to foreign investment;
> [and]
> [t]o nationalize, expropriate or transfer ownership of foreign property in which case appropriate compensation *should* be paid by the State adopting such measures, taking into account its relevant laws and regulations and all circumstances that the State considers pertinent. In any case where the question of compensation gives rise to a controversy, it shall be settled under the domestic law of the nationalizing State and

---

21 Except France.
22 UNGA, 'Permanent Sovereignty over Natural Resources', 25 November 1966, Resolution No. 2158 (XXI); UNGA, 'Permanent Sovereignty over Natural Resources', 17 December 1973, Resolution No. 3171 (XXVIII).
23 Resolution No. 3171 (XXVIII), para. 3.
24 UNGA, 'Declaration on the Establishment of a New International Economic Order', 1 May 1974, Resolution No. 3201 (S-VI), Art. 4 (e).

by its tribunals, unless it is freely and mutually agreed by all States concerned that other peaceful means be sought on the basis of the sovereign equality of States and in accordance with the principle of free choice of means.[25]

The Charter, mainly sponsored by developing countries and rejected *en bloc* by the western world, crystallized the highly polarized views on the issue of the duties of host States towards foreign investors.[26] As Andreas Lowenfeld underlines, 'At a minimum, the Charter on the Rights and Duties of States was a concerted effort by the developing countries to repudiate a system of law in whose creation they had played little or no part.'[27] Developing countries took the view that a country's right to regulate investment into its territory is a corollary of the conception it has of its public interest, which is subject to its domestic law alone, to the exclusion of international law. The addition that foreign investors could not claim any preferential treatment evidenced the rejection of any international minimum standard of treatment. The elaboration of compensation measures was considered a matter of national law, which *de facto* might not provide for any indemnification, rather than international law.[28] Western countries contended that the Charter had left untouched the existing CIL principles as embodied in the Declaration on Permanent Sovereignty over Natural Resources, and kept arguing that a State's treatment of aliens was subject to international rules and responsibility.[29] At that moment, consensus over any CIL rule had definitely evaporated, despite many allegations to the contrary.[30]

The dissimilarity in visions resulting from decolonization and the emergence of the socialist bloc precluded the conclusion of global investment standards. Bloc voting in the General Assembly, culminating in the two political declarations in 1974, illustrated the contrast between the numerical majority and the global economic powers at the time.[31] Their impact on international investment law is marginal and, despite repeated references to the 1974 Declarations in the General Assembly,[32] they never

25 UNGA, 'Charter on the Economic Rights and Duties of States', 12 December 1974, Resolution No. 3281 (XXIX), Art. 2, para. 2, (a) and (c). Emphasis added.

26 C.M. Ryan, 'Discerning the Compliance Calculus: Why States Comply with International Investment Law', *Ga. J. Int'l & Comp. L.* 38, 2009, 69.

27 Lowenfeld, *International Economic Law*, op. cit., p. 492.

28 Vandevelde, op. cit., p. 168.

29 Ibid.

30 Concerning the customary character of the Hull Formula, see Schachter, op. cit., and P. Gann, 'Compensation Standard for Expropriation', *Colum. J. Transnat'l L.* 23, 1984–1985, 615.

31 S. M. Schwebel, 'The Influence of Bilateral Investment Treaties on Customary International Law', *Am. Soc'y Int'l L. Proc.* 98, 2004, 28.

32 See e.g. the preambles of UNGA, 'Effective mobilization of women in development, 21 December 1976, Resolution No. 31/175; UNGA, 'Economic co-operation among developing countries', 19 December 1977, Resolution No. 32/180; UNGA, 'World social

gained State recognition in bilateral relations nor in judicial and arbitrational proceedings.[33]

2.3 The emergence of bilateral investment treaties

Partly as a result of this uncertainty concerning the customary rules on the standard of treatment of aliens' properties abroad, but also of the steady increase in FDI during the twentiety century, and in light of waves of expropriations in certain countries, capital-exporting States started, from 1959 on, to intensify a practice consisting in agreeing with host countries on protective terms for their national investors, by way of BITs,[34] double taxation treaties (DTTs) and Regional Integration Agreements containing provisions on investment.[35] These treaties unmistakeably created rules of law in a more advanced and detailed way, which enabled the parties to rely more on the abidance by the conditions and norms agreed upon.[36] In what follows, we focus on the first kind of agreements, which directly and solely concern FDI.

Several attempts at concluding a comprehensive multilateral agreement on foreign investment, which would have settled most questions regarding the status of CIL in this regard, have failed over the years. They include the Havana Charter of the International Trade Organization, which was focused on trade but also contained provisions on investment protection.[37] It was envisioned for the Havana Charter to create a liberal investment regime by shifting international investment relations from bilateral to multilateral agreements, and thus instigating similar effects to international investment as those which followed from the (provisional) entry into force of the General Agreement on Tariffs and Trade (GATT) for international trade relations.[38] Still, it only contained Article 12 on international investment for economic development and reconstruction, which is generally seen as a rather weak compromise on

development', 14 December 1978, Resolution No. 33/48; UNGA, 'International Development Strategy for the Third United Nations Development Decade', 5 December 1980, Resolution No. 35/56; UNGA, 'Development of the energy resources of developing countries', 21 December 1982, Resolution No. 37/251; UNGA, 'Economic measures as a means of political and economic coercion against developing countries', 5 December 1986, Resolution No. 41/165.

33 Schwebel, 'The Influence of Bilateral Investment Treaties on Customary International Law', op. cit., p. 28.

34 The ancestors of BITs were the Treaties of Friendship, Commerce and Navigation, the first of which was signed by the United States and France in 1778. See Treaty of Amity and Commerce Between the United States of America and His Most Christian Majesty, concluded on 6 Feb. 1778, 1778 WL 38 (US Treaty), 8 *Stat* 12.

35 Vandevelde, op. cit., p. 168–9.

36 Schwebel, 'The Influence of Bilateral Investment Treaties on Customary International Law', op. cit., p. 28.

37 See Final Act of the United Nations Conference on Trade and Employment, held at Havana, Cuba from 21 November 1947 to 24 March 1948, UN doc. E/Conf. 2/78.

38 Vandevelde, op. cit., p. 162.

investment issues between developed and developing countries, lacking concrete obligations.[39]

More recently, there were the attempts for the OECD-sponsored Multilateral Agreement on Investment (MAI), whose failure showed again that divisions on the subject were deep, even between industrialized countries.[40] Certain successes were, however, recorded, such as the International Centre for the Settlement of Investment Disputes (ICSID) Convention.[41] The significance of the ICSID Convention lies in the provision of facilities and an institutional and procedural framework for conciliation, arbitration and resolution of legal disputes. It does not entail any substantive norms nor a regime for FDI. In 1985, the MIGA Convention was signed,[42] which sets up the Multilateral Investment Guarantee Agency, an institution of the World Bank System which insures foreign investment against non-economic risks, such as expropriation by the host State or negative effects of regime changes for investors.[43] The MIGA aims to enhance the flow of capital and technology to developing countries for productive purposes and on the basis of fair and stable standards for the treatment of foreign investment.[44] However, no legal obligations for States in bilateral investment relations were specified. None of these multilateral achievements could therefore settle the debate on the substance of the international law on investment.

The proliferation of BITs most certainly goes hand in hand with the need to create legal certainty in international investment.[45] The trend to resort to BITs goes back to 1959.[46] The number of signed BITs grew regularly until the 1990s, when it literally exploded, before returning to more reasonable

39 Wouters, De Man and Chanet, op. cit., p. 269; J.E. Spero, *The Politics of International Economic Relations*, London: Routledge, 1990, p. 137.

40 See Organization for Economic Co-operation and Development (OECD), Negotiating Group on the Multilateral Agreement on Investment (MAI), the multilateral agreement on investment draft consolidated text, 22 April 1998, DAFFE/MAI(98)7/REV.

41 Convention on the Settlement of Investment Disputes between States and Nationals of Other States, signed in Washington DC on 18 March 1965, entry into force on 14 October 1966.

42 Convention Establishing the Multilateral Investment Guarantee Agency, signed in Washington DC on 11 October 1985, entry into force on 12 April 1988, last amended November 2010.

43 Art. 2 MIGA Convention.

44 See Preamble, Art. 12 (e) MIGA Convention.

45 M. Sornarajah, *The International Law on Foreign Investment*, Cambridge: Cambridge University Press, 2010, 3rd edn, pp. 183–187.

46 The first proper BIT to have been signed is the Treaty for the Promotion and Protection of Investments, with protocol and exchange of notes between the Federal Republic of Germany and Pakistan, signed on 25 November 1959, entry into force on 28 April 1962, 457 UNTS 23; UNCTAD, 'Bilateral Investment Treaties 1959–1999', UNCTAD/ITE/IIA/2, 2000, p. 1, Online. Available HTTP <http://www.unctad.org/en/docs/poiteiiad2.en.pdf> (accessed 3 January 2012).

proportions from the year 2000.[47] The BITs boom generally is associated with two developments: the economic growth of Asian markets and the loss of alternatives to foreign investment as a source of capital following the debt crisis in the 1980s.[48] Since 2001 the number of BITs concluded annually has constantly diminished. This trend contrasts with the upsurge in free trade agreements and other treaties on economic cooperation containing investment provisions.[49] Right now, the total number of BITs signed amounts to more than 2,800[50] and, to date, they constitute the preferred instrument for the international protection of FDI.[51] An interesting aspect of this evolution is that developing countries are now signing BITs amongst themselves, the share of such treaties representing about a third of the total at present.[52] However, BITs between developed countries are virtually non-existent, but investment provisions may be included in free trade agreements.[53]

Bilateral investment treaties are concluded between two States and give prospective third parties – private investors and nationals of one of the signatory States – certain legal safeguards in relation to the investment projects they (plan to) have in the other State. The stated rationale of BITs is usually the encouragement of capital flows and the promotion of economic cooperation between the signatory States, while the practical advantages are in the protection of foreign investment in the host State.[54] Indeed, for the capital-exporting country, the main purpose of BITs is to ensure that the other party grants a certain standard of treatment to its national investors, which until that point had proven uncertain due to the absence of both a consensus in CIL and of a substantive multilateral treaty on the matter.

47 In 2008, eleven BITs were even denunciated; in nine of these Ecuador was involved. The other denounced BITs are the one between El Salvador and Nicaragua and the one between the Netherlands and the Bolivarian Republic of Venezuela. UNCTAD, 'Recent Developments in International Investment Agreements (2008–June 2009)', *IIA Monitor* No. 3 (2009), p. 6.
48 Vandevelde, op. cit., p. 177.
49 UNCTAD, 'Non-Equity Modes of Production and Development – World Investment Report 2011', 2011, p. 100. Online. Available HTTP <http://www.unctad-docs.org/files/UNCTAD-WIR2011-Full-en.pdf> (accessed 3 January 2012).
50 The total number of BITs rose to 2,807 at the end of 2010. See UNCTAD, 'World Investment Report 2011', op. cit., p. 100.
51 C. McLachlan, L. Shore and M. Weiniger, *International Investment Arbitration: Substantive Principles*, Oxford: Oxford University Press, 2007, p 26.
52 Twenty of the 54 BITs signed in 2010 were between developing countries and/or transition economies; UNCTAD, 'World Investment Report 2011', op. cit., p. 100; M. Herdegen, *Internationales Wirtschaftsrecht*, München: Verlag C.H. Beck, 2011, p. 301.
53 See the US–Australia free trade agreement's investment chapter, which has the peculiarity of not containing a dispute settlement clause, possibly because both developed countries are inclined to trust each other's judicial system: Free Trade Agreement between Australia and the United States, done at Washington DC on 18 May 2004, Online. Available HTTP <http://203.6.168.65/fta/ausfta/final-text/> (accessed 3 January 2012).
54 Lowenfeld, *International Economic Law*, op. cit., p. 555.

For capital-importing countries, however, agreeing on these inroads into their sovereignty was mainly motivated by the desire to develop an investment-friendly environment and to attract foreign investors. The view has become widespread that FDI is a vector of development and that it therefore needed to be liberalized. Signing BITs allowed such countries to build a competitive advantage against other capital-importing countries.

Aside from more general clauses on the scope and definition of investment and, at times, conditions of admission and establishment, (a number of) the following investor-protective clauses can usually be found in BITs: (i) application of 'fair and equitable treatment' to the investment (often substantiated by a vague reference to principles of CIL); (ii) protection of the investor against unreasonable interference by other private entities (commonly labelled 'full protection and security'); (iii) a commitment to only expropriate the investor for a public purpose and against satisfactory compensation (the substantiation of such clauses has often proved quite contentious); (iv) guarantees of free transfers of funds and investments; (v) the guarantee that the host State will observe any obligation undertaken vis-à-vis the investor ('umbrella clause'); (vi) the interdiction of performance requirements imposed by the host State such as export quotas, the employment of local labour or local purchase obligations; (vii) taxation measures; and (viii) dispute settlement provisions allowing for the investor to directly sue the host State before an international tribunal in case of breach of the BIT,[55] most often without exhaustion of domestic remedies.[56]

Under the current BIT system, host States carry the burden of protecting foreign investments without being granted corresponding rights apart from their ability to prohibit certain economic activities.[57] Neither is it common in BITs to include clauses granting host States policy space to pass regulation and pursue what they see as the public interest, even though this practice is more and more frequent (see *infra*). For this reason it is hard to conclude that BITs contain substantive reciprocal undertakings.[58]

---

55 Recourse to such a dispute settlement avenue by investors is arguably on the rise. As of 31 December 2011, ICSID had registered 369 cases since 1972. In 63 per cent of those cases a BIT was invoked as the basis of ICSID jurisdiction. ICSID, 'The ICSID Caseload – Statistics', Issue 1, 2012, Online. Available HTTP <http://icsid.worldbank. org/ICSID/FrontServlet?requestType=ICSIDDocRH&actionVal=ShowDocument& CaseLoadStatistics=True&language=English31> (accessed 20 July 2012). It should be noted that ICSID is but one of the 'institutionalized' forums before which investment disputes may be brought. See: UNCTAD, 'World Investment Report 2011', op. cit., p. 102.

56 For an overview of the clauses enumerated above, see Lowenfeld, *International Economic Law*, op. cit., pp. 555–572.

57 S.F. Halabi, 'Efficient Contracting between Foreign Investors and Host States: Evidence from Stabilization Clauses', *NW. J. Int'l L. & Bus* 31, 2011, 271.

58 Sornarajah, *The International Law on Foreign Investment*, op. cit., p. 188.

2.4 The effect of bilateral investment treaties on customary international law

2.4.1 Arguments that the BIT network is conducive to customary international law

In light of the proliferation of BITs, many of which are 'remarkably similar', certain authors have 'inferred' that the BITs network now represents to a large extent the state of CIL in the area of investment law.[59] Such a finding is, of course, not neutral for practice. Great economic stakes are associated with it, as it generalizes the protective regime of investors which predominates in BITs and makes it applicable even in the absence of a treaty.[60] Investors the world over would enjoy the same level of protection, irrespective of their being able to rely on a BIT or not. As a proof that the debate is gaining ground, arbitral awards have considered on a number of specific points whether State practice as evidenced in BITs affects the state of 'general international law'.[61]

The following arguments are typically advanced in support of such affirmations. First, as treaty-making is a form of State practice relevant for identifying norms of CIL,[62] it is said that the phenomenon of BITs is so

---

59 Lowenfeld, *International Economic Law*, op. cit., pp. 555 and 584. The arbitral tribunal in Pope & Talbot also stated that 'applying the ordinary rules for determining the content of custom in international law, one must conclude that the practice of states is now represented by those treaties'. *Pope & Talbot Inc. v The Government of Canada*, UNCITRAL, Award on Damages, 31 May 2002, para. 62.

60 O. Schachter, 'Entangled Treaty and Custom', in Y. Dinstein (ed.), *International Law in a Time of Perplexity: Essays in Honour of Shabtai Rosenne*, Leiden: Brill, 1989, p. 718: there is 'an increasing tendency on the part of governments and lawyers to consider the rules in international agreements as customary law on one ground or another, and therefore binding on States not party to the agreement'. The classic rule under international law remains, however, that a treaty obligation is not binding upon third parties (*res inter alios acta nec nocet nec prodest*) unless it has become a rule of international custom; H. Thirlway, 'The Sources of International Law', in Malcolm Evans (ed.), *International Law*, Oxford: Oxford University Press, 2010 (3rd edn), p. 100.

61 For example, *CMS Gas Transmission Co. v Argentina*, ICSID Case No. ARB/01/8, Decision of the Tribunal on Objections to Jurisdiction, 17 July 2003, paras 43 ff, examines whether minority shareholders can also benefit from investor protection when the corporation in question benefits from a specific protective regime, contrary to the famous finding of the *Barcelona Traction* case. The tribunal found the following: 'The Tribunal . . . finds no bar in current international law to the concept of allowing claims by shareholders independently from those of the corporation concerned, not even if those shareholders are minority or non-controlling shareholders. Although it is true, as argued by the Republic of Argentina, that this is mostly the result of *lex specialis* and specific treaty arrangements that have so allowed, the fact is that *lex specialis* in this respect is so prevalent that it can now be considered the general rule, certainly in respect of foreign investments and increasingly in respect of other matters. To the extent that customary international law or generally the traditional law of international claims might have followed a different approach – a proposition that is open to debate – then that approach can be considered the exception.'

62 A. Boyle and C. Chinkin, *The Making of International Law*, New York: Oxford University Press, 2007, pp. 236–237.

widespread and the contents of these treaties so similar, that a consensus among BIT-signatory nations can be found to exist, such consensus amounting to general law which should also apply to situations where no BIT is applicable.[63] Moreover, such consensus would have been strengthened by the demise of communist doctrines around the world and by the fall of the USSR and the conversion of the eastern bloc to market economies.[64] These authors, however, add that one should not confuse the specific clauses of BITs with their underlying principles which have 'ripened into customary international law', as only the latter have a general scope.[65] Therefore BITs would be of a 'double nature': on the one hand they would contain customary principles on the protection of investment, and on the other hand, they would represent the *lex specialis* of the relationship between their signatories.[66]

From the viewpoint of *opinio juris*, the widespread signing of BITs by developed and developing countries alike would be evidence of the existence of a protective legal framework for FDI which all countries find desirable and even necessary. In 2004 Steffen Hindelang argued that '[t]he States have left us today with a network of more than 2,300 BITs – a broad statement that almost the whole community of States views foreign investment favourably and its protection by international law not only desirable but necessary. Can this, however, also be viewed as a statement in favour of common principles embodied in customary international law? The answer is almost certainly yes.'[67]

2.4.2 Arguments that the BIT network is lex specialis and largely leaves customary international law unchanged

2.4.2.1 Concerning the existence of opinio juris

Counterarguments abound against the arguments outlined above, and are no less compelling. First of all, many authors stigmatize the overreliance of these theories on the simple existence of a large number of like BITs, without considering the reasons underlying the conclusion of such BITs. In other words,

---

63 A. Lowenfeld, 'Investment Agreements and International Law', *Colum. J. Transnat'l L.* 42, 2003–2004, 128–129.

64 Ibid., p. 127.

65 Lowenfeld, *International Economic Law*, op. cit., p. 586.

66 S. Hindelang, 'Bilateral Investment Treaties, Custom and a Healthy Investment Climate – The Question of Whether BITs Influence Customary International Law Revisited', *Journal of World Investment and Trade* 5, 2004, 805 and 809. See at 805: 'In fact, BITs are of a double nature. In regard to the particular rights and obligations – the details – contained in the treaty, each treaty is and remains *lex specialis* or *quid pro quo* between the parties. Those specific rights and obligations, however, originate and are deduced from general principles or concepts and it is open to question whether those general principles, may in the intention of the parties, apply only to approved investment or to any investment.'

67 Ibid., p. 806.

can mere mimicry make custom? The UN International Law Commission, in the context of the customary law of consular relations, stated:

> An international convention admittedly establishes rules binding the contracting parties only, and based on reciprocity; but it must be remembered that these rules become generalized through the conclusion of other similar conventions containing identical or similar provisions, and also through the operation of the most-favoured-nation clause.[68]

There are, however, many examples of legal fields in which plenty of similar treaties were signed, without giving rise to the creation of CIL: extradition, air law, etc.[69]

Also, such theories are said to downplay the motives pushing developing countries to sign BITs, with a view to demonstrating the existence of the so-called consensus. While developed countries use BITs for defensive motives, most BITs were signed by developing countries for reasons of economic expediency, in order to attract foreign investment likely to boost their economic development, and from fear that, if staying out of the BIT network, they would disappear from the investment map. This difference in approach resulted in a weaker bargaining position of the developing countries and scepticism towards the perceived non-reciprocal nature of the agreements. In general, BITs are drafted by the developed country and offered to the developing country for signature, with the final agreement typically only reflecting minor modifications from the model agreements.[70]

The wave of economic liberalism which culminated in the 1990s certainly reinforced that feeling and did not leave developing countries much choice in this respect: they felt they had to build a competitive advantage for themselves.[71] However, no developing country, to our knowledge, has ever admitted contributing to the creation of custom by signing a BIT, and developing countries have always considered BITs as necessary concessions to be made to their sovereignty. It is widely accepted that the main purpose of developing countries in signing BITs was political and economic expediency rather than the replication or generation, in treaty form, of rules of CIL.[72] Andreas

---

68 Report of the International Law Commission Covering the Work of its 12th Session, (1960) *Yearbook of the International Law Commission*, UN Doc A/4425, para. 21, p. 145.

69 B. Kishoiyian, 'The Utility of Bilateral Investment Treaties in the Formulation of Customary International Law', *Journal of International Law and Business* 14, 1994, 341.

70 Vandevelde, op. cit., p. 170.

71 A. Guzman, 'Why LDCs Sign Treaties that Hurt Them: Explaining the Popularity of Bilateral Investment Treaties', *Va. J. Int'l L.* 38, 1998, 648.

72 'In the competition to attract foreign investment, potential host states end up in a bidding contest for foreign capital. Developing countries are pressured to give up their interests and concerns in exchange for greater incentives to investors, such as tax breaks, reduced pollution controls, and relaxed employment regulations. UN resolutions passed by the General Assembly demonstrate that developing countries want the ability to regulate

Lowenfeld asks the question, 'Does it matter whether the acceptance of BITs reflects genuine conversion or merely opportunism?'[73] We would answer that it does.

If the widespread adoption of BITs were to be interpreted as contributing to CIL on investment, this would imply that, in adhering to them, developing countries act out of a sense of legal obligation, or *opinio juris*, and that they feel compelled to abide by the rules contained in BITs even in the absence of such treaties.[74] *Opinio juris* serves to distinguish custom from standardized patterns of practice which are not binding on State parties.[75] It is highly debatable whether such *opinio juris* can be effectively detected in the behaviour of developing countries in the BIT context. The least one can say is that, if ever there were indications of this at the time when BITs were skyrocketing, the current international spirit is no longer of this kind. In Latin America, for instance, a number of countries have started retreating from commitments that they made earlier.[76] In addition, doubts are currently being expressed as to the real impact of FDI on economic development,[77] and as to the actual contribution of BITs in attracting such investment.[78] The repeated failures of the international community to agree on substantive multilateral treaties on investment likewise signal that many countries do not see such endeavours as a mere codification of existing customary rules, but rather as a norm-creating effort which would produce new general rules they are not ready to accept at any price.[79]

For certain authors, the existence of the vast network of BITs is so compelling as State practice that *opinio juris* could almost be presumed. It is also sometimes argued that the adoption, before the explosion of BITs, of UNGA resolutions

foreign investment compatibly with their development goals and desire for greater sovereignty over their resources.' O. Chung, 'The Lopsided International Investment Law Regime and its Effect on the Future of Investor-State Arbitration', *Va. J. Int'l L.* 47, 2007, 957–958.

73 Lowenfeld, 'Investment Agreements and International Law', op. cit., p. 126.

74 Schachter, 'Entangled Treaty and Custom', op. cit., p. 725.

75 Ibid., p. 732.

76 UNCTAD, 'Recent Developments in International Investment Agreements (2007–June 2008)', op. cit., p. 6.

77 See M. Crakovic and R. Levine, 'Does Foreign Direct Investment Accelerate Economic Growth?', in T. Moran et al. (eds), *Does Foreign Direct Investment Promote Development?*, Washington DC, Institute for International Economics/Center for Global Development, 2005, p. 195. See further L. Colen, M. Maertens and J. Swinnen, 'Foreign Direct Investment as an Engine for Economic Growth and Human Development: A Review of the Arguments and Empirical Evidence', *Human Rights & Int'l Legal Disc.* 3, 2009, 177–228.

78 See M. Hallward-Driemeier, 'Do Bilateral Investment Treaties Attract Foreign Direct Investment? Only a Bit . . . And They Could Bite', *World Bank Policy Research Working Paper No. 3121*, August 2003, Online. Available HTTP <http://econ.worldbank.org/external/default/main?pagePK=64165259&piPK=64165421&theSitePK=469372&menuPK=64216926&entityID=000094946_03091104060047> (accessed 3 January 2012).

79 See P. Daillier, M. Forteau and A. Pellet, *Droit International Public*, 8th edn, Paris: L.G.D.J., 2009, p. 1209.

(or at least of the 1962 Resolution on the Permanent Sovereignty over Natural Resources, which was supported by a wide range of developed and developing countries alike – see *supra*) on the issue of investment could be analysed as 'instant custom'.[80] These contentions appear dubious: the first one because even State practice so widespread cannot dispense with at least some expression of the conviction that this is based on binding international norms, which the position of developing countries seems to negate;[81] the second, because the extent to which UN Member States adopting the UNGA resolutions in question were expressing *opinio juris* is far from evident. The 1962 Resolution was the result of fierce debate and several unilateral declarations by States qualify its contents in non-consensual ways.[82]

One must be wary of the temptation to equate a succession of bilateral treaty consents with *opinio juris*. Consent is given in relation to 'specially negotiated regimes' applicable among a defined set of actors, such as BITs,[83] while *opinio juris* derives from the conviction of being bound by a general obligation.[84] The interwovenness of treaty rules and CIL is much more evident in multilateral treaties than in a maze of bilateral ones. Again, the failure to conclude substantive multilateral agreements on investment is telling in this respect. It should also be pointed out that the normative value of the rules expressed in treaties has an impact on their being capable of reflecting CIL. Norm-declaring treaties are more likely to give rise to general regulation than 'contractual' terms negotiated in a bilateral relationship.[85] The political and economic nature of BITs and the bargaining position of developing countries in their adoption are strong indicators against such norm-declaring character.

One evolution in the BIT network must, however, be brought into the debate, namely the fact that developing countries are now increasingly signing BITs among themselves. As indicated above, BITs concluded among developing

---

80 Sornarajah, *The International Law on Foreign Investment*, op. cit., p. 82.
81 Kishoiyian, op. cit., p. 332: 'The argument that these treaties strengthen the now antiquated "customary law" on investment protection cannot be supported in the context in which such treaty-making has taken place which usually involves the exchange of *quid pro quo* between the contracting parties. Each treaty is bound to be different from the other as each depends on the internal political order and the economic aspirations of each developing country.'
82 Lowenfeld, *International Economic Law*, op. cit., p. 489.
83 R. Dolzer and C. Schreuer, *Principles of International Investment Law*, Oxford: Oxford University Press, 2008, p. 21.
84 See Kishoiyian, op. cit., p. 337. In this connection also, '[i]nvestment rule-making is evolving towards more bilateralism and regionalism – which is the opposite of a harmonized, collective approach.' UNCTAD, 'International investment rule-making: stocktaking, challenges and the way forward', UNCTAD Series on International Investment Policies for Development, New York and Geneva, 2008. Online. Available HTTP <http://unctad.org/en/docs/iteiit20073_en.pdf> (accessed 20 July 2012), p. 64.
85 On the characteristics of treaties conducive to customary international law, see J. Charney, 'International Agreements and the Development of Customary International Law', *Wash. L. Rev.*, 1986, Vol. 61, p. 983.

countries amounted for about 26 per cent of the total at the end of 2008.[86] In 2010, 20 of the 54 BITs signed were between developing countries and/or transition economies.[87] Developing countries are therefore also becoming 'host and home economies',[88] and in that sense they seem to buy into the protective framework set up by BITs, possibly moving towards a recognition of certain customary principles. If all countries, developed and developing, had the same stakes in protecting investment and their sovereignty both as home and host States, the way to CIL would be much easier to find. The 2011 issue of UNCTAD's World Investment Report shows clear signs that the FDI gap is getting more narrow between developed and a certain segment of the developing – 'emerging' – world. In 2010, for the first time, more than half of FDI inflows were received by developing and transition economies, and the latter were also responsible for a record proportion of world FDI outflows (29 per cent). These statistics must, however, be qualified in that they are unevenly distributed among regions (with Africa and parts of Asia lagging behind), and definitely do not concern least-developed countries, whose numbers keep falling year after year.[89] Therefore, one cannot conclude that all developing countries – in particular least-developed countries – are there yet. Moreover, the levelling of bargaining positions may give way to diverging opinions on the issue of investment protection, preventing the emergence of consensus.[90]

2.4.2.2 On the extent of state practice reflected by BITs

Critics of the theories outlined above also tend to argue that they overestimate the consistency of BIT clauses which would not meet the 'general State practice' threshold necessary for custom. As M. Sornarajah points out:

> [t]hough the repetition of the rule in numerous treaties may create customary law, regard must also be had to the variations in the structure of such treaties in which the rule is embedded. Bilateral investment

86 UNCTAD, 'Recent Developments in International Investment Agreements (2008–June 2009)', IIA MONITOR No. 3 (2009), UNCTAD/WEB/DIAE/IA/2009/8, p. 4.
87 UNCTAD, 'World Investment Report 2011', op. cit., p. 100.
88 UNCTAD, 'International Investment Rule-Making: Stocktaking, Challenges and the Way Forward', op. cit., pp. 36–37.
89 UNCTAD, 'World Investment Report 2011', op. cit., pp. 3 ff.
90 'One possible consequence of this development could be a growing convergence of views among emerging economies and some developing countries, as emerging economies increasingly see themselves as capital exporters and seek to protect their interests. This, in turn, could strengthen consensus-seeking in support of core principles of investment protection. At the same time, however, it may also increase the diversity of views among developing countries that increasingly will no longer have monolithic interests as capital importing countries.' UNCTAD, 'International Investment Rule-Making: Stocktaking, Challenges and the Way Forward', op. cit., p. 38.

treaties, though similar in structure, vary as to detail to such an extent that it would be difficult to argue that they are capable of giving rise to customary international law.[91]

The issue of the standard of compensation to be applied in cases of expropriation is a good example of such fundamental deviations. Even though many BITs use the Hull formula, not all of them do so,[92] and one must thus guard oneself from jumping to conclusions as to customary value.[93] Similarly, the standard of 'fair and equitable treatment', vague by nature as it is, has been drafted in many different versions, arguably explaining in part the unsettled character of the case law applying the standard.[94] More generally, as evidenced by the latter standard, the content of BITs protections is often vague and open-ended, giving arbitral tribunals a hard time in finding coherent interpretations, thereby also reducing the actual generality of the rules contained in BITs for the purpose of establishing CIL.[95] An example of these difficulties can be found in the discrepancies in arbitral case law about the meaning of 'umbrella clauses'. In these 'observation of commitment' clauses the contracting parties commit themselves to observe any obligation they may have assumed with regard to foreign investors. As such, the clause is generally understood as an attempt to elevate all possible violations of investment contracts from the national to the international level and to engage the international responsibility of the host State for any breach of contract.[96] Yet, while such clauses are present in many BITs, their wording often differs, causing divergent lines of interpretation in arbitral decisions. In the 2003 *SGS v Pakistan* case, the ICSID Tribunal took a 'prudential approach' and rejected, failing express language as to this in the BIT concerned, the far-reaching meaning of the umbrella clause purported by the claimant that it 'elevated' any breach of an investment contract to the level of a BIT breach, therefore opening the way to BIT arbitration.[97]

---

91 Sornarajah, *The International Law on Foreign Investment*, op. cit., p. 82. In the same vein, see also C. Cai, 'International Investment Treaties and the Formation, Application and Transformation of Customary International Law Rules', *Chin. J. Int'l L.* 7, 2008, 664; P. Muchlinski, 'Policy Issues', in P. Muchlinksi, F. Ortino and C. Scheurer (eds), *The Oxford Handbook of International Investment Law*, Oxford: Oxford University Press, 2008, p. 16.
92 Lowenfeld, *International Economic Law*, op. cit., p. 564.
93 See Schachter, 'Compensation for Expropriation', op. cit.; Sornarajah, *The International Law on Foreign Investment*, op. cit., p. 418.
94 A. Joubin-Bret, 'The Growing Diversity and Inconsistency in the IIA System', in K.P. Sauvant, *Appeals Mechanism in International Investment Disputes*, Oxford: Oxford University Press, 2008, p. 138.
95 See Chung, op. cit., pp. 959–962.
96 Dolzer and Schreuer, op. cit., pp. 153–5 and P. Weil, 'Problèmes relatifs aux contrats passés entre un Etat et un particulier', *Recueil des cours de l'Académie de droit international de La Haye*, Vol. 128, Leiden: Martinus Nijhoff Publishers, 1969, p. 124.
97 *SGS Société Générale de Surveillance S.A. v Islamic Republic of Pakistan*, ICSID Case No. ARB/01/13, Decision of the Tribunal on Objections to Jurisdiction, 6 August 2003, paras 163–174.

This interpretation was explicitly rejected as 'unconvincing' by another arbitral tribunal in *SGS v Philippines*, which accepted that the umbrella clause – in that case drafted in a more affirmative manner – could have the 'elevator effect' sought by the claimant.[98]

Subsequent arbitral decisions diversely reflected the interpretative frictions, leaving the debate open to this day.[99] The various examples of conflicting interpretations of like though not identical BIT clauses by tribunals therefore cannot be said to support, in relation to BITs, the claim to consistency required by the customary 'State practice' requirement.[100]

Perhaps as a result of the above, the trend is now to use increased detail in BIT clauses so as to define their scope and meaning more precisely.[101] BITs are therefore becoming increasingly complex, but at the same time ever more diversified. As a result, the BITs network is becoming even less coherent, which undermines any affirmative finding as to the existence of CIL.[102] A recent report of UNCTAD states:

> In substance, the agreements reflect a *considerable degree of consensus* with respect to the principal content. Provisions relating to treatment and protection of investment such as national and MFN treatment, compensation for expropriation, the right to free transfers, and consent to investor–State and State–State dispute resolution appear in a very large majority of agreements. However, the actual wording or these provisions shows great and sometimes surprising diversity. Other provisions, however, such as guarantees of national treatment and MFN treatment with respect to the right to establish investment and prohibitions on performance

98 *SGS Société Générale de Surveillance S.A. v Republic of the Philippines*, ICSID Case No. ARB/02/6, Decision of the Tribunal on Objections to Jurisdiction, 29 January 2004, paras 113–129; Herdegen, op. cit., pp. 306–307.

99 See e.g. *Eureko v Poland*, in which the Tribunal determined that it had jurisdiction to consider whether actions taken by the government related to a contract can amount to violations of treaty provisions, considering the ordinary maximum meaning of the umbrella clause, stating '"Any" obligations is capacious; it means not only obligations of a certain type, but "any" – that is to say, all – obligations'; *Eureko v Poland*, 12 ICSID Reports (2005) 518, Partial Award, 19 August 2005, para. 246. Shortly after, in *Noble Venture v Romania*, the ICSID Tribunal held that while there were certain breaches of contract and violations of the treaty, there were factual findings that did not link these treaty breaches with the claimant's damages; *Noble Venture v Romania*, ICSID Case No. ARB/01/11, Award, 12 October 2005.

100 M. Wendlandt, 'SGS v Philippines and the Role of ICSID Tribunals in Investor-State Contract Disputes', *Texas International Law Journal* 43, 556.

101 On the fair and equitable treatment clauses, 'while most BITs contain a straightforward provision on fair and equitable treatment, some more recent agreements elaborate in more detail on the content of this article. This raises the question as to whether the substantive content of both variations differ.' UNCTAD, 'International Investment Rule-Making: Stocktaking, Challenges and the Way Forward', op. cit., p. 56.

102 See generally ibid., pp. 29–31; and p. 31: 'it has become difficult to speak in any meaningful way of a "typical" [International Investment Agreement].'

requirements, appear only in a minority of agreements, sometimes with considerable variation among treaties.[103]

In light of this, it is rather doubtful that the threshold of a sufficiently 'extensive and virtually uniform' State practice has been reached, let alone that there is enough evidence of 'a belief that this practice is rendered obligatory by the existence of a rule of law requiring it'.[104]

2.4.3 Interim conclusion

In the face of all this criticism, the proponents of the customary character of the BITs network had to recognize that only very broad principles enshrined in BITs are probably of a customary nature, most notably the principle that expropriation can only be for a public purpose, and against compensation, failing which diplomatic protection can be resorted to.[105] However, such a principle already existed before BITs emerged, and was only weakly challenged by the Calvo doctrine and some UNGA resolutions, which have never imposed themselves strongly enough to modify CIL on these issues. To be sure, expropriations without compensation have historically been very rare.[106] Other major issues dealt with in BITs have clearly remained out of the customary sphere, such as the principle of arbitrability of investor–State disputes,[107] or the national treatment and most-favoured nation treatment standards.[108] The contribution of BITs to CIL would therefore be reduced to the codification of a few loose principles which have been around for a long time already. In this respect, the binding interpretation by NAFTA's Free Trade Commission given to the 'minimum standard of treatment' contained in Article 1105 of NAFTA, as not requiring more than the customary international law minimum standard of treatment of aliens, can serve as an example.[109] For

---

103 Ibid., p. 43. Emphasis in original.
104 To use the terms of the ICJ in the *North Sea Continental Shelf Cases* (Germany/Denmark and The Netherlands), Judgment, *ICJ Reports 1969*, 4, paras 74 and 77, respectively.
105 Hindelang, op. cit., p. 805.
106 Lowenfeld, *International Economic Law*, op. cit., p. 485.
107 Kishoiyian, op. cit., p. 368.
108 C. Crépet Daigremont, 'Traitement national et traitement de la nation la plus favorisée dans la jurisprudence arbitrale récente relative à l'investissement international', in Ch. Leben (ed.), *Le contentieux arbitral transnational relatif à l'investissement: nouveaux développements*, Paris and Louvain-la-Neuve: L.G.D.J. and Anthemis, 2006, pp. 108–109.
109 NAFTA Free Trade Commission, 'Clarifications Related to NAFTA Chapter 11', July 31, 2001, Online. Available HTTP <http://www.worldtradelaw.net/nafta/chap11interp.pdf> (accessed 3 January 2012), clarifying that although Article 1105(1) simply refers to 'treatment in accordance with international law', it 'prescribes the customary international law minimum standard of treatment of aliens as the minimum standard of treatment to be afforded to investments of investors of another Party'. This interpretation is particularly controversial since it effectively overruled interpretations previously adopted; see A. Roberts, 'Power and Persuasion in Investment Treaty Interpretation: The Dual Role of States', *Am. J. Int'l L.* 104, 2010, 180.

the remainder, BITs largely fail to crystallize or generate new customary international rules.

We submit that theories contending that the BITs network as a whole contributes to the formation of an encompassing customary regime on investment do not constitute a sensible approach. Any analysis as to the existence of CIL, notably in the field of investment, so much characterized by polarization of views and interests, should start with a bottom-up, case-by-case, rule-by-rule examination from the viewpoint of State practice and *opinio juris*, rather than by conducting a large-scale analysis of the impact of the BITs network as a whole on a possible customary regime. In other words, the proper test is: do like clauses in many BITs evidence sufficient State practice and *opinio juris* on the issues that they address? This test will yield different results according to the rule considered, due notably to the prior state of CIL on the issue, the state of BITs on that matter, the scope of compliant and deviant practice, and countless psychological and political elements that surround the BIT clauses at hand. The BITs network is thus relevant in finding custom on investment, but as such is not conclusive. Any different approach will inevitably lose itself in fallacious approximations. Often, such approaches fail to distinguish between the different ways treaty and custom may interact: codification, crystallization and generation.[110] This has led to dubious statements which rather contribute to a devaluation of the notion of CIL altogether, such as the qualification of the BITs network as 'something like customary law' or submissions that the definition of CIL itself is wrong.[111]

Admittedly, one can also argue that the question of the extent to which investment treaties have contributed to the development of the customary law on international investment was much more important before the BITs boom of the 1990s. In that period, with only a limited number of BITs in force, protection for international investment rested more largely on customary law, which made the question of whether provisions appearing in non-applicable BITs had achieved customary legal status much more pressing. Today, with thousands of investment treaties in place covering a majority of investment disputes, attention has rather shifted to the arbitral interpretation of clauses where CIL remains marginally relevant, notably under Article 31(3)(c) of the Vienna Convention on the Law of Treaties, and the scope of treaty protection available. Nevertheless, the network of investment treaties is far from complete and situations remain where customary protection is all that is available.

2.5 Bilateral investment treaties, customary international law and the host state's policy space

It has become clear that the dominant practice of BIT-making falls short of gathering unanimous satisfaction, let alone a consensus conducive to customary

110 As in A. D'Amato, 'Treaties as a Source of General Rules of International Law', *Harvard J. Int'l L.* 3, 1962, p. 1.
111 Lowenfeld, 'Investment Agreements and International Law', op. cit., p. 130.

status. With the globalization-induced redistribution of economic power, which is reshuffling the cards among capital-importing and exporting countries, the international investment legal regime, and in particular the BITs network, was bound to evolve. In this section, we take stock of a new trend in investment treaty practice, which arguably finds its origins in the seemingly unequal positions of host States and investors in the BITs network. It has been observed that, in a number of situations, the firm protections enshrined in BITs in favour of investors are constraining host States' policy space, thereby running afoul of international law's foundational principle of State sovereignty. The new treaty practice in the field of investment, as we shall see in our analysis of a 'new generation' of Model BITs, seeks to re-equilibrate the level of protection that investors can legitimately claim, and the breadth of policy space for host States.[112] Through a close scrutiny of the evolution of the most important clauses in the new generation of BITs, we will analyse the extent to which this renovated approach seeks to stick closer to traditional customary standards, and whether it could offer the prospect of letting a wider consensus emerge in the future.

2.5.1 *The overall issue of policy space and its importance for development*

It is interesting at this juncture to study the impact of BITs on host States' sovereign right to regulate in their territories, as this question, as we shall see, is now a major factor in the evolution of treaty practice in the field of investment. It is one of the cornerstones of international law that States are entitled to sovereignly pursue any policy they deem appropriate, save what is prohibited by international law.[113] This issue is particularly relevant to the impact of FDI on human development, as developing countries, which most often play the role of the host State in relation to FDI, have as a major objective to pursue their economic and social development. In doing so, they must pass legislation and put policies in place. The creation of a healthy investment climate, *inter alia*, through the conclusion of BITs, is one of them. However, as indicated above, BITs have, in practice, mainly been concerned with investor protection, rather than with the development of the host State.[114] As a result, host States, among which are a majority of developing countries, have agreed to a number of clauses prohibiting them from negatively affecting foreign investments through a variety of measures, thereby seriously curtailing their

---

112 See generally Daillier, Forteau and Pellet, op. cit., pp. 1213–1216, also discussing similar evolutions in the case-law.

113 PCIJ, *Case of the S.S. 'Lotus'*, 7 September 1927, PCIJ Series A – No. 10.

114 Even if BITs are often entitled 'Agreement for the promotion and protection of investment', specific promotion provisions in BITs are scarce and often much less operative than other clauses protective of investors. See UNCTAD, 'International Investment Rule-Making: Stocktaking, Challenges and the Way Forward', op. cit., pp. 79 ff. See also J.E. Alvarez, 'The Return of the State', *Minn. J. Int.'l L.* 20, 2011, 231.

sovereign right to regulate within their territories. Under the early customary standard of protection of aliens' property, the impact of investment protection rules on the right of the host State to regulate in the general interest was rather limited.[115] Can it be that the BITs network has modified this to such an extent as to create a customary regime of investor protection which encroaches significantly on host States' sovereignty?[116] It is submitted this is not the case. As argued above, the BITs network has not had such an overall impact on the state of CIL, and it has not become by itself an expression of CIL providing for extended investor protection which impinges on public policy-making in the host State.[117]

An important sign in this respect is the emphasis which is currently given to the notion of 'national policy space' for achieving a host State's development. The evolution of international investment law in the last two decades has indeed revealed a worrying trend: BITs have become so protective of investors that they sometimes prohibit host States from passing laws and regulations which were designed *bona fide* with a view to economic and social development, were clearly in the public interest, and did not even have any connection with investment.[118] Recent examples of the operation of investor protections against host States' sovereign regulatory measures include the arbitration claims mounted by the tobacco industry against domestic anti-smoking policies, such as laws imposing standard packaging for tobacco products.[119] Countries such as Uruguay,[120] but also powerful first-world countries like Canada, have yielded to the pressure of investors, and given up (or relaxed) their health policies in order to avoid having to pay damages.[121] This trend has been intensified by the

---

115 Lowenfeld, *International Economic Law*, op. cit., p. 481.
116 See e.g. C. Leben, 'La liberté normative de l'Etat et la question de l'expropriation indirecte', in Leben, (ed.), op. cit., pp. 163 ff.
117 See UNCTAD, 'International Investment Rule-Making: Stocktaking, Challenges and the Way Forward', op. cit., p. 69: 'provided that host countries respect their international commitments deriving from IIAs, e.g. the principle of non-discrimination, the standard of fair and equitable treatment, and the obligation to compensate in case of an expropriation, they remain free to subject TNCs in their territories to social, fiscal, environmental and other regulations that they deem necessary to meet their national development objectives.'
118 For a more detailed assessment, see: J. Wouters and N. Hachez, 'When Rules and Values Collide: How can a Balanced Application of Investor Protection Provisions and Human Rights be Ensured?', *Human Rights & Int'l. Legal Disc.* 3, 2009, 301–344.
119 See very recently, *Philip Morris Asia Limited v Australia*, UNCITRAL, Notice of Claim, 22 June 2011.
120 R. Carroll, 'Uruguay bows to pressure over anti-smoking law amendments', *The Guardian*, 27 July 2011. Online. Available HTTP <http://www.guardian.co.uk/world/2010/jul/27/uruguay-tobacco-smoking-philip-morris> (accessed 3 January 2012).
121 M. Porterfield and C. Byrnes, 'Philip Morris v. Uruguay: Will investor-State arbitration send restrictions on tobacco marketing up in smoke?', *Investment Treaty News*, International Institute for Sustainable Development, 12 July 2011. Online. Available HTTP <http://www.iisd.org/itn/2011/07/12/philip-morris-v-uruguay-will-investor-state-arbitration-send-restrictions-on-tobacco-marketing-up-in-smoke/> (accessed 3 January 2012).

vagueness in the wording of many BITs' clauses, which, for example, do not specify what exactly 'fair and equitable treatment' means, or do not define what constitutes an 'expropriation'. Arbitral tribunals have contributed to this imbalance by an extensive interpretation of such open-ended provisions, which has further reduced the host State's policy space.

2.5.2 *A new generation of BITs*

The aforementioned tendencies have certainly triggered a reaction on the part of BIT-signing countries, some of which have sought to rebalance their national policy space with their obligations to protect foreign investment. Certain activist countries, including developed countries like the United States and Canada (which have had to face fierce and unexpected challenges from investors against some of their – notably environmental – policies[122]) have therefore started to negotiate what is called a 'new generation' of BITs. These new BITs add more detail as to what the obligations of the host State are with regard to investor protection.[123] The recent growth in the numbers of revised Model BITs is of interest in the context of the possible evolution of CIL. In 2003 and 2004, the Slovak Republic, Finland, India, the United States and Canada presented new Model BITs, followed by Turkey, the United Kingdom, Latvia, France, Germany, Spain, the Czech Republic and China.[124] Numerous other countries are currently in the process of reviewing their own model investment agreements and renegotiating former BITs.[125]

The United States seems to have engaged in a progressive turn compared to its 1984 to 1987 Model BITs, which were generally considered as very investor-protective, by revising its Model BIT to provide for greater limits on

122 See R. Moloo and J. Jacinto, 'Environmental and Health Regulation: Assessing Liability Under Investment Treaties', *Berkeley J. Int'l L.* 29, 2011, 1–65.

123 UNCTAD, 'Recent Developments in International Investment Agreements', *IIA Monitor No. 2 (2005)*, 2006, p. 4. Online. Available HTTP <http://www.unctad.org/en/docs/webiteiit20051_en.pdf> (accessed 3 January 2012).

124 OECD, International Investment Perspectives 2006, OECD Publishing, Paris, 2006, Table 6.1, p. 146 and UNCTAD, IIA Compendium: Investment instruments. Online. Available HTTP <www.unctadxi.org/templates/DocSearch.aspx?id=780> (accessed 3 January 2012). Other countries are also in the process of developing new model BITs (Argentina, Venezuela, Ecuador, Morocco, Bolivia) or are planning a review process (Thailand and India). UNCTAD, World Investment Report, p. 85.

125 OECD, *International Investment Perspectives 2006*, OECD Publishing, Paris, 2006, p. 144. In 2007, 10 of the 44 new BITs replaced earlier treaties, which brought the share of renegotiated agreements to less than 5 per cent of the total number of BITs. Germany renegotiated the largest number of BITs (16), followed by China (15), Morocco (12) and Egypt (11), and more countries are revising their Model BITs to reflect new concerns related to environmental and social issues, including the host country's right to regulate; see UNCTAD, 'Recent Developments in International Investment Agreements (2007–June 2008)', *IIA Monitor* No. 2 (2008), p. 5.

investor protections.[126] The 2010 World Investment Report indicates that over 30 per cent of investment-related national policy changes now provide for greater regulation.[127] As José Alvarez underlines: 'UNCTAD's examples of these restrictions reveal how some countries are re-asserting their "sovereign rights" vis-à-vis foreign investors.'[128] It is remarkable that, next to these efforts introduced by the United States, others, like China, traditionally a proponent of national policy space, have been leaning towards the creation of a more investment-friendly climate.[129]

Concrete efforts by countries to rebalance BITs have, on the other hand, not always been welcomed by stakeholders. For example, in 2009 Norway renounced its proposed Model BIT, a very progressive attempt at creating equitable and transparent conditions based on mutual benefits, even comprising obligations for investors related to corporate social responsibility. This effort was sadly abandoned, following protests by non-governmental organizations (NGOs) and business groups alike.[130] The former claimed that the Model BIT had the potential to diminish the policy space of developing countries by 'locking in Norway's developing country treaty partners into a relationship of economic inequality and dependence'.[131] The latter groups felt that the model did not provide investors with enough substantive protection.[132] As a result, Norway expressed doubts regarding the BITs regime and its inability to create certainty for States as well as investors.[133]

In the following subsections, we focus on a selection of traditional BIT provisions as they are now approached in the new generation of BITs, so as to assess the impact of this evolution on national policy space and possibly CIL. In doing so, we will equally highlight tendencies in international arbitral dispute settlement, for – while not 'making law on its own' – it plays a decisive

126 Alvarez, 'The Return of the State', op. cit., p. 231; S.M. Schwebel, 'The United States 2004 Model Bilateral Investment Treaty: An Exercise in the Regressive Development of International Law', *Transnat'l DisP. Man.* 3, 2006, 3–7.
127 United Nations Conference on Trade and Development, 2010, World Investment Report 2010: Investing in a Low-Carbon Economy, p. 76.
128 Alvarez, 'The Return of the State', op. cit., p. 233.
129 Roberts, op. cit., pp. 196–197.
130 Preamble Norwegian draft Model BIT. Online. Available HTTP <http://www. regjeringen.no/upload/NHD/Vedlegg/hoeringer/Utkast%20til%20modellavtale2. doc> (accessed 3 January 2012); Ryan, op. cit., p. 88; Alvarez, 'The Return of the State', op. cit., p. 241.
131 South Center, 'Comments on Norway's Draft Model Bilateral Investment Treaty (BIT): Potentially Diminishing the Development Policy Space of Developing Country Partners', 15 April 2008, Geneva, Switzerland. Online. Available HTTP <http://www.regjeringen. no/upload/NHD/Vedlegg/hoeringer/2008/Modellavtale/South%20Centre.doc> (accessed 3 January 2012).
132 D. Vis-Dunbar, 'Norway Shelves Its Draft Model Bilateral Investment Treaty', *Inv. Treaty News*, 8 June 2009. Online. Available HTTP <http://www.iisd.org/itn/2009/06/08/ norway-shelves-its-proposed-model-bilateral-investment-treaty/> (accessed 19 July 2012).
133 Ryan, op. cit., p. 88.

role in the interpretation and determination of the scope of those clauses; and most BITs contain arbitral dispute settlement clauses.[134]

2.5.2.1 Fair and equitable standard

The 'fair and equitable standard' (FET) serves as a first example: virtually all BITs contain provisions specifying the treatment a contracting party is obliged to provide to investors of the other party. The standard of treatment is, moreover, the most commonly invoked standard in investors' claims before arbitral tribunals.[135] The FET standard has an absolute character: it must be guaranteed according to the BIT and regardless of the existence of other standards in the host country's domestic law.[136] The standard itself, however, lacks a precise meaning. Proponents of a strict approach to the standard argue that FET is no more than a reproduction of the customary international minimum standard.[137] In customary international law a breach of the minimum standard has been argued to occur only in the case of gross misconduct or manifest injustice following the interpretation given to it in the context of the 1926 *Neer* case,[138] thereby rejecting any claim as to the expansion of the customary standard by subsequent BIT practice. For example, the arbitral tribunal in *Glamis Gold v USA* stated that:

> although situations presented to tribunals are more varied and complicated today than in the 1920s, the level of scrutiny required under *Neer* is the same. Given the absence of sufficient evidence to establish a change in the custom, the fundamentals of the *Neer* standard thus still apply today: to violate the customary international law minimum standard of treatment codified in Article 1105 of the NAFTA, an act must be sufficiently egregious and shocking – a gross denial of justice, manifest arbitrariness, blatant unfairness, a complete lack of due process, evident discrimination,

---

134 P. Dumberry, 'Are BITs Representing the "New" Customary International Law in International Investment Law?', *Penn St. Int'l L. Rev.* 28, 2009–2010, 679. See also S.W. Schill, *The Multilateralization of International Investment Law*, Cambridge: Cambridge University Press, 2009, p. 331, note 156; J.E. Alvarez, 'A Bit on Custom', *N.Y.U. J. Int'l L. & Pol.* 42, 2009, 45.

135 S.A. Spears, 'The Quest for Policy Space in a New Generation of International Investment Agreements', *J. Int'l Econ. L.* 13, 2010, 1052.

136 See UNCTAD, 'Bilateral investment treaties 1995–2006: Trends in investment rulemaking', p. 28.

137 See in this regard the FTA's official interpretation of Article 1105 of NAFTA (above).

138 *Neer v Mexico* – Mexico General Claims Commission, 15 October 1926, *Am. J. Int'l L..*, Vol. 21, 1927, p. 555: 'the propriety of governmental acts should be put to the test of international standards ... [T]he treatment of an alien, in order to constitute an international delinquency should amount to *an outrage, to bad faith, to wilful neglect of duty*, or to an insufficiency of governmental action so far short of international standards that every reasonable and impartial man would readily recognize its insufficiency.' United Nations, Reports of International Arbitral Awards, 1926, IV, p. 60.

or a manifest lack of reasons – so as to fall below accepted international standards and constitute a breach of Article 1105(1).[139]

As a result, equalizing the FET standard with the minimum standard imposes a relatively small burden on the policy space of host governments.[140] Indeed, a number of arbitral tribunals, following the *Glamis Gold* arbitrators, have given content to the FET standard by explicit reference to its ordinary meaning based on the *Neer* standard.[141]

A different interpretation leading to a greater limitation of the host State's policy space can be found in cases in which the FET standard is given an autonomous meaning. A 2002 NAFTA arbitral award justifies such approach as follows:

> [T]he vast number of bilateral and regional investment treaties (more than 2000) almost uniformly provide for fair and equitable treatment of foreign investments, and largely provide for full security and protection of investments. Investment treaties run between North and South, and East and West, and between States in these spheres *inter se*. On a remarkably widespread basis, States have repeatedly obliged themselves to accord foreign investment such treatment. In the Tribunal's view, such a body of concordant practice will necessarily have influenced the content of rules governing the treatment of foreign investment in current international law. It would be surprising if this practice and the vast number of provisions it reflects were to be interpreted as meaning no more than the *Neer* Tribunal (in a very different context) meant in 1927.[142]

Arbitral decisions supporting this second approach in their turn have never reached consensus on FET's concrete reach. An autonomous meaning thereof has the potential to encompass all sorts of different treatments.[143] Many different situations,[144] such as for example the lack of transparency in an administrative process, have been considered to be in violation of the fair and equitable treatment standard.[145] There have been criticisms that the dominant case law

---

139 *Glamis Gold, Ltd v The United States of America*, UNCITRAL, Award, 8 June 2009, para. 22.

140 UNCTAD, 'Bilateral investment treaties 1995–2006: Trends in investment rulemaking', p. 29.

141 Spears, op. cit., p. 1055; M.C. Ryan, 'Glamis Gold Ltd v The United States and the Fair and Equitable Treatment Standard', *McGill L.J.* 56, 2011, p. 934.

142 *Mondev International Ltd v United States of America*, ICSID Case No. ARB(AF) 99/2, Award, 11 October 2002, para. 117.

143 For an analysis, see Wouters and Hachez, op. cit., pp. 301–344.

144 For an overview, see A. Reinisch, 'Internationales Investitionsschutzrecht', in C. Tietje (ed.), *Internationales Wirtschaftsrecht*, Berlin: De Gruyter Recht, 2009, p. 357.

145 *Metalclad Corporation v United Mexican States*, ICSID Case No. ARB(AF)/97/1, Award of the Tribunal, 30 August 2000, paras 99–101.

on fair and equitable treatment is following an expansionary trend, limitlessly extending the scope of this standard of treatment.[146]

In this regard, the current controversy about the fact that the FET standard would be breached when 'legitimate expectations' of investors are frustrated is of interest.[147] More concretely, the debate revolves around the question of whether the host State's conduct creates such reasonable and justifiable expectations for the investor regarding his investment, that a failure of the host State to act in conformity with those expectations could cause the investor to be unduly surprised and to suffer damages in relation to his investment.[148] The 'legitimate expectations' test is controversial as it risks imposing a limit to the host State's ability to change its course of action, notably by passing new regulation. Yet, this test has been applied in a more or less flexible manner by arbitral tribunals. In *ADF v The United States*, a refusal of the Federal Highway Administration to follow prior judicial and administrative rulings was not considered grossly unfair or unreasonable in this respect.[149] On the other hand, the tribunal in *Tecmed v Mexico* adopted a very high interpretive threshold for the obligation to provide fair and equitable treatment, based on the following interpretation of investors' legitimate expectations:

> The foreign investor expects the host State to act in a consistent manner, free from ambiguity and totally transparently in its relations with the foreign investor, so that it may know beforehand any and all rules and regulations that will govern its investments, as well as the goals of the relevant policies and administrative practices or directives, to be able to plan its investment and comply with such regulations.[150]

Remarkably, this harsh interpretation turns out to be quite popular and has been cited in numerous awards.[151] Still, the requirement for host States to pass

---

146 See M. Sornarajah, 'A Coming Crisis: Expansionary Trends in Investment Arbitration', in Sauvant, op. cit., pp. 39–80.

147 This criterion finds its origins in general principles of law since it is often applied in domestic administrative law. In the BIT context, it was also introduced in expropriation discussions. For further reading, see Dolzer and Schreuer, op. cit., pp. 104–106 and J. Cazala, 'La protection des attentes légitimes de l'investisseur dans l'arbitrage international', *Revue internationale de droit économique* 23, 2009, 5.

148 See the definition of 'legitimate expectations' as put forward by the tribunal in *International Thunderbird Gaming Corporation v The United Mexican States*, NAFTA Tribunal, Award, 26 January 2006, para. 149.

149 The tribunal in *ADF Group Inc. v United States of America*, ICSID Case No. RB(AF)/00/1, Award, 23 January 2003, para. 189, found that the legitimate expectations indicated were not raised by the defendant State.

150 *Tecmed Tecnicas Medioambientales S.A. v The United Mexican States*, ICSID Case No. ARB(AF)/00/2, Award, 29 May 2003, para. 154.

151 Herdegen, op. cit., p. 310 refers to *Occidental Exploration and Production Company v The Republic of Ecuador*, LCIA Case No. UN 3467, para. 185; According to Steinberg and Kotuby, at least twelve investment tribunals have held that the FET standard is violated

policies in the general interest, and in political and economic contexts which may have evolved since the time the BIT was signed, was also taken into account by some tribunals so as to mitigate the stringency of the 'legitimate expectations' criterion.[152] In *Saluka v Czech Republic*, the tribunal upheld a policy-space-inspired argument, warning that if the legitimate expectations criterion 'were to be taken too literally, [it] would impose upon host States' obligations which would be inappropriate and unrealistic'[153] as they would preclude any modification of the regulatory framework applicable to foreign investors.

As stated *supra*, some of the world's most influential capital exporters brought about a new generation of BITs protecting domestic regulatory action. The BITs concluded in the last decade to which these 'reforming' States are a party generally support the 'minimum standard' interpretation of FET. The intent to reduce regulatory and jurisprudential discretion is reflected in the Canadian Model BIT and the 2004 Model BIT of the United States.[154] The latter expressly defines in its Article 5, paragraph 2:

> For greater certainty, paragraph 1 prescribes the customary international law minimum standard of treatment of aliens as the minimum standard of treatment to be afforded to covered investments. The concepts of 'fair and equitable treatment' and 'full protection and security' do not require treatment in addition to or beyond that which is required by that standard, and do not create additional substantive rights. The obligation in paragraph 1 to provide:
>
> (a) 'fair and equitable treatment' includes the obligation not to deny justice in criminal, civil, or administrative adjudicatory proceedings in accordance with the principle of due process embodied in the principal legal systems of the world; and
> (b) 'full protection and security' requires each Party to provide the level of police protection required under customary international law.[155]

when a state frustrates an investor's legitimate expectations; A.B. Steinberg and C.T. Kotuby, 'Bilateral Investment Treaties and International Air Transportation: A New Tool for Global Airlines to Redress Market Barriers', *Journal of Air Law and Commerce* 76, 2011, 481; Moloo and Jacinto, op. cit., p. 46.

152 See e.g. *S.D. Myers, Inc. v Canada*, UNCITRAL, First Partial Award, 13 November 2000, paras 261–3.

153 *Saluka Invs. B.V. v Czech Republic*, UNCITRAL, Partial Award, 17 March 2006, para. 301–302. See also *Parkerings-Compagniet AS v Lithuania*, ICSID Case No. ARB/05/8, Award, 11 September 2007.

154 K.J. Vandevelde, 'A Comparison of the 2004 and 1994 U.S. Model BITs', *Y.B. Int'l L. & Pol'y* 1, 2009, 298; Spears, op. cit., p. 1043; Schwebel, 'The United States 2004 Model Bilateral Investment Treaty: An Exercise in the Regressive Development of International Law', op. cit.; Alvarez, 'The Return of the State', op. cit., p. 235.

155 Annex A of the US Model BIT clarifies that 'with regard to Article 5 [Minimum Standard of Treatment], the customary international law minimum standard of treatment of aliens refers to all customary international law principles that protect the economic rights and interests of aliens'.

The United States and Canada clearly opposed the catch-all character given to FET in certain arbitral decisions. As such, they objected in a very persistent way to the more expansive interpretation of FET clauses interfering with the sovereign rights of States. Both the American and Canadian recent Model BITs, moreover, exclude claims based on lack of transparency in administrative proceedings from investor–State dispute settlement.[156] It is submitted that China and the United States share the same understanding of the FET standard, notwithstanding the Chinese hesitation, based on historical discrepancies between East and West in the formation of CIL, to explicitly refer to CIL when defining the FET standard.[157] The Norwegian Draft Model BIT solely referred to customary law in general and not to the minimum standard interpretation of FET.[158] Other countries, such as France, Belgium and Luxembourg, include the FET standard as in accordance with the 'principles of international law'.[159] These countries thus agree to follow whatever the current international standard for FET is, and their treatment must therefore minimally respect customary international law and possibly additional international rules when in force. This is probably also the implicit approach taken in the many (Model) BITs that refer to FET without clarifying its content.[160]

2.5.2.2 Expropriation

The right of States to expropriate property within their territory for public purposes is at the very core of State sovereignty.[161] In virtually all BITs, the host

---

156 Art. 24, 1 (a) (i) (A) 2004 US Model BIT excluding Art. 11 on Transparency; Article 19 2004 Canada Model BIT.

157 For example, Art. 143(1) of China–New Zealand FTA uses the term 'commonly accepted rules of international law' to avoid the wording 'customary international law' included in Article 5(1) of 2004 US BIT Model; C. Congyan, 'China–US BIT Negotiations and the Future of Investment Treaty Regime: A Grand Bilateral Bargain with Multilateral Implications', *J. Int'l Econ. L.* 12, 2009, 468.

158 Art. 5 Norwegian draft Model BIT (2007).

159 See Belgium–Luxembourg Model BIT (2002) and Art. 3 French Model BIT (2006). The latter reads: 'Either Contracting Party shall extend fair and equitable treatment in accordance with the principles of International Law to investments made by nationals and companies of the other Contracting Party on its territory or in its maritime area, and shall ensure that the exercise of the right thus recognized shall not be hindered by law or in practice. In particular though not exclusively, shall be considered as de jure or de facto impediments to fair and equitable treatment any restriction on the purchase or transport of raw materials and auxiliary materials, energy and fuels, as well as the means of production and operation of all types, any hindrance of the sale or transport of products within the country and abroad, as well as any other measures that have a similar effect.'

160 See e.g. Art. 2(2) of the UK Model BIT (2005) which states: 'Investments of nationals or companies of each Contracting Party shall at all times be accorded fair and equitable treatment and shall enjoy full protection and security in the territory of the other Contracting Party.' Article 2(2) of the German Model BIT (2009) contains similar wording.

161 The right to exercise policy powers is part of the internal policy discretion States have following their internal sovereignty. Also see: Military and Paramilitary Activities in and against Nicaragua (*Nicaragua v United States of America*), Judgment, *ICJ Reports* 1986, p. 133; Reinisch, op. cit., p. 357.

countries agree to set limits on this right by spelling out conditions for lawful expropriations and by subjecting themselves to arbitral dispute settlement. It does not come as a surprise that numerous discussions arose where BITs limited the rights of host States to use compulsory acquisitions as a means to pursue legitimate non-investment policy objectives.[162] Customary international law does not preclude host States from expropriating foreign investments, provided the taking of the investment is for a public purpose, as provided by law, in a non-discriminatory manner and with compensation, language which is reprinted in most BITs around the world.[163]

Both the definition of and appropriate compensation for expropriation by host States[164] have formed the object of discussion, leading to variations in international practice and dispute settlement decisions.[165] Two main points have caused the most debate in relation to expropriation.

First, the question of whether expropriation clauses were only applicable to situations of removal by the host State of property rights *stricto sensu*, or whether they also extended to so-called 'regulatory takings' or 'indirect expropriations' by host governments, which 'arise . . . where government legislation or a regulatory measure deprives a property owner of the use or benefit of property, limits or prohibits the transfer or disposition of property or has the effect of destroying the value of property, but where the State does not acquire title to the property in question'.[166] It now seems settled that expropriation can occur as a result of regulatory measures which do not deprive the investor of its property title but nullify the value of the investment.

Second, and connected to this first question, comes the question of whether the purpose of the measures taken by a host State is relevant in the characterization of the latter as a regulatory taking or not. A number of arbitral tribunals have held that only the effect of the measure – that is, the deprivation of the reasonably expected profit of the investment – should be taken into consideration to conclude to an expropriation and therefore give rise to an obligation to

---

162 Spears, op. cit., p. 1049.

163 OECD, '"Indirect Expropriation" and the "Right To Regulate" in International Investment Law', *Working Papers on International Investment*, 2004, p. 3.

164 China has always insisted on using the wording 'appropriate compensation', rejecting the Hull Rule, which has, according to many other States – most notably the United States – become a rule of customary international law; see Congyan, op. cit., p. 476. The Resolution on Permanent Sovereignty over Natural Resources required 'appropriate' compensation while Art. 2(2)(c) of the Charter of Economic Rights and Duties of States, as indicated *supra*, stated that States have a right '[t]o nationalize, expropriate or transfer ownership of foreign property' provided compensation is paid to the State pursuant to the State's laws, and disputes regarding compensation will be resolved under domestic law unless another agreement has been reached.

165 Spears, op. cit., p. 1051.

166 A.P. Newcombe, 'Regulatory Expropriation, Investment Protection and International Law: When Is Government Regulation Expropriatory and When Should Compensation Be Paid?', 1999, at 3–4. Online. Available HTTP <http://ita.law.uvic.ca/documents/RegulatoryExpropriation.pdf> (accessed 3 January 2012).

compensate (sole effect doctrine).[167] The *Metalclad* case, in which the tribunal ruled that in order to decide on an indirect expropriation it 'need not decide or consider the motivation, nor intent of the adoption' of the measure, is often referred to as a classic example of this doctrine.[168] Others however, concerned with host States' right to regulate and to take measures to promote human development, argue that the public purpose of the measure prevents characterizing it as an expropriation (public powers doctrine). Only a number of arbitral cases have recognized as lawful (and therefore not requiring compensation) the good faith resort by States to (indirectly) expropriatory measures in order to achieve, through non-discriminatory actions, public interest objectives.[169]

An interesting trend to be observed is that in the recent generation of BITs expropriation provisions have been drafted in a manner that grants States extended policy space to undertake public interest regulatory measures with a lesser risk of having to compensate investors. The United States and Canada have accepted the case-by-case approach of international tribunals deciding in expropriation cases, but nevertheless considered it useful to include interpretative guidance for arbitrators in annexes to their 2004 Model BITs.[170] Annex B of the 2004 US Model BIT points out that Article 6 (on

---

167 Dolzer and Schreuer, op. cit., pp. 101–104, describing that authority for the sole effect doctrine is among others to be found in the case law of the Iran–US Claims Tribunal; Reinisch, op. cit., p. 368. See also *Tecmed S.A. v The United Mexican States*, op. cit.

168 *Metalclad v United Mexican States*, op. cit., para. 111. In this case, a US company, although granted permission from the central Mexican government to operate a hazardous waste landfill, had been refused a construction permit by the local government due to ecological reasons. In para. 49 of the award, which ruled in favour of the investor, it was furthermore stated: 'Indeed, a finding of expropriation on the basis of the Ecological Decree is not essential to the Tribunal's finding of a violation of NAFTA, Art. 1110. However, the Tribunal considers that the implementation of the Ecological Decree would, in and of itself, constitute an act tantamount to expropriation.'

169 OECD, '"Indirect Expropriation" and the "Right To Regulate" in International Investment Law', *Working Papers on International Investment*, 2004, p. 22. See e.g. *Methanex Corporation v United States of America*, Final Award of the NAFTA Tribunal, 7 August 2005, which ruled that '[a] non-discriminatory regulation for a public purpose, which is enacted in accordance with due process and, which affects, *inter alios*, a foreign investor or investment is not deemed expropriatory and compensable unless specific commitments had been given by the regulating government to the then putative foreign investor contemplating investment that the government would refrain from such regulation'. For further reading, see Moloo and Jacinto, op. cit., pp. 1–65.

170 OECD, '"Indirect Expropriation" and the "Right To Regulate" in International Investment Law', op. cit., p. 21; see Art. 6 and Annex B (4)(b) 2004 US Model BIT and Art. 13 and Annex B(13)(1(c) 2004 Canada Model BIT. Art. 6 of the US Model BIT reads: 'Neither Party may expropriate or nationalize a covered investment either directly or indirectly through measures equivalent to expropriation or nationalization ("expropriation"), except: (a) for a public purpose; (b) in a non-discriminatory manner; (c) on payment of prompt, adequate, and effective compensation; and (d) in accordance with due process of law and Art. 5 [Minimum Standard of Treatment] (1) through (3).' Article 13 of the Canada Model BIT stipulates: 'Neither Party shall nationalize or

expropriation and compensation) is intended to reflect customary international law concerning the obligation of States with respect to expropriation and that 'except in rare circumstances' non-discriminatory regulatory actions that are designed and applied to protect legitimate public welfare objectives, such as public health, safety, and the environment, do not constitute indirect expropriations.[171] The Canadian model mirrors this provision and even accentuates the extraordinary character of situations in which domestic regulations will be considered indirect expropriations.[172] The example and wording of interpretative provisions was soon to be followed by China in its Model BIT.[173] Some (multilateral) agreements take it a step further. The often quoted 2007 COMESA Common Investment Area Agreement (CIAA) and the 2009 ASEAN Comprehensive Investment Agreement view regulatory measures taken for a public purpose as not falling under the rules on indirect expropriation.[174] The former refers to this approach as consistent with CIL and reads:

> Consistent with the right of states to regulate and the customary international law principles on police powers, *bona fide* regulatory measures taken by a Member State that are designed and applied to protect or enhance legitimate public welfare objectives, such as public health, safety

expropriate a covered investment either directly, or indirectly through measures having an effect equivalent to nationalization or expropriation (hereinafter referred to as "expropriation"), except for a public purpose, in accordance with due process of law, in a non-discriminatory manner and on prompt, adequate and effective compensation.'

171 Comparing the American and Canadian Model BITs to the 2009 German Model BIT, Jörn Griebel argues that, although he does not necessarily agree with the content of the annexes to the first mentioned BITs, the latter fails to provide legal certainty for investors by not establishing any criteria. See J. Griebel, 'Einführung in den Deutschen Mustervertrag über die Förderung und den gegenseitigen Schutz von Kapitalanlagen von 2009', *Praxis des Internationalen Privat- und Verfahrensrechts* 30, 2010, 418.

172 Annex B.13(1)(c) reads: 'Except in rare circumstances, such as when a measure or series of measures are so severe in the light of their purpose that they cannot be reasonably viewed as having been adopted and applied in good faith, non-discriminatory measures of a Party that are designed and applied to protect legitimate public welfare objectives, such as health, safety and the environment, do not constitute indirect expropriation.'

173 See Art. 7 (1) of the Chinese Model BIT, in line with international law, placing similar conditions on expropriation: 'Neither Contracting Party may expropriate or nationalize an investment either directly or indirectly through measures tantamount to expropriation or nationalization ("expropriation"), except: (a) for a public purpose; (b) on a non-discriminatory basis; (c) in accordance with due process of law; and (d) on payment of compensation in accordance with paragraph 2 below [paragraph on compensation].' Paragraph 3 copies the interpretative language from the American and Canadian annexes: 'Except in rare circumstances, non-discriminatory regulatory actions by a Party that are designed and applied to protect legitimate public welfare objectives, such as public health, safety, and the environment, do not constitute indirect expropriations.'

174 See also: Sornarajah, *The International Law on Foreign Investment*, op. cit., p. 397; Spears, op. cit., p. 1052.

and the environment, shall not constitute an indirect expropriation under this Article.[175]

The French Model BIT allows direct and indirect expropriation in cases of public interest while referring to fixed elements of the Hull formula on compensation in these cases.[176] The strongest language is to be found in Article 6 of the former draft Norwegian Model BIT, which expressly grants the right to regulate to the host State.[177] Other countries, such as the United Kingdom, have not altered their official position on the Hull formula. In practice, however, it appears that this standard was not applied so strictly when the UK was the capital-importing State that had to compensate foreign investors.[178] The British Government's nationalization of the shares of the banks Northern Rock and Bradford & Bingley in 2008 failed to respect the protection owed to the banks' non-UK investors by calculating the compensation according to the 'liquidation value' instead of other calculation methods such as the 'fair market value'.[179] In light of the above, and taking into account the new generation of BITs, the hypothesis of a customary compensation practice supporting the Hull formula may not be established firmly.[180]

2.5.2.3 *Most favoured nation*

The principle that investors of one State may not be discriminated against in comparison with the investors of any third State and their investments (most favoured nation or MFN) is central in the protection of investors' rights. The MFN requirement is a well-known concept in investment and trade law

---

175 Article 20(8) CIAA. The interpretative Annex 2 of the 2009 ASEAN Comprehensive Investment Agreement does not explicitly refer to customary international law and reads: 'non-discriminatory measures of a Member State that are designed and applied to protect legitimate public welfare objectives, such as public health, safety and the environment, do not constitute an expropriation of the type referred to in sub-paragraph 2(b) [on indirect expropriation]'.
176 See Art. 5 French Model BIT (2006).
177 Article 6 of the Norwegian Model BIT reads: '(1) A Party shall not expropriate or nationalize an investment of an investor of the other Party except in the public interest and subject to the conditions provided for by law and by the general principles of international law. (2) The preceding provision shall not, however, in any way impair the right of a Party to enforce such laws as it deems necessary to control the use of property in accordance with the general interest or to secure the payment of taxes or other contributions or penalties.'
178 For a detailed discussion, see N. Jansen Calamita, 'The British Bank Nationalisations: An International Law Perspective', *Int'l & Comp. L. Q* 58, 2009, 119–149.
179 'Adequacy', a component of the Hull formula, is generally understood as 'fair market value'. On this notion, see M. Waibel, 'Opening Pandora's Box: Sovereign Bonds in International Arbitration', *American Journal of International Law* 101, 2007, 754; I. Marboe, 'Compensation and Damages in International Law: The Limits of Fair Market Value', *J. of World Investment & Trade* 7, 2006, 723; Jansen Calamita, op. cit., pp. 126–127.
180 Sornarajah, *The International Law on Foreign Investment*, op. cit., p. 418.

but it has also found its way into other fields, most notably diplomatic and consular law. Most-favoured-nation clauses in bilateral agreements have significant effects, as they may be used to endow the network of BITs with the multilateral role and non-discriminatory function a multilateral treaty was never able to provide.[181] The International Law Commission (ILC) in 1978 adopted draft articles on the MFN clause, which were, however, never taken up by the General Assembly.[182] The ILC's Draft Article 7 underlined the conventional rather than customary international law status of MFN treatment.[183] Yet circumstances are no longer the same as they were in 1978: the inclusion of MFN clauses in customs unions and regional organizations, and the spread of BITs, all containing some sort of MFN clause and their arbitral interpretations, have had a great impact on the contents of the principle.[184] While it is a well-known standard in international relations, and despite the fact that MFN in the GATT/WTO trade regime evolved into a standard consistently interpreted by the Dispute Settlement Body,[185]

181 J.A. Maupin, 'MFN-Based Jurisdiction in Investor-State Arbitration: Is there any Hope for a Consistent Approach?', *J. Int'l Econ. L.* 14, 2011, 158; Alvarez, 'A Bit on Custom', op. cit., p. 55.

182 United Nations International Law Commission, Report of the International Law Commission, Doc. No. A/63/10, Sixtieth Session, 2008, para. 14, p.394. The Commission, at its sixtieth session (2008), decided to include the topic 'The Most Favoured Nation clause' in its programme of work and to establish a Study Group on the topic at its sixty-first session. In 2010 the Study Group decided to try to identify further the normative content of the MFN clauses in the field of investment, and to undertake a further analysis of the case law, including the role of arbitrators, factors that explain different approaches to interpreting MFN provisions, the divergences, and the steps taken by States in response to the case law. At its sixty-third session in 2011, the Commission reconstituted the MFN Study Group, which held a comprehensive discussion on the interpretation and application of MFN clauses in investment agreements while also taking into account recent arbitral decisions. In preparing a programme of work for the future, the Study Group affirmed its intention not to formulate any draft articles or to revise the 1978 draft articles: United Nations International Law Commission, Report of the International Law Commission, Doc. No. A/66/10, Sixty-Third Session, 2011, paras 345–346 and 362, p.288.

183 Article 7, Draft Articles on most-favoured-nation clauses with commentaries, *Yearbook of the International Law Commission*, 1978, vol. II, Part Two, spells out: 'Nothing in the present articles shall imply that a State is entitled to be accorded most-favoured-nation treatment by another State otherwise than on the basis of an international obligation undertaken by the latter State.' In the commentaries to the draft article it is clarified that 'Although the grant of most-favoured-nation treatment is frequent in commercial treaties, there is no evidence that it has developed into a rule of customary international law. Hence it is widely held that only treaties are the foundation of most-favoured nation treatment.'

184 Paragraph 16, Report of the International Law Commission, op. cit., p. 394.

185 See e.g. interpretations of MFN given in EC–Regime for the Importation, Sale and Distribution of Bananas, WT/DS27/AB/R (WTO), 25 September 1997 (on Art. 1 GATT); Canada – Certain Measures Affecting the Automotive Industry, WT/DS139/AB/R (WTO), 31 May 2000 (on Art. 2 GATS), which are consequently referred to, see e.g. Columbia – Indicative Prices and Restrictions on Ports of Entry, WT/DS366/R, 27 April 2009, paras 7.320–7.323.

its inclusion in BITs has not resulted in a similar outcome in the investment context.[186]

The case law on the matter is divided.[187] In the often quoted 2004 *Maffezini* award, MFN is given a very broad scope, as applicable not only to substantive but also to procedural issues. The central question in this case – whether a claim should first be brought before domestic courts under a BIT containing an MFN clause whereas this was not a requirement in other bilateral agreements of the host country – was answered negatively:

> [T]he Tribunal is satisfied that the Claimant has convincingly demonstrated that the most favored nation clause included in the Argentine–Spain BIT embraces the dispute settlement provisions of this treaty. Therefore, relying on the more favorable arrangements contained in the Chile–Spain BIT and the legal policy adopted by Spain with regard to the treatment of its own investors abroad, the Tribunal concludes that Claimant had the right to submit the instant dispute to arbitration without first accessing the Spanish courts.[188]

The tribunal decided that the MFN clause included procedural rights for investors, including the right to seek arbitration without first submitting the dispute to local courts. This interpretation was criticized for significantly reducing the policy space of host States and encouraging 'treaty shopping' by investors.[189] Moreover, it is debatable whether States actually intended to confer such an extent to their obligations when signing BITs.[190] The approach taken in *Maffezini* was not followed unanimously by investment tribunals, leading to a vivid discussion on the actual content of MFN clauses in BITs, which is still not settled today.[191]

---

186 Paragraph 10, Report of the International Law Commission, op. cit., p. 392.
187 Most strikingly, tribunals have come to very different conclusions, even in cases involving the same question and in relation to the same BIT; see Maupin, op. cit., p. 160.
188 *Maffezini v Kingdom of Spain*, ICSID Case No. ARB/97/7, Award on Jurisdiction, 25 January 2000, para. 64. Conversely, in the ILC draft articles, MFN was limited to substantive issues; Art. 9, Draft Articles on most-favoured-nation clauses with commentaries, op. cit.
189 On the question of 'treaty-shopping' related to MFN in BITs, see A.F. Rodriguez, 'The Most-Favored-Nation Clause in International Investment Agreements: A Tool for Treaty Shopping?', *Journal of International Arbitration* 25, 2008, 89–102.
190 Ryan, op. cit., p. 65; para. 26 Report of the International Law Commission, op. cit., p. 398.
191 For a detailed study based on 17 publicly available awards, see Maupin, op. cit., pp. 157–189. Cases following a more narrow interpretation of MFN include *Tecmed v Mexico*, op. cit.; *Salini* and *Plama* arbitrations; *CMS Gas Transmission Company v Argentina*, ICSID Case No. ARB 701/08, Award, 25 April 2005. For cases supporting the broad approach, see *Siemens* arbitration; *MTD Equity Bhd v Chile*, ICSID Case No. ARB/01/7, Award, 25 May 2004; *Bayindir Insaat Turizm Ticaret Ve Sanayi AS v Islamic Republic of Pakistan*, ICSID Case No. ARB/03/29, Decision on Jurisdiction, 14 November 2005. In *Wintershall*, after considering *Maffezini* and the related discussions, it is stated: 'In the absence of language or context to suggest the contrary, the ordinary meaning of

The tribunal in the 2009 *Renta* Arbitration summarized the current state of the case law as follows:

> A considerable number of awards under BITs have dealt with the jurisdictional implications of MFN. . . . They are of uneven persuasiveness and relevance. The present Tribunal would find it jejune to declare that there is a dominant view; it is futile to make a head-count of populations of such diversity. What can be said with confidence is that a *jurisprudence constante* of general applicability is not yet firmly established.[192]

Faced with such uncertainty, the new generation of BITs have undergone some remarkable modifications, in quite a number of cases leaning towards greater policy space for the State parties involved. Here too, however, it is difficult to say that any consistent practice has emerged. France, for example, included in its 2006 Model BIT a quasi-absolute MFN provision, only excluding tax matters and 'privileges granted by the host State to nationals or companies of a third-party State by virtue of its participation or association in a free trade zone, customs union, common market or regional economic organization'.[193] Other new (Model) BITs on the contrary restrained the scope of MFN clauses so as to reduce the uncertainty that the stream of prior arbitration decisions had brought about.

Most of the BITs, however, remain silent on the issue of whether the MFN clause allows parties to make use of dispute settlement provisions contained in other BITs.[194] The United Kingdom chose to expressly extend the scope of its MFN clause to the dispute settlement provisions contained in its 2005 Model BIT.[195] The 2007 Norwegian draft Model BIT conversely states in

---

"investments shall be accorded treatment no less favourable than that accorded to investments made by investors of any third State" is that the investor's substantive rights in respect to the investments are to be treated no less favourable than under a BIT between the host State and a third State. It is one thing to stipulate that the investor is to have the benefit of MFN treatment but quite another to use an MFN clause in a BIT to bypass a limitation in the settlement resolution clause of the very same BIT . . .'. See *Wintershall Aktiengesellschaft v Argentine Republic*, ICSID, Case No. ARB/04/14, Award, 8 December 2008.

192 *Renta 4 S.V.S.A. et al v The Russian Federation*, Arbitration V (024/2007), Arbitration Institute of the Stockholm Chamber of Commerce, Award on Preliminary Objections (20 March 2009), para. 94.

193 See Art. 4 French Model BIT (2006).

194 See for example the German Model BIT; Y. Radi, 'The Application of the Most-Favoured-Nation Clause to the Dispute Settlement Provisions of Bilateral Investment Treaties: Domesticating the "Trojan Horse"', *European Journal of International Law* 18, 2007, 763; D.H. Freyer and D. Herlihy, 'Most-Favored-Nation Treatment and Dispute Settlement in Investment Arbitration: Just How "Favored" is "Most-Favored"?', *ICSID Rev. For. Inv. L.J.* 58, 2005, 60.

195 Article 3(3) of the UK Model BIT provides: 'For avoidance of doubt it is confirmed that the treatment provided for in paragraphs (1) and (2) above shall apply to the provisions

its Article 4(3) that 'for greater certainty, treatment referred to in paragraph 1 [on MFN] does not encompass dispute resolution mechanisms provided for in this Agreement or other International Agreements'. Another example of fine-tuning of MFN clauses can be found in the 2008 BIT Modification Agreement between China and Cuba, in which the MFN clause is expressly made inapplicable to issues concerning enforcement or annulment of an arbitral award.[196]

Certain countries have opted for a general distinction between substantive and procedural rights in relation to the MFN clause. The United States and Canada Model BITs limit the MFN standards to 'the establishment, acquisition, expansion, management, conduct, operation, and sale or other disposition of investments in its territory', thereby excluding procedural issues such as those discussed in the *Maffezini* case.[197] Furthermore, in its 2004 amended Model BIT Canada accords parties the possibility of reducing the level of protection by including an annex exempting prior agreements from the MFN obligation included in Article 4 of the new Model BIT.[198]

2.5.2.4 *National treatment*

A fourth very important clause regularly (if not always) found in BITs is the 'national treatment' standard. The prohibition of discrimination between nationals and aliens has been part of the customary rules on the treatment of aliens for many years (see *supra*).[199] As a general standard of treatment in investment law, national treatment places the non-discriminatory application of domestic laws in tension with the 'international minimum standard' which must be afforded in any event to aliens. Historically, it therefore faced doubts from capital-exporting States, who feared it would supersede the minimum standard and thus subject their investments to the whims of foreign

---

of Articles 1 to 11 of this Agreement' [Articles 8 and 9 of the UK Model BIT provide for dispute settlement].

196 Article 10(8)(6) of the China-Cuba Modification Agreement (2008) states 'Neither contracting party shall resort to any treaty or convention, to which the contracting parties are members, to apply for enforcement or annulment of the arbitration award according to the provisions of most-favoured-nation treatment of this Agreement.' See also Congyan, op. cit., p. 474.

197 Article 4, 2004 US Model BIT and Art. 4 2004 Canada Model BIT.

198 See Annex III(1) of the Canadian Model BIT (2004) which states: 'Article 4 shall not apply to treatment accorded under all bilateral or multilateral international agreements in force or signed prior to the date of entry into of this Agreement.'

199 The national treatment and MFN standards are often discussed together. The 2007 Colombian Model BIT even combines both in its Art. 4(1): 'Each Contracting Party shall grant to the investments of investors of the other Contracting Party made in its territory, a not less favourable treatment than that accorded, in like circumstances, to investments of its own investors or to investors of any other third State, whichever is more favourable to the investor.' The same language can be found in the German 2009 Model BIT (Art. 3), the 2003 Indian Model BIT (Art. 4) and the Dutch Model BIT (Art. 3) in their provisions on non-discrimination.

governments.[200] On the other hand, host countries could legitimately wish to favour the domestic economic operators through targeted measures, for example to protect a nascent industry. In recent times, the national treatment standard has caused much discussion and has evolved significantly. Many host States have sought to provide national economic sectors with tax or other advantages and privileges, which were soon to be claimed by foreign investors, demanding national treatment.[201] Conversely, the standard also at first glance prevents the host State from imposing measures on foreign investments solely based on a nationality criterion.[202]

The standard is now widely understood as the prohibition to treat national and foreign investors differently in 'like circumstances'.[203] Despite the language that is generally used in BITs,[204] the standard is never interpreted in absolute terms. First, the protection afforded to the foreign investor varies according to the rights granted to (legal) persons in the host State. Second, the majority of investment agreements, in accordance with general international law, preserve the host State's control over the admission and establishment of FDI.[205]

200 Sornarajah, *The International Law on Foreign Investment*, op. cit., p. 335.
201 See e.g. *de facto* discrimination by Mexico denying an American company tax rebates during periods when national corporations were receiving these in comparable circumstances; *Marvin Feldman (CEMSA) v The United Mexican States*, ICSID Case No. ARB(AF)/99/1, Award, 16 December 2002.
202 See e.g. *ADF v United States*, op. cit., paras 147–174, where the tribunal did not find the performance standards imposed by the US, requiring all investors to purchase steel originating from the US, to be a violation of the national treatment standard.
203 This may thus encompass both the 'right of admission and establishment' and 'national treatment in the post-establishment phase'; UNCTAD, 'World Investment Report 2003', 2003, 102. Online. Available HTTP <http://www.unctad.org/en/docs/wir2003 light_en.pdf> (accessed 3 January 2012). The term 'in like circumstances' is common in international trade law, and was reprinted in the language of many BITs and Art. 1102 NAFTA. See N. DiMascio and J. Pauwelyn, 'Nondiscrimination in Trade and Investment Treaties: Worlds Apart or Two Sides of the Same Coin?', *Am. J. Int'l L.* 102, 2008, 48–89, at 71.
204 Some BITs, however, have tended to become more sophisticated. For example, Anne Van Aaken and Jurgen Kurtz point out that some US BITs (e.g. the 1994 Argentinian–US BIT and the 1996 Ukraine–US BIT) contain national treatment exceptions for the financial sector: A. Van Aaken and J. Kurtz, 'Prudence or discrimination? Emergency measures, the global financial crisis and international economic law', *Journal of International Economic Law* 12, 2009, 859–894, note 160. Article 4 of the Dutch Model BIT in its turn excludes 'special fiscal advantages'; Art. 4 of the 2006 French Model BIT and of the 2003 Indian Model BIT, for example, do not apply to tax matters. Intellectual Property Rights are mentioned as an exception in Art. 6 of the 2002 Korea–Japan BIT.
205 UNCTAD, 'World Investment Report 2003', op. cit., 107. This is done by excluding certain sectors from the scope of the 'national treatment' standard in the admittance to a national market stage; see Dolzer and Schreuer, op. cit., p. 320. In other BITs, no reference to the establishment phase is included; for an example see the Agreement between the Government of the Republic of France and the Government of the United Mexican States on the Reciprocal Promotion and Protection of Investments, 12 November 1998, and the Agreement between Japan and The Republic of Colombia for the Liberalization, Promotion and Protection of Investment, 12 September 2011.

In contrast to European and Latin American BITs, this is not the case for the US and Canada Model BITs.[206] The Belgium–Luxembourg Model BIT also stands out: it does not include a reference to the pre-establishment phase but also does not limit the national treatment obligation to the post-establishment phase, leaving room for discussion regarding how such a provision would be interpreted if an investor were to rely on it to claim discrimination in its pre-establishment activities.[207] Third, measures that have to be taken for reasons of public order or public security are often excluded from the national treatment standard. Finally, it may happen that, in the post-establishment phase, BITs contain language preserving policy space in relation to national treatment, notably by excluding certain measures (e.g. subsidies) or sectors from the standard's application.[208]

National treatment is indeed an important point in the 'preservation of policy space' debate. The balance to be found in respect of the national treatment standard is to protect foreign investors from discrimination by host States without overly constraining the latters' sovereign right to regulate.[209] As has been said, the development of developing countries may require targeted policy measures favouring domestic actors, in order to support national enterprises, to protect infant industries in certain sectors and to build and upgrade domestic capabilities.[210] Various tribunals have accepted host States' public policy considerations to defend measures supporting national businesses in becoming fully competitive and encouraging human development. As such, it was submitted that the assessment of the 'like circumstances' phrase must also 'take into account circumstances that would justify governmental regulations that treat [non-national investors] differently in order to protect the public interest'.[211] Reflecting this line of interpretation, the observation that a differentiated treatment can be legitimate was expressly included in a footnote of the (failed) Norwegian Draft Model BIT:

---

206 See Art. 3 of the 2004 US Model BIT and Art. 3 of the 2004 Canada Model, which explicitly include non-discrimination in the 'establishment' of the investment, a phrase that is not found in e.g. Art. 2 of the UK Model BIT and Art. 4 of the 2006 French Model BIT. One explanation is that, in the EU context, market access issues are dealt with at the EU level (freedom of establishment/free movement of capital), rather than that of the Member States.

207 N. Bernasconi-Osterwalder and L. Johnson, 'Belgium's Model Bilateral Investment Treaty: A review', International Institute for Development Working Paper, March 2010, p. 14. Online. Available HTTP <http://www.iisd.org/pdf/2011/belgiums_model_bit.pdf> (accessed 3 January 2012).

208 Dolzer and Schreuer, op. cit., p. 179; Sornarajah, *The International Law on Foreign Investment*, op. cit., p. 336.

209 DiMascio and Pauwelyn, op. cit., p. 89.

210 UNCTAD, 'World Investment Report 2003', op. cit., 102.

211 *S.D. Myers, Inc. v Canada*, First Partial Award, NAFTA arbitration, 13 November 2000, para. 250.

> The Parties agree/are of the understanding that a measure applied by a government in pursuance of legitimate policy objectives of public interest such as the protection of public health, safety and the environment, although having a different effect on an investment or investor of another Party, is not inconsistent with national treatment and most favoured nation treatment when justified by showing that it bears a reasonable relationship to rational policies not motivated by preference of domestic over foreign owned investment.

The challenge for host governments and arbitrators remains to determine which policy objectives are sufficiently important and legitimate to justify a deviation from strict national treatment.[212] The German Model BIT is helpful in this regard, as it explains what treatment will be deemed less favourable within the meaning of the MFN and national treatment article.[213]

2.5.3 *The comeback of sovereignty in BITs and its effect on CIL*

The evolutions in the provisions discussed in this chapter all share a number of features. First, a certain re-affirmation of the policy space of the host governments, affecting the scope of the protections afforded to investors, was observed in the new generation of BITs, notably by some traditionally capital-exporting States. The rebalancing of policy space and investors protections was most explicit in the now abandoned Norwegian draft Model BIT, but is also a recurring characteristic in Model BITs that are in use today, though probably in a less radical fashion. Second, and contrasting with the growing and seemingly popular 'institutionalization' of international arbitration in investment law,[214] the variation in arbitral decisions has certainly led the new generation of BITs to redress expansionist trends which have been observed in a significant share of the investment case law.[215] Interpretative clauses in certain BITs indeed directly seek to counter controversial arbitral precedents and to limit arbitral discretion. Other States are taking a more radical turn, and are exiting the investment arbitration regime, such as a number of Latin American

---

212 N. F. Diebold, 'Standards of non-discrimination in international economic law', *International & Comparative Law Quarterly* 60, 2011, 841 and 852.

213 Article 3 para. 2 of the 2009 German Model BIT lists (1) different treatment in the event of restrictions on the procurement of raw or auxiliary materials, of energy and fuels, and of all types of means of production and operation; (2) different treatment in the event of impediments to the sale of products at home and abroad; and (3) other measures of similar effect. For a general analysis of the 2009 German Model BIT, see Griebel, op. cit., 414–419.

214 See J. Wouters and N. Hachez, 'The Institutionalization of Investment Arbitration and Sustainable Development', in M-C Cordonier Segger, M. Gehring and A. Newcombe (eds), *Sustainable Development in World Investment Law*, Alphen: Kluwer Law International, 2011, pp. 615–639.

215 Sornarajah, 'A Coming Crisis', op. cit.

States who, expressing their dissatisfaction with investment arbitration, denounced the ICSID Convention and a number of BITs.[216]

The rebalancing of the rights of investors and host States is to a large extent still an ongoing process, of which only certain characteristics have been described in this chapter. Apart from this, a number of remarkable developments in international investment law, treaty-making and compliance mechanisms have taken place against the background of the further liberalization of international markets and the ever-increasing economic links between steadfastly developing economies and traditional capital-exporting countries.

First, the network of BITs has brought about a sort of 'multilateralism by default' that was never achieved through the conclusion of a proper multilateral treaty on investment.[217] The intention of BITs is to liberalize investment flows and as such contribute to globalization processes.[218] Virtually all countries in the world do indeed accept that the conclusion of investment treaties is worthwhile and certain recurrent trends across these agreements can be observed.[219] However, it remains impossible to view the network of BITs as a mature legal regime. Even where States enter into new-generation BITs, this does not cover up the larger picture of the thousands of older BITs that are still in force. The very same States continue to apply numerous older BITs, which vary greatly in form, length and substance.[220]

Second, the trends observed in the new generation of BITs do indicate a certain reduction of the gap between the positions of capital-importing and capital-exporting countries. The lead taken by the United States in promoting less one-sided BITs and the qualification of investor protections in a number of respects has been followed by States around the world.[221] The Norwegian Model BIT went even further in promoting parties' reciprocal legal obligations, and fuelled some hopes of seeing BITs turning into dynamic

---

216 On 6 July 2009 the World Bank received a written notice of denunciation of the Convention on the Settlement of Investment Disputes between States and Nationals of Other States (the ICSID Convention) from the Republic of Ecuador. In May 2007, Bolivia, Venezuela and Nicaragua agreed to denounce the ICSID Convention, but only Bolivia carried out the threat. Venezuela, for its part, refused to renew its BIT with the Netherlands in April 2008 and introduced significant changes to its national laws in derogation of the rights of foreign investors. See Alvarez, 'The Return of the State', op. cit., p. 240; Spears, op. cit., p. 1040; S.W. Schill, 'W(h)ither Fragmentation? On the Literature and Sociology of International Investment Law', *European Journal of International Law* 22, 2011, 895; K.F. Gomez, 'Latin America and ICSID: David versus Goliath?', *Law & Business Review of the Americas* 17, 2011, 185–230.

217 Schill, *The Multilateralization of International Investment Law*, op. cit., p. 63.

218 Vandevelde, op. cit., p. 183.

219 See also A. Mills, 'Antinomies of Public and Private at the Foundations of International Investment Law and Arbitration', *J. Int'l Econ. L.* 14, 2011, 473.

220 Dumberry, op. cit., p. 683.

221 Alvarez, 'The Return of the State', op. cit., pp. 237–238.

and powerful instruments of economic development.[222] As positions on the global economic chessboard are progressively shifting as a result of the fast development of some nations, the interests of host and home States no longer seem so entrenched. What could the impact of such evolutions be on the formation of CIL?

It is clear that BITs rely on, interact with, and influence CIL. But it is quite another thing, as Patrick Dumberry noted, 'to simply say that BITs now represent the new custom in international investment law'.[223] Consequently, we reiterate that the formation process of CIL should be assessed in light of the State practice and *opinio juris* elements, with the new generation of BITs simply being another variable in the equation. Neither of the two elements can currently be discerned in the recent generation of BITs. While a pattern of international treaties undoubtedly contributes to the formation of usages,[224] practice at the very least needs to be widespread and consistent,[225] which is not yet the case in investment law.[226] In the recent past, we did observe tendencies to tone down investor protections, or at least leave more policy space to host States. This tendency is reflected in the recent BIT practice of both developed and developing countries. Exemplary evidence can be found in the changing treaty language concerning some of the most crucial provisions, such as the fair and equitable treatment standard, the most favoured nation clause, as well as in expropriation and compensation provisions (the Hull formula). But the extended policy space for host countries at the same time inevitably leads to a greater differentiation of State practice regarding investment.[227] Finally, the new generation of BITs form but a tiny share of the several thousand BITs currently in force. Consequently, for the time being it rather evidences a further breakdown in the consistency of State practice than an emerging consensus leading to CIL formation.

2.6 Conclusion

Questions such as the shape, contents and evolution of the international legal regime on investment and interrogations on the customary status of international

222 R. Sarkar, 'A "Re-Visioned" Foreign Direct Investment Approach from an Emerging Country Perspective: Moving from a Vicious Circle to a Virtuous Cycle', *ILSA J. Int'l & Comp. L.* 17, 2011, 388.
223 Dumberry, op. cit., p. 681.
224 I. Brownlie, *Principles of Public International Law*, Oxford: Oxford University Press, 2008 (7th edn), p. 6. Thirlway explains that, while treaties may serve as acts of practice significant for the development of custom, they remain purely declaratory. The very fact that States have recourse to treaties to establish certain rules shows that they consider that those rules would not be applicable if no treaty were concluded. Thirlway, op. cit., p. 112.
225 Military and Paramilitary Activities in and against Nicaragua (*Nicaragua v United States of America*), Judgment, ICJ Reports 1986, p. 14, para. 186. See also, in greater detail, *North Sea Continental Shelf Cases*, para. 75, as referred to *supra*, note 104.
226 See *supra* the discussion of FET, MFN and expropriation clauses; Dumberry, op. cit., pp. 685–690; Sornarajah, *The International Law on Foreign Investment*, op. cit., p. 176.
227 Spears, op. cit., p. 1039.

rules on foreign investment are highly political. They shed light on the profound divisions between States which export capital and States which import it. Home States want to protect their investors as much as possible and therefore are in favour of a liberal and protective legal framework, whereas host States, while keen on attracting investment and creating a trustworthy climate for investors, are reluctant to agree to overly strong inroads into their sovereign rights. This fault line has arguably prevented the emergence of a comprehensive customary regime or of a multilateral treaty on foreign investment. The dense network of BITs which has emerged has not been able to significantly affect that stalemate, as it has largely ratified the position of capital-exporting States (mainly developed countries), which developing host States kept trying to resist but felt compelled to accept. The network of BITs therefore seems as yet imbalanced. It is submitted that no customary international legal framework is likely to emerge from it as long as the interests of home States and host States are so far apart. If, and to what extent, the great majority of States become both home and host States, they will have a common interest in forming a general regime for investment, and the agreeable distribution of rights and obligations between investors and of the host States would be easier to determine. As noted above, this progressive shift in the positions of developed and developing countries with regard to FDI may well be in the making, at least for emerging economies. In the current state of the law, however, the most realistic hope for the emergence of CIL through BITs is the rejuvenation of the current network of BITs by consensual treaties striking a fairer balance between the rights of investors and the rights of host States. The emerging new generation of BITs, perhaps evidencing a convergence in the interests of the community of States as alternatively home and host States, and resulting in a rebalancing of respective rights and responsibilities, hopefully involves just such a development.

3 Foreign direct investment as an engine for economic growth and human development

A review of the arguments and empirical evidence*

Liesbeth Colen, Miet Maertens and Johan Swinnen

3.1 Introduction

Until the 1970s many developing countries – in Latin America and South-East Asia as well as Africa – were rather reluctant to accept foreign investment and pursued a policy of import substitution. But during the past three decades – mainly as a result of the structural adjustment programmes that started in the late 1970s – most developing countries have opened up their economies.[1] Countries in Eastern Europe and the former Soviet Union also opened up during the process of transition from state-controlled to market economies during the 1980s and 1990s. As part of the liberalization policies, and stimulated by international donors such as the World Bank and the IMF, low-income countries are increasingly adopting policies to attract foreign direct investment (FDI).[2] Such policies are based on the belief that FDI could contribute significantly to the growth and development of these nations. This chapter critically assesses the contribution FDI has made – so far – to economic growth and human development in low-income countries. We will review

* This chapter was originally published as L. Colen, M. Maertens and J. Swinnen, 2009, 'Foreign direct investment as an engine for economic growth and human development: A review of the arguments and empirical evidence', *Human Rights and International Legal Discourse* 3(2) 177–227. The authors would like to thank Matthias Sant'Ana and Lode Berlage for valuable comments.

1 P. Nunnenkamp, 2004, 'To What Extent can Foreign Direct Investment Help Achieve International Development Goals?' *The World Economy* 27(5): 657–677.
2 The United Nations defines FDI as 'investment involving a long-term relationship and reflecting a lasting interest and control of a resident entity in one economy in an enterprise resident in an economy other than that of the foreign direct investor' (UNCTAD, 2002. *World Investment Report: Transnational Corporations and Export Competitiveness*, United Nations, New York). FDI implies a form of international inter-firm co-operation that involves a significant equity stake and effective management decision-making power in, or ownership control of, foreign enterprises (L. de Mello, 1997, 'Foreign Direct Investment in Developing Countries: A Selective Survey', *The Journal of Development Studies*, 34(1): 1–34).

theoretical arguments and assess their empirical validity, using evidence from the available literature.

Since the publication of the first Human Development Report in 1990 there has been a general shift in focus from 'economic growth' as an indicator of development towards the broader concept of 'human development'. Human development is defined as the process of widening people's choices in a way which enables them to enjoy long, healthy and creative lives.[3] This broad concept includes attention to income, education, health care, employment, human rights, nutrition, gender equality, democracy, etc. Yet, economic growth, poverty and inequality remain essential components of human development and their economic measures are strongly correlated with the Human Development Index (HDI), developed by the United Nations (UN).[4] In this chapter we therefore focus in the first place on the impact of FDI on economic growth, then we look at poverty alleviation and income inequality, and finally we expand on some non-economic components of human development such as human rights, labour standards and the environment. This economic perspective on FDI and human development can shed light on the type and importance of the links that exist between FDI and economic outcomes. This can inform the identification of regulatory mechanisms for the promotion of human development through FDI and therefore this economic perspective is extremely relevant for the legal discourse on human development and FDI.

After this introduction we continue with an overview of FDI trends and flows and a discussion of the importance of FDI for developing countries. In the third section we assess the theoretical arguments and empirical evidence concerning the direct impact of FDI on economic growth through capital accumulation and technological advance. The fourth section deals with the indirect effects of FDI on growth. In this section, economic theory and empirical analysis on the spillover of technology and know-how from foreign-owned firms to the host economy are studied. Empirical findings on the impact of FDI on growth are very heterogeneous. The sources of this heterogeneity are studied in more detail in the fifth section. The next section deals with the poverty-reducing and inequality impact of FDI. In section seven we briefly discuss the effect of FDI on human rights, education and environmental standards. Finally, in section eight we turn to the quality of the growth that is stimulated by FDI. We look at how FDI affects some non-economic components of human development. The last section concludes.

---

3 UNDP, 1990, *Human Development Report: Concept and Measurement of Human Development*, United Nations, New York.
4 UNDP, 1996, *Human Development Report: Economic Growth and Human Development*, United Nations, New York; G. Ranis, F. Stewart and A. Ramirez, 2000, 'Economic Growth and Human Development', *World Development* 28(2): 197–219; S. Anand and A. Sen, 2000, 'The Income Component of the Human Development Index', *Journal of Human Development* 1(1): 83–106.

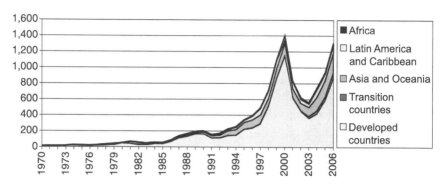

Figure 3.1 Yearly FDI inflows (US $ billion) per region, 1970–2006

Source: UNCTAD, FDI/TNC database (www.unctad.org/fdistatistics)

Note
The developing economies are classified by region. Asia and Oceania include the Middle East, but not CIS, Australia, New Zealand, Japan and Israel. The developed world contains Europe (except for South-East Europe), North America, Australia, New Zealand, Japan and Israel.

3.2 FDI in developing countries

We start with an overview of the evolution of FDI flows to and FDI stocks in the developing world. Both yearly flows of FDI – the new investments made during that year – and FDI stocks – the total value of accumulated investments over a long period – have increased largely, but their growth has been unevenly distributed among the developing regions. We look at the importance of FDI for these regions and potential ways to differentiate between various types of FDI.

3.2.1 Trends in FDI flows

During recent decades, FDI has increased exponentially: the yearly global flows of FDI increased from 55 billion US dollars in 1980 to 1,306 billion US dollars in 2006 (Figure 3.1 and Table 3.1). During the 1980s and 1990s FDI inflows increased continuously – with the sharpest growth in the late 1990s – to reach a peak in 2000. Between 2001 and 2003 the developed economies experienced a sharp decline in FDI inflows, associated with a general global economic recession.[5] Developing countries were affected only to a small

5 The sudden drop in FDI flows in 2001 is related to depressed stock market sentiment and business cycles, both of which led to a massive decline in merger and acquisition (M&A) investments, especially in the developed countries (UNCTAD, 2002, op. cit.). The relatively

Table 3.1 Global and developing countries' FDI inflows, 1980–2006

	Share in global FDI inflows (%)						
	1980	*1985*	*1990*	*1995*	*2000*	*2003*	*2006*
Developed countries	86.1	75.5	82.2	64.8	81.2	64.0	65.7
Developing countries	13.9	24.5	17.8	33.8	18.1	31.7	29.0
Transition countries	0.04	0.03	0.04	1.4	0.64	4.3	5.3
Asia & Oceania	1.4	9.5	11.6	23.6	10.5	20.4	19.9
Lat. Am. & Caribbean	11.7	10.7	4.8	8.6	6.9	7.9	6.4
Africa	0.7	4.2	1.4	1.7	0.7	3.3	2.7
	Total FDI inflows (US $ billion)						
	1980	*1985*	*1990*	*1995*	*2000*	*2003*	*2006*
World FDI inflows	55.3	58.0	201.5	342.6	1,411.4	564.1	1,305.9
Developed countries	47.6	43.7	165.6	222.0	1,146.2	361.2	857.5
Developing countries	7.7	14.2	35.9	116.0	256.1	178.7	379.1

Source: UNCTAD, FDI/TNC database (www.unctad.org/fdistatistics)

extent. The FDI flows started to recover in 2004 and were back at their 2000 level in 2006.[6]

High-income countries receive the lion's share of global FDI flows (more than two-thirds in 2006). The sharp increase of FDI flows in the late 1990s can be mainly attributed to cross-border investments in developed countries (Figure 3.1). However, developing countries' share in global FDI inflows has more than doubled, from less than 14 per cent in the 1980s to 30 per cent in more recent years (Table 3.1). During the period from 2000 to 2006 FDI inflows into developing countries increased by almost 50 per cent – from 255 billion US dollars in 2000 to 378 billion US dollars in 2006 (Table 3.1) – while developed countries' FDI inflows stagnated during that period. Also, since 1990 FDI has started to emerge in the former state-controlled economies of Eastern Europe and the former Soviet Union, i.e. the transition countries (Figure 3.1).

mild drop in developing countries is presumably due to the fact that a large fraction of FDI in developing countries is greenfield investment (UNCTAD, 2002, op. cit.).
6 UNCTAD, 2007, *World Investment Report: Transnational Corporations, Extractive Industries and Development*, United Nations, New York.

However, FDI flows are not evenly distributed among the developing regions. First, Asia and the Pacific have become quite successful in attracting FDI in recent decades and now receive two-thirds of total developing countries' FDI inflows, while in the early 1980s Latin America was the developing region receiving most FDI (Table 3.1). Second, Africa receives the smallest share of global FDI flows – around 3 per cent in recent years. Nevertheless, Africa's share in global FDI has doubled since the early 1990s. Third, since the 1980s almost half of developing countries' FDI inflows have been concentrated in only three countries: China, Brazil and Mexico.[7]

3.2.2 Trends in FDI stocks

Increasing FDI inflows contributed to a large and continuous increase in the total stock of FDI worldwide, reaching 11,999 billion US dollars in 2006 (Table 3.2). The distribution of the global stocks of FDI between the developed and developing economies did not change drastically and the developed world still holds about three-quarters of the total FDI stocks. Nevertheless, in absolute terms the stocks of FDI increased enormously everywhere: over the past three decades all regions have experienced at least a tenfold increase in the stock of inward FDI.

Within the developing world, the distribution of foreign investment between the regions has changed over recent decades. Africa's share declined from more than 7 per cent in 1980 to less than 3 per cent in 2006, while Asia and the transition countries increased their share in FDI stocks. The share of Latin America and the Caribbean also slightly increased.

3.2.3 The importance of FDI for developing countries

Although only a quarter of the global inward FDI stock is situated in developing countries, FDI is of increasing importance for these countries. One indication of the increasing importance of FDI is the rising intensity of FDI, i.e. the share of FDI in GDP (Figure 3.2). While in the 1980s FDI accounted only for less than 10 per cent of GDP, the share of FDI in GDP now reaches more than 20 per cent in the developed world, 25 per cent in Asia, and 30 per cent or more in Africa and Latin America. Within only 15 years, transition countries started from zero FDI and reached the same level as the other regions.

In addition, FDI also rapidly gained importance with respect to other sources of capital. Critics argue that FDI still accounted for only 13 per cent of overall capital formation in developing countries between 1998 and 2000 and that domestic savings remain more important than FDI.[8] However, the share of FDI

---

7 UNCTAD, 2007, op. cit.
8 Nunnenkamp, 2004, op.cit.

Table 3.2 Global and developing countries' FDI stocks, 1980–2006

	Share in global FDI stocks (%)						
	1980	*1985*	*1990*	*1995*	*2000*	*2003*	*2006*
Developed countries	74.5	72.3	79.5	75.1	69.4	73.7	70.5
Developing countries	25.5	27.7	20.5	24.4	29.4	24.2	26.3
Transition countries	0.00	0.00	0.01	0.46	1.23	2.11	3.24
Asia & Oceania	11.9	14.8	11.3	15.1	18.5	14.1	16.1
Lat. Am. & Caribbean	6.36	7.68	5.88	6.21	8.28	7.58	7.57
Africa	7.23	5.19	3.35	3.14	2.64	2.48	2.63

	Total FDI stocks (US $ billion)						
	1980	*1985*	*1990*	*1995*	*2000*	*2003*	*2006*
World FDI stocks	551.2	804.2	1,779.2	2,761.3	5,810.2	8,185.4	11,998.8
Developed countries	410.9	581.6	1,414.4	2,073.3	4,031.3	6,034.7	8,453.9
Developing countries	140.4	222.6	364.7	675.2	1,707.6	1,978.1	3,155.9

Source: UNCTAD, FDI/TNC database (www.unctad.org/fdistatistics)

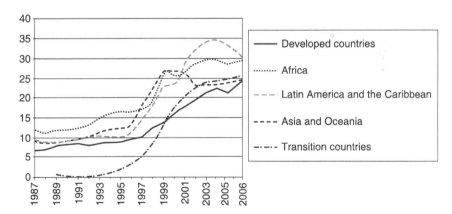

Figure 3.2 Inward FDI stock as a percentage of GDP across regions, 1980–2006

Source: UNCTAD, FDI/TNC database (www.unctad.org/fdistatistics)

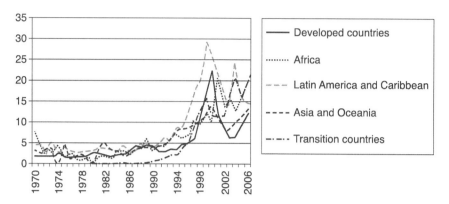

Figure 3.3 Inward FDI stock as a percentage of Gross Fixed Capital Formation across regions, 1970–2006

Source: UNCTAD, FDI/TNC database (www.unctad.org/fdistatistics)

Note
Gross Fixed Capital Formation is a measure that summarises the total value of net new investment in fixed capital assets (factories, buildings, land improvements, infrastructure, etc.) by enterprises, the government and households during the period of a year.

in total capital formation is increasing very rapidly, and even more in low-income countries than in developed countries (Figure 3.3).

Apart from FDI, portfolio investment, official bank loans and official development assistance (ODA) also add to international capital flows. Until the early 1990s ODA was the most important source of external capital for developing countries, but since 1994 FDI has taken over (Table 3.3). In 2006 FDI accounted for 50 per cent of total developing countries' capital inflows while the contribution of ODA was less than 10 per cent. Portfolio investment and official bank loans have also increased in the past couple of years but FDI has remained the largest component of international capital flows into developing countries.

3.2.4 Differentiation of FDI flows

We can differentiate between different types of FDI, either (1) according to the specific objective of transnational companies (TNCs) to invest in developing countries, (2) according to the entry mode of the FDI company, or (3) according to the sector of investment. As will become apparent in the following sections, this heterogeneity in the motives for cross-border investment, the entry modes of FDI (i.e. greenfield investment or mergers and acquisitions (M&As)) and the sectoral composition of FDI gives rise to differential impacts on growth

Table 3.3 Inward FDI flows and Official Development Assistance to developing countries (US $ billion), 1970–2006

	Resource flows to developing countries (US $ billion)								
	1970	*1975*	*1980*	*1985*	*1990*	*1995*	*2000*	*2003*	*2006*
FDI	3.9	9.7	7.7	14.2	35.9	116.0	256.1	178.7	379.1
ODA	5.4	9.2	17.0	21.2	38.5	40.5	36.1	49.7	77.0

Source: Based on UNCTAD, 2007, *World Investment Report: Transnational Corporations, Extractive Industries and Development*, United Nations, New York and World Bank, 2006, *Global Development Finance: The Development Potential of Surging Capital Flows*, The World Bank, Washington DC.

and development. We therefore discuss these differentiations in FDI flows in more detail.

3.2.4.1 Differentiation in the motives for FDI

Four different types of FDI are identified by UNCTAD: natural-resource-seeking, market-seeking, efficiency-seeking and strategic-asset-seeking foreign investment.[9]

- *Natural-resource-seeking FDI* is investment in the exploitation of raw materials, which are mainly exported without being transformed. This corresponds mainly to investment in extractive industries such as mining, quarrying and petroleum, thus in the primary sector. Natural-resource-seeking FDI is believed to be more volatile than other investments, given the sensitivity to the fluctuating world prices of oil and minerals.
- *Market-seeking FDI* is mainly situated in the manufacturing sector and the services sector (telecommunication and electricity) in developing countries. In the 1960s and 1970s, when many developing countries introduced import substitution policies, setting up a production site in the developing country itself became an important alternative to exporting goods to that country. Besides trade barriers, high transportation costs or country-specific consumer preferences or market structures can also be a reason for market-seeking investment.
- *Efficiency-seeking FDI* occurs when part of the value chain is located abroad in order to improve profitability. Traditionally, these investments take advantage of lower labour costs in developing countries by allocating the

9 UNCTAD, 1999, *World Investment Report: Foreign Direct Investment and Development*, United Nations, New York.

labour-intensive parts of the production processes there. Efficiency-seeking investment is situated in the manufacturing and service sectors.

- *Strategic-asset-seeking FDI* usually takes place at a more advanced stage of globalization and concerns investment in research-and-development capabilities, mainly in the more advanced developing countries (e.g. software development in India).

3.2.4.2 Differentiation in the entry modes of FDI

When a firm wants to invest in a foreign country, there are two possible entry modes: greenfield investment or M&As. Greenfield FDI refers to the establishment of new production facilities such as offices, buildings, plants, factories and the movement of intangible capital (mainly services) to a foreign country. Greenfield FDI thus directly adds to production capacity in the host country and, other things remaining the same, contributes to capital formation and employment generation in the host country. Cross-border M&As involve the partial or full takeover or the merging of the capital and assets of an existing enterprise in the host country by TNCs from the home country. Mergers and acquisitions represent a change in ownership that does not necessarily involve any immediate additions to investment or employment in the country.[10]

Greenfield investment is more important in developing countries than in industrialized economies (Table 3.4). But the surge of FDI flows to developing economies in the 1990s was accompanied by a marked change in its composition. The M&A investments grew much more rapidly than the greenfield investments and since the mid-1990s M&As have accounted for a third of total FDI flows to developing countries. Latin America and transition countries are above the average, while Asia and Africa tend to have a significantly lower share of their inflows in M&As.

3.2.4.3 Sectoral composition of FDI

Over the past 25 years, FDI has increased significantly in absolute terms in all three major sectors: primary production, manufacturing and services. With an increase from 40 per cent of global FDI inflow in the 1990s to about 60 per cent in 2006, the services sector became the most important sector for foreign investment.[11] In the developing world the services sector can even reach up to about 70 per cent of total M&As (Figure 3.4). Investment in the primary sector experienced a decline in the 1990s, but re-emerged in developing and transition countries due to a significant rise in FDI inflow into extractive industries such as mining, quarrying and petroleum.

---

10 UNCTAD, 2006, *World Investment Report: FDI from Developing and Transition Economies: Implications for Development*, United Nations, New York.
11 UNCTAD, 2007, op. cit.

Table 3.4 FDI flows, greenfield investment and M&As as a percentage of GDP (weighted average), 1987–2001

% of GDP	Industrial countries			Developing countries		
	Total FDI	Greenfield	M&A	Total FDI	Greenfield	M&A
1987–89	0.99	0.23	0.76	0.86	0.77	0.09
1990–94	0.76	0.26	0.50	1.43	1.12	0.30
1995–99	1.74	0.26	1.48	2.80	1.87	0.93
2000–01	3.67	0.46	3.21	3.63	2.10	1.53

Source: C. Caldéron, N. Loayza and L Serven, 2004, 'Greenfield Foreign Direct Investment and Mergers and Acquisitions: Feedback and Macroeconomic Effects', World Bank Policy Research Working Paper 3192, based on the UNCTAD database.

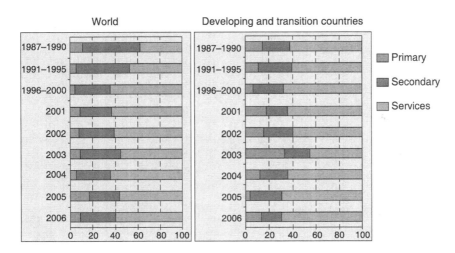

Figure 3.4 Sectoral distribution of cross-border M&As in the world and in developing and transition countries (1987–2006)

Source: UNCTAD, 2007, op. cit.

The sectoral distribution is characterized by a large geographical variation. The share of primary sector investment, especially, is extremely variable. In Africa, 55 per cent of investment is located in the primary sector, reaching up to 80 per cent in some years. This is due to the fact that TNCs are still largely attracted by the abundance of natural resources rather than the market or host-country investment climate. This also explains the uneven distribution of FDI in Africa: all the top ten recipients of FDI in 2003 have large mineral and petroleum reserves. The increase in FDI in the services sector was especially high in the Latin American and Caribbean region, while Asia exhibits a large and stable share of FDI in the manufacturing sector.[12]

3.3 The direct impact of FDI on economic growth

The main idea underlying the FDI liberalization policies of many developing countries and the FDI promotion efforts of international donors such as the World Bank and the IMF is the notion that FDI inflows foster economic growth. As FDI is a composite bundle of capital stock, know-how and technology, its impact on economic growth is expected to be manifold.[13] In the ways through which FDI can affect economic growth we can distinguish direct and indirect effects. In this section we review the economic arguments and empirical evidence on the direct contribution of FDI to economic growth while section 3.4 deals with the indirect or spillover effects.

3.3.1 *Capital accumulation, technological advances and long-term growth*

Foreign direct investment can contribute to economic growth by expanding the capital stock, just like all other types of capital inflow. Following the traditional neoclassical approach to growth, this capital accumulation can affect growth only in the short run.[14] Long-run growth is only possible through a permanent increase in the level of technology and is taken to be exogenous in neoclassical growth models. Yet, more recent models, such as the endogenous growth model, consider technology as internal to the economic growth process, and see a role for capital in the creation of technological advance.[15] Capital allows for investment in the development of new ideas and skills, and since knowledge is – to some extent at least – a public good, it raises the level of technology not only within the firm but in the entire economy. These externalities account for the permanent advance in the level of technology, which is needed to promote growth in the long run. Thus, according to the new growth theories, capital – including FDI – can permanently affect output growth through increased investment in technology and know-how, thereby increasing the overall level of knowledge and technology in the economy.

12 UNCTAD, 2007, op. cit.
13 De Mello, 1997, op. cit.; J.H. Dunning, 1992, 'The Global Economy, Domestic Governance, Strategies of Transnational Corporations: Interactions and Policy Implications', *Transnational Corporations*, 1(3): 7–46.
14 R.M. Solow, 1956, 'A Contribution to the Theory of Economic Growth'. *Quarterly Journal of Economics*, 70: 65–94; R.M. Solow, 1957, 'Technical Change and the Aggregate Production Function', *Review of Economics and Statistics*, 39: 312–320.
15 P. Romer, 1990, 'Endogenous Technological Change', *The Journal of Political Economy*, 98(5): 71–102.

In particular, FDI is believed to be more important for growth than other sources of capital. Besides a general provision of capital – which can be invested in the adoption and imitation of more advanced technologies and knowledge – FDI in itself often embodies higher levels of technology and know-how. It is described as a whole package of resources: physical capital, modern technology and production techniques, managerial and marketing knowledge, entrepreneurial abilities and business practices.[16] Therefore FDI is said to contribute directly – and more strongly than domestic investment – to accelerated levels of growth in an economy because of the more advanced levels of technology, managerial capacity and know-how, resulting in higher levels of efficiency and productivity.

However, others have argued that the assumption that foreign firms are more efficient than domestic firms is not necessarily true.[17] When FDI takes the form of M&As the inflow of capital might not always be accompanied by improved technologies, managerial capacity and entrepreneurial ability. Foreign investment can take place because foreigners have a superior cash position and can take advantage of liquidity-constrained domestic investors' fire sales, rather than because of a technological advantage. Nevertheless, the superior position of FDI companies in terms of technology and know-how has underlain many of the arguments in favour of FDI liberalization policies.

3.3.2 Cross-country evidence on the overall growth impact of FDI

Macro-economic studies using aggregate FDI flows for a cross-section of countries suggest a positive link between FDI and growth. For example, De Gregorio shows, using panel data from twelve Latin American countries, that the effect of foreign investment on GDP growth is about three times larger than for domestic investment.[18] Other papers confirm the finding that FDI contributes more to GDP growth than does domestic investment and they conclude that FDI can be a powerful instrument for economic development.[19]

---

16 M.P. Todaro, 1985, *The Economic Development in the Third World*, New York: Longman; de Mello, 1997, op. cit.

17 P. Krugman, 2000, 'Fire-sale FDI', in S. Edwards (ed.) *Capital Flows and the Emerging Economies: Theory, Evidence and Controversies*, Chicago: University of Chicago Press, pp. 43–60. Online. Available HTTP <http://www.nber.org/chapters/c6164> (accessed 30 July 2012); R. Hausmann and E. Fernández-Arias, 2000, 'Foreign Direct Investment: Good Cholesterol?' *Working Paper* 417, Inter-American Development Bank, 27p.

18 J. De Gregorio, 1992, 'Economic Growth in Latin America', *Journal of Development Economics* 39: 58–84.

19 V.N. Balasubramanyam, 1998, 'The Multilateral Agreement on Investment (MAI) and Foreign Direct Investment in Developing Countries', *Discussion Paper* 16, Lancaster University; B. Xu, 2000, 'Multinational Enterprises, Technology Diffusion, and Host Country Productivity Growth', *Journal of Development Economics* 62(2): 477–493.

3.3.2.1 Identifying causality

The positive link that is mostly found between FDI inflows and economic growth is very likely to be highly endogenous. Theoretically the causality can run in both directions: FDI can cause growth through various effects, but on the other hand a growing economy is likely to attract more FDI since it provides new market and profit opportunities. It has been argued that several of the empirical studies on FDI and economic growth do not account for this endogeneity and therefore fail to identify causality between FDI and economic growth. Country-specific and convergence effects are often not accounted for.[20] More recent studies try to control for these biases using causality tests or simultaneous equation systems, and use panel data to account for country-specific effects.

A study by Kholdy indicates no causality from FDI to productivity, while Nair-Reichert and Weinhold find that FDI on average causes growth, although the relationship is highly heterogeneous across countries.[21] Other studies detect a two-way causal link between FDI and growth, but the effects are more apparent from growth to FDI.[22] Bende-Nabende and co-authors find both negative and positive direct effects of FDI on output for the APEC countries.[23] Their results indicate that growth effects are more likely to be positive in the less developed countries of the sample. The results of Chowdury and Mavrotas suggest that in the case of Chile GDP growth attracts FDI, while for Thailand and Malaysia there is evidence of causality in both directions.[24] Hansen and Rand assess the causal relationship between FDI and GDP for 31 developing countries.[25] The results show a bidirectional causality but also indicate that FDI has a lasting impact on the level of GDP, while GDP has only a short-run impact on FDI, suggesting that FDI causes growth rather than the other way around. Overall, we can say that macro-economic studies indicate a positive

20 M. Carkovic and R. Levine, 2002, 'Does Foreign Direct Investment Accelerate Economic Growth?', in: T.H. Moran, E.M. Graham and M. Blomström (eds), *Does Foreign Direct Investment Promote Development?*, Washington DC: Institute for International Economics, pp. 195–220.

21 S. Kholdy, 1995, 'Causality Between Foreign Investment and Spillover Efficiency', *Applied Economics*, 27: 745–749; U. Nair-Reichert and D. Weinhold, 2001, 'Causality Tests for Cross-Country Panels: a New Look at FDI and Economic Growth in Developing Countries', *Oxford Bulletin of Economics and Statistics* 63(2): 153–171.

22 K.H. Zhang, 2001, 'How Does Foreign Direct Investment Affect Economic Growth in China?' *Economics of Transition*, 9(3): 679–693; J.I. Choe, 2003, 'Does Foreign Direct Investment and Domestic Investment Promote Economic Growth?' *Review of Development Economics* 7(1): 44–57.

23 A. Bende-Nabende, J. L. Ford, B. Santoso and S. Sen, 2003, 'The Interaction Between FDI, Output and the Spillover Variables: Co-Integration and VAR Analyses for APEC, 1965–1999', *Applied Economics Letters* 10(3): 16–172.

24 A. Chowdury and G. Mavrotas, 2006, 'FDI and Growth: What Causes What?' *The World Economy* 26(1): 9–19.

25 H. Hansen and J. Rand, 2006, 'On the Causal Links between FDI and Growth in Developing Countries', *The World Economy* 29: 21–41.

relationship between FDI and growth, but that the causality is likely to run in both directions.

3.3.3 Micro-economic evidence on technological advances in FDI firms

Another body of empirical literature, using micro-economic company data, which allow for a better identification of the causal effects, has tested the hypothesis of FDI companies being technologically more advanced and more productive. Based on panel data from Venezuelan plants, foreign equity participation is indeed found to be positively correlated with plant productivity.[26] Foreign establishments in Sweden are found to have high levels of labour productivity compared with domestic firms.[27] Konings finds evidence that foreign firms perform better than domestic ones in Poland, but not in Romania and Bulgaria, and Czech enterprises with foreign ownership have higher total factor productivity growth and higher labour productivity.[28] These micro-findings support the hypothesis that FDI companies are more productive and that they contribute to productivity growth in developing countries.

3.3.4 The type of growth promoted by FDI

3.3.4.1 Stability of capital accumulation and sustainable growth

Another argument on the beneficial impact of FDI on economic growth relates to the stability of FDI flows. It has been argued that FDI has a larger impact on growth than other international capital flows – such as portfolio investment and bank loans – because of the limited volatility of FDI. This relates to the fact that FDI cannot easily be withdrawn while profits, losses and risks are shared among the foreign and host entities. Thus FDI is attracted by the long-term prospects of the country and its policies, and is therefore more stable than other types of capital investment,[29] which are known to be more volatile and shorter term, thereby hindering sustainable growth.[30]

26 B. Aitken and A. Harrison, 1999, 'Do Domestic Firms Benefit from Foreign Direct Investment? Evidence from Venezuela', *The American Economic Review* 89(3): 605–618.
27 M. Blomström and F. Sjöholm, 1999, 'Technology Transfer and Spillovers: Does Local Participation with Multinationals Matter?', *European Economic Review* 43: 915–923.
28 J. Konings, 2001, 'The Effects of Foreign Direct Investment on Domestic Firms: Evidence from Firm-level Panel Data in Emerging Economies', *Economics of Transition*, 9: 619–633; S. Djankov and B. Hoekman, 2000, 'Foreign Direct Investment and Productivity Growth in Czech Enterprises', *World Bank Economic Review* 14(1): 49–64.
29 R. Albuquerque, 2003, 'The Composition of International Capital Flows: Risk Sharing through Foreign Direct Investment', *Journal of International Economics* 61 (2): 353–383.
30 J. Stiglitz, 2000, 'Capital Liberalization, Economic Growth, and Instability', *World Development* 28(6): 1075–1086.

On the other hand, it is argued that the stability of FDI is often overstated since there are other ways than repatriating FDI to flee a country in financial crisis, for example through changes in the capital account.[31] Empirical evidence on the stability of FDI is contradictory. For example, Claessens, Dooley and Warner argue that FDI is indistinguishable from other capital flows in terms of its volatility and predictability.[32] Sarno and Taylor, to the contrary, find that FDI is more persistent than other components of capital flows.[33]

3.3.4.2 The current account and balanced growth

Foreign direct investment is often associated with increased international trade and therefore has an impact on the current account of the host economy. The main argument is that foreign-owned companies export more because they have better access to international markets through their links with the home economy. In particular, efficiency-seeking and strategic-asset-seeking FDI into the manufacturing (and services) sector would lead to increased exports.[34] The impact of FDI on the current account is difficult to assess but it is estimated that exports by foreign-owned companies are very high in certain developing countries. For example, FDI accounts for around half of total exports in China, Malaysia, Costa Rica and some Eastern European countries, and for a quarter or more in Latin America, Slovenia and Romania.[35] Also, multinationals in Mexican manufacturing are more likely to export than domestic firms.[36] Through its contribution to exports FDI may positively affect the balance of payments, which is important for countries with a large current account deficit, such as many African and South-East Asian countries – and bring about more balanced growth. In Botswana, for example, mineral exports by TNCs have enabled the country to run current account surpluses and to accumulate substantial foreign exchange reserves.[37]

On the other hand, FDI in extractive industries can cause adverse macro-economic effects, particularly through appreciating exchange rates, which may damage other sectors such as manufacturing; FDI in extractive industries had a negative effect on the balance of payments in some African economies because of profit remittances surging above new FDI inflows.[38]

31 Nunnenkamp, 2004, op. cit.; Haussman and Fernandez-Aria, 2000, op. cit.
32 S. Claessens, M.P. Dooley and A. Warner, 1995, 'Portfolio Capital Flows: Hot or Cold?', *World Bank Economic Review* 9(1): 153–74 .
33 L. Sarno and M.P. Taylor, 1999, 'Hot Money, Accounting Labels and the Permanence of Capital Flows to Developing Countries: An Empirical Investigation', *Journal of Development Economics*, 59(2): 337–364.
34 B. Aitken, G. Hanson and A. Harrison, 1997, 'Spillovers, Foreign Investment and Export Behavior', *Journal of International Economics* 43(1–2): 103–132.
35 A. Sumner, 2005, 'Is Foreign Direct Investment Good for the Poor? A Review and Stocktake', *Development in Practice*, 15(3–4): 269–285.
36 Aitken et al., 1997, op. cit.
37 UNCTAD, 2007, op. cit.
38 Nunnenkamp, 2004, op. cit.

3.3.5 Some conclusions

Theoretical arguments assign a key role to FDI in economic growth. While these theoretical arguments are quite straightforward and widely accepted, the empirical evidence is less clear, or as de Mello puts it: 'whether FDI can be deemed to be a catalyst for output growth, capital accumulation, and technological progress, seems to be a less controversial hypothesis in theory than in practice.'[39] Micro-economic studies indicate that FDI firms are often more productive than domestic firms. Yet, while the empirical macro-economic literature shows a clear link between FDI and GDP growth, the direction of causality is more difficult to assess.[40] Moreover, when the heterogeneity of the host economies is recognized in empirical studies, the link between FDI inflows and growth becomes ambiguous,[41] as will be discussed in detail in section 3.5. Research has therefore turned towards the mechanisms responsible for the predicted growth effect – including indirect and spillover effects – and the factors conditioning the growth impact of FDI. These issues are discussed in the following sections.

3.4 Indirect effects of FDI on economic growth

As explained in the previous section, FDI is argued to affect economic growth in a different way than domestic investment because FDI entails – besides the accumulation of physical capital – a bundle of potentially growth-enhancing attributes, including technology, managerial know-how, entrepreneurial ability, and access to global distribution networks and international markets.[42] These attributes may not only foster productivity and growth from within the entering multinational corporations (MNCs) – as discussed above – but may additionally spill over to other companies in the host economy and further benefit economic growth in these countries through indirect or spillover effects. In this section we discuss the different types of such potential spillover effects and the channels through which they occur, and review the available empirical evidence on their importance.

3.4.1 Typology of FDI spillover effects

3.4.1.1 Productivity and market access spillovers

Blomström and Kokko identify two types of spillover effect from FDI to the host country: productivity spillovers and market access

39 De Mello, 1997, op. cit.
40 Nunnenkamp, 2004, op.cit.; Carkovic and Levine, 2002, op. cit.
41 P. Nunnenkamp and J. Spatz, 2004. 'FDI and Economic Growth in Developing Economies: How Relevant are Host-economy and Industry Characteristics', *Transnational Corporations*, 13(3): 52–86.
42 Dunning, 1992, op. cit.

spillovers.[43] *Productivity spillovers* take place when the entry of MNCs into the host country leads to productivity or efficiency benefits in the local firms. *Market access spillovers* take place when the entry of multinational firms improves access to export markets for local firms.

3.4.1.2 Vertical and horizontal spillovers

Multinational corporations are among the most technologically advanced firms and account for a substantial part of the world's investment in research and development.[44] When starting up a foreign affiliate, MNCs are not likely to give the source of their competitive advantage away for free. They will thus try to limit *horizontal spillovers* (intra-industry) of productivity and market access advances to competing domestic firms that operate in the same market. Yet, technology and knowledge are characterized by imperfect markets with important externalities, so horizontal spillover of technology or trained labour to domestic competitors can never be completely prevented.

In contrast, *vertical spillovers* (inter-industry) through forward and backward linkages with domestic companies are desirable for the MNC and it is thought that these spillovers to suppliers and buyers can play a very important role. While MNCs tend to prevent the transfer of technologies to home country competitors, they are likely to increase the efficiency of domestic suppliers or customers voluntarily through vertical input–output linkages. The MNCs provide incentives to local firms by imposing high standards and help them to increase productivity and quality.[45]

3.4.2 Spillover channels

Productivity and market access spillovers are generally difficult to distinguish in practice as they take place through similar spillover channels. We identify five channels through which spillover effects from FDI companies to domestic firms can occur: imitation, formation of human capital, competition, crowding-in and export effects.[46]

43 M. Blomström and A. Kokko, 1998, 'Multinational Corporations and Spillovers', *Journal of Economic Surveys* 12(2): 1–31.

44 R. Caves, 1974, 'Multinational Firms, Competition and Productivity in Host-Country Markets', *Economica* 41(6): 176–193.

45 H. Görg and D. Greenaway, 2004, 'Much Ado about Nothing? Do Domestic Firms Really Benefit from Foreign Direct Investment?' *The World Bank Research Observer* 19(2): 171–197; H. Gow. and J. Swinnen, 1998, 'Up- and Downstream Restructuring, Foreign Direct Investment, and Hold-up Problems in Agricultural Transition', *European Review of Agricultural Economics* 25(3): 331–350.

46 This classification is based on based on Blomström and Kokko, 1998, op. cit. and Görg and Greenaway, 2004, op. cit.

3.4.2.1 Imitation

Imitation is simply the copying of products, technologies and production processes by a local firm, often referred to as reverse engineering.[47] Such reverse engineering can result in horizontal productivity spillovers and growth advances for the economy. For the imitation of advanced technologies, a certain level of technical skills in the imitating domestic firm may be required, while managerial and organizational innovations may be easier to imitate.

3.4.2.2 Formation of human capital

Foreign direct investment can contribute to the formation of human capital – resulting in spillover effects to the rest of the economy – both by demanding and by supplying skills.[48] A large share of FDI in developing countries is attracted by the relatively low wages in these countries. Nevertheless, multinational firms are generally more skill-intensive than local firms.[49] When MNCs enter the market they may increase the *demand for skilled workers* if they do not substitute the local demand for employment. An increased demand for skills is expected to raise the wage and employment opportunities of skilled workers, creating incentives for overall investment in human capital.

On the other hand, multinational firms might affect the *supply side of skills* by investing in training their workers and the development of human capital. The type of training can range from informal on-the-job training to official training, seminars or even investment in formal education. Foreign-owned firms may organize informal and official training for their own employees. In addition, MNCs may involve themselves in general education by the voluntary provision of grants and assistance to community development, including formal education. The MNCs may, for example, engage in the start-up of research and development (R&D) or education centres to develop local skills for their high-tech industries or business education.[50]

The importance of training depends on the motive for foreign investment.[51] Natural resource investment is usually capital-intensive and requires the training of only a small number of highly skilled workers. Efficiency-seeking manufacturing MNCs usually search for low-skilled low-wage labour and their

---

47 J.-Y. Wang and M. Blomström, 1992, 'Foreign Investment and Technology Transfer: A Simple Model', *European Economic Review*, 36(1): 137–155.

48 M. Slaughter, 2002, 'Skill Upgrading in Developing Countries: Has Inward Foreign Direct Investment Played a Role?', *OECD Working Paper* No. 192, p. 35.

49 D.W. te Velde and O. Morrissey, 2002, 'Foreign Direct Investment: Who Gains?', *ODI Briefing Paper* April 2002, Overseas Development Institute, London; D.W. te Velde, 2002, 'Government policies for inward foreign direct investment in developing countries: implications for human capital formation and income inequality', *OECD Working Paper* No. 193, p. 37.

50 Te Velde, 2002, op. cit.

51 Ibid.

need for training is limited. In particular, strategic-asset-seeking FDI organizes training in very specific skills for a relatively well-educated workforce. Finally, market-seeking FDI might involve technological or marketing training of local people.

Spillovers resulting from the training of employees and general investment in education can be horizontal or vertical. Horizontal spillovers can take place through externalities or through labour turnover. When MNCs support industrial or regional skill development institutions, it is expected that skills will spill over to domestic firms that receive training at these MNC-supported institutions. Another important form of horizontal spillovers consists of employees who move to domestic firms after having been employed and trained at a MNC. Spin-offs occur when such employees decide to use the acquired skills to start up a new company.[52] These types of horizontal spillover effect may only become apparent after some time.[53] Vertical spillover effects through human capital formation may be more immediate, for example when training is provided by a MNC to its local suppliers. Such training and learning by downstream suppliers and upstream buyers may result in immediate productivity gains for these companies.

3.4.2.3 Competition and crowding out

The entry of a foreign firm or affiliate generally increases competition. Even if local firms are unable to imitate the technology of multinational firms, greater competition forces them to increase the efficiency of existing technologies, to adopt or develop new, more efficient technologies, or to invest in human capital – generally benefiting productivity and growth.[54] Young states that the innovations embodied in FDI may create rents accruing to older technologies, making domestic investment more profitable.[55]

However, increased competition can also result in the crowding out of local firms and reduce domestic investment. For example, multinationals may have lower marginal costs due to some firm-specific advantages, which allow them to attract demand away from domestic firms. This effect can offset the positive productivity spillover effects of increased competition.[56]

52　K. Miyamoto, 2003, 'Human Capital Formation and Foreign Direct Investment in Developing Countries', *Working Paper* No. 211, 49p.

53　A. Fosfuri, M. Motta and T. Ronde, 2001, 'Foreign Direct Investment and Spillovers through Workers' Mobility', *Journal of International Economics* 53(1): 205–222; Blomström and Kokko, 2002, op. cit.

54　Wang and Blomström, 1992, op. cit.; A.J. Glass and K. Saggi, 2002, 'Multinational Firms and Technology Transfer', *The Scandinavian Journal of Economics*, 104(4): 495–514; H. Gow and J. Swinnen, 2001, 'Private Enforcement Capital and Contract Enforcement in Transition Countries', *American Journal of Agricultural Economics*, 83(3): 686–690.

55　A. Young, 1993, 'Substitution and Complementarity in Endogenous Innovations', *Quarterly Journal of Economics* 108: 775–807.

56　Aitken and Harrison, 1999, op. cit.

3.4.2.4 Crowding in domestic investment

Some argue that, rather than creating competition that crowds out local firms, FDI stimulates domestic investment and leads to a crowding-in of domestic firms. The technologies, know-how and new market opportunities brought in by MNCs may attract domestic investors into the sectors entered by MNCs.[57] Yet, in poor countries, crowding-in may be hampered since governments lack the ability to direct FDI projects such that they do not displace local firms.[58] Additionally, policies offering preferential treatment and incentives to attract FDI – such as export-free zones and other tax incentives – may introduce a distortion that negatively affects domestic investment and limits growth spillover effects through crowding-in.[59]

3.4.2.5 Export effects

A last source of spillovers arises from the export activity of foreign firms.[60] Multinational corporations link local suppliers and subcontractors to international markets, provide information on foreign market conditions and consumer preferences, and offer distribution networks, transport infrastructure and export management skills.[61]

3.4.3 Empirical evidence on spillover effects

3.4.3.1 Horizontal productivity spillovers

A large empirical literature has tried to find evidence of the above identified spillover effects. Görg and Greenaway give an overview of 40 studies on horizontal productivity spillovers in manufacturing industries in developing, developed and transition economies.[62] Twenty-two of these studies find positive and statistically significant spillovers from foreign to domestic firms, but most of them use cross-sectional data, often aggregated at the sectoral level.[63] If foreign investment is attracted towards the more productive sectors, then cross-sectional data will show a positive relationship between FDI and productivity. But this does not allow us to conclude that the higher productivity

57 E. Borensztein, J. De Gregorio and J.W. Lee, 1998, 'How Does Foreign Direct Investment Affect Economic Growth?', *Journal of International Economics*, 45: 115–135
58 M. Agosin and R. Mayer, 2000, 'Foreign Investment in Developing Countries: Does it Crowd in Domestic Investment?', *UNCTAD Discussion Paper* No. 146, Geneva.
59 Borensztein et al., 1998, op. cit.
60 Aitken et al., 1997, op. cit.
61 Blomström and Kokko, 1998, op. cit.
62 Görg and Greenaway, 2004, op. cit.
63 Cross-sectional data contain information at one point in time. The use of such data has limitations, especially to identify causality. Also the use of data aggregated at the sector level, for which information is available only for the industrial or agricultural sectors as a whole, has limitations in identifying relations within certain sub-sectors or industries.

is due to spillovers from FDI. When we look only at those studies using a panel of firm-level data, seven of them find positive evidence of spillovers, mostly in developed economies (e.g. Castellani and Zanfei for Italy; Görg and Strobl for Ireland; Damijan and co-authors for Romania; Driffield for the UK).[64] Blalock and Gertler also find positive horizontal spillovers from FDI for a sample of Indonesian firms.[65] Other empirical studies find evidence of a decrease in productivity for Morocco; Venezuela; Spain; Bulgaria and Romania; and for the Czech Republic.[66] But most studies find no significant impact by multinationals on domestic productivity. Thus, while the empirical literature provides fairly robust evidence of the beneficial effects of the presence of foreign companies in developed countries, the large number of studies on productivity spillovers in transition and developing economies finds no or even negative spillovers for domestic firms.

Several explanations have been put forward to explain the negative results that have been found. Aitken and Harrison and Konings suggest that foreign firms may reduce the productivity of domestic firms through a negative competition effect.[67] However, while some firms may experience negative competition effects, at the same time other firms may succeed in improving their efficiency as a response to the increased competition. The overall impact from competition is thus the result of aggregating both positive and negative effects. Another explanation for not finding positive spillover effects may be the fact that it takes time for domestic firms to learn, which is not captured by short-run analyses. Or multinational firms might try to prevent their technology from spilling over to competitors. Other literature has argued that the assumption that foreign firms are more efficient than domestic firms is not necessarily true, especially when FDI takes the form of M&As.[68]

3.4.3.2 Vertical spillover effects in manufacturing

More recent literature has focused on the importance of vertical spillover effects, through technology and know-how spillovers. In an early study, Lall found

64   D. Castellani and A. Zanfei, 2002, 'Multinational Companies and Productivity Spillovers: Is there a Specification Error?', *SSRN working paper* 303392. Online. Available HTTP < http://papers.ssrn.com> (accessed 25 July 2012); Damijan et al., 2003, op. cit.; H. Görg and E. Strobl, 2003, 'Multinational Companies, Technology Spillovers and Plant Survival', *Scandinavian Journal of Economics* 105(4): 581–595; N. Driffield, 2001, 'The Impact on Domestic Productivity of Inward Investment in the UK', *Manchester School* 69(1): 103–119
65   G. Blalock and P. Gertler, 2009, 'How Firm Capabilities Affect Who Benefits from Foreign Technology', *Journal of Development Economics* 90(2): 192–199.
66   M. Haddad and A. Harrison, 1993, 'Are There Positive Spillovers from Direct Foreign Investment? Evidence from Panel Data for Morocco', *Journal of Development Economics*, 42: 51–74; Aitken and Harrison, 1999, op. cit., Castellani and Zanfei, 2002; op. cit., Konings, 2001, op. cit.; Djankov and Hoekman, 2000, op. cit.
67   Aitken and Harrison, 1999, op. cit.; Konings, 2001, op. cit.
68   Krugman, 1998, op. cit.; Hausmann and Fernandez-Aria, 2000, op. cit.

significant backward productivity linkages for truck manufacturing in India.[69] Positive vertical spillovers are found for Indonesia and Hungary.[70] For Lithuania, positive backwards spillovers were found, while in Romania there is evidence of negative vertical spillovers.[71]

Some studies have specifically compared the importance of horizontal and vertical spillover effects. Kugler finds very clear evidence of positive inter-industry (vertical) spillovers in ten manufacturing industries in Colombia, while only in one of these industries was evidence of intra-industry (horizontal) spillovers also found.[72] Other empirical studies come to similar conclusions. Javorcik, and Blalock and Gertler find no evidence of horizontal spillovers but do indicate productivity spillovers through backward linkages.[73] For UK manufacturing industries positive spillovers through forward linkages were found, but no significant spillovers through backward linkages.[74] And for ten transition countries the impact of FDI on firms' productivity is estimated to be ten times larger through vertical rather than horizontal spillovers.[75]

3.4.3.3 Vertical spillover effects in the agri-food sector

Vertical spillover effects from FDI in the agri-food sectors of developing and transition countries has recently received a lot of attention in the empirical literature. Foreign direct investment in the agri-food sector of developing countries is thought to be particularly important because of the existence of vertical links with local farmers. Such vertical links in the agri-food sector entail the potential for creating poverty-reducing effects in rural areas of developing countries, where poverty rates are often very high (this is further discussed in section 3.6).

69 S. Lall, 1980, 'Vertical Inter-firm Linkages in LDCs: An Empirical Study', *Oxford Bulletin of Economics and Statistics*, 42: 203–226.
70 K. Schoors and B. Van Der Tol, 2002, 'Foreign Direct Investment Spillovers within and between Sectors: Evidence from Hungarian Data', *Ghent University Working Paper* 02/157; G. Blalock, 2001, 'Technology from Foreign Direct Investment: Strategic Transfer through Supply Chains', mimeo, University of California, Berkeley.
71 B.S. Javorcik, 2004, 'Does Foreign Direct Investment Increase the Productivity of Domestic Firms? In Search of Spillovers Through Backward Linkages', *American Economic Review* 94: 605–627; B.S. Javorcik, K. Saggi and M. Spatareanu, 2004, 'Does It Matter Where You Come From? Vertical Spillovers from Foreign Direct Investment and the Nationality of Investors', *World Bank Policy Research Working Paper* No. 3449.
72 M. Kugler, 2006, 'Spillovers from Foreign Direct Investment: Within or Between Industries?', *Journal of Development Economics* 80: 444–477.
73 Javorcik, 2004, op. cit.; G. Blalock and P. Gerlter, 2009, 'How Firm Capabilities Affect Who Benefits from Foreign Technology', *Journal of Development Economics* 90(2): 192–199.
74 N. Driffield, M. Munday and A. Roberts, 2002, 'Foreign Direct Investment, Transaction Linkages and the Performance of the Domestic Sector', *International Journal of the Economics of Business* 9(3): 335–351.
75 Damijan et al., 2003, op. cit.

Many studies provide evidence of positive productivity spillover effects from FDI in the agri-food sector to domestic farmers in low-income countries. For example, Dries and Swinnen find that dairy farmers in Poland have significantly higher levels of output and productivity when they are vertically linked to modern FDI milk companies.[76] Similar effects are found for the broiler, dairy and fruit and vegetable sectors in Thailand, the Philippines and India.[77] These studies indicate that such productivity spillover effects are created because technology and know-how are transferred directly from FDI companies to supplying farms through contract-farming schemes, including extensive farm assistance programmes. In addition, such programmes include the provision of inputs and credit to farmers.

3.4.3.4 Education, training and human capital formation

There is quite a lot of evidence that MNCs provide more training than their local counterparts. In Nigeria, training expenses per employee were five times higher in MNCs compared to domestic firms and were aimed more at white-collar workers.[78] Similar results are found for Kenya.[79] More recent empirical studies show that higher foreign equity shares are indeed an important determinant of employee training in Mexico, Indonesia and Malaysia.[80] However, evidence on how TNCs affect general education is lacking.

In Mexico training of domestic suppliers occurred in the auto industry[81] and training spillovers through vertical linkages were also observed in Costa Rica.[82] Examples of horizontal human capital spillovers through labour turnover and

76   L. Dries and J. Swinnen, 2004, 'Foreign Direct Investment, Vertical Integration and Local Suppliers: Evidence from the Polish Dairy Sector', *World Development* 32: 1525–1544.

77   A. Gulati, N. Minot, C. Delgado and S. Bora, 2005, 'Growth in High-Value Agriculture in Asia and the Emergence of Vertical Links with Farmers', Paper presented at the workshop *Linking Small-scale Producers to Markets: Old and New Challenges*, The World Bank; P.S. Birthal, P.K. Joshi and A. Gulati, 2005, 'Vertical Coordination in High-Value Food Commodities: Implications for Smallholders', *MTID Discussion Paper* No. 85, International Food Policy Research Institute, Washington DC.

78   O. Iyanda and J. Bello, 1976, *Employment Effects of Multinational Enterprises in Nigeria*, International Labour Office, Geneva.

79   I. Gershenberg, 1987, 'The Training and Spread of Managerial Know-how: A Comparative Analysis of Multinational and other Firms in Kenya', *World Development* 15: 931–939.

80   H. Tan and G. Batra, 1996, *Enterprise Training in Developing Countries*, World Bank, Washington DC; H. Tan and G. Lopez-Acevedo, 2003, 'Mexico: In-Firm Training for the Knowledge Economy', *World Bank Policy Research Working Paper* 2957, World Bank, Washington DC; K. Miyamoto and Y. Todo, 2003, 'Enterprise Training in Indonesia: The Interaction between Worker's Schooling and Training', *OECD Developing Centre Working Paper*, OECD, Paris.

81   E. Lim, 2001, 'Determinants of, and the Relations between, Foreign Direct Investment and Summary of the Recent Literature', *IMF Working Paper* WP/01/175, Washington DC.

82   B.F. Larrain, L.F. Lopez-Calva and A. Rodriguez-Clare, 2000, 'Intel: A Case Study of Foreign Investment in Central America', *CID Working Paper* No. 58.

spin-offs are found in Costa Rica and Malaysia.[83] Todo and Miyamoto provide evidence that a larger absorptive capacity of domestic firms enhances training transfers.[84]

Gershenberg finds some evidence of the movement of managers from foreign to domestic firms for Kenya.[85] And there is evidence of training spillovers through workers' mobility in the manufacturing sector in Ghana.[86] They find that firms which are run by owners who worked for multinationals in the same industry immediately prior to opening up their own firm have higher productivity levels than other firms.

3.4.3.5 Export spillover effects

Empirical evidence of export spillover effects is limited. In the Venezuelan manufacturing sector, positive export spillover effects were found.[87] The probability that a domestic firm engages in export activities is positively correlated with proximity to multinational firms, while for domestic exporting firms no export spillovers are found. Greenaway, Sousa and Wakelin find that MNCs' exports have a positive effect on domestic firms' probability of being exporters but do not find evidence that such spillovers impact on the export ratio of domestic firms.[88]

3.4.3.6 Crowding in or out?

The empirical evidence on the impact of FDI on domestic investment is quite mixed. Some find that FDI stimulates domestic investment while others find that FDI creates competition, leading to crowding-out effects. Most of the evidence comes from manufacturing. For example, Agosin and Mayer find mixed results, with crowding-out effects dominating in most developing countries except for certain Asian countries.[89] On the contrary, others report FDI in developing countries to result in crowding-in of domestic investment.[90]

83 A. Rodriguez-Clare, 2001, 'Costa Rica's Development Strategy Based in Human Capital and Technology: How it Got There, the Impact of Intel and Lessons for Other Countries', *Journal of Human Development*. 2(2) : 311–324; Lim et al., 2001, op. cit.

84 Y. Todo. and K. Miyamoto, 2002, 'Knowledge Diffusion from Multinational Enterprises: The Role of Domestic and Foreign Knowledge-Enhancing Activities', *Technical Paper* No. 196, OECD Development Centre, Paris.

85 Gershenberg, 1987, op. cit.

86 H. Görg and E. Strobl, 2005, 'Spillovers from Foreign Firms through Worker Mobility: An Empirical Investigation', *Scandinavian Journal of Economics* 107(4): 693–709.

87 Aitken et al., 2007, op. cit.

88 D. Greenaway, N. Sousa and K. Wakelin, 2004, 'Do domestic firms learn to export from multinationals?', *European Journal of Political Economy* 20: 1027–1043.

89 Agosin and Mayer, 2000, op. cit.

90 Borenzstein et al., 1998, op. cit.; B. Bosworth and S. Collins, 1999, 'Capital Flows to Developing Countries: Implications for Saving and Investment', *Brookings Papers on Economic Activity* 1, 143–169.

These studies find a one-to-one relationship between FDI and domestic investment – meaning that a \$1 increase in FDI raises domestic investment by \$1 – which is significantly larger than for other forms of external capital flow.

A particularly important case of FDI and crowding-in effects is in the agrifood sectors of developing countries (again because of the link to poverty reduction; see further section 3.6). Some argue that FDI in food processing, exporting and distribution in developing countries leads to the exclusion of small and resource-poor farmers from profitable opportunities.[91] This crowding-out or exclusion of local farmers happens because FDI companies replace small-scale farmers or because they prefer to establish vertical links with large commercial farms, creating increased competition with the smallholder sector. However, others have presented evidence, for Senegal, Madagascar and Kenya, that this is not the case or that there are important benefits through employment creation.[92]

3.4.4 Some conclusions

Economic theory predicts that FDI will create growth multiplier effects through horizontal and mainly through vertical spillover effects, including the transfer of technology and know-how to domestic firms and the formation of human capital. The empirical evidence casts doubt on the intensity of horizontal (or intra-industry) spillover effects but provides convincing evidence of the existence and importance of vertical (or inter-industry) spillover effects, in the manufacturing as well as the agricultural sectors.

3.5 Causes of heterogeneous growth effects

Empirical studies on the implications of FDI for economic growth in the host economies – whether through direct or indirect effects – often come to very different conclusions. The empirically observed effects seem to be heterogeneous across countries and regions while certain theoretical arguments might hold only for certain types of FDI inflow. The recent literature has recognized that

91 C. Dolan and J. Humphrey, 2000, 'Governance and Trade in Fresh Vegetables: The Impact of UK Supermarkets on the African Horticulture Industry', *Journal of Development Studies* 37(2): 147–176; E. Farina and T. Reardon, 2000, 'Agrifood Grades and Standards in the Extended Mercosur: Their Role in the Changing Agrifood System', *American Journal of Agricultural Economics* 82: 1170–1176; S. Jaffee and S. Henson, 2005, 'Agro-food Exports from Developing Countries: The Challenges Posed by Standards', in M.A. Aksoy and J.C. Beghin (eds), *Global Agricultural Trade and Developing Countries*, Washington DC: The World Bank; B. Minten, L. Randrianarison and J.F.M. Swinnen, 2009, 'Global Retail Chains and Poor Farmers: Evidence from Madagascar', *World Development* 37(11): 1728–1741.
92 M. Maertens and J. Swinnen, 2009, 'Trade, Standards and Poverty: Evidence from Senegal', *World Development*, 37(1), 161–178; M. Maertens, L. Colen and J. Swinnen, 2011, 'Globalization and Poverty in Senegal: A Worst Case Scenario?', *European Review of Agricultural Economics*, 38(1): 31–54.

certain factors may condition the growth effect of FDI in developing countries. In this section, we briefly assess these factors – theoretically as well as empirically.

3.5.1 Factors conditioning the growth effect of FDI

3.5.1.1 The technological gap

Since the imitation of technology is typically cheaper than the invention of new ideas, less developed countries will grow relatively faster and catch up with the developed nations.[93] As a result, the impact of FDI on growth is expected to be larger where there is a wider technological gap between leaders and followers. Since developing countries generally lag behind in terms of technological development, FDI inflows might be a particularly important way of spurring economic growth in the least advanced nations.

In contrast, other theories state that the rate of this 'catch-up process' depends on the level of human capital in the developing country,[94] and thus on the ability to absorb the positive spillovers from FDI. A large technological gap between home and host country can thus hamper the knowledge and technology spillovers. As a result, the impact of FDI on growth is expected to depend inversely on the technological gap between the investing and the receiving country.

3.5.1.2 Macro-economic conditions

From a theoretical point of view it is widely agreed that technological spillovers are the most important form through which FDI can create growth. Yet, the magnitude of this effect can depend on country-specific characteristics. Apart from the technological gap and the difference in the level of income or human capital between home and host country, other macro-economic conditions may determine the growth effect of FDI inflows. For example, Bhagwati hypothesized that the beneficial effect of FDI in terms of enhancing economic growth is stronger in countries that pursue an outwardly oriented trade policy than in countries adopting an inwardly oriented policy.[95]

3.5.1.3 The type of FDI

Nunnenkamp emphasizes that the effect of FDI on growth depends on the motivation for and sector of investment.[96] He argues that efficiency-seeking

---

93 P. Romer, 1993, 'Idea Gaps and Object Gaps in Economic Development', *Journal of Monetary Economics* 32: 543–573; R.J. Barro and X. Sala-i-Martin, 1997, 'Technological Diffusion, Convergence, and Growth', *Journal of Economic Growth* 2(1): 1–26.

94 R. Nelson and E. Phelps, 1966, 'Investment in Humans, Technological Diffusion, and Economic Growth', *The American Economic Review* 56(1–2): 69–75.

95 J. Baghwati, 1978, 'Anatomy and Consequences of Exchange Control Regimes', *Studies in International Economic Relations* 10, NBER, New York.

96 Nunnenkamp, 2004, op. cit.

FDI is superior to market-seeking FDI in stimulating higher growth in host countries with favourable conditions. And while FDI in the manufacturing sector is expected to have a growth effect, natural-resource-seeking FDI in the primary sector is expected to have only a limited impact on growth. Kojima predicts that FDI will be more growth-enhancing when directed to more labour-intensive and less technology-intensive industries, thus when investment is made in industries where the technological gap between foreign and domestic firms is limited.[97] In contrast, Dutt argues that investment in less advanced industries worsens the terms of trade and that the impact of FDI is thus larger when directed towards the more technologically advanced industries.[98]

It is argued by UNCTAD that in the primary sector, the scope for linkages between foreign affiliates and local suppliers is often limited and mining firms often operate as 'enclaves'.[99] The manufacturing sector has a broad variety of linkage-intensive activities, while in the tertiary sector the scope for subcontracting and creating strong linkages is also limited.

The different entry modes of FDI may also cause differential impacts. Most developing countries prefer greenfield investment because it immediately and directly adds to their existing industrial capacity, whereas M&As transfer ownership of local assets from domestic to foreign interests. Concerning the creation of jobs, it is similarly argued that M&As are less likely to create new jobs. However, in the longer term, M&As may receive supplementary capital and employment may rise.[100] On the other hand, greenfield investment is more likely to operate as an enclave with close links to other units in their international corporate network but limited interaction with the host economy, thereby limiting spillovers to domestic firms. In contrast, M&As tend to have a more developed network of local and regional suppliers, since they are simply a takeover of domestically developed companies.[101]

3.5.2 Empirical evidence

3.5.2.1 Heterogeneous effects in cross-country studies

Many studies do not find an unequivocally positive growth effect related to FDI inflows but find instead that certain conditions need to be fulfilled for FDI to generate benefits (Table 3.5). Some studies find that FDI contributes more to

97 K. Kojima, 1973, 'A Macroeconomic Approach to Foreign Direct Investment', *Hitotsubashi Journal of Economics* 14: 1–21

98 A.M. Dutt, 1997, 'The Pattern of Direct Foreign Investment and Economic Growth', *World Development* 25: 1925–1936.

99 UNCTAD, 2005, *Economic Development in Africa. Rethinking the Role of Foreign Direct Investment*, United Nations, New York.

100 UNCTAD, 1998, *World Investment Report: Trends and Determinants*, United Nations, New York.

101 M. Szanyi, 2001, 'Privatization and Greenfield FDI in the Economic Restructuring of Hungary', *Transnational Corporations* 10(3): 25–38.

Table 3.5 Overview of the empirical studies explaining the heterogeneous effect of FDI across countries

	Sign of the direction in which the conditional factor influences the growth impact of FDI		*Controlling for causality*
Borensztein et al. (1998)	Education	+	No
Xu (2000)	Education	+	No
Blomström et al. (1994)	Education	No effect	No
	GDP/capita	+	
Balasubramanyam (1998)	Level of human capital level	+	No
	Well developed infrastructure	+	
	Stable economic climate	+	
Balasubramanyam et al. (1996)	Export-oriented trade regime	+	No
Alfaro et al. (2004)	Developed financial markets	+	No
Bende-Nabende et al. (2003)	Technology gap	+	Simultaneous equation
Li and Liu (2005)	Level of human capital	+	Simultaneous equation
	Technology gap	–	
Carkovic and Levine (2002)	Education	No effect	Simultaneous equation
	GDP/capita	No effect	
	Export-oriented trade regime	No effect	
	Developed financial markets	No effect	
Hansen and Rand (2006)	Education	No effect	Granger causality
	GDP/capita	No effect	
	Export-oriented trade regime	No effect	
	Developed financial markets	No effect	

growth than domestic investment when the country has a highly educated workforce that can exploit the FDI spillovers.[102] Balasubramanyam finds similar results and concludes that FDI can be a strong instrument of development, but only if a certain threshold of human capital, well-developed infrastructure facilities and a stable economic climate is attained in the host country.[103] In another study (together with Salisu and Sapsford) Balasubramanyam shows that the impact of FDI on growth is larger for countries that pursue a policy of export promotion rather than import substitution.[104] In the context of export-promoting trade regimes they find that FDI is more growth-enhancing than domestic investment. There is evidence that FDI promotes economic growth

---

102 Borenzstein et al, 1998, op. cit.; Xu, 2000, op. cit.
103 Balasubramanyam, 1998, op. cit.
104 V. N. Balasubramanyam, M. Salisu, and D. Sapsford, 1996, 'Foreign Direct Investment and Growth in EP and IS Countries', *Economic Journal*, 106: 92–105.

where financial markets are sufficiently developed.[105] Blomström, Lipsey and Zejan find no evidence of the importance of education but they argue that FDI has a positive growth effect only when the country is rich enough.[106] Li and Liu support the theory of a positive growth effect from FDI and indicate that a sufficient level of human capital is needed and that the technology gap may not be too large if a positive growth impact from FDI is to be experienced.[107] These findings indicate that a threshold of development, or absorptive capacity, needs to be attained before a country is able to take advantage of the spillover effects of FDI.

However, there is also contrasting empirical evidence suggesting that the technological gap is not important or confirming the hypothesis that less-developed countries can benefit more from FDI because of a larger 'catch-up effect'. Some studies do not find evidence of the suggested thresholds when accounting for heterogeneity and country-specific effects.[108] Another study finds a positive impact of FDI on output for the less advanced Philippines and Thailand, but a negative effect in the more economically developed Japan and Taiwan.[109] These results generally indicate that spillover effects are more likely to be positive in the less developed countries.

3.5.2.2 Heterogeneous effects across sectors and entry mode

In contrast to the theoretical models, Dutt finds no difference in the growth impact of FDI between high-technology and low-technology industries.[110] However, he does not account for different sectors. Nunnenkamp and Spatz find in a cross-country study that the link between FDI and growth is larger for services than for manufacturing industries.[111] Within the manufacturing sector efficiency-seeking FDI turns out to be more growth-enhancing than market-seeking FDI. Chakraborty and Nunnenkamp also find for India that the growth effect of FDI varies across sectors.[112] Positive growth effects are found in the manufacturing sector, no causal relationship is found in the primary sector and for FDI in the services sector the direction seems to run from growth to FDI and not the opposite way. Alfaro and Charlton find that the overall

105 L. Alfaro, A. Chanda, S. Kalemi-Ozcan and S. Sayek, 2004, 'FDI and Economic Growth: The Role of Local Financial Markets', *Journal of International Economics* 64(1): 89–112.
106 M. Blomström, R.E. Lipsey and M. Zejan, 1994, 'What Explains the Growth of Developing Countries?', in W. Baumol, R. Nelson and E. Wolff (eds) *Convergence of Productivity: Cross-National Studies and Historical Evidence*, Oxford: Oxford University Press, pp. 243–259.
107 X. Li and X. Liu, 2005, 'Foreign Direct Investment and Economic Growth: An Increasingly Endogenous Relationship', *World Development* 33: 393–407.
108 Carkovic and Levine, 2002, op. cit.; Hansen and Rand, 2006, op. cit.
109 Bende-Nabende et al. 2003, op. cit.
110 Dutt, 1997, op. cit.
111 Nunnenkamp and Spatz, 2004, op. cit.
112 C. Chakraborty and P. Nunnenkamp, 2006, 'Economic Reforms, Foreign Direct Investment and its Economic Effects in India', *Kiel Working Paper* No. 1272, 45p.

growth effect of FDI is ambiguous, while the impact is negative for the primary sector, positive for the manufacturing sector and ambiguous for investment in the services sector.[113]

On the differential impact of greenfield investment or M&A, empirical evidence is limited. Wes and Lankes find for a set of firms in transition countries that M&A creates more employment and attracts more unskilled labour, while greenfield FDI looks mainly for skilled workers.[114] Zemplinerova and Jarolim find higher productivity growth for M&A than for greenfield investment in the Czech Republic.[115] The positive results of investments in the agri-food sector are also all from greenfield investments.

3.5.2.3 Heterogeneous effects across firms

A lot of attention has been paid to the fact that not all firms benefit equally from the spillovers and that their positive effect is lost by aggregating the data of all firms. Recent theoretical work has highlighted the importance of firm heterogeneity in understanding FDI.[116] Differences in absorptive capacity, regional dimensions and vertical linkages may explain why certain local firms do and others do not benefit from FDI. It is hypothesized that whether a firm can benefit depends on the technology gap with the foreign firm and its capacity for absorbing new knowledge and technology.[117] Yet, it is not clear in which direction this technology gap affects technology adoption. On the one hand, firms with a large gap have more to gain from adoption and therefore have a higher incentive to learn from the foreign firm. For firms with a higher level of technology it might be costly to make further productivity improvements. On the other hand, firms with a large technology gap may be too far behind and lack the technical competency to catch up.[118]

Some empirical studies have addressed this need for *absorptive capacity* at firm level. Kokko and co-authors find evidence of productivity spillovers to those domestic firms with moderate technology gaps, but not for firms that use considerably lower levels of technology.[119] Other studies come to similar

113 L. Alfar and Charlton, 2007, 'Growth and the Quality of Foreign Direct Investment: Is All FDI Equal', *HBS Finance Working Paper*, No. 07–072.
114 M. Wes and H.P. Lankes, 2001, FDI in economies in transition: M&As versus greenfield investment, *Transnational Corporations*, 10(3): 113–130.
115 A. Zemplinerova and M. Jarolim M., 2001, 'Mode of Entry and Firm Performance: The Czech Case', *Transnational Corporations* 10(3): 95–112.
116 E. Helpman, M. Melitz and S. Yeaple, 2004, 'Export Versus FDI with Heterogeneous Firms', *American Economic Review* 94: 300–316.
117 A similar argument on the need for absorptive capacity was made at country level, stating that countries which are technologically behind or have a low level of human capital are not able to experience growth resulting from FDI.
118 Blalock and Gertler, 2009, op. cit.
119 A. Kokko, R. Tansini and M. Zejan, 1996, 'Local Technological Capability and Productivity Spillovers from FDI in the Uruguayan Manufacturing Sector', *Journal of Development Studies* 32: 602–611.

results.[120] In contrast, Blalock and Gerlter find that it is the firms with a lower prior level of technology that benefit most from the presence of multinational competitors for a sample of Indonesian firms.[121] *Regional dimensions* may also play a role, since domestic firms that are located close to MNCs may be more likely to experience spillovers from human capital acquisition and imitation. Several empirical studies do not find clear evidence for this hypothesis.[122] Yet, findings for Mexico suggest that proximity to MNCs, in general, provides domestic plants with better access to foreign markets.[123]

3.5.3 Some conclusions

Empirical evidence suggests that the potential growth impact of FDI is not self-evident, but conditional on a number of factors such as the technological and absorptive levels of the home economy, macro-economic stability and the location of the firm. This explains why the impact of FDI on growth is largely heterogeneous across host countries, sectors and firms.

3.6 The impact of FDI on poverty reduction and inequality

In the previous sections we showed that there are sound theoretical arguments and convincing empirical evidence for believing that under certain conditions FDI can further economic growth in developing countries. However, the question remains as to whether FDI is really contributing to development that enlarges and equalizes opportunities for people in the developing world. Do FDI flows to developing countries reduce poverty? Does FDI reduce inequality between countries? Does FDI reduce existing inequalities or does it worsen the income distribution of the host country?

3.6.1 Can FDI contribute to poverty reduction?

While some argue that FDI is one of the most effective tools in the fight against poverty,[124] others say that the role of FDI in poverty reduction is highly overestimated.[125] Except for 'socially responsible' investment in poverty-

---

120 S. Girma, 2005, 'Absorptive Capacity and Productivity Spillovers from FDI: A Threshold Regression Analysis', *Oxford Bulletin of Economics and Statistics*, 67(3): 281–306; S. Barrios and E. Strobl, 2002, 'Foreign Direct Investment and Productivity Spillovers: Evidence from the Spanish Experience', *Wolfwirtshaftliches Archiv* 138: 159 81.

121 Blalock and Gertler, 2009, op. cit.

122 Aitken and Harrison, 1999, op. cit.; F. Sjöholm, 1999, 'Technology Gap, Competition and Spillovers from Direct Foreign Investment: Evidence from Establishment Data', *Journal of Development Studies* 34(1): 53–73.

123 Aitken et al., 1997, op. cit.

124 M. Klein, C. Aaron, B. Hadjimichael, 2001, 'Foreign Direct Investment and Poverty Reduction', *World Bank Policy Research Working Paper* 2613, The World Bank.

125 Nunnenkamp, 2004, op. cit.

reducing projects out of charity or image-building, there is no direct link between FDI and poverty. Yet, there are four possible indirect channels through which FDI affects poverty: (1) the economic growth channel; (2) the employment channel; (3) the wage channel; and (4) the tax revenue channel.[126] We discuss these mechanisms for poverty reduction in turn.

3.6.1.1 Economic growth and poverty reduction

First, to the extent that FDI enhances economic growth and increases national income, it thereby offers a potential to benefit the poor. The relationship between economic growth and poverty has been the subject of an extensive economic literature and the link between growth and poverty reduction – especially in the long run – has become a well-established fact. Dollar and Kraay show, using country panel data over four decades, that growth is inequality neutral and leads to proportional income rises for the poorest income quintile.[127] In a critique of this study, Ashley agrees that in periods of economic growth the poor also benefit from this growth, although not in equal proportion.[128] Ravallion and Chen also show that poor people benefit from rising average income, using micro-econometric analysis and household survey data from more than 40 countries.[129] Ravallion and Datt find that economic growth is positively related to poverty reduction across Indian states, using survey data over about four decades.[130] In a recent paper Kraay investigates the cross-country variation in changes in the headcount measure of poverty in a large set of developing countries for the 1980s and 1990s.[131] He finds that average income growth is the main source of poverty reduction, accounting for 70 per cent of the variation in poverty in the short run and for 97 per cent in the long run. These results[132] all underscore the importance of economic growth for poverty reduction.

126 Te Velde and Morrissey, 2002, op. cit.; Klein et al., 2001, op. cit.

127 D. Dollar and A. Kraay, 2002, 'Growth is Good for the Poor', *Journal of Economic Growth*, 7(3): 195–225.

128 R. Ashley, 2008, 'Growth may be Good for the Poor, but Decline is Disastrous . . .', *International Review of Economics and Finance* 17: 333–338.

129 M. Ravallion and S. Chen, 1997, 'What Can New Survey Data Tell Us about Recent Changes in Distribution and Poverty?', *World Bank Economic Review* 11: 357–382.

130 M. Ravallion and G. Datt, 2002, 'Why has Economic Growth been More Pro-poor in some States of India than Others?', *Journal of Development Economics* 68: 381–400.

131 A. Kraay, 2006, 'When is Growth Pro-poor? Evidence from a Panel of Countries', *Journal of Development Economics* 80: 198–227.

132 Many other influential empirical studies have investigated the link between economic growth and poverty reduction in developing countries, resulting in similar conclusions, e.g. W. Easterly, 1999, 'Life during Growth', *Journal of Economic Growth* 4: 239–276; M. Ravallion, 2001, 'Can High-inequality Developing Countries Escape Absolute Poverty?', *Economics Letters* 56(1): 51–57; Besley T. and R. Burgess, 2003, 'Halving Global Poverty', *Journal of Economic Perspectives* 17: 3–22; R. Adams, 2004, 'Economic Growth, Inequality and Poverty: Estimating the Growth Elasticity of Poverty', *World Development* 32: 1989–2014; M. Bruno, M. Ravallion and L. Squire, 1995, 'Equity and Growth in Developing

Yet, in the short run there might be a trade-off between growth and poverty reduction. Economic growth might indeed not directly benefit the poor. Especially in countries characterized by high inequality of income and assets, economic growth might not be related to poverty reduction in the short run.[133] Income growth will generally not immediately and directly benefit those who are trapped in poverty because of initial asset inequality coupled with market failures and because of spatial externalities.

Whether or not the economic growth promoted by FDI benefits poverty reduction remains an empirical question. Yet, very few empirical studies have tackled the question of the link between FDI, growth and poverty. Cross-country research on FDI and changes in income poverty and inequality is very limited. None of the available studies have provided strong evidence of a positive link between FDI, growth and poverty reduction.[134]

3.6.1.2 Employment creation

A second channel through which FDI could indirectly affect poverty in the host countries is through the creation of employment. Additional investments are likely to create employment. Increased employment benefits workers by adding to their per capita income, which can help some people to move out of poverty. In addition, FDI might cause employment multiplier effects. Through vertical linkages with local suppliers or crowding-in effects, additional employment might be created in the sector as a whole or in downstream and upstream sectors.

Not all types of FDI are likely to create substantial additional employment in the host economies. When FDI represents additional investment (greenfield investment), it generally provides employment, while M&As are less likely to create additional jobs.[135] Also, especially in the case of efficiency-seeking investment, FDI might be associated with increased employment since such investment is often motivated by the low wages and abundant labour force in low-income countries. On the other hand, in mining sectors local job creation is expected to be very limited.

Countries: Old and New Perspectives on the Policy Issues' World Bank Policy Research Working Paper 1563, World Bank, Washington DC; P. Timmer, 1997, 'How Well Do the Poor Connect to the Growth Process', CAER Discussion Paper 17, Harvard Institute of International Development.

133 H.A. Pasha and T. Palanivel, 2004, *Pro-poor Growth and Policies: The Asian Experience*, United Nations Development Program; M. Ravallion, 2004, 'Pro Poor Growth: A Primer', *World Bank Policy Research Working Paper* No. 3242, The World Bank, Washington DC.

134 R.P. Agénor, 2004, 'Does Globalization Hurt the Poor?', *International Economics and Economic Policy*, 1(1), 21–51; B. Milanovic, 2002, 'Can We Discern the Effect of Globalization on Income Distribution? Evidence from Household Budget Surveys', *World Bank Policy Research Working Paper* 2876, World Bank, Washington DC.

135 UNCTAD, 2003, op. cit.

However, since foreign firms are usually more capital-intensive than domestic firms and have more advanced technologies than local firms, it is possible that they increase employment only for the relatively better-skilled workers while excluding the poorest, uneducated people from employment benefits. Moreover, when foreign firms compete with local firms resulting in crowding-out, employment in domestic companies and in the sector as a whole may be reduced. Hence, the magnitude and sign of the employment effect will depend on the industry of investment, mode of entry of FDI and country characteristics.

Estimating the employment effect of FDI in developing countries is difficult because of a lack of data and because of the difficulty of disentangling simultaneous effects such as indirect effects and employment displacement. Hence, the empirical evidence on employment effects is very poor.[136] In 1999 it was estimated that 50 million people globally are directly employed by foreign affiliates of multinationals, accounting for only 1 to 2 per cent of the global workforce.[137] However, when taking into account also indirect effects the overall figures may be much higher. It is estimated that in developing countries for each worker employed by the local affiliate of a foreign-based firm, at least one or two jobs are created indirectly.

3.6.1.3 Pressure on wages

Third, FDI can alleviate poverty if foreign firms pay higher wages than local firms and invest more in training, thereby benefiting employees and creating incentives that can benefit the entire economy. The reason why multinationals would pay higher wages is related to the multinational firms' ownership, implying that they use higher levels of technology than domestic firms. By entering the market, domestic firms will also be forced to pay higher wages to attract workers. However, wage spillovers can also be negative if productivity spillovers are negative, for example due to negative competition effects.[138]

Empirical evidence exists of multinational firms paying higher wages, even after controlling for size and other firm and sectoral characteristics.[139] Negative wage spillovers have been found for Venezuela and Mexico and positive wage spillovers in the United States.[140] In Indonesia a higher foreign presence in a sector is found to lead to higher wages in domestic firms in that sector.[141]

---

136 UNCTAD, 2005, op. cit.
137 UNCTAD, 1999, op. cit.
138 Görg and Greenaway, 2004, op. cit.
139 Haddad and Harrison, 1993, op. cit.; Girma et al., 2001, op. cit.; Lipsey and Sjöholm, 2001, op. cit.
140 Aitken et al., 1996, op. cit.
141 Lipsey and Sjöholm, 2001, op. cit.

3.6.1.4 Increasing tax revenues

A fourth way in which FDI can affect poverty is by contributing to the governments' tax revenue, which can be used for redistributive measures benefiting the poor or be spent on the development of social safety nets for the poorest.[142] In some developing countries, the importance of FDI in overall tax revenue is quite high, creating opportunities for poverty-reducing policy measures. For example, 50 per cent of Botswana's government budget results from the mining industry.[143] However, in countries where, in order to attract FDI, governments extend tax exemptions to MNCs – as is the case in many developing countries – the potential for poverty-reducing effects through tax revenues and redistributive measures is limited.

The impact of FDI on growth, employment, wages and government revenue is very heterogeneous between countries, sectors, firms and individuals (see section 3.5), and thus so is the impact of FDI on poverty. When FDI is only directed to more developed countries, creates spillovers to the more advanced firms and hires and trains more highly skilled workers, the poverty-alleviating effects of FDI may be limited. Even when on average the income of the poor increases with growth, it does not mean that the poor are benefiting as much as the rich, and inequality might increase.[144]

3.6.2 Is FDI inequality reducing?

Critics argue that FDI enhances inequality *between* countries and worsens income distribution *within* countries. Gender inequality might also be affected by FDI inflows.

3.6.2.1 Across-country inequality

Does FDI increase inequality *between countries*? First of all, the largest share of FDI is still directed to the developed world, and within the developing world the FDI stock is concentrated in a small number of large and relatively advanced countries.[145] In per capita terms both FDI inflows and FDI stocks are significantly lower in countries with a high incidence of absolute poverty.[146] Hence, a first condition for FDI to contribute to increased equality is that developing countries – and especially poverty-stricken countries – need to do better in attracting FDI.

Moreover, several studies have found that the impact of FDI on growth depends on certain conditions: the type of FDI, industry and host country characteristics (see the evidence presented in section 3.5). More developed

---

142 Klein et al., 2001, op. cit.
143 UNCTAD, 2007, op. cit.
144 Klein et al., 2001, op. cit.
145 UNCTAD, 2007, op. cit.
146 Nunnenkamp, 2004, op. cit.

countries with a good investment climate, a highly skilled labour force and developed infrastructure are more likely to absorb spillover effects and to translate FDI into growth than poor countries. On the other hand, the larger the technology gap, the more and faster technology and knowledge can spill over, which would predict that FDI contributes to convergence among countries. Evidence is limited, but Choi finds that the level and growth of per capita income converges as bilateral FDI flows increase between two countries.[147] More empirical literature exists on the impact of trade and openness on inequality between countries. Both positive[148] and negative[149] impacts on convergence were found.

3.6.2.2 Within-country inequality

How does FDI affect inequality *within a country*? FDI can help to reduce income inequality when its benefits favour the poor and those in the lowest income categories. Inequality is likely to be reduced when FDI employs abundant unskilled labour,[150] such as in agriculture, or when the positive impact on economic growth is spread throughout the whole economy.

On the other hand, FDI can also worsen income distribution by raising wages in the corresponding sector relative to wages in traditional sectors.[151] Except for agribusiness investment, FDI is mainly directed to the urban areas, leaving out the rural poor. Moreover, it is unclear whether FDI benefits the poorest segment of the population working in the informal sector. Thus, since FDI has been mainly directed towards the skill-intensive sectors it is unlikely to have reduced wage inequality.[152] Also the provision of training is likely to be biased towards the better-educated workforce, which is not the poorest group in society.[153] Wood hypothesizes that following openness, inequality in very poor countries might increase by helping those with basic education (rather than the highly skilled) and leaving even further behind those without education.[154]

147 C. Choi, 2004, 'Foreign Direct Investment and Income Convergence', *Applied Economics Letters* 36: 1045–1049.

148 D. Ben-David, 1996, 'Trade and the Rate of Income Convergence', *Journal of International Economics* 40: 279–298; D. Ben-David, 2001, 'Trade Liberalization and Income Convergence: A Comment', *Journal of International Economics*, 55: 229–234.

149 M.J. Slaughter, 1997, 'Per Capita Income Convergence and the Role of International Trade', *American Economic Review* 194–199; M.J. Slaughter, 2001, 'Trade Liberalization and Per Capita Income Convergence: A Difference-in-differences Analysis', *Journal of International Economics* 55(1): 203–228.

150 A.V. Deardorff and R.M. Stern, 1994, *The Stolper-Samuelson Theorem: A Golden Jubilee*, Ann Arbor, NI: University of Michigan Press.

151 P. Tsai, 1995, 'Foreign Direct Investment and Income Inequality: Further Evidence', *World Development* 23(3): 469–483.

152 Te Velde and Morrissey, 2002, op. cit.

153 Miyamoto, 2003, op. cit.

154 A. Wood, 1995, 'How Trade Hurt Unskilled Workers', *The Journal of Economic Perspectives* 9(3): 57–80.

Thus only when at least basic education becomes the norm is inequality likely to fall.

The empirical literature shows mixed results for the impact of FDI on inequality. Tsai argues unambiguously that FDI inflows are very likely to worsen income distribution in developing countries.[155] Studies on Korea and China find that FDI inflows worsen income distribution.[156] Choi finds for a sample of 119 countries that FDI is positively associated with income inequality.[157] Other studies, in contrast, find no significant relationship between FDI and income inequality.[158] And Tsai argues that the significant relationship found between FDI and inequality might be due to geographical differences in inequality rather than to a causal effect of foreign investment.[159]

Some studies focus specifically on wage inequality between skilled and unskilled workers. Feenstra and Hanson find that foreign capital inflows in Mexico are associated with rising wage inequality.[160] Taylor and Driffield find that inward flows of FDI contribute to wage inequality in the UK manufacturing sectors.[161] Another study finds no evidence for a consistent relationship between FDI and wage inequality in a large sample of developing countries.[162] Te Velde and Morrissey find evidence that the wage premium paid by foreign firms is higher for skilled workers in five African countries.[163]

3.6.3 Some conclusions

Hence, although the evidence is mixed it seems likely that FDI increases inequality within a country. The impact of FDI on gender equity in the host country seems to be heterogeneous. Yet, even though inequality might increase

155 Tsai, 1995, op. cit.
156 J.S. Mah, 2002, 'The Impact of Globalization on Income Distribution: The Korean Experience', *Applied Economics Letters*, 9(15): 1007–1009; X. Zhang and K.H. Zhang, 2003, 'How Does Globalisation Affect Regional Inequality Within A Developing Country? Evidence from China', *Journal of Development Studies* 39(4): 47–67.
157 Choi, 2004, op. cit.
158 P. Lindert and J. Williamson, 2001, 'Does Globalization Make the World More Unequal?', *NBER Working Papers* 8228, National Bureau of Economic Research, Inc.; B. Milanovic, 2002, 'Can We Discern the Effect of Globalization on Income Distribution? Evidence from Household Budget Surveys', *World Bank Policy Research Working Paper* 2876, World Bank, Washington DC.
159 Tsai, 1995, op. cit.
160 R.C. Feenstra and G.H. Hanson, 1997, 'Foreign Direct Investment and Relative Wages: Evidence from Mexico's Maquiladoras', *Journal of International Economics* 42: 371–393.
161 K. Taylor and N. Driffield, 2005, 'Wage Inequality and the Role of Multinationals: Evidence from UK Panel Data', *Labour Economics* 12(2): 223–249.
162 R. Freeman, R. Oostendorp and M. Rama, 2001, 'Globalization and Wages', World Bank, Development Research Group, Washington DC.
163 D.W. te Velde and O. Morrissey, 2001, 'Foreign Ownership and Wages: Evidence from Five African Countries', *CREDIT Discussion Paper*.

in the short run, this does not exclude the possibility that FDI may nevertheless contribute importantly to poverty reduction when directed towards sectors with low-skilled labour in rural areas.

3.7 FDI, human development and human rights

3.7.1 Economic vs. human development

So far we have discussed in detail the impact of FDI on the economic components of human development: economic growth, income poverty and income inequality. The concept of human development includes economic development, but is much broader than that. The UN Development Programme (UNDP) defines human development as 'the process of widening people's choices in a way which enables them to enjoy long, healthy and creative lives'.[164] Its main purpose is to look beyond these economic indicators, by taking into account a series of non-economic factors such as education, health, employment, human rights, democracy and gender issues. Yet, it should be emphasized that economic growth, income poverty and inequality should not be underestimated as indicators of human development: even though income may not be the final purpose of human development itself, it does create opportunities for development and enlarges choices.[165] The 1996 Human Development Report emphasizes the positive two-way relationship between human and economic development.[166] There exists a strong connection between economic growth and human development: economic growth provides the resources to permit sustained improvement in human development, and on the other hand improvements in human capital contribute to economic development.[167] Hence, our findings on indicators of economic development – economic growth, poverty and income inequality – in the previous sections do indicate that FDI may enhance human development when the conditions are right. In the remainder of this section we look into the impact of FDI on the non-economic components of human development. First, we discuss two opposing views on the relationship between FDI and human development. Then we look at the empirical evidence for some non-economic components of human development such as labour standards, education, the environment and gender issues. Finally, we expand on the effect of foreign investment on human rights in the host country.

164 UNDP, 1999, op. cit.
165 S. Anand and A. Sen, 2000, 'The Income Component of the Human Development Index', *Journal of Human Development* 1(1): 83–106.
166 UNDP, 1996, *Human Development Report: Economic Growth and Human Development*, United Nations, New York, p. 113.
167 G. Ranis, F. Stewart and A. Ramirez, 2000, 'Economic Growth and Human Development', *World Development* 28(2): 197–219.

3.7.2 Race to the bottom or climb to the top?

With respect to the impact of FDI on human development there exist two basic hypotheses. The first, critical perspective states that FDI leads to a 'race to the bottom': foreign companies tend to locate production in countries or regions with low wages, low taxes and weak social and environmental regulations. In order not to lose investment and jobs, developing countries are thus forced to lower their standards, and corrupt governments are supported as long as they favour the company's objectives.[168] Moreover, when FDI is motivated by the search for raw materials, the control of these resources might be better ensured when the company has close links with the (autocratic) host government.[169] In this case, benefits for the general population – either directly or through reinvestment of the acquired capital by the government – are likely to be very limited. In this perspective FDI causes a 'race to the bottom'.

A second perspective argues that foreign firms are attracted to places where net profitability is highest, not where costs are lowest.[170] For example, the property rights of MNCs might be better insulated in democratic rather than authoritarian regimes.[171] In addition, low labour costs may be an advantage, but there is also the need for a certain quality of labour: the disadvantage of higher wages can be offset by the higher productivity of labour.[172] Moreover, foreign investors have a strong interest in preserving their brand reputation.[173] Especially when firms are selling to developed country markets, they are held responsible for the behaviour not only of their own company but also that of local subcontractors.[174] Global information networks play a very important role in driving the 'corporate social responsibility' idea of multinational companies. This 'spotlight phenomenon' helps NGOs to direct media attention to malpractices of multinational firms, which can hence influence consumer behaviour. Consequently, foreign investors bring not only capital and technological know-how, but also a specific corporate culture of setting higher

168 S. Hymer, 1979, 'The Multinational Corporation and the Law of Uneven Development', in J.W. Bhagwati (ed.), *Economics and World Order*, New York: Macmillan, pp. 113–140; T. Collingsworth, J. W. Goold and P.J. Harvey, 1994, 'Labor And Free Trade: Time For A Global New Deal', *Foreign Affairs* 73(1): 8–13.
169 D. Spar, 1999, 'Foreign Investment and Human Rights', *Challenge* 24(1): 55–80.
170 Klein et al., 2001, op. cit.
171 N.M. Jensen, 2003, 'Democratic Governance and Multinational Corporations: Political Regimes and Inflows of Foreign Direct Investment', *International Organization* 57(3): 587–616; Q. Li and A. Resnick, 2003, 'Reversal of Fortunes: Democratic Institutions and Foreign Direct Investment Inflows to Developing Countries', *International Organization* 57: 175–211.
172 D. Kucera, 2002, 'Core Labour Standards and Foreign Direct Investment', *International Labour Review* 141(1–2): 31–69.
173 C.P. Oman, 1999, *Policy Competition for Foreign Direct Investment: A Study of Competition among Governments to Attract FDI*, OECD, Paris.
174 Spar, 1999, op. cit.

social and environmental standards for their operations, compared to local competitors. Therefore, over time, FDI is a force for raising standards in developing countries and creates a 'climb to the top'.

3.7.3 *Some non-economic indicators of human development*

The holistic definition of human development and the lack of a simple measure make it difficult to assess the overall human development impact of FDI. Regardless of these difficulties, attempts have been made to assess the relationship between foreign investment and non-economic components of human development. We look at the limited empirical evidence on the impact of FDI on some of these human development indicators, before going into more detail on the relationship between FDI and human rights.

3.7.3.1 *Human Development Index*

Two studies have analysed the effect of foreign investment on human development as a whole by making use of the Human Development Index (HDI), which consists of three components: life expectancy; adult literacy and education enrolment; and per capita income. The study by Sharma and Gani finds no significant impact of FDI on the HDI, but their results should be treated with caution since they use limited data and do not account for endogeneity.[175] The study of Letnes also does not claim to resolve the question of causality, but uses a more detailed analysis.[176] This study finds a positive relationship between FDI and the HDI, but attributes this result mainly to the fact that GDP per capita is an important component of the HDI.

3.7.3.2 *Education*

In sections 3.4.2 and 3.4.3 we discussed the impact of FDI on human capital through spillovers, which then contribute to economic growth. Foreign firms can supply training and education to improve the quality of their labour force and in addition their demand for highly skilled labour increases the incentives for individuals and the government to invest in education. There is clear evidence that foreign firms provide more training than domestic companies.[177] However, besides some anecdotal evidence of firms supporting local schooling programmes or building a school, evidence on how transnational corporations affect general education is lacking.

175 B. Sharma and A. Gani, 2004, 'The Effects of Foreign Direct Investment on Human Development', *Global Economy Journal* 4(2): Article 9.
176 B. Letnes, 2002, 'Foreign Direct Investment and Human Rights: An Ambiguous Relationship', *Forum for Development Studies*, 29(1): 33–61.
177 Miyamoto and Todo, 2003, op. cit.; Lim, 2001, op. cit.

3.7.3.3 Labour standards

Some studies have analysed whether foreign firms make use of the lack of social and labour standards in developing countries. There have been some high-profile cases showing that MNCs do at times subcontract to enterprises that employ children. Yet, especially with respect to child labour, reputational damage can be very large.[178] Empirical studies find no effect of globalization on primary school non-attendance and generally indicate that more FDI is associated with a lower incidence of child labour.[179] Mosley and Uno find that FDI is positively and significantly related to workers' rights,[180] while Kucera finds no significant correlation.[181]

3.7.3.4 Environment

While multinationals have been accused of investing in developing countries to take advantage of weak environmental regulations – the 'pollution haven' hypothesis – they have more recently been seen as leaders in the introduction of good environmental practices and 'green technologies' into developing countries.[182] The existing literature has found little evidence to support the pollution haven hypothesis.[183] Eskeland and Harrison find some evidence that foreign investors are concentrated in sectors with high levels of air pollution, although evidence is weak at best.[184] They find that foreign plants are significantly more energy efficient and use cleaner types of energy. Other studies also contradict the pollution haven hypothesis.[185] Javorcik and

178 E. Neumayer and I. De Soysa, 2004, 'Trade Openness, Foreign Direct Investment and Child Labor', *World Development* 33(1): 43–63.
179 R.B. Davies and A. Voy, 2009, 'The Effect of FDI on Child Labor', *Journal of Development Economics*, 88(1): 59–66; A. Cigno, F.C. Rosati and L. Guarcello, 2002, 'Does Globalization Increase Child Labor?', *World Development* 30(9): 1579–1589; Neumayer and De Soysa, 2004, op. cit.
180 L. Mosley and S. Uno, 2007, Racing to the Bottom or Climbing to the Top? Economic Globalization and Collective Labor Rights. *Comparative Political Studies*, 40(8): 923–948.
181 Kucera, 2002, op. cit.
182 D. Chudnovsky and A. López, 1999, 'Globalization and Developing Countries: Foreign Direct Investment and Growth and Sustainable Human Development', *Paper for the UNCTAD/UNDP Global Programme on Globalization, Liberalization and Sustainable Development*, Geneva.
183 J.M. Dean, 1992, 'Trade and the Environment: A Survey of the Literature', *World Bank Policy Research Working Paper* No. 966, The World Bank, Washington DC; L. Zarsky, 1999, 'Havens, Halos and Spaghetti: Untangling the Evidence about Foreign Direct Investment and the Environment', in *Foreign Direct Investment and the Environment*, The Hague: OECD, pp. 47–74.
184 G. Eskeland and A. Harrison, 2003, 'Moving to Greener Pastures? Multinationals and the Pollution Haven Hypothesis', *Journal of Development Economics* 70: 1–23.
185 R. Letchumanan and F. Kodama, 2000, 'Reconciling the Conflict between the "Pollution-haven" Hypothesis and an Emerging Trajectory of International Technology Transfer', *Research Policy* 29; D. Wheeler, 2001, 'Racing to the Bottom? Foreign Investment and Air Pollution in Developing Countries', *World Bank Development Research Group Working Paper* No. 2524: 59–79.

Wei find some support for the hypothesis which is, however, relatively weak and not robust.[186]

3.7.3.5 Gender equity

Foreign direct investment might also have an impact on gender equity in developing countries. When FDI is directed to sectors with a high share of women in employment, it might improve opportunities for women. When women's labour participation increases with foreign investment, it is likely that their economic independence and their control over income resources in the household will improve.[187] In addition, it is known that income controlled by women has a superior development impact, since women tend to spend a larger share of the household income on child nutrition, children's education, health care, etc.[188] On the other hand, when FDI is benefiting the better-educated workers, women are typically disadvantaged in developing countries because of their lower level of education. Braunstein argues that women tend to be concentrated in sectors (electronics, textiles) where there is particular pressure to keep labour costs down.[189] In that case, effects through employment creation may improve gender equity, while negative wage pressure from FDI may have the opposite effect.

Empirical studies find that an increase in foreign investment, especially in labour-intensive, export-oriented industries, has been accompanied by a rising share of women in employment.[190] Studies by the International Labour Organization (ILO) and by Heyzer on East Asia find that women do indeed benefit from sustained growth through increased employment in the formal sector, which offers them an independent wage.[191] Ghosh finds that the share of women in India's industrial sector is declining, but attributes this to the rising importance of subcontracting to women working at home.[192] Other studies find that gender wage inequality increases with foreign

186 B.S. Javorcik and S-J. Wei, 2001, 'Pollution Havens and Foreign Direct Investment: Dirty Secret or Popular Myth?', *NBER Working Paper* 8465.

187 A. Quisumbing, 2003, *Household Decisions, Gender, and Development: A Synthesis of Recent Research*, International Food Policy Research Institute, Washington DC.

188 A. Quisumbing and B. McClafferty, 2006, *Using Gender Research in Development*, International Food Policy Research Institute, Washington DC.

189 E. Braunstein, 2006, 'Foreign Direct Investment, Development and Gender Equity: A Review of Research and Policy', *Occasional Paper* 12, United Nations Research Institute for Social Development (UNRISD), Geneva.

190 S. Joekes and A. Weston, 1994, *Women and the New Trade Agenda*, UNIFEM, New York.

191 N. Heyzer, 1995, *A Commitment to the World's Women: Perspectives on Development for Beijing and Beyond*. New York: UNIFEM; ILO, 1995, 'Women at Work in Asia and the Pacific – Recent Trends and Future Challenges', in *Briefing Kit on Gender Issues in the World of Work*, ILO, Geneva.

192 J. Ghosh, 2001, 'Globalisation, Export-oriented Employment for Women and Social Policy: A Case Study of India', Paper prepared for United Nations Research Institute for Social Development (UNRISD), Geneva.

investment.[193] This might be related to the wage gap between skilled and unskilled labour, since men in developing countries tend to have a higher education and end up in better-paid jobs. A study by Davin finds that, relative to locally owned firms, the wages paid to women are high.[194]

3.7.4 FDI, democracy and human rights

There has been considerable research interest in the relationship between foreign investment and human rights. Meyer clearly explains the two main opposing hypotheses with respect to this relationship: one argues that foreign investment and multinational firms act as an 'engine of development' and 'promoter of human rights', while the 'Hymer thesis' is more critical and argues that multinationals are detrimental for human rights in developing countries.[195]

Stephen Hymer states that MNCs directly contribute to violations of human rights in developing countries.[196] Huntington and Dominguez claim that autocratic governments are more able to enforce efficiency-enhancing policies, thereby providing a better economic environment for domestic and foreign investment.[197] If this is true, foreign firms would support autocratic governments, which would lead to a 'race to the bottom' with respect to human rights.

A more optimistic view states that MNCs are attracted by regions where democracy and human rights are respected. Autocratic regimes are associated with a high risk of policy reversal and a lack of credibility, and FDI is attracted by more stable, democratic governments.[198] In addition, the increased awareness of human rights abuses has made multinational firms vulnerable to reputational costs, as they are increasingly held responsible for their actions.[199] To avoid these

193 G. Berik, Y. van der Meulen Rodgers and J. Zveglich, 2003, 'International Trade and Wage Discrimination: Evidence from East Asia', *World Bank Policy Research Working Paper* No. 3111, World Bank, Washington, DC; S. Seguino, 2000, 'The Effects of Structural Change and Economic Liberalization on Gender Wage Differentials in South Korea and Taiwan', *Cambridge Journal of Economics,* 24(4): 437–459.

194 D. Davin, 2001, 'The Impact of Export-Oriented Manufacturing on Chinese Women Workers', Paper prepared for United Nations Research Institute for Social Development (UNRISD), Geneva.

195 W.H. Meyer, 1996, 'Human Rights and MNCs: Theory Versus Quantitative Analysis', *Human Rights Quarterly*, 18(2): 368–397; S. Hymer, 1979, 'The Multinational Corporation and the Law of Uneven Development', in J.W. Bhagwati (ed.), *Economics and World Order*, New York: Macmillan, pp. 113–140.

196 Humer, 1979, op. cit.

197 S.P. Huntington. and J.I. Dominguez, 1975, 'Political Development', in F.I. Greenstein and N.W. Polsby (eds), *Handbook of Political Science*, 3, Reading: Adison-Wesley, pp. 1–114.

198 M.C. McGuire and M. Olson, 1996, 'The Economics of Autocracy and Majority Rule: The Invisible Hand and the Use of Force', *Journal of Economic Literature* 34(1): 72–96; M. Olson, 1993, 'Dictatorship, Democracy, and Development', *American Political Science Review* 87: 567–575.

199 Spar, 1999, op. cit.

reputational risks, MNCs would be more likely to locate in regions where human rights are respected and thereby support democracies rather than autocratic regimes. Moreover, the MNCs would directly promote economic and social rights through the creation of better employment and labour conditions and indirectly support civil and political rights through their potential for enhancing economic development.

Spar argues that the relationship between FDI and human rights has changed over time from rather pessimistic to more positive.[200] This shift would in the first place be associated with a parallel shift in the sectoral composition and motives of FDI. Initially, FDI was mainly determined by the search for raw materials, low-cost unskilled labour and/or weak social and social legislation. Foreign firms would be mainly concerned about ensuring access to these resources, which would be best achieved through tight linkages with an (autocratic) government. Yet, new types of FDI in the secondary and tertiary sector require a certain quality of labour and are therefore concerned about the training, wages and health of their workers in order to increase the quality of their output. A second explanation for this shift in the relationship between foreign investment and human rights is attributed to the impact of the revolution of international information flows and the increased ethical and environmental concerns of home country consumers. Easy access to and diffusion of information allows NGOs to direct media attention to malpractices by multinational firms in developing countries, 'the spotlight phenomenon'. Through foreign investment social, ethical and environmental standards are promoted in the developing world. A number of studies have empirically examined the relationship between political and civil liberties and the motives for FDI. Different measures of human rights are used, but those most commonly used are the Freedom House indicators for political rights and civil liberties and the Political Terror Scale (PTS). Despite some anecdotal evidence that foreign companies support repressive governments,[201] there is only limited support for the view that FDI is more attracted to countries with autocratic regimes because of lower profitability or restrictive labour standards in democracies.[202] Rodrik shows that countries with weaker democratic rights attract less US capital and recent studies seem to confirm these results.[203] Other studies do not support the idea that multinational firms have a preference for

200 Spar, 1999, op. cit.
201 ITT played a role in overthrowing the popularly elected Allende government in Chile and international extractive industries supported authoritarian regimes in Nigeria (Shell), Myanmar (Unocal) and Columbia (British Petroleum) (Spar, 1999, op. cit.).
202 Neumayer and De Soysa, 2004, op. cit.; J.R. Oneal, 1994, 'The Affinity of Foreign Investors for Authoritarian Regimes', *Political Research Quarterly*, 47(3): 565–588.
203 D. Rodrik, 1996, 'Labor Standards in International Trade: Do They Matter and What Do We Do About Them?', in R. Lawrence, D. Rodrik and J. Whalley (eds), *Emerging Agenda For Global Trade: High States for Developing Countries*, Baltimore: Johns Hopkins University Press, pp. 35–79; P. Harms and H. Ursprung, 2002, 'Do Civil and Political Repression Really Boost Foreign Direct Investment?', *Economic Inquiry*, 40: 651–663.

undemocratic regimes, but rather that FDI is attracted by more individual freedom.[204] Busse goes back to the early 1970s to assess the link between FDI and democratic rights and finds that there is an increased tendency over time for multinational firms to direct their investments towards countries with a broader protection of political rights.[205] His findings support the earlier hypothesis of Spar, who argues that there has been a shift over time in the relationship between FDI and human rights.[206] Li and Resnik find a positive relationship between increased democracy and FDI inflows, but they argue this relationship is indirect and is explained by the effect of improved private property rights.[207] They use a sample of 53 developing countries over the period from 1982 to 1995 and show that, after controlling for the impact of property rights protection, the final relationship between democracy and foreign investment is negative and highly significant. However, Jakobson and de Soysa doubt the robustness of these results and find a positive relationship, also after controlling for property rights, by enlarging the sample.[208] Although the empirical studies do not reveal the direction of causality, overall, and especially more recently, foreign investment rather seems to have contributed to a 'climb to the top' with respect to human rights.

3.7.5 *Some conclusions*

When looking at non-economic indicators of human development, opposing views also exist. The hypothesis that FDI leads to a 'race to the bottom' finds little support in general, although it might be true for certain sectors or countries and there definitely exist examples of negative effects from foreign investment. However, in general, the hypothesis that FDI promotes human development directly or indirectly – through its impact on economic development – seems to find more support. It appears that FDI is generally directed towards regions where human rights are respected and through its accountability in the home country, FDI might enhance the spread of human rights and social and environmental standards to developing regions.

204 S.L. Blanton and R.G. Blanton, 2006, 'Human Rights and Foreign Direct Investment: A Two-Stage Analysis', *Business Society* 45(4): 464–485; N.M. Jensen, 2003, 'Democratic Governance and Multinational Corporations: Political Regimes and Inflows of Foreign Direct Investment', *International Organization* 57(3): 587–616; M. Busse, 2004, 'Transnational Corporations and Repression of Political Rights and Civil Liberties: An Empirical Analysis', *Kyklos* 57(1): 45–66.
205 Busse, 2004, op. cit.
206 Spar, 1999; op. cit.
207 Q. Li and A. Resnick, 2003, 'Reversal of Fortunes: Democratic Institutions and Foreign Direct Investment Inflows to Developing Countries', *International Organization* 57: 175–211.
208 J. Jakobson and I. de Soysa, 2006, 'Do Foreign Investors Punish Democracy? Theory and Empirics, 1984–2001', *Kyklos* 59(3): 383–410.

3.8 Conclusion

In this chapter we have tried to give an overview of the economic arguments and the empirical evidence of the impact of FDI on human development. While economic theory unequivocally predicts a positive impact by FDI on economic growth, empirical evidence is mixed. There seems to be no doubt that there is a strong correlation between FDI and growth, but the direction of causality is less clear. Micro-economic studies reveal that foreign firms are more productive than domestic firms and that there are important vertical spillovers to suppliers and buyers. Horizontal spillovers, on the other hand, seem to be less important and can even be negative. Yet, these firm-level results indicate that FDI can have a causal positive impact on productivity growth, even though the effect may be largely dependent on conditional factors such as the absorptive capacity of the host economy, macro-economic stability, the technology gap between the home and host economies and the type of FDI. The impact of FDI on other components of human development – most importantly poverty and inequality – can also differ in terms of these factors. When foreign investment is directed towards the more advanced developing countries or when foreign companies employ the relatively richer and skilled part of the population, inequality may be increased in the short run. Yet, when FDI is directed towards the least developed countries and associated with the creation of employment for unskilled workers, FDI may contribute importantly to poverty reduction. In particular, FDI in the agricultural sector can contribute to poverty alleviation by enhancing development in rural areas, where the incidence of poverty is the largest. When looking at some non-economic indicators of human development, there are two opposing views. One states that FDI causes a 'race to the bottom' while the other argues that FDI contributes to a 'climb to the top'. Empirical evidence is again heterogeneous, but in general, the optimistic view seems to find more support. The same holds for the impact of transnational corporations on the promotion of democracy and human rights. Attracting FDI is thus not a simple solution for enhancing economic growth and human development. But when policy-makers succeed in setting the right conditions, FDI can provide an important contribution to economic and human development.

4 Determinants of foreign direct investment flows to developing countries

The role of international investment agreements

Liesbeth Colen, Miet Maertens and Johan Swinnen

4.1 Introduction

Given that foreign direct investment (FDI) can create important benefits for developing countries (see Chapter 3), it is crucial to understand what determines the flows of FDI to the developing world and how developing country policy-makers can influence these determinants. There is a large literature on this subject, with reviews by Agarwal, Schneider and Frey, and more recently by Chakrabarti and Blonigen.[1] In this chapter, we first review this literature and summarize key conclusions from conceptual and empirical studies. In the second part of the chapter we analyse in more detail the impact of investment treaties on FDI. This issue has received less attention so far in the literature and is increasingly important.

In the process of increased openness towards FDI, there have been a large number of policy reforms over the past decades. Since 1992, 80 to 90 per cent of national policy changes have been in favour of foreign investment, and although in the second half of the last decade restrictive policies became somewhat more frequent, still more than 70 per cent are in the direction of further liberalization and promotion of foreign investment.[2] One important policy element is that since the 1980s policy-makers in developing countries have increasingly engaged in international investment agreements (IIAs) with other countries to attract foreign investment by providing security and favourable treatment for foreign investors. In addition, clauses on investment might be included in other international agreements (e.g. free trade agreements).

---

1 J.P. Agarwal, 1980, 'Determinants of Foreign Direct Investment: A Survey', *Weltwirtschaftliches Archiv*, 116:739–773; A. Chakrabarti, 2001, 'The Determinants of Foreign Direct Investment: Sensitivity Analysis of Cross-country Regressions', *Kyklos*, 54(1): 89–113, F. Schneider and B.S. Frey, 1985, 'Economic and Political Determinants of Foreign Direct Investment', *World Development* 13: 161–175; B.A. Blonigen, 2005, 'A Review of the Empirical Literature on FDI Determinants', *Atlantic Economic Journal* 33: 383–403.
2 UNCTAD, 2010, 'World Investment Report 2010. Investing in a low-carbon economy', United Nations, New York and Geneva.

The most common agreements are bilateral investment treaties (BITs) and double taxation treaties (DTTs). Signing such treaties also entails costs for the developing countries, since the country gives up some of its sovereignty and foregoes tax revenues. Therefore, the question whether these treaties effectively succeed in attracting foreign investors is a very relevant one. In this chapter we will show that the evidence is mixed and that the effect of IIAs on FDI inflows seems to be rather small, especially compared to the more fundamental economic determinants of FDI.

This chapter is organized as follows. We start by introducing a conceptual framework that summarizes the different factors that can act as a determinant of FDI flows. In the third section we discuss the empirical evidence on the importance of these different determinants of FDI. In the fourth section we focus on the role of international investment treaties in attracting FDI and we discuss the existing empirical evidence. The final section concludes.

4.2 The determinants of FDI: conceptual framework

The exponential growth of FDI flows and the belief that FDI can contribute to development have attracted a lot of interest from researchers. A large body of empirical literature has focused on the driving factors behind this rapid increase in foreign investment. In this section we give an overview of the economic arguments for these determinants.

4.2.1 A conceptual framework

There are many reasons why foreign investors would decide to invest in a particular location. Following the OLI paradigm,[3] multinationals decide to invest abroad rather than to trade, because they have an ownership (O), locational (L) and internalization (I) advantage.[4] The *ownership advantage* refers to an asset obtained by the firm which gives it an advantage over local firms in the foreign country. The firm could use this ownership advantage to export to the foreign market or it could decide to carry out production in the foreign market by starting a foreign affiliate. *Locational advantages* will determine whether the company decides to produce at home and to export, or to produce in the foreign country. Finally, the importance of *internalization advantages* will then determine whether the production in the foreign country will take the form of FDI. The alternative would be that local firms produce after having

---

3 J.H. Dunning, 1980, 'Toward an Eclectic Theory of International Production: Some Empirical Tests', *Journal of International Business Studies* 11: 9–31
4 Other theories explaining the FDI decision of firms are based on the new trade literature (J.R. Markusen and A.J. Venables, 1998, 'Multinational Firms and the New Trade Theory', *Journal of International Economics* 46: 183–203). These theories primarily focus on explaining market-seeking FDI, although the framework is useful for explaining different types of FDI too.

acquired the asset that gives the ownership advantage (e.g. a copyright). When the ownership advantage is related to intangible assets (e.g. marketing strategies, managerial techniques, innovations that are easy to copy), the firm may prefer to keep the foreign production under its own control. The firm can do this in order to keep control over key sources of competitiveness or to avoid transaction costs related to the regulation and enforcement of contracts related to the transfer of these intangible assets.

The ownership and internalization advantage have merely to do with firm and product characteristics (often proxied by research-and-development intensity, advertising expenditures and managerial skills). Once these two conditions are fulfilled, the locational advantages related to the foreign country will determine whether the firm decides to invest in this country rather than in another country. These locational advantages are related to the economic, political, institutional and investment climate of the host country and will determine to which country the FDI is directed. Since we are specifically interested in how developing countries can attract foreign investment, we will focus on these locational determinants of FDI.

We follow the framework proposed in UNCTAD[5] and Dunning[6] to give an overview of the locational determinants of FDI. Host country determinants of FDI are divided into (1) the policy framework for FDI, (2) economic determinants and (3) business facilitation. The policies set the rules for foreign investment. Once the policies create an attractive setting for FDI to enter the country, economic factors can create incentives for investors to locate their activities in the host country. When the main economic determinants are favourable, policies or initiatives that lower entry barriers and improve the business climate can start to play a role.

4.2.2 The policy framework of FDI

The main FDI policies consist of rules and regulations – including international investment treaties – concerning the entry and operations of foreign investors, the treatment of FDI (e.g. versus domestic investment), the functioning of the markets in which they operate and the legal framework for FDI. These policies aim at restricting or promoting foreign investment, directing it to certain sectors, influencing the geographical origin of FDI or promoting its contributions to the local economy. It is obvious that foreign investment can only take place if the policy of the host country allows FDI to enter. In this sense, restrictive FDI policy is very efficient in keeping FDI out of the country. Since most investment is directed towards the tradable sector, more open trade

---

5 UNCTAD, 1998, *World Investment Report 1998: Trends and Determinants*, United Nations publications, NY and Geneva.

6 J.H. Dunning, 2002, 'Determinants of Foreign Direct Investment: Globalization Induced Changes and the Role of FDI Policies', World Investment Prospects, Economist Intelligence Unit, London

policies are expected to favour FDI. Yet, whether the investment actually takes place will also depend on a lot of other factors. The best examples of the importance of an open trade and investment policy in determining the location of FDI are several countries in Central and Eastern Europe, and Guandong province in China in the 1990s, where liberalization was followed by an immediate exponential increase in FDI inflows. On the other hand, most African countries pursue a quite open policy towards foreign investment, but nevertheless FDI inflows remain very low. Overall, it seems that the negative effects of restrictive policies are very strong, while liberal policies only lead to an increase in FDI inflows if the economic and institutional factors are also favourable for foreign investment.[7]

The importance of liberal FDI policies seems to have declined as the world has become more globalized. As more countries open up towards FDI, the effectiveness of these policies in attracting FDI reduces.[8] While open FDI policies lose importance, host countries start to compete by a broader set of investment-related policies. They increasingly implement policies that affect the economy and business climate in a way that favours foreign investment. Examples are monetary and fiscal policies that affect taxes, exchange rates and economic stability, investment agreements specifying legal commitments of the host country towards foreign investors (BITs), policies affecting the structure and organization of the economy (sectoral and spatial composition of FDI, increased investment in human capital), and policies to facilitate business (Figure 4.1).

4.2.3 Economic determinants

Once a policy framework that allows for the entry of FDI is in place, economic factors are clearly the most important ones in determining the location of FDI. Moreover, the more FDI policies converge to a common open attitude towards investment from abroad, the more economic factors get the upper hand in determining the location of investment. Lall argues that 'FDI location decisions will increasingly depend on economic factors (reflecting underlying cost competitiveness) rather than on policy interventions that can only temporarily skew such decisions'.[9]

The economic determinants of FDI are largely dependent on the motives for foreign investment: market-seeking, resource-seeking or efficiency-seeking.[10] Historically, the main motive for investment, especially into developing countries, was the availability of natural resources. Yet, *resource-seeking FDI* can also be motivated by non-natural type of resources that are abundant in the host

7 UNCTAD, 1998, op. cit.

8 Ibid.

9 S. Lall, 2000, 'FDI and Development: Research Issues in the Emerging Context', Policy Discussion Paper 20, Centre for International Economic Studies, University of Adelaide.

10 UNCTAD, 1998, op. cit.

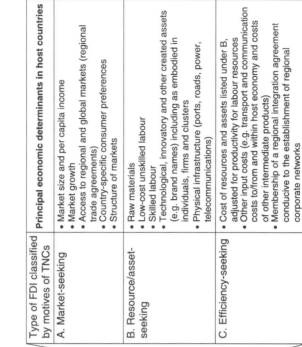

- **Ownership advantage**
- **Locational advantage (host country determinants)**

I. Policy framework for FDI
- Economic, political and social stability
- Rules regarding entry and operations
- Standards of treatment of foreign affiliates
- Policies on functioning and structure of markets (especially competition and M&A policies)
- International agreements on FDI (including BITs)
- Privatization policy
- Trade policy (tariffs and NTBs) and coherence of FDI and trade policies
- Tax policy

II. Economic determinants

III. Business facilitation
- Investment promotion (including image-building and investment-generating activities and investment-facilitating services)
- Investment incentives
- Hassle costs (related to corruption, administrative efficiency, etc.)
- After-investment services

- **Internalization advantage**

Type of FDI classified by motives of TNCs	Principal economic determinants in host countries
A. Market-seeking	• Market size and per capita income • Market growth • Access to regional and global markets (regional trade agreements) • Country-specific consumer preferences • Structure of markets
B. Resource/asset-seeking	• Raw materials • Low-cost unskilled labour • Skilled labour • Technological, innovatory and other created assets (e.g. brand names) including as embodied in individuals, firms and clusters • Physical infrastructure (ports, roads, power, telecommunications)
C. Efficiency-seeking	• Cost of resources and assets listed under B, adjusted for productivity for labour resources • Other input costs (e.g. transport and communication costs to/from and within host economy and costs of other intermediate products) • Membership of a regional integration agreement conducive to the establishment of regional corporate networks

Figure 4.1 Determinants of FDI (based on UNCTAD, 1998)

country, such as cheap labour, specific high-skilled labour and a well-developed physical infrastructure. *Market-seeking FDI* looks for a market to sell its products and decides to locate its production close to the market it is aiming at. The market-size hypothesis states that a large market is necessary for efficient utilization of resources and exploitation of economies of scale. Likely determinants for this type of investment are the market size and per capita income of the host country, market growth and access to regional and global markets. *Efficiency-seeking FDI* is attracted by low production costs or efficient production methods. Costs of resources and the productivity of labour, input costs, transaction and transport costs and corporate networks affect the efficiency of locating the production process in the host country. The currency of the host country can also play a role, although several theories come up with different predictions.[11]

Policies can alter the impact of certain economic determinants to some extent.[12] For example, export barriers can undo the attractiveness of efficiency-seeking FDI that wants to serve its home market. Tariffs on intermediate goods can undo the cost advantage of producing abroad. An increase in import tariffs can favour 'tariff-jumping' market-seeking FDI when the host country market is sufficiently large. 'Tariff-jumping' FDI refers to the shifting of production to the country the product is destined for rather than exporting it to that country in order to avoid the import tariffs. And monetary policies can help to stabilize exchange rates.[13] Resource-seeking FDI is more difficult to influence by host country policies. Yet, as will be argued in Chapter 5, policies that protect investors might be especially effective for FDI in natural resources. Natural resources cannot be created, but they can be managed by the government in a way that is more or less favourable to FDI. Human resources and infrastructure are hard to influence in the short run, but in the long term, governments can add to the countries' assets by investing in education to improve quality of the labour force or by improving the infrastructure and communication facilities.

4.2.4 Business climate

The ease of doing business in a country is likely to play a role in the decision on where to locate investment. Poor institutions, corruption and long and complex administrative procedures raise the cost of doing business significantly and discourage investment. Moreover, due to high sunk costs, FDI is especially

---

11 Blonigen, 2005, op. cit.
12 In particular, trade policies can largely alter the impact of other economic determinants. For this reason Nunnenkamp classifies trade policy among the economic determinants rather than in the policy framework (P. Nunnenkamp, 2001, 'Foreign Direct Investment in Developing Countries: What Policymakers Should Not Do and What Economists Don't Know', Kiel Discussion Paper No. 380, Kiel: Institute for World Economics.
13 UNCTAD, 1998, op. cit.

vulnerable to any form of uncertainty, including uncertainty stemming from poor government efficiency, policy reversals, corruption or a weak enforcement of the legal system.[14]

Therefore, FDI policies are increasingly complemented by proactive measures that improve the business climate and facilitate the business activities by foreign investors in the home country. These business facilitation measures include promotion efforts, incentives to foreign investors, and reduction of corruption and administrative inefficiency. These measures are not new, but have proliferated rapidly with globalization. Although FDI policies became much more liberalized, several countries were still perceived not to be FDI-friendly. Therefore, liberalization policies have often been accompanied by promotion activities, executed by investment promotion agencies (IPAs) to alter this negative image. In addition, IPAs have increasingly started to look for new investment based on detailed firm-specific research. They directly target firms that are likely to invest in the country.[15] Investment-facilitating services and after-investment services aim at lowering bureaucratic barriers and simplifying the administrative process. Also the use of financial investment incentives has increased. These include economic advantages granted by the government to a specific enterprise or category of firms in order to persuade them to invest in the host country. In developing countries these are mainly fiscal incentives. As economies opened up, the competition in terms of incentives among countries wanting to attract FDI has rapidly increased.[16] These business facilitation efforts mainly play a role at the margin. If the basic economic determinants are not in place, or FDI policies are not favourable, promotional activities will not be very successful.

4.2.5 Institutions

Particularly for less-developed countries, the quality of institutions is likely to be an important determinant of FDI activity.[17] Institutions affect all the other determinants discussed above. First, poor institutions are usually related to weak enforcement of policies and a high risk of policy reversals. Because FDI incurs a lot of sunk costs, it is particularly vulnerable to these types of risk. When the legal protection of assets is poor, the risk of expropriation of a firm's assets increases and investment becomes less likely. International investment agreements on FDI try to improve and secure this legal framework for

---

14 A. Bénassy-Quéré, M. Coupet and T. Mayer, 2007, 'Institutional Determinants of Foreign Direct Investment', *The World Economy* 30(5): 764–782.

15 L.T. Wells and A.G. Wint, 1990, 'Marketing a Country. Promotion as a tool for attracting foreign investment', FIAS Foreign Investment Advisory Service – Occasional Paper 1, Washington DC.

16 J.P. Morisset, 2003, 'Does a Country Need a Promotion Agency to Attract Foreign Direct Investment? A small analytical model applied to 58 countries', World Bank Policy Research Working Paper No. 3028, World Bank, Washington DC.

17 Blonigen, 2005, op. cit.

investment. Poor institutions and corruption also increase the cost of doing business and, thus, should also reduce FDI inflows. Finally, a country's low institutional quality is associated with a poor provision of public goods, such as infrastructure and communication facilities, thereby reducing the profitability of moving activities to this country.

4.3 The determinants of FDI: empirical evidence

A very large number of studies have searched for empirical evidence on the importance of each determinant of FDI. In this section we give an overview of the major findings of this large body of literature.[18] Table 4.1 summarizes the existing empirical evidence for the main FDI determinants.[19]

A look at the wide range of studies on the determinants of foreign investment reveals that the *market size* of the host country is the most important explanation for the country's propensity to attract FDI.[20] Chakrabarti finds that it is the only determinant that is robust over the large number of empirical studies.[21] For other variables empirical evidence is more mixed. Quite a lot of the empirical evidence supports the hypothesis that a *growing economy* creates better profit-making opportunities and is therefore more attractive for investment,[22] though this evidence seems not to be equally strong for all periods and regions. A study by Nigh finds a weak positive correlation for the less-developed and a weak negative correlation for developed countries.[23] For *host country wages* the

---

18 For other studies reviewing the empirical evidence on FDI determinants, refer to Agarwal, 1980, op., cit., Chakrabarti, 2001, Blonigen, 2005, op. cit. and H. Singh and K.W. Jun, 1995, 'Some New Evidence on Determinants of Foreign Direct Investment in Developing Countries', Policy Research Working Paper No. 1531, The World Bank, Washington DC.

19 Sources cited in Table 4.1 include the following (all other sources are cited elsewhere in the footnotes): D.L Swenson, 1994, 'The Impact of U.S. Tax Reform on Foreign Direct Investment in the United States', *Journal of Public Economics* 54: 246–626; V.M. Gastanaga, J.B. Nugent and B. Pashamova, 1998, 'Host Country Reforms and FDI Inflows: How Much Difference Do They Make?', *World Development* 26: 1299–1313; D.G. Hartman, 1984, 'Tax Policy and Foreign Direct Investment in the United States', *National Tax Journal* 37: 475–487; J.H. Dunning, 1980, 'Toward an Eclectic Theory of International Production: Some Empirical Tests', *Journal of International Business Studies* 11: 9–31; R.E. Lipsey, 1999, 'The Location and Characteristics of US Affiliates in Asia', NBER Working Paper No. 6876; K.A. Froot and J.C. Stein, 1991, 'Exchange Rates and Foreign Direct Investment: An Imperfect Capital Markets Approach', NBER Working Paper No. 1141; R. Lucas, 1993, 'On the Determinants of Direct Foreign Investment: Evidence from East and Southeast Asia', *World Development* 21(3): 391–406.

20 Agarwal, 1980, op. cit; Singh and Jun, 1995, op. cit.; Bloningen, 2005, op. cit.

21 A. Chakrabarti, 2001, 'The Determinants of Foreign Direct Investment: Sensitivity Analysis of Cross-country Regressions', *Kyklos*, 54(1): 89–113.

22 F. Schneider and B.S. Frey, 1985, 'Economic and Political Determinants of Foreign Direct Investment', *World Development* 13: 161–175.

23 D. Nigh, 1988, 'The Effect of Political Events on United States Direct Foreign Investment: A Pooled Time-series Cross-sectional Analysis', *Journal of International Business Studies* 16: 1–17.

Table 4.1 Overview of the empirical evidence for the determinant of FDI

Determinants of FDI	Positive	Negative	Insignificant
Policy framework			
Openness	Culem (1988) Edwards (1990) Gastanaga et al. (1998) Asiedu (2002) Singh and Jun (1995): export-orientation		Wheeler and Mody (1992)
Taxes	Swenson (1994)	Hartman (1984) Loree and Guisinger (1995)	Wheeler and Mody (1992)
IIAs	See Table 4.2		
Economic determinants			
Market size	Dunning (1980) Nigh (1988) Wheeler and Mody (1992) Tsai (1994) Culem (1988)		
GDP per capita	Schneider and Frey (1985) Tsai (1994) Lipsey (1999)	Edwards (1990) Jaspersen et al. (2000)	Loree and Guisinger (1995) Wei (2000)
Growth rate	Schneider and Frey (1985) Culem (1988)		Nigh (1988) Tsai (1994)
Labour cost	Wheeler and Mody (1992)	Schneider and Frey (1985) Culem (1988)	Tsai (1994) Loree and Guisinger (1995) Lipsey (1999)
Trade deficit	Culem (1988) Tsai (1994)	Schneider and Frey (1985) Lucas (1993)	
Exchange rate	Edwards (1990)	Froot and Stein (1991)	Blonigen (1997)
Infrastructure	Wheeler and Mody (1992) Loree and Guisinger (1995) Asiedu (2002), non-SSA		Asiedu (2002), SSA
Human capital	Noorbakhsh et al. (2001)		Nunnenkamp and Spatz (2002)

Determinants of FDI	Positive	Negative	Insignificant
Business facilitation			
Investment promotion agencies	Morisset (2003) Wells and Wint (1990)		
Institutions			
Corruption		Wei (2000)	
Political instability		Schneider and Frey (1985) Edwards (1990)	Loree and Guisinger (1995) Jaspersen et al. (2000)

Source: Based on Chakrabarti (2001), Asiedu (2002) and Blonigen (2005)

effect on FDI goes from positive over insignificant to negative.[24] These results may be due to differences in productivity which undo the cost–benefit of low wages. *Trade openness* (usually measured by exports plus imports over GDP) is generally found to have a positive link with FDI. Asiedu finds that the impact of openness to trade is larger for non-Sub-Saharan African than for Sub-Saharan African countries.[25] Chakrabarti concludes that, leaving out market size, trade openness is the variable most likely to be positively associated with FDI.[26] For *exchange rate volatility*, *trade deficit* and *tax incentives*, different empirical results have been found (see Table 4.1).[27] With respect to the role of *human capital* as a determinant of FDI, results are mixed. Nunnenkamp and Spatz do not find a significant effect of schooling.[28] Noorbakhsh, Paloni and Youssef do conclude that human capital attracts FDI and they find an increased importance of

24 D. Wheeler and A. Mody, 1992, 'International Investment Location Decisions: The Case for U.S. Firms', *Journal of International Economics*, 33: 57–76; C.G. Culem, 1988, 'The Locational Determinants of Direct Investments Among Industrialized Countries', *European Economic Review* 32, 885–904; D.W. Loree and S. Guisinger, 1995, 'Policy and Non-policy Determinants of US Equity Foreign Direct Investment', *Journal of Business Studies* 35: 281–299.

25 E. Asiedu, 2002, 'On the Determinants of Foreign Direct Investment to Developing Countries: Is Africa Different?', *World Development*, 30(1): 107–119.

26 Chakrabarti, 2001, op. cit.

27 S. Edwards, 1990, 'Capital Flows, Foreign Direct Investment and Debt-equity Swaps in Developing Countries', NBER Working Paper No. 3497; B.A. Blonigen, 1997, 'Firm-specific Assets and the Link between Exchange Rates and Foreign Direct Investment', *American Economic Review* 87: 447–465.

28 P. Nunnenkamp. and J. Spatz, 2002, 'Determinants of FDI in Developing Countries: Has Globalization Changed the Rules of the Game?' *Transnational Corporations* 11(2).

human capital over time.[29] The role of *international investment treaties* as determinants of FDI will be discussed in detail in the next section.

Several studies have asked whether globalization has altered the importance of certain FDI determinants. Some have argued that the importance of traditional determinants for FDI, market size and trade openness being the most important ones, has declined due to globalization forces and the changing motives for FDI. The size of national markets would have become less important due to a shift from national-market-oriented to more world-market-oriented FDI,[30] and UNCTAD argues that determinants such as cost differences, the availability of skills, the quality of institutions and the ease of doing business have become more important.[31] Similarly, Dunning states that there has been a shift from market-seeking and resource-seeking FDI to more efficiency-seeking FDI,[32] that is rather determined by these so-called 'non-traditional' variables.[33] Yet, according to the empirical results surprisingly little has changed. Most studies find that market size-related variables remained the dominant determinant of FDI throughout the 1970s, 1980s and 1990s.[34]

For the *quality of infrastructure* a positive relation with FDI has been found.[35] Asiedu finds that infrastructure development promotes FDI to non-SSA countries, but not to SSA countries.[36] A possible explanation is the fact that FDI to SSA countries is still mainly based in extractive industries, where the infrastructure measure they use – availability of telephones – is not very relevant. Very few econometric studies have focused on the impact of business facilitation activities. The *effectiveness of promotion agencies* in attracting FDI is found to have a positive effect,[37] although further research and better econometric techniques would be necessary.

The hypotheses on the impact of *institutions* on FDI are non-controversial, but empirical studies have to deal with the lack of accurate measures of institutions. Moreover, analysis might be hampered by the limited variation over time within a country. Wei shows that FDI is strongly negatively

29 F. Noorbakhsh, A. Paloni and A. Youssef, 2001, 'Human Capital and FDI Inflows to Developing Countries: New Empirical Evidence', *World Development*, 29(9): 1593–1610.
30 Loree and Guisinger, 1995, op. cit.
31 UNCTAD, 1996, *World Investment Report 1996: Investment, Trade and International Policy Arrangements*, United Nations publications, New York and Geneva, p. 97
32 Dunning, 2002, op. cit.
33 Though, in contrast to FDI in industrial host countries, FDI in developing countries is still predominantly directed to accessing natural resources and national or regional markets (J.II. Dunning, 1999, 'Globalization and the theory of MNE activity', University of Reading, Discussion Papers in International Investment and Management No. 264).
34 P-L. Tsai, 1994, 'Determinants of Foreign Direct Investment and Its Impact on Economic Growth', *Journal of Economic Development*, 19(1), pp. 137–163; UNCTAD, 1998, op. cit.; Dunning, 2002, op. cit.; Nunnenkamp and Spatz, 2002, op. cit.
35 Wheeler and Mody, 1992, op. cit.; Loree and Guisinger, 1995, op. cit.
36 Asiedu, 2002, op. cit.
37 Morisset, 2003, op. cit.; Wells and Wint, 2001, op. cit.

correlated with *corruption*, using a number of different corruption indices.[38] The empirical relationship between *political instability* and FDI flows is unclear. Some studies find a negative relation,[39] while more recent studies find no significant effect.[40]

Overall, the empirical evidence points to economic factors and open policies as the most important determinants of FDI. Market size, trade openness, growth rates and infrastructure have the strongest empirical support. The findings for other investment determinants seem to depend on the countries or regions under study, the type of investment, and the methodology used.

4.4 International investment treaties

Over the past few decades, developing country policy-makers have increasingly implemented policies to attract foreign investors to their countries. One way of doing this is to engage in international investment treaties (IITs). In this section we give an overview of the arguments and empirical evidence for the effectiveness of two types of international investment treaties (IITs): bilateral investment treaties (BITs) and double taxation treaties (DTTs). Figures 4.2 and 4.3 illustrate the rapidly increasing number of BITs and DTTs signed worldwide, and the increasing participation of developing countries in these treaties. We will describe shortly how BITs and DTTs are supposed to attract FDI and give a detailed overview of the empirical evidence so far.

4.4.1 BITs and DTTs

International investment treaties are signed to attract foreign investment from one signatory partner to the other, by providing investment protection or favourable regulations for foreign investors. Most treaties are signed between a developed and a developing country, where institutions and the legal framework for investment may be poor and where the additional provisions of investment treaties might be needed in order to convince foreigners from developed countries to invest.

Bilateral Investment Treaties (BITs) provide a number of guarantees to private foreign investors, including minimum treatment standards, rights to freely transfer funds and assets, and protection from expropriation. An important element is the incorporation of a direct investor–state dispute mechanism with an arbitration tribunal outside of the host state (mostly the ICSID, the

38 S-J. Wei, 2000, 'How Taxing is Corruption on International Investors?' *Review of Economic and Statistics* 82: 1–11.
39 Schneider and Frey, 1985, op. cit.; Edwards, 1990; op. cit.
40 Loree and Guisinger, 1995, op. cit.; F.Z. Jaspersen, A.H. Aylward and A.D. Knox, 2000, 'The Effects of Risk on Private Investment: Africa Compared with Other Developing Areas', in P. Collier and C. Patillo (eds), *Investment and Risk in Africa*, New York: St Martin's Press, pp. 71–95.

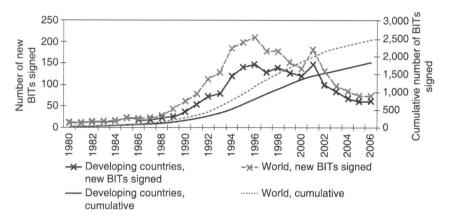

Figure 4.2 Number of new BITs and cumulative number of BITs signed worldwide and by developing countries (1980–2007)

Source: UNCTAD, FDI/TNC database

International Centre for the Settlement of Investment Disputes), providing credibility to the commitments made. The number of BITs signed by developing countries increased from about 200 in 1990 to about 2,000 in 2009 (Figure 4.2).

Double taxation treaties (DTTs) have existed for a long time and prevent foreign investors from being taxed both in their home country and in the host country where the investment takes place. Double tax rates and uncertainty over the future taxation of foreign investors may prevent foreign investment from taking place. By signing a DTT, the developing country agrees that the foreign company will not have to pay taxes, as it already pays taxes in its home country. The reduced tax burden is then expected to attract foreign investment. Obviously, signing such a DTT means that the developing country foregoes some of its revenues from taxation. The number of DTTs is smaller than the number of BITs, but in the case of DTTs developing countries have increasingly engaged in signing these agreements in the 1990s. By 2007 about 1,300 DTTs had been signed by developing countries (Figure 4.3).

Developing countries invest time and resources to set up, negotiate and sign BITs and DTTs, and they give up part of their sovereignty and tax revenues in signing these binding international treaties. Yet, as discussed in the previous section, the political and economic factors such as market size, skilled labour and trade policies seem to be more important for the locational decision of foreign investment than the legal structure for protection and the rate of taxation. So the question arises as to whether these international treaties effectively succeed in attracting more FDI inflows and whether it is worthwhile for the host country to incur these costs. The concurrent increase in FDI and

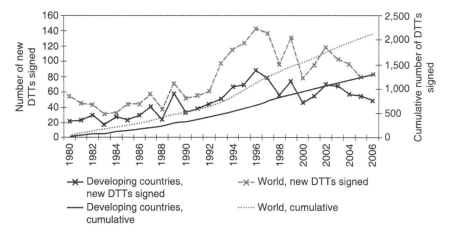

Figure 4.3 Number of new DTTs and cumulative number of DTTs signed
worldwide and by developing countries (1980–2007)

Source: UNCTAD, FDI/TNC database

IITs during the last decades clearly indicates a strong positive correlation
between the two. Yet it is not clear how much of this correlation is due to a
causal effect of IITs on investment decisions.

First, it might be that the causal relation runs rather in the other direction
and that treaties merely protect and benefit the investment that has already
been sunk. Then IITs would result from the demand for increased protection
and a more favourable tax regime by current rather than by future investors.
There is some evidence that foreign investors encourage their home country
governments to conclude BITs with host countries in which they already have
FDI.[41] For example, Salacuse and Sullivan write that, historically, BITs were
first developed by developed countries looking to protect their home investors
and that only more recently have developing countries such as China proactively
addressed potential BIT partners.[42]

Second, the effect of BITs and DTTs is not necessarily limited to the FDI
flows with the signatory counterparts. In principle, the provisions specified in
the treaty protect only investors from the signatory country. This 'commitment
effect' would suggest that signing a treaty with a country that invests a lot
abroad, such as Germany or the United States, has a larger impact on FDI
flows than signing a treaty with countries that export less capital. Yet, when
an IIT is signed, a signal is sent to potential investors in all countries that the

41 UNCTAD, 1998, op. cit.
42 J.W. Salacuse and N.P. Sullivan, 2005, 'Do BITs Really Work? An Evaluation of Bilateral
    Investment Treaties and Their Grand Bargain', *Harvard International Law Journal* 46:
    67–130.

developing country is seriously willing to protect and promote foreign investment.[43] It is therefore likely that there are positive spillover effects from signing IITs. The importance of this signalling effect can of course depend on the effective commitment made. For example, a BIT with the United States possibly sends a more credible signal than a BIT signed with a country that is less engaged in international investment. Yet, this signalling effect may lose importance as more treaties are signed. Salacuse and Sullivan state that the signalling effect of BITs may have eroded during the 1990s as they had become a normal feature of the institutional structure.[44]

Finally, the relation may run through other factors that affect both IITs and FDI. For example, it could be that a country that pursues open FDI policies, or has better institutions and thereby attracts more FDI, is also more willing or able to set up an international treaty such as a BIT or DTT. The positive correlation between IITs and FDI is then attributable to the large effects of FDI determinants such as market size, openness and investment climate on both FDI and IITs. Once controlled for this endogeneity, the potential positive effect from signing IITs may be found to be marginal, especially in comparison to more important determinants of FDI.

4.4.2 Empirical evidence: BITs

Some early non-econometric studies formulated little belief in the effectiveness of BITs in attracting FDI.[45] Sornarajah suggests that 'in reality attracting foreign investment depends more on the political and economic climate for its existence rather than on the creation of a legal structure for its protection'.[46] An argument is found in the fact that some major receivers of FDI, such as Brazil or Mexico, have long been reluctant to sign BITs.[47] Yet, it is likely that these more advanced developing countries do not need BITs as other conditions are sufficient to attract FDI, while for less-developed countries the legal structure of BITs may influence foreign investors' decisions. If this is the case, BITs act as substitutes for a good investment climate. Some empirical studies have analysed how BITs interact with the institutional quality of the host country in order to identify whether BITs act as substitutes for, or rather complement, good institutions and a favourable investment climate.[48]

43 E. Neumayer and L. Spess, 2005, 'Do Bilateral Investment Treaties Increase Foreign Direct Investment to Developing Countries?', *World Development* 33(10): 1567–1585.
44 Salacuse and Sullivan, 2005, op. cit.
45 UNCTC, 1988, *Bilateral Investment Treaties*, United Nations Centre on Transnational Corporations, Geneva; UNCTAD, 1992, *Bilateral Investment Treaties, 1959–1991*, United Nations, New York and Geneva.
46 M. Sornarajah, 1986, 'State Responsibility and Bilateral Investment Treaties', *Journal of World Trade Law* 20: 79–98.
47 UNCTAD, 1998, op. cit.
48 Neumayer and Spess, 2005, op. cit.

An important question in the literature on the effectiveness of BITs is that of which investors are affected by signing these types of treaties.[49] Some authors argue that only investors from signatory partners of the treaties are affected, since in principle, the host country only commits to protect investors from the signatory country when it signs the treaty.[50] This 'commitment effect' would suggest that signing a BIT increases the FDI inflows only from the country the BIT was signed with. Others argue that when a BIT is signed, a signal is sent to potential investors in all countries. Signing a BIT signals that the developing country is seriously willing to protect foreign investment.[51] Kerner argues that the signing of a BIT is related to significant *ex ante* costs, which sends a signal that the country is serious about investors' protection, not only vis-à-vis the signatory partner but to investors over the entire world.[52] In addition, the signing of a BIT also involves *ex post* costs, when the state effectively needs to commit to respecting the treaty, which would predict that there is an additional effect on investors from signatory countries. Based on these arguments he hypothesizes that both the signalling and the commitment effect have a positive effect on investment flows, and that the commitment effect is larger.

A number of studies have tried to isolate statistically the causal effect of BITs on FDI inflows, whether BITs act as substitutes or complements to institutional quality, and to what extent there is a signalling and a commitment effect. Evidence hereto is mixed. Table 4.2 gives a schematic overview of the empirical studies that we describe in more detail below.

Three United Nations studies have analysed the fast evolution in the number of BITs.[53] The first and second reports take a non-econometric look at FDI flows and investment treaties between 1970 and 1985. They find 'no apparent relationship' between the number of bilateral agreements and the volume of FDI flows and are rather sceptical about the value of BITs as a means of protecting and promoting FDI. The third study includes both a cross-country and a time-series analysis. The time-series study indicates a significant but weak effect of BITs on FDI flows. The effect is found to be larger for BITs signed by African countries. In the cross-country study, BITs are found to have a significant (lagged) effect in two of the nine regressions. The overall conclusion is that BITs play a minor and secondary role. Yet, this study uses minimal control variables and does not control for the strong upward trend in FDI.

The first serious econometric study on the impact of BITs on FDI flows is Hallward-Driemeier, using data on bilateral FDI flows from 20 OECD countries

49 Kerner, A., 2009, 'Why Should I Believe You? The Costs and Consequences of Bilateral Investment Treaties', *International Studies Quarterly* 53: 73–102.
50 M. Busse, J. Königer and P. Nunnenkamp, 2010, 'FDI Promotion Through Bilateral Investment Treaties: More Than A Bit?', *Review of World Economics* 146: 147–177.
51 Neumayer and Spess, 2005, op. cit.
52 Kerner, 2009, op. cit.
53 UNCTC, 1998, op. cit.; UNCTAD, 1992, op. cit.; UNCTAD, 1995, op. cit.

to 31 developing countries over the period from 1980 to 2000.[54] Using fixed effects estimations, she finds no increase in the bilateral flow of FDI from the developed to the developing country due to the signing of a BIT. When the BIT variable is interacted with various components of institutional quality, a positive coefficient is found, which suggests that BITs complement rather than substitute for institutional quality.

A study by Tobin and Rose-Ackerman analyses the impact of BITs for the same period but for 63 developing countries.[55] As dependent variable they use the share of global FDI flows directed to the country, rather than only the FDI flows coming from the signatory partner in the BIT. In this way they take into account the potential signalling effect of a BIT with one country on investors from a third country. A different impact of BITs is found for different levels of risk. At high levels of risk, a BIT lowers FDI, while for low levels of risk a BIT raises FDI flows. This suggests, again, that BITs seem to complement institutional quality and security. Yet, the obtained negative impact of BITs found casts some doubts, since there is no reasonable explanation why BITs would reduce FDI flows.

Salacuse and Sullivan perform a cross-sectional analysis of FDI flows coming from the United States for the years 1998, 1999 and 2000, for a larger sample size of 99 developing countries.[56] They also provide a 'fixed effects' estimation of bilateral FDI flows from the United States over the period from 1991 to 2000 for 31 developing countries. They find that US BITs have a positive impact of inflows of FDI from the US, using both cross-sectional and time series analysis. The effect of the number of OECD-BITs is insignificant.

Neumayer and Spess dispose of a larger sample of bilateral FDI flows for 119 developing countries and for a longer period (1970 to 2001).[57] As dependent variables they use absolute FDI flows and FDI inflow in the host country relative to the total FDI going to developing countries. As explanatory variable they weight the BIT signed with a certain country by the share of this country in total outward FDI. Hereby they anticipate that both the commitment and the signalling effect may be more important when the signatory partner is a major capital exporter. The results of their estimations show a positive impact of BITs on foreign investment for different model specifications and sample sizes. They also show some limited evidence that BITs act as substitutes for institutional quality. Neumayer and Spess conclude that countries that have signed more BITs with major capital-exporting countries are likely to receive more FDI.

54 M. Hallward-Driemeier, 2003, 'Do Bilateral Investment Treaties Attract FDI? Only a Bit ... and they could bite', World Bank Policy Research Paper WPS 3121, World Bank, Washington DC.
55 J. Tobin and S. Rose-Ackerman, 2005, 'Foreign Direct Investment and the Business Environment in Developing Countries: the Impact of Bilateral Investment Treaties', Yale Law School Center for Law, Economics and Public Policy Research No. 293.
56 Salacuse and Sullivan, 2005, op. cit.
57 Neumayer and Spess, 2005, op. cit.

Aisbett attributes the different results of previous studies to differences in country selection and methodology.[58] First she looks at the possible effect of selection bias, but when including country-pair fixed effects this turns out to be less of a concern than expected. Second, she stresses that policy adoption, such as signing a BIT, is endogenously determined, due to omitted variables or reverse causality. Increased FDI flows might induce a BIT to be signed, or improvement in the investment climate may positively affect both FDI and BIT participation. Aisbett finds a positive and significant correlation between BITs and FDI. Yet, after accounting for the endogeneity of the decision to form a BIT, she finds that the correlation is not attributable to a causal effect of BITs. She uses the number of BITs signed with other OECD countries as a proxy for the signalling effect of a BIT, but finds no evidence that BITs signal a safe investment climate.

More recent studies make use of the availability of longer series of data and bilateral FDI flows, and apply new methods to account for endogeneity. These studies use either an instrumental variables approach or the GMM approach developed by Arellano and Bond[59] to come to a more convincing estimate of the causal impact of BITs on FDI inflows. This method can be summarized as first-differencing the FDI regressions to remove the fixed effects, and subsequently using lags of potentially endogenous variables as instruments for the equation in differences.

Egger and Merlo analyse the effect of BITs on dyadic FDI flows for 24 home and 28 host countries.[60] The host countries they consider are OECD countries and ten transition countries. Taking into account the dynamic nature of FDI, they find that BITs have a short-term effect of about 5 per cent and a long-term effect of about 9 per cent on FDI.

Kerner uses a larger sample including dyadic data for 127 developing countries over the period from 1982 to 2000.[61] This study uses a two-stage-least-squares approach to account for the endogeneity of signing BITs. The percentage of the host state's neighbours that have ratified a BIT with the home state is used as an instrument for the existence of a BIT with this home state. Using this method, Kerner finds evidence that BITs attract foreign investment. He also finds evidence for a signalling effect: he shows that BITs have a positive impact on both protected and non-protected investors' decisions, but that the signalling effect is smaller than the commitment effect. In line with his theory,

58 E. Aisbett, 2009, 'Bilateral Investment Treaties and Foreign Direct Investment: Correlation Versus Causation' in K.P. Sauvant and L.E. Sachs (eds), *The Effect of Treaties on Foreign Direct Investment: Bilateral Investment Treaties, Double Taxation Treaties, and Investment Flows*, Oxford: Oxford University Press.

59 M. Arellano and S. Bond, 1991, 'Some Tests of Specification for Panel Data, Monte Carlo Evidence and an Application to Employment Equations', *The Review of Economic Studies* 58(2): 277–297.

60 P. Egger and V. Merlo, 2007, 'The Impact of Bilateral Investment Treaties on FDI Dynamics', *The World Economy* 30(10): 1536–1549.

61 Kerner, 2009, op. cit.

he finds that the higher the *ex ante* costs related to the signing of a BIT, the more credible and the more effective is the signal sent to other investors.

Busse, Königer and Nunnenkamp analyse the effectiveness of BITs using dyadic data for 83 developing host countries between 1978 and 2004.[62] As source countries they include both OECD and non-OECD countries, thereby capturing the recent increase in FDI flows and BITs signed between two developing countries. Using the system GMM estimator to solve the endogeneity problem they find that BITs have a significantly positive effect on bilateral FDI flows. They find that BITs may substitute for weak host country institutions.

Berger, Busse, Nunnenkamp and Roy add to the existing literature by looking at the actual content of BITs, while earlier studies treat them as 'black boxes'.[63] They analyse the importance of the guarantees of market access for foreign investors and credible dispute settlement clauses for the effectiveness of a BIT. The period and countries covered are the same as in the previously discussed paper. Using the GMM estimator to account for endogeneity, they find that FDI responds positively to BITs. Their results indicate that foreign investors respond positively to BITs but that the specific content of BITs seems not to matter much.

Concluding, the empirical impact of BITs remains contested and the result is very sensitive to the methodology used, the countries included in the sample and the period covered. The most recent studies, accounting for the endogeneity of signing BITs in a more sophisticated way, attribute a significantly positive, although not very large, increase of FDI to the signing of a BIT. Several, although not all, studies find that the effect of BITs is larger for countries with a weak institutional environment, and thus that BITs can act as substitutes for poor institutional quality or a bad business environment. Some studies suggest that BITs do not only affect the decisions of investors in countries that are the signatory partners of the treaty, but also for investors for other countries, which is referred to as the 'signalling effect' of BITs.

4.4.3 Empirical evidence: DTTs

On the effectiveness of DTTs in attracting FDI to developing countries there is much less empirical evidence. Several studies do not specifically focus on DTTs, but look at the overall determinants of FDI flows, including tax regulation. They do find some evidence that DTTs might effectively increase FDI inflows. In an overview of the literature, a paper by Davies lists a number of studies that find bilateral tax treaties to have a positive effect

---

62 Busse et al., 2010, op. cit.
63 A. Berger, M. Busse, P. Nunnenkamp and M. Roy, 2010, 'Do trade and investment agreements lead to more FDI? Accounting for key provisions inside the black box', *Kiel Working Papers No. 1647*, Kiel Institute for the World Economy.

Table 4.2 Overview of the empirical evidence for the impact of BITs on FDI flows

Study	Period	Cross-section/time series	Impact
Hallward-Driemeier (2003)	1980–2000	Cross-section (dyadic) 31 countries	n.s. (interaction term with institutional quality: +)
Tobin and Rose-Ackerman (2005)	1980–2000 (5-year average)	Time series 31 countries	(−) for high risk (+) for low risk (log BITs as dep var)
Salacuse and Sullivan (2005)	1998, 1999, 2000	Cross-section 63 countries	(+) for overall and US BITs n.s. for OECD BITs
	1991–2000	Time series 31 countries	(+) for overall and US BITs n.s. for OECD BITs
Neumayer and Spess (2004)	1970–2001	Time series 119 countries	(+) for different model specifications Interaction term with institutional quality (−) BIT weighted by share of signatory partner in FDI flows to DC
Aisbett (2009)	1980–1999	Time series 28 low- and middle-income countries	(+) not accounting for endogeneity n.s. accounting for endogeneity of BIT adoption signalling effect: n.s.
Egger and Merlo (2007)	1980–2001	Time series (dyadic) 28 countries (OECD and transition)	(+) accounting for endogeneity (GMM) Larger effect in long run than in short run
Kerner (2009)	1982–2001	Time series (dyadic) 127 countries	(+) accounting for endogeneity (2SLS) Signalling effect + but smaller than commitment effect
Busse et al. (2010)	1978–2004	Time series (dyadic) 83 countries	(+) accounting for endogeneity (GMM) More positive for weak institutions
Berger et al. (2010)	1978–2004	Time series (dyadic) 83 countries	(+) accounting for endogeneity (GMM) Content of BITs does not matter much

Source: Partly based on Neumayer and Spess (2004) and Aisbett (2008)

on FDI inflows.[64] For example, Hines finds an effect of 'tax sparing',[65] a provision contained in most DTTs.[66] Di Giovanni finds a positive effect of DTTs on mergers and acquisitions deals[67] and Egger et al. find that FDI flows between two countries are higher when bilateral effective tax rates are lower.[68] However, unilateral tax reductions by the host country are predicted to reduce FDI, which can be explained by their positive effect on competing national enterprises in the host country. Since DTTs provide special tax benefits for foreign companies, this study would suggest that they positively affect FDI inflows.

Most of these studies, however, focus on developed economies and evidence for developing countries is more limited. Blonigen and Davies include an analysis of the effects of bilateral tax treaties on FDI activity from the United States, including to developing countries, over the period from 1980 to 1999.[69] They find very little evidence that bilateral tax treaties increase FDI activity. Neumayer was the first study to look specifically at middle and low income countries.[70] The data covers the period from 1970 to 2011. He finds that DTTs are effective in middle-income countries, but not in low-income countries. This last study looks both at the effect on bilateral FDI flows between developing countries and the United States, and at the effect on aggregate FDI flows, thereby avoiding the problem of missing observations in dyadic data. He finds a positive and significant effect for both approaches. More recently, Barthel, Busse and Neumayer have made use of a large dataset on bilateral FDI flows provided by UNCTAD, including 105 FDI host countries, of which 84 are developing countries.[71] The period covered is 1978 to 2004. Using the system GMM estimator to solve for endogeneity, they find a significant and substantial effect of DTTs on FDI flows.

Overall, although there is some contradictory evidence, it seems that the more recent papers, making use of large dyadic panel datasets, find that DTTs

64 R.B. Davies, 2004, 'Tax Treaties and Foreign Direct Investment: Potential Versus Performance', *International Tax and Public Finance*, 11(6): 775–802.
65 J.R. Hines, 1998, '"Tax sparing" and direct investment in developing countries', NBER Working Paper 6728, National Bureau of Economic Research, Cambridge, MA.
66 Tax sparing is an agreement where the residence country agrees to grant relief from residence taxation on the extra income that a firm has earned due to tax reduction incentives in the host country.
67 J. Di Giovanni, 2005, 'What Drives Capital Flows? The Case of Cross-border M&A Activity and Financial Deepening', *Journal of International Economics* 65(2): 127–149.
68 P. Egger, S. Loretz, M. Pfaffermayr and H. Winner, 2009, 'Firm-specific Forward Looking Effective Tax Rates', *International Tax and Public Finance* 16: 822–849.
69 B.A. Blonigen and R.B. Davies, 2004, 'The Effects of Bilateral Tax Treaties on US FDI Activity', *International Tax and Public Finance* 11(5): 601–622.
70 E. Neumayer, 2007, 'Do Double Taxation Treaties Increase Foreign Direct Investment to Developing Countries?', *Journal of Development Studies*, 43(8): 1501–1519.
71 F. Barthel, M. Busse and E. Neumayer, 2010, 'The Impact of Double Taxation Treaties on Foreign Direct Investment: Evidence from Large Dyadic Panel Data', *Contemporary Economic Policy* 28(3): 366–377.

succeed in attracting FDI and that the magnitude of the effect is not negligible. Overall, the evidence seems to be stronger for DTTs than it is for BITs.

4.5 Conclusion

An enormous body of – mainly empirical – literature has studied the factors affecting the decision on whether and where to invest. Host country determinants of FDI can be divided into the policy framework, the economic determinants and business facilitation. Open FDI policies are likely to be a prerequisite for attracting FDI. Yet, as soon as FDI policies are not restrictive, economic determinants take the upper hand. Business facilitation and investment incentives may play a role at the margin, once other conditions are satisfied. Empirical studies indeed find that the major determinants of FDI are economic factors. Market size is the only variable agreed upon across datasets and methodologies. The evidence for trade openness as a determinant of FDI is also quite robust. Yet for other variables the evidence is less strong.

One of the policy tools to attract FDI that has increasingly been used by developing countries is international investment treaties. These are – mostly bilaterally – signed contracts that offer a legal framework to protect foreign investment or to reduce the tax burden on foreign investors. A number of empirical studies have used different datasets and specifications to test for the effectiveness of BITs and DTTs in attracting foreign investment. Although not all studies point in the same direction, overall it seems that DTTs are more effective than BITs in attracting FDI. In general, the empirical literature suggests that international investment agreements might play some – although probably only a small – role in attracting FDI. Economic determinants and trade policy clearly dominate the investor's decisions on where to locate investment.

5 What type of foreign direct investment is attracted by bilateral investment treaties?

Liesbeth Colen and Andrea Guariso[1]

5.1 Introduction

Foreign direct investment (FDI) is widely believed to stimulate development,[2] yet the range of policies that can enhance the inflow of FDI in the short run is limited. As the previous chapter shows, economic factors such as market size, openness, economic growth and political institutions are the most important determinants of FDI. Although policy can affect these dimensions, it usually takes time for changes to materialize. Therefore, many policy-makers have increasingly turned towards alternative solutions that may improve the attractiveness of their countries in the short run. These include the adoption of reduced tax regimes for foreign companies, investment promotion activities and international investment agreements (IIAs).

Since the 1980s, developing countries have increasingly engaged in such IIAs, mostly bilateral investment treaties (BITs) and double taxation treaties (DTTs), thereby committing to certain obligations concerning, for instance, the legal protection of foreign investors, dispute settlement, the repatriation of profits and taxation. More specifically, BITs guarantee the fair and equitable treatment of foreign investors and include guarantees on compensation in case of expropriation. Moreover, by signing a BIT, the host country commits to submit to a binding dispute-settlement mechanism in case of disputes between investors and the state.[3] Developing countries invest time and resources to set up, negotiate and sign these treaties, by which they give up part of their sovereignty. An important question is therefore whether BITs actually succeed in attracting more FDI inflows and whether it is worthwhile for a developing country to incur these costs.

The existing literature so far has provided mixed answers to the question concerning the actual effectiveness of BITs. On the one hand, the sceptical

---

1 The authors would like to thank Damiaan Persyn, Wijnand Stoefs and Lucia Mitariu for useful comments and ideas.
2 An overview of the theoretical arguments and the available empirical evidence can be found in Chapter 3 of this volume.
3 UNCTAD, 1998, *Bilateral Investment Treaties in the mid-1990s*, United Nations, New York and Geneva.

attitude that several authors have towards BITs[4] was reinforced by most of the early studies, which did not find any positive effect of BITs on FDI inflows.[5] On the other hand, more recent empirical studies, by exploiting new estimation techniques, longer series of data, and bilateral FDI flows, generally find that BITs do actually stimulate the inflow of FDI.[6,7] However, one thing that all the existing studies have in common is their focus on overall FDI inflows. In this chapter we want to contribute to this literature by looking for the first time at the potentially heterogeneous impact that BITs have on the different types of FDI. There are two main reasons for looking at such heterogeneous effects. First of all, as Chapter 4 emphasized, the beneficial impact of FDI likely depends on the type of FDI concerned. In general, FDI is expected to contribute more to poverty alleviation when it is targeted at labour-intensive industries and when interactions with local firms can create spillovers.[8] On the other hand, the enclave character of investments in resource extraction seems unlikely to significantly contribute to growth and poverty reduction.[9] When BITs are signed in order to stimulate growth and development through incoming FDI, it is therefore important to analyse whether it is indeed the development-enhancing type of FDI that is attracted through signing these agreements.

Second, by studying the heterogeneous impact of BITs we will contribute to 'opening the black box' of these treaties. While early studies were mostly interested in studying whether or not BITs effectively attracted FDI, more recent studies started investigating also some of the mechanisms through which these effects are likely to happen. Egger and Merlo,[10] for instance, distinguish a short-term and long-term impact, while Kerner[11] compares

---

4 M. Sornarajah, 1986, 'State Responsibility and Bilateral Investment Treaties', *Journal of World Trade Law* 20: 79–98; J.W. Yackee, 2007, 'Conceptual Difficulties in the Empirical Study of Bilateral Investment Treaties'. Online. Available HTTP <http://works.bepress.com/jason_yackee/1> (accessed 26 July 2012).

5 See for instance M. Hallward-Driemeier, 2003, 'Do bilateral investment treaties attract investment? Only a bit . . . and they could bite', *World Bank Research Working Paper* 3121, Washington DC: The World Bank.

6 See for instance P. Egger and V. Merlo, 2007, 'The Impact of Bilateral Investment Treaties on FDI Dynamics', *The World Economy*, 30(10): 1536–1549; M. Busse, J. Königer and P. Nunnenkamp, 2010, 'FDI Promotion through Bilateral Investment Treaties: More Than a Bit?', *Review of World Economics*, 146: 147–177; A. Berger, M. Busse, P. Nunnenkamp and M. Roy, 2010, 'Do Trade and Investment Agreements Lead to More FDI? Accounting for Key Provisions Inside the Black Box', *Kiel Working Papers* No. 1647, Kiel Institute for the World Economy.

7 For a more detailed overview of the empirical literature on the effect of BITs and DTTs on FDI, refer to Chapter 4 of this volume.

8 OECD, 2002, 'Foreign Direct Investment for Development: Maximising Benefits, Minimizing Costs', OECD, Paris.

9 P. Nunnenkamp, 2004. 'To What Extent Can Foreign Direct Investment Help Achieve International Development Goals?', *World Economy*, 27(5): 657–677.

10 Egger and Merlo, 2007, op. cit.

11 A. Kerner, 2009, 'Why Should I Believe You? The Costs and Consequences of Bilateral Investment Treaties', *International Studies Quarterly* 53: 73–102.

protected and non-protected investors, to see whether, in addition to providing legal protection to investors from the signatory country, the signing of a BIT also acts as a signal to investors from other countries, by indicating that the country is serious about protecting and promoting foreign investment. Kerner finds evidence for such a 'signalling effect' – although the effect of a BIT is found to be larger for investors that are effectively protected by the BIT. Finally, Berger et al.[12] look into the different provisions of BITs and RTAs (Regional Trade Agreements), concluding that the actual provisions matter for RTAs, but not for BITs, since foreign investors react positively to BITs independently from the specific modalities.

On the basis of the prevailing arguments in the literature on how BITs are expected to affect investors' decisions, in the following sections we derive more specific hypotheses concerning the heterogeneous effect that BITs are expected to have on different types of FDI. The validity of these hypotheses will then be tested empirically in the subsequent section of the chapter. A serious concern, when one wants to study heterogeneous effects on FDI flows, is the limited availability of disaggregated FDI data. We will rely on data on FDI stocks disaggregated by industry for twelve countries in the Former Soviet Union and Central and Eastern Europe, collected by the Vienna Institute for International Economic Studies (WIIW).[13] While this relatively small dataset obviously imposes constraints on our empirical analysis as well as on the geographical representativeness of our results, so far it is – at least to our knowledge – the only source of available disaggregated FDI data that has been collected in a systematic way. Moreover, the specific set of countries in our sample seems to be especially relevant for a study on BITs, given that these countries have increasingly engaged in signing investment treaties since the early 1990s, with 800 BITs entering into force between 1990 and 2009. Moreover, previous empirical studies have revealed that BITs may be particularly important for transition countries. Busse et al. and Berger et al.[14] find a positive effect of BITs for a large sample of countries, but report that this result is highly driven by the large effect of BITs for transition countries, and their results lose significance once this group of countries is excluded. And in a survey among managers by UNCTAD in 2007, BITs were reported to be among the most important decision factors when undertaking FDI in transition countries, more important than for developing countries. The fact that BITs are especially important for these countries might be related to the lack of credibility that usually follows regime change.

Overall, the results of our empirical analysis confirm the findings of the recent literature on BITs: the effect of BITs on the inflow of FDI is statistically significant and non-negligible. Moreover, our findings confirm our hypothesis

12　Berger et al., 2010, op. cit.
13　WIIW, 2010, *WIIW Handbook of Statistics 2010: Central, East and Southeast Europe*, Vienna Insitute for International Economic Studies, Vienna, Austria.
14　Berger et al., 2010, op. cit.

that BITs have a heterogeneous effect on FDI in different sectors. These results should, however, be considered as a first step in the analysis of the heterogeneous impact of BITs on FDI and they will have to be confirmed by further research, once more disaggregated information on (preferably dyadic) FDI flows for a wider set of countries becomes available.

In the next section we develop the hypotheses for the heterogeneous impact of BITs across different sectors of FDI. The third section describes the data and section four discusses the empirical estimation strategy. The fifth section contains the results and the sixth concludes.

5.2 The heterogeneous effects of BITS on FDI: conceptual framework

The existing literature on BITs suggests several hypotheses on how certain aspects of these treaties are supposed to have an impact on foreign investors' decisions. In this section we analyse conceptually how different types of FDI may be affected differently by each one of these aspects and we formulate hypotheses on the sectors for which the impact of BITs and DTTs is expected to be larger.

5.2.1 Bilateral investment treaties

Bilateral investment treaties (BITs) specify a number of guarantees to foreign investment, such as rights to freely transfer funds and assets, minimum treatment standards and protection from expropriation. In particular, several authors have referred to the protection from expropriation – and the provision of the dispute-settlement mechanism to ensure this protection – as the crucial elements in BITs.[15] The need for an external arbitration mechanism, which allows investors to bring claims of treaty violations to international arbitration tribunals (mostly the International Centre for Settlement of Investment Disputes, ICSID) is the result of a time-inconsistency problem:[16] in order to attract foreign investment, a government can assure investors that it will not expropriate the investments or raise taxes after the investment is made; yet, once the costs of investments are borne by the investors, the optimal policy for the host country government is to breach its promises and extract rents or expropriate property or funds. Anticipating these incentives, investors will not

---

15 T. Büthe and H.V. Milner, 2008, 'The Politics of Foreign Direct Investment into Developing Countries: Increasing FDI through International Trade Agreements?', *American Journal of Political Science* 52: 741–762; Z. Elkins, A. Guzman and B. Simmons, 2006, 'Competing for Capital: The Diffusion of Bilateral Investment Treaties, 1960–2000', *International Organization*, 60, 811–846. Kerner, 2009. op. cit.

16 R. Vernon, 1971, *Sovereignty at Bay: The Multinational Spread of US Enterprises*, New York: Basic Books; B.A. Simmons, 2000, 'International Law and State Behavior: Commitment and Compliance in International Monetary Affairs', *The American Political Science Review* 94(4): 819–835.

trust the promises made by the government in the first place and will refrain from investing in the country. Since many types of FDI typically imply large sunk costs, they are likely to be very susceptible to such time-inconsistent behaviour and this hold-up problem will ultimately lead to underinvestment.[17,18] Bilateral investment treaties are believed to provide a credible commitment to overcome this problem of time-inconsistency,[19] thereby reducing the risk of investment and, ultimately, attracting more FDI.

If this is the main argument for BITs to be effective – as the literature suggests – we should expect foreign investments that are more susceptible to discriminatory treatment and expropriation to react to the signature of a new BIT relatively more strongly than investments that are less vulnerable to such threats.

5.2.2 BITs and the sector of investment

A number of studies have analysed the expropriation risk of FDI and the sectors in which this risk is concentrated. Hajzler shows that after a period of frequent expropriation acts[20] in the 1960s and 1970s (which corresponds to the period of colonial independence), expropriations went down in the 1980s. Yet, since about 1995 the number of expropriation acts has increased again, mostly in Latin America and Central and Eastern Europe.[21] Hajzler studies the frequency of expropriation of foreign investment in different sectors relative to the importance of these sectors in total FDI and he finds that most expropriation acts are more frequent in mining and petroleum, which appears to be in line with the results of earlier studies.[22] Expropriations in the services sector seem

17 Busse et al. (2010, op. cit.) correctly point out that the need for such an external arbitration option is necessary in a one-time game, while in a dynamic setting, the deterring effect of violating earlier promises on future FDI inflows should be sufficient to ensure compliance. However, even in a dynamic setting, policy reversals may not only lead to the violation of guaranteed rights, but also to an overall negative attitude towards future foreign investment flows. In case of such a policy reversal, a binding bilateral treaty still provides external arbitration options to the investor.
18 See for instance E. Neumayer and L. Spess, 2005, 'Do Bilateral Investment Treaties Increase Foreign Direct Investment to Developing Countries?', *World Development* 33(10), 1567–1585; Büthe and Milner, 2008, op. cit.
19 K.J. Vandevelde, 1998, 'Investment Liberalization and Economic Development: The Role of Bilateral Investment Treaties', *Columbia Journal of Transnational Law* 36: 501–527; Elkins et al., 2006, op. cit.
20 Expropriation in this chapter is measured by the frequency of 'expropriation acts' where an 'act' may refer to: (1) explicit confiscations of property; (2) breaches of contract including forced renegotiation of contract terms; (3) extra-legal interventions or transfers of ownership by private actors and not resolved by the government; (4) forced sale of property. C. Hajzler, 2010, 'Expropriation of Foreign Direct Investments: Sectoral Patterns from 1993 to 2006', *University of Otago Economic Discussion Papers* No. 1011.
21 Hajzler, 2010, op. cit.
22 F.J. Truitt, 1970, 'Expropriation of Foreign Investment: Summary of the Post-World War II Experience of American and British Investors in the Less Developed Countries', *Journal*

to have increased during the 1990s, while the expropriation risk seems to be considerably lower in the manufacturing sector. A look at the list of the arbitration cases of the ICSID, provided by UNCTAD,[23] supports these findings: most cases concern expropriation of resource extraction industries and utilities such as electricity provision, water and communication.

In the literature, a number of explanations have been put forward for why resources and, to some extent, utilities would be more vulnerable to expropriations than other types of foreign investment. First of all, technologies used in these sectors may be less dependent on foreign-owned knowledge and capacities, which may result in a higher return to expropriated capital. This is in line with the theories of Eaton and Gersovitz and of Raff, who consider that a host country government can expropriate capital but not foreign managerial expertise,[24] which may be especially important in many manufacturing and service industries. This explanation finds confirmation in the findings of Kobrin, who estimates a negative effect of firm-specific knowledge on expropriation.[25] A second explanation is related to the importance of sunk costs in resource extracting industries and utilities provision. Mineral extraction requires large investments in exploration and excavation infrastructure before revenues are realized and, once the profitability and the quality of mineral deposits is clear, expropriation becomes particularly profitable for the government.[26] Moreover, a sudden increase in mineral prices may result in governments wanting to renegotiate contracts that are suddenly perceived as much more generous than expected.[27] Thus, the combination of large initial investments and high fluctuations in mineral and petroleum prices makes the mining sectors especially vulnerable. In the case of utilities, costs are mainly related to the initial establishment of network infrastructures, as in the case of water and electricity distribution. Finally, foreign ownership in utilities and extractive industries is very often politically sensitive. Extractive industries, utilities, rail, communications and national defence are indeed seen as important to political and economic independence and

of International Business Studies, 1(2): 21–34; S.J. Kobrin, 1980, 'Foreign Enterprise and Forced Divestment in LDCs', *International Organization*, 34(1): 65–88; C.R. Kennedy Jr., 1993, 'Multinational Corporations and Expropriation Risk', *Multinational Business Review*, 1(1): 44–55.

23 UNCTAD, FDI/TNC database (www.unctad.org/fdistatistics) , consulted February 2012.

24 J. Eaton and M. Gersovitz, 1984, 'A Theory of Expropriation and Deviations from Perfect Capital Mobility', *The Economic Journal* 50(1): 85–101; H. Raff, 1992, 'A Model of Expropriation with Asymmetric Information', *Journal of International Economics*, 33(3–4), 245–265.

25 Kobrin, 1980, op. cit.

26 Vernon, 1971, op. cit.

27 E. Engel and R.D. Fischer, 2010, 'The Natural Resources Trap: Private Investment without Public Commitment', in *Optimal Resource Extraction Contracts under Threat of Expropriation*, Cambridge, MA: MIT Press, pp. 161–196; R. Duncan, 2006, 'Price or Politics? An Investigation of the Causes of Expropriation', *The Australian Journal of Agricultural and Resource Economics*, 50: 85–101.

Foreign Direct Investment and Human Development

national security.[28] Utilities may be considered as basic provisions that should be in public ownership, therefore being susceptible to policy reversals, while natural resources are owned by the host country itself. Some authors also argue that extractive industries may become subject to high political pressure when a period of overall poor economic performance in the country coincides with a period of prosperity in industries that are dominated by foreign-owned firms.[29]

Overall, these arguments suggest that the increased protection provided by BITs benefits FDI especially in the resource sector and in utilities. Our hypothesis is therefore that BITs would have a stronger effect for FDI in these sectors compared to others.

5.2.3 BITs and alternative classifications of FDI

A similar line of reasoning to the one presented in the previous paragraph could apply to alternative classifications of FDI, such as by different components (equity capital, reinvested earnings or intra-company loans) or by different forms of ownership (joint venture or complete ownership).

The values of FDI usually reported by institutions such as the IMF, UNCTAD and OECD is the sum of three components: equity capital, reinvested earnings, and intra-company loans.[30] The argument that FDI is vulnerable to the time-inconsistent behaviour of governments appears to be best suited for equity investment. The decision of equity investment is indeed the most likely to bring along a large share of primary investment and to be susceptible to policy reversals. Intra-company loans and reinvested earnings might also be affected by such a threat, but are more likely to be used for current than initial investments. Hence, BITs are predicted to have a significant positive effect on equity investment, a potentially weaker positive effect on loans and a small or non-significant one on reinvested earnings.

Concerning the different forms of ownership, Asiedu and Esfahani prove that US multinationals are more likely to choose complete ownership if the country risk of expropriation declines.[31] In this case we would therefore predict that BITs – by reducing expropriation risk – would enhance complete ownership. This, in turn, could potentially enhance the long-term involvement of foreign

28 M. Shafer, 2009, 'Capturing the Mineral Multinationals: Advantage or Disadvantage?', *International Organization*, 37(1): 93–119; Kobrin, 1980, op. cit.
29 D.A. Jodice, 1980, 'Sources of Change in Third World Regimes for Foreign Direct Investment, 1968–1976', *International Organization* 34(2): 177–206; S.J. Kobrin, 1984, 'Expropriation as an Attempt to Control Foreign Firms in LDCs: Trends from 1960–1979', *International Studies Quarterly*, 28: 329–348.
30 IMF and OECD, 2000, *Report on the survey of implementation of methodological standards for direct investment. Report by IMF and OECD*. Online. Available HTTP <http://www.imf.org/external/bopage/pdf/mar2000.pdf> (accessed 26 July 2012).
31 E. Asiedu and H.S. Esfahani, 2001, 'Ownership Structure in Foreign Direct Investment Projects', *The Review of Economics and Statistics* 83(4): 647–662.

investment, strengthening spillover effects and contributing to the host country's development.

Unfortunately, the data we have currently available do not allow a proper disaggregation of FDI along these lines. In the empirical part of this chapter we will therefore focus on the heterogeneous effects of BITs on FDI in different sectors and we leave the exploration of these other questions to further research.

5.3 Data

We empirically estimate the impact of BITs on the inflow of FDI in different sectors for twelve countries in Central and Eastern Europe and the Former Soviet Union over the period from 1995 to 2009.[32] We use FDI data disaggregated by industry, collected by the Vienna Institute for International Economic Studies.[33] We have classified the FDI data by industry into six economic sectors: agriculture and fisheries, mining, manufacturing, utilities, services and banking.[34] For some countries, information is missing for a number of years or sectors, resulting in an unbalanced panel. The dependent variable will be the stock of FDI of each country. Given that we will rely on a fixed effects estimator or first-difference model, the use of FDI stocks allows us to consider the effect on the net inflow of FDI, which is the difference of FDI stocks.[35]

Contrary to the more recent papers that estimate the effect of BITs on FDI[36] we do not use bilateral FDI information, but we consider a measure of overall incoming FDI in the host country. This choice is in the first place driven by data availability, as there are no FDI data available that are disaggregated both by sending country and by sector. However, the use of a dyadic versus non-dyadic approach comes down to the discussion of whether BITs have a 'signalling effect', in addition to a 'commitment effect' on the investors' decision.[37] It is argued that a dyadic approach underestimates the effects of BITs, since it ignores the spillovers that a BIT (especially when signed with an important capital exporter) might have on FDI from other source countries. Investors from other source countries – even though not protected by the BIT themselves – may indeed see the BIT as a signal that this host country wants to engage in the protection of FDI and is willing to formally commit thereto. Kerner uses dyadic data and estimates both the effect on the bilateral inflow of FDI from the signatory partner country (the commitment effect) and the effect on other investors (the signalling effect). He finds evidence for both, but the former is – as expected – stronger. Given that we use non-dyadic data, our analysis

---

32 See Appendix A for the full list of countries and years considered in the analysis.
33 WIIW, 2010, op. cit.
34 See Appendix B for the list of industries assigned to each of the six sectors.
35 Egger and Merlo, 2007, op. cit.
36 See for instance Egger and Merlo, 2007, op. cit; Busse et al., 2010, op. cit.
37 Kerner, 2009, op. cit.

estimates the overall effect (commitment and signalling) without being able to distinguish between the two.

Information on the signing and ratification of BITs is taken from UNCTAD's IIA database.[38] Given our fixed effects estimation approach, we use the cumulative number of BITs entered into force to estimate the effect of one additional BIT on FDI. We use the year of entry into force, rather than the moment of signature, as between signature and ratification several years may pass, and it is only upon ratification that the actual commitments are made. Moreover, states tend to publish the text of treaties and submit them to the United Nations only after ratification.[39]

We include in the analysis a number of control variables that may explain part of the variation in FDI in the host country over time (see the next section for a more detailed explanation of the choice of the variables). Data on real GDP and real per capita GDP, inflation rate and trade openness (sum of exports and imports relative to GDP) are taken from the World Development Indicators.[40] Our measure of political institutional quality is taken from the Polity IV project.[41] It is a composite index of the political regime ranging from +10 (strongly democratic) to −10 (strongly autocratic).

5.4 Empirical specification

We use fixed effects models to estimate the effect of BITs on FDI. We start by estimating a simple static model and we then move to a dynamic one, in order to properly take into account the sluggish adjustment of FDI. The dynamic fixed effects model takes the following form (the static one simply does not include the lagged FDI variable):

$$FDI_{it} = FDI'_{i.t-1}\,\alpha + BIT'_{it}\,\beta + x'_{it}\gamma + t_t + \mu_i + \upsilon_{it},$$
$$i = 1, \ldots, N; t = 2, \ldots, T,$$

where i indicates the home country, t indicates the year and $\mu_i + \upsilon_{it}$ is the error term. The parameters to be estimated are α, β, and the vector γ. The error term is composed by an idiosyncratic component υ_{it} and a country-specific component μ_i. The former is specific to each country-year observation, while the latter varies only across countries and contains unobserved time-invariant differences between countries. The fixed-effects estimation allows us to get rid of this

38 UNCTAD, 2011, *IIA database*. Online. Available HTTP <http://unctad.org/en/pages/DIAE/International%20Investment%20Agreements%20(IIA)/IIA-Tools.aspx> (accessed 30 July 2012).
39 Yackee, 2007, op. cit.
40 World Bank, 2011, *World Development Indicators*. Online. Available HTTP <http://data.worldbank.org/indicator/> (accessed 26 July 2012).
41 Polity IV Political Regime Characteristics and Transitions, 1800–2010. Online. Available HTTP <http://www.systemicpeace.org/polity/polity4.htm> (accessed 26 July 2012).

second component, through first-differencing, leaving only within-country variation over time in the error term. Year dummies t_t are included in the regression to capture eventual common time-trends in FDI across host countries.

The FDI variable (FDI_{it}) is the logarithm of FDI in stocks. As already mentioned, using stock values in a fixed-effects estimation (or first-differenced model), effectively allow us to look at differences in stocks over time, which is actually a measure of net FDI flows.[42] A separate estimation will be performed for every sector of FDI, but we also estimate the effect on the overall (aggregated) stock of FDI. The lagged value of FDI ($FDI_{i,t-1}$) allows us to take into account the sluggish adjustment of FDI over time and its coefficient is expected to be positive. The explanatory variable of interest is the cumulative number of BITs (BIT) by host country i in year t. The vector x consists of a standard set of controls, already anticipated in the previous paragraph. The logarithm of real GDP accounts for market size and is expected to be positively related to FDI. The logarithm of the inflation rate is meant to control for macroeconomic distortions generated by poor monetary policies and is expected to be negatively related to FDI. However, it should be noted that there seems to be an unclear relationship between inflation and economic growth and the actual impact of inflation might therefore be ambiguous.[43] The logarithm of real per capita GDP can be considered both a measure for purchasing power parity – in which case we would expect a positive coefficient – and a proxy for labour costs – in which case we would instead expect a negative coefficient. Also the coefficient of the variable capturing openness to trade is expected to have an ambiguous sign. On the one hand, a high value of openness is expected to enhance FDI by signalling a positive attitude towards foreign investors. On the other hand, market-seeking FDI might be negatively related to increased openness, as openness decreases incentives for investors to move production to the host country rather than to export goods to that country in order to avoid tariffs. The final sign of the coefficients of these last two variables is thus an empirical matter. Finally, we include a measure of political institutional quality, taken from the Polity IV project. This variable takes larger values for stronger institutional environments, which are likely to attract more FDI. A positive coefficient is therefore expected for this variable. We will also interact this variable with the variable containing the number of BITs. As suggested by earlier studies, BITs might be more effective in countries with a lower level of institutional quality, as the need for investment protection is higher. In that case we would expect a negative coefficient on the interaction term and BITs are said to work as complements to institutional quality. If the contrary is true, they act as substitutes.

42 Egger and Merlo, 2007, op. cit.
43 M. McGillivray, S. Feeny, N. Hermes and R. Lensink, 2005, 'It Works; It Doesn't; It Can, But That Depends?: 50 Years of Controversy over the Macroeconomic Impact of Development Aid', Working Papers RP2005/54, World Institute for Development Economic Research (UNUWIDER).

While our dynamic fixed effects model takes into account the fact that FDI stocks adjust slowly, it brings along another problem. Indeed the inclusion of lagged variables of the dependent variable in a 'fixed effects' estimation causes the so-called 'Nickell bias'.[44] This bias decreases as the number of time periods increases, but, given the limitations of our dataset, it is likely to affect our estimates. A possible solution is represented by the first-differenced GMM (General Method of Moments) estimator by Arellano and Bond,[45] in which lagged variables of the explanatory and dependent variables are used as 'internal' instruments for the first-differenced equation. More recently, Arellano and Bover[46] and Blundell and Bond[47] proposed a system GMM approach in which lagged first-differences are also used as instruments for the levels. However, the last approach imposes the additional assumption of stationarity of the dependent variable,[48] which is unlikely to hold for FDI stocks in a period of increasing FDI inflows. Moreover, tests on instrument validity perform better in our analysis using a difference GMM rather than a system GMM approach. We will therefore use the first-differenced GMM estimator next to the dynamic fixed effects model. In order to avoid a problem of too many instruments, we collapse the vector of instruments.[49]

5.5 Results

The results from the static fixed effects model are reported in Table 5.1. Tables 5.2 and 5.3 report the results from the dynamic fixed effects regression, with and without interaction term with the democracy index. Tables 5.4 and 5.5 show the results from the Arellano-Bond estimation using lags 3 and 5 to instrument for the difference in FDI stocks. Our main results from the GMM estimation are robust to alternative specifications (available on request), such as using lags 2 to 4, 2 to 5 or 2 to 6, not collapsing instruments or using system GMM instead of difference GMM (although Sargan tests perform less well for some sectors when using system GMM).

The coefficients from the static fixed effects estimation (Table 5.1) are in line with our expectations. A higher number of BITs is associated with a higher FDI

44 S. Nickell, 1981, 'Biases in Dynamic Models with Fixed Effects', *Econometrica*, 49, 1417–1425.

45 M. Arellano and S. Bond, 1991, 'Some Tests of Specification for Panel Data, Monte Carlo Evidence and an Application to Employment Equations', *The Review of Economic Studies* 58(2): 277–297.

46 M. Arellano and O. Bover, 1995, 'Another Look at the Instrumental Variables Estimation of Error-components Models', *Journal of Econometrics* 68: 29–51.

47 R. Blundell and S. Bond, 1998, 'Initial Conditions and Moment Restrictions in Dynamic Panel Data Models', *Journal of Econometrics* 87: 11–143.

48 D. Roodman, 2009, 'How to Do Xtabond2: An Introduction to "Difference" and "System" GMM in STATA', *The Stata Journal* 9(1): 86–136.

49 D. Roodman, 2009, 'A Note on the Theme of Too Many Instruments', *Oxford Bulletin of Economics and Statistics* 71(1): 135–158.

Table 5.1 Static fixed effects model

VARIABLES	(1) Total	(2) Agriculture	(3) Mining	(4) Manufacturing	(5) Utilities	(6) Services	(7) Banking
Nr of BITs	0.0366***	0.0149	0.113***	0.0318***	0.00296	0.0461***	0.0447***
	[4.714]	[0.884]	[4.480]	[4.673]	[0.0761]	[4.321]	[3.005]
Ln(GDP per cap)	-0.164	11.23*	-30.24***	-8.183***	1.368	3.247	-1.681
	[-0.0529]	[1.674]	[-2.996]	[-3.017]	[0.0883]	[0.764]	[-0.284]
Ln(GDP)	1.228	-10.61	33.85***	8.773***	-1.476	-4.375	3.394
	[0.361]	[-1.439]	[3.051]	[2.942]	[-0.0866]	[-0.936]	[0.521]
Democracy	0.188***	0.110	0.469***	-0.0224	0.00481	0.290***	0.302***
	[3.751]	[1.009]	[2.871]	[-0.510]	[0.0192]	[4.213]	[3.148]
Ln(Inflation)	-0.0905**	0.0745	-0.0829	-0.0358	0.0473	-0.0997*	-0.183**
	[-2.178]	[0.827]	[-0.612]	[-0.982]	[0.227]	[-1.746]	[-2.297]
Openness	-0.00432*	0.00572	-0.0189**	-0.00350†	0.0191†	0.00179	-0.00976**
	[-1.723]	[1.054]	[-2.316]	[-1.594]	[1.525]	[0.522]	[-2.038]
Observations	107	107	107	107	107	107	107
R-squared	0.955	0.822	0.704	0.944	0.790	0.895	0.918
Number of countries	12	12	12	12	12	12	12

t-statistics in brackets

*** p<0.01, ** p<0.05, * p<0.10, † p<0.15

stock in the mining, manufacturing and services. Note that the estimate for the regression of FDI in the mining sector is substantially larger than the estimates for the other sectors of FDI. The logarithm of per capita GDP is negatively related to FDI in mining and manufacturing, suggesting that FDI is attracted by lower labour costs, while it is positively related to FDI in agriculture. The logarithm of total GDP has a positive coefficient which is statistically significant in the regressions of FDI in mining and manufacturing. A higher level of democracy is associated with more FDI, and is significantly different from zero for the total FDI stock, for mining, services and banking. The logarithm of inflation has a negative and significant coefficient for total FDI stock, services and banking. Trade openness is found to have a negative effect (although often only significant at the 0.15 level) for total FDI, mining, manufacturing and banking. For manufacturing and banking this last result could be explained by the fact that FDI in these sectors is mostly market-seeking and that greater openness reduces the need for moving production or financial operations physically to the host country. For FDI in utilities larger openness is instead associated with more FDI.

The results from the dynamic fixed effects model (Table 5.2), which includes the lag of the dependent variable FDI stock, suggest that the static model indeed overestimated the role of BITs and of the other determinants in explaining FDI stocks. As expected, FDI decisions are found to be dynamic and the past level of FDI stocks explains an important part of the current stock of FDI for all sectors. The dynamic model finds a significant effect of BITs for mining and services, with a larger estimate for the former than for the latter sector. For the other variables, the results are in line with what was found in the static model, although for some of the variables the coefficients lose significance in the dynamic specification. The only exception is the unexpected significantly negative effect of overall GDP on total FDI stock. It seems that this negative relation is mostly driven by FDI in the utilities and banking sector, but a further investigation of this rather counterintuitive result would be necessary. In Table 5.3 an interaction term of BITs and the level of democracy is added in order to test whether BITs complements or substitutes a safe institutional environment. In line with earlier studies[50] we find that BITs act as substitutes. The higher the level of democracy, the less strong is the effect of signing an additional BIT on attracting FDI in mining and services. In the regression of total FDI the interaction term also has a negative sign, but is not statistically significant. Note that the effect of BITs loses significance in the regression of FDI in manufacturing.

Tables 5.4 and 5.5 show the results for the first-differenced GMM estimation, which address the bias that we introduced in the model when adding a lagged dependent variable to the controls. The Sargan test statistic does not reject the null hypotheses that the moment conditions are jointly satisfied, except for the

---

50 See for instance Neumayer and Spess, 2005, op. cit.

Table 5.2 Dynamic fixed effects model

VARIABLES	(1) Total	(2) Agriculture	(3) Mining	(4) Manufacturing	(5) Utilities	(6) Services	(7) Banking
Nr of BITs	0.00520	−0.00287	0.0629***	0.0132†	−0.000683	0.0121†	0.00789
	[0.782]	[−0.185]	[2.897]	[1.622]	[−0.0214]	[1.536]	[0.576]
Ln(GDP per cap)	5.287*	−1.180	−15.12†	−0.247	19.62	0.311	5.846
	[1.940]	[−0.167]	[−1.578]	[−0.0737]	[1.383]	[0.0926]	[0.982]
Ln(GDP)	−5.809*	2.582	16.74†	0.204	−21.43	−0.645	−6.119
	[−1.978]	[0.339]	[1.615]	[0.0563]	[−1.394]	[−0.177]	[−0.954]
Democracy	−0.0459	0.0688	0.520***	−0.0555	0.252	−0.0216	−0.0169
	[−0.953]	[0.632]	[3.609]	[−1.133]	[1.173]	[−0.380]	[−0.162]
Ln(Inflation)	0.0106	−0.0391	0.0433	0.00487	−0.0382	0.0133	−0.0241
	[0.315]	[−0.476]	[0.402]	[0.133]	[−0.234]	[0.331]	[−0.323]
Openness	−0.00341**	0.00618	−0.00585	−0.00313†	0.00459	−0.00267	−0.00679*
	[−2.054]	[1.455]	[−0.996]	[−1.640]	[0.511]	[−1.280]	[−1.872]
FDI (t−1)	0.774***	0.520***	0.388***	0.445***	0.407***	0.788***	0.588***
	[8.460]	[5.296]	[5.187]	[4.153]	[5.065]	[10.71]	[5.429]
Year dummies	Yes	Yes	Yes	Yes	Yes	Yes	Yes
Observations	94	94	94	94	94	94	94
R-squared	0.977	0.872	0.819	0.952	0.902	0.955	0.944
Number of countries	12	12	12	12	12	12	12

t-statistics in brackets

*** p<0.01, ** p<0.05, * p<0.10, † p<0.15

Table 5.3 Dynamic fixed effects model including interaction term of BITs and democracy index

VARIABLES	(1) Total	(2) Agriculture	(3) Mining	(4) Manufacturing	(5) Utilities	(6) Services	(7) Banking
Nr of BITs	0.0383†	-0.00166	0.343***	0.00459	0.0746	0.0570*	0.0388
	[1.569]	[-0.0267]	[4.385]	[0.162]	[0.550]	[1.936]	[0.704]
Nr of BITs*democracy	-0.00384	-0.000141	-0.0321***	0.00105	-0.00897	-0.00524†	-0.00356
	[-1.408]	[-0.0201]	[-3.701]	[0.318]	[-0.572]	[-1.582]	[-0.579]
Ln(GDP per cap)	6.087**	-1.151	-10.66	-0.571	22.18†	1.384	6.645
	[2.203]	[-0.158]	[-1.211]	[-0.162]	[1.483]	[0.408]	[1.082]
Ln(GDP)	-6.950**	2.540	9.544	0.633	-24.93†	-2.201	-7.214
	[-2.298]	[0.319]	[0.990]	[0.163]	[-1.499]	[-0.591]	[-1.074]
Democracy	0.0768	0.0732	1.546***	-0.0877	0.535	0.143	0.101
	[0.773]	[0.297]	[5.039]	[-0.779]	[0.991]	[1.211]	[0.441]
Ln(Inflation)	0.0143	-0.0390	0.0777	0.00332	-0.0313	0.0196	-0.0231
	[0.427]	[-0.468]	[0.788]	[0.0893]	[-0.190]	[0.490]	[-0.308]
Openness	-0.00317*	0.00619	-0.00505	-0.00320†	0.00438	-0.00231	-0.00659*
	[-1.911]	[1.437]	[-0.944]	[-1.655]	[0.485]	[-1.118]	[-1.798]
FDI (t–1)	0.765***	0.520***	0.331***	0.435***	0.429***	0.786***	0.575***
	[8.420]	[5.253]	[4.734]	[3.876]	[4.786]	[10.82]	[5.161]
Year dummies	Yes	Yes	Yes	Yes	Yes	Yes	Yes
Observations	94	94	94	94	94	94	94
R-squared	0.978	0.872	0.852	0.952	0.903	0.957	0.945
Number of countries	12	12	12	12	12	12	12

t-statistics in brackets

*** p<0.01, ** p<0.05, * p<0.10, † p<0.15

regression for FDI in services. Hence, we need to be cautious in interpreting the results for these specific regressions. There is some significant first-order autocorrelation in the first-differenced residuals in some of the regressions (AR1), but there is no significant second-order serial correlation (AR2), except for utilities. This is why we decide to use lags starting from order 3, rather than 2. The results from the difference GMM estimation show that BITs have a significantly positive effect on the total level of FDI and on FDI in mining, with a larger estimate for the latter. Again, the results for the other variables are in line with earlier results, although significance levels may differ somewhat. Note that the democracy indicator gets a negative sign in some of these regressions, while remaining positive for mining. After adding an interaction term of BITs with democracy (Table 5.5), these negative effects for the democracy variable disappear and the interaction term in the GMM estimation confirms that BITs are more effective when levels of political institutional quality are low.

Although further analysis for a larger sample of countries and a longer time series would be desirable, these results do suggest that the effect of a BIT may be very different for FDI in different sectors. The results discussed above indicate that FDI in mining, in particular, is attracted by the additional protection provided in BITs. We moreover find a positive effect also for the aggregate regression, in which we analyse the overall effect of BITs on FDI. This is in line with the most recent studies showing that BITs are effective, and especially so in transition countries.[51] The magnitude of the effect for mining and for total FDI is substantial. Our most conservative estimate is a coefficient of 0.04 for mining and 0.02 for total FDI. Hence, when a new BIT enters into force overall FDI stock is expected to increase by 2 per cent, while the stock of FDI in mining increases by 4 per cent. The magnitude of these results is in line with the results of recent studies.[52]

5.6 Conclusion

Over the past decades, developing countries have increasingly engaged in the signing of bilateral investment treaties with developed countries in order to attract FDI. Besides the time and effort developing countries invest in negotiation process of these treaties, they also give up part of their sovereignty. It is therefore relevant to know whether these treaties really fulfil expectations. Do these treaties succeed in attracting FDI and, if they do so, do they succeed in attracting the type of FDI that is desirable to spur economic growth and development?

While several studies have recently addressed the first part of this question, nobody looked into the potential heterogeneous effects of BIT on different

---

51 Busse et al., 2010, op. cit.
52 Egger and Merlo, 2007, op. cit.; Busse et al., 2010, op. cit.; F. Barthel, M. Busse and E. Neumayer, 2011, 'The Impact of Double Taxation Treaties on Foreign Direct Investment: Evidence from Large Dyadic Panel Data', *Contemporary Economic Policy*, 28: 366–377.

Table 5.4 Difference GMM model

VARIABLES	(1) Total	(2) Agriculture	(3) Mining	(4) Manufacturing	(5) Utilities	(6) Services	(7) Banking
Nr of BITs	0.0211*	-0.0166	0.0436†	0.00709	-0.0104	0.0196	0.0349
	[1.943]	[-0.312]	[1.483]	[0.468]	[-0.163]	[0.989]	[1.346]
Ln(GDP per cap)	0.159	-25.89	-28.04**	0.712	11.23	-5.042	-14.14†
	[0.0428]	[-1.157]	[-2.467]	[0.107]	[0.338]	[-0.877]	[-1.526]
Ln(GDP)	-0.649	26.16	28.77**	-1.419	-14.93	5.373	14.15
	[-0.163]	[1.171]	[2.387]	[-0.205]	[-0.423]	[0.875]	[1.428]
Democracy	-0.163**	-0.247	0.417***	-0.134***	0.512*	-0.0989	-0.425**
	[-1.968]	[-0.718]	[3.101]	[-2.773]	[1.801]	[-0.836]	[-2.140]
Ln(Inflation)	0.0694*	-0.117	0.234**	0.0471	0.153	0.0592	0.0975
	[1.803]	[-0.616]	[2.153]	[1.151]	[0.647]	[1.013]	[1.084]
Openness	-0.00545***	0.00582	-0.00340	-0.00411**	0.00663	-0.00384	-0.00775†
	[-2.828]	[0.679]	[-0.580]	[-2.227]	[0.513]	[-1.261]	[-1.608]
FDI (t−1)	0.736**	1.382	0.349**	0.150	0.982**	1.069**	0.783***
	[2.233]	[1.263]	[2.440]	[0.296]	[2.179]	[2.022]	[2.697]
Year dummies	Yes	Yes	Yes	Yes	Yes	Yes	Yes
Observations	79	79	79	79	79	79	79
Number of countries	12	12	12	12	12	12	12
Sargan test statistic	3.041	1.120	2.476	0.465	0.318	5.692	1.265
p-value	0.219	0.571	0.290	0.793	0.853	0.0581	0.531
AR 1	-1.407	-1.277	-1.001	-0.174	-2.733	-2.068	-1.685
p-value	0.159	0.201	0.317	0.862	0.00628	0.0386	0.0920
AR2	-1.063	0.544	-0.748	0.802	1.686	-0.178	-1.298
p-value	0.288	0.587	0.455	0.423	0.0917	0.859	0.194

t-statistics in brackets

*** p<0.01, ** p<0.05, * p<0.10, † p<0.

Table 5.5 Difference GMM model with interaction of BITs and democracy index

VARIABLES	(1) Total	(2) Agriculture	(3) Mining	(4) Manufacturing	(5) Utilities	(6) Services	(7) Banking
Nr of BITs	0.0689**	0.134	0.190**	0.000701	0.0387	0.0715†	-0.0534
	[2.207]	[1.305]	[2.316]	[0.0242]	[0.201]	[1.513]	[-0.451]
Nr of BITs*Democracy	-0.00550†	-0.0175	-0.0180*	0.000727	-0.00616	-0.00598	0.0103
	[-1.603]	[-1.402]	[-1.873]	[0.230]	[-0.271]	[-1.188]	[0.788]
Ln(GDP per cap)	0.688	-16.66	-25.32**	0.823	9.553	-3.796	-15.62†
	[0.199]	[-0.985]	[-2.386]	[0.140]	[0.307]	[-0.706]	[-1.509]
Ln(GDP)	-1.409	16.13	24.71**	-1.490	-13.40	3.600	16.08
	[-0.377]	[0.934]	[2.163]	[-0.242]	[-0.403]	[0.615]	[1.436]
Democracy	0.0610	0.377	0.967***	-0.157†	0.696	0.114	-0.842
	[0.402]	[0.924]	[3.133]	[-1.510]	[0.970]	[0.554]	[-1.403]
Ln(Inflation)	0.0467	-0.112	0.213**	0.0500	0.150	0.0411	0.121
	[1.210]	[-0.749]	[2.116]	[1.229]	[0.644]	[0.735]	[1.155]
Openness	-0.00592***	0.00477	-0.00490	-0.00409**	0.00607	-0.00416†	-0.00691
	[-3.315]	[0.694]	[-0.914]	[-2.255]	[0.485]	[-1.494]	[-1.283]
FDI (t–1)	0.458	1.016	0.215†	0.177	0.927**	0.877†	0.973**
	[1.364]	[1.413]	[1.639]	[0.403]	[2.176]	[1.739]	[2.231]
Year dummies	Yes	Yes	Yes	Yes	Yes	Yes	Yes
Observations	79	79	79	79	79	79	79
Number of countries	12	12	12	12	12	12	12
Sargan test statistic	3.006	0.740	1.720	0.421	0.345	5.974	1.136
p-value	0.223	0.691	0.423	0.810	0.842	0.0504	0.567
AR1	-0.754	-1.448	-0.494	-0.242	-2.734	-1.811	-1.507
p-value	0.451	0.148	0.621	0.809	0.00626	0.0702	0.132
AR2	-0.602	0.575	-0.729	0.826	1.664	-0.238	-1.217
p-value	0.547	0.566	0.466	0.409	0.0961	0.812	0.224

t-statistics in brackets

*** $p<0.01$, ** $p<0.05$, * $p<0.10$, † $p<0.15$

forms of FDI. In this chapter we make a first step in that direction by analysing the effect of BITs on FDI in different economic sectors. We argue that BITs have a larger effect on investment decisions for those sectors that involve large sunk costs and are susceptible to expropriation. The literature on expropriation and the records of investor–state dispute settlement suggest that FDI in resource extraction and utilities are the most vulnerable to expropriation. These sectors typically involve large sunk costs, require relatively low levels of know-how, and are often politically sensitive to foreign ownership. We therefore expect – FDI in mining and utilities – to be more responsive to BITs compared to other sectors. We empirically test this hypothesis using disaggregated FDI data for twelve countries in Central and Eastern Europe and the Former Soviet Union. Using different estimation models, including static and dynamic fixed effects models and GMM estimations, we find partial support to our hypothesis: BITs have a larger impact on FDI in the mining sector (and on overall FDI). Contrary to our hypotheses, however, FDI in the utilities sector is not found to be responsive to BITs. For FDI in the services sector some of our models find a significant effect of BITs, but it is not robust to alternative specifications. In other sectors FDI does not seem to respond to new BITs.

While the small sample of countries that we use in this study clearly limits the geographical relevance of our findings, we do think they are important in that they are the first results to point to a differential impact of investment treaties on different types of FDI. Overall, our results suggest that BITs do not attract the most development-enhancing FDI. Investments in the mining sector often have limited linkages with the local economy, create little knowledge transfer and are likely to repatriate the majority of profits made. Although more detailed studies for a larger set of countries are required before formulating strong policy conclusions, our results do challenge the idea that BITs are a desirable policy tool to enhance development through increased foreign investments.

6   The host state

Improving the monitoring of
international investment
agreements at the national level

Olivier De Schutter

6.1 Introduction

There is no certain, necessary relationship between foreign direct investment (FDI) and human development in the receiving country. And whether FDI contributes to human development depends, to a large extent, on the quality of governance in the host State. Where negotiations with investors are conducted in full transparency, with the involvement of the communities directly affected, and with appropriate procedural safeguards to ensure that the public interest will be served and that the benefits will accrue to the population, FDI can be a powerful tool for human development. Conversely, however, where investment treaties or host government agreements[1] are negotiated without parliamentary scrutiny and without participation of the local communities concerned, in weakly governed States, the consequences may be highly detrimental: some local elites may benefit, in particular through side-payments or by capturing the benefits from the investment, but the linkages to the local economy and the increase in fiscal revenues can remain minimal, and the situation of the local communities worsen, not improve, in particular as a result of the increased competition for the natural resources on which these communities depend.

The importance of establishing robust mechanisms at the domestic level to ensure that FDI will serve development goals has been acknowledged primarily in the context of the extractive industries. Mineral-rich but capital-poor countries that depend on foreign technologies to exploit the resources in their

---

1 In this chapter, the expression 'investment treaties' will refer to agreements concluded between States, and imposing obligations under international law (see Art. 2 para. 1(a) of the Vienna Convention on the Law of Treaties (1155 UNTS 331), signed in Vienna on 23 May 1969); the expression 'host government agreements' will serve to designate agreements between one private investor and the host State: such agreements are often also called 'concession agreements' in the extractive industry sector or when a private company acquires the right to exploit a resource or to provide a service at conditions determined by the government, who retains ultimate control of the resource or the right (Nicholas Miranda, 'Concession Agreements: From Private Contracts to Public Policy', *Yale L.J.*, vol. 107 (2007), p. 510).

subsoil need foreign investors in order to do so. But the exploitation of mineral resources typically takes the form of large-scale projects in which a small number of individuals control vast amounts of wealth. The capture of the benefits can therefore be highly unequal, unless affirmative measures are taken to ensure that they will be fairly distributed across a large number. Moreover, natural resources are non-renewable: they are 'assets in the ground' whose value depends on technology, market prices and political risk. The exploitation of mineral resources thus should be seen as the consumption of capital, rather than only of a stream of incomes.[2] The temptation is thus huge for those in power both to exploit those resources in order to create as much wealth as possible within the shortest possible time (for they do not know for how long they will stay in power), and to sell off the right to exploit resources to the highest bidder (in order to cash in immediately the equivalent of all future income streams that could result from exploiting the resource). As a result, the leaders holding power may be reluctant to cede it to rivals (for instance, by organizing fair and transparent elections and accepting their results when they are voted out of office), simply because the exploitation of natural resources represents such an opportunity for fast personal enrichment. Together, these factors contribute to what came to be known as the 'resource curse': the paradox of countries that suffer from weak governance and poor human development, not only despite, but *because of*, having a subsoil rich in natural resources.[3]

Much of the emerging literature on the risks and opportunities associated with the exploitation of mineral resources focuses on the importance of institutions in guiding the relationship between natural resources and growth. Whether the presence of natural resources is a curse or a blessing would depend, according to this analysis, on the strength of institutions, in particular those ensuring democratic accountability, as well as on the incentives for diversification beyond the exploitation of the resources.[4] The analysis, however, should not necessarily be limited to the extractive industry. To the extent that a government in power at a certain moment in time adopts decisions related to an investment that will have a lasting impact, generally far beyond its time in office, there will be a natural tendency to discount the long-term losses and to overvalue the short-term benefits, especially when, whether legally or illegally, such benefits disproportionately accrue to the elites controlling the State apparatus.

2 M. Humphreys, J. Sachs and J. Stiglitz (eds), *Escaping the Resource Curse* (New York: Columbia University Press, 2007), p. 8.
3 See, for instance, P. Collier and A. Hoeffler, 'On Economic Causes of Civil War', 50 *Oxford Economic Papers* 563 (1998), pp. 563–573; J.D. Sachs and A.M. Warner, 'Natural Resource Abundance and Economic Growth', NBER Working Paper no. 5398 (originally 1995, revised 1997, 1999). For a useful literature survey, see F. Van der Ploeg, 'Challenges and Opportunities for Resource Rich Economies', CEPR Discussion Paper no. 5688 (2006).
4 See Thad Dunning, 'Resource Dependence, Economic Performance, and Political Stability', 49 *Journal of Conflict Resolution* 451 (2005); T. Dunning, 'Crude Democracy: Natural Resource Wealth and Political Regimes', in R.H. Bates, S. Hanson et al. (eds), *Cambridge Studies in Comparative Politics* (Cambridge and New York: Cambridge University Press, 2008).

The question of accountability for the choices made by governments with respect to FDI arrival is raised even in the most unlikely contexts, where the said governments have a reputation for making decisions that benefit the populations. On 6 December 2011, for instance, President Ellen Johnson Sirleaf of Liberia visited communities affected by the development of a large palm tree plantation in the north-western part of the country. The first African female head of State, Johnson Sirleaf was awarded the Nobel Peace Prize for her contributions to rebuilding the country after 14 years of civil conflict, and she had been recently re-elected as the head of the country. Her visit and that of the ministers of her government accompanying her was triggered by the protests against a large concession for palm oil development that went to a Malaysian company, Sime Darby, a subsidiary of a New York-based investment fund, to which the Liberian government had ceded a total of 1.6 million acres between 2009 and 2011.[5] The rural communities affected by the first stages of implementation in north-western Liberia complained that the salaries paid to those employed on the plantations were below the wages promised, and that the planting of palm trees led to environmental degradation. The response of President Johnson Sirleaf, as reported in the Liberian press, was this:

> When your government and the representatives sign any paper with a foreign country, the communities can't change it. With that, the Constitution gives the government the authority to do so. Therefore if the government makes mistake, let us come back and talk it. . . . You are trying to undermine your own government. You can't do that. If you do so all the foreign investors coming to Liberia will close their businesses and leave, then Liberia will go back to the old days.[6]

The episode is illustrative in a number of ways. First, the response of President Johnson Sirleaf to the rural communities she visited suggests a reverse relationship between the protection of the rights of the local communities affected by an investment, on the one hand, and the attractiveness of a particular location for the investor, on the other hand. But that commonly held assumption only holds true when insufficient precautions have been taken, at a sufficiently early stage, to ensure that the rights of the communities will be respected and

5 S. Kpanan'Ayoung Siakor and R. Knight, 'A Nobel Laureate's Problem at Home', *The New York Times*, 20 January 2012. Online. Available HTTP <http://www.nytimes.com/2012/01/21/opinion/in-liberia-a-nobel-laureates-problem.html> (last consulted on 21 January 2012). The same op-ed piece claims that 'Between 2006 and 2011, Mrs. Johnson Sirleaf granted more than a third of Liberia's land to private investors to use for logging, mining and agro-industrial enterprises. Today, more than seven million acres have become forestry and agricultural concessions.'
6 'Ellen Ends Deadlock at Sime Darby Plantation in Grand Cape Mount', *Daily Observer*, 14 January 2012. Online. Available HTTP <http://www.liberianobserver.com/index.php/news/item/207-ellen-ends-deadlock-at-sime-darby-plantation-in-grand-cape-mount> (last consulted on 21 January 2012).

their interests taken into account, and that they will participate in shaping the investment: in that case, indeed, it may be true that correcting mistakes committed during the early stages of the process may be costly in terms of credibility and send the message to potential investors that their investments may not be safe or immune to challenge.

The lesson, therefore, is not that investments should proceed without all the appropriate safeguards, including participation of the local communities: it is, quite to the contrary, that a framework should be established to ensure that no such mistakes shall be committed, and that no investment shall be allowed to proceed unless adequate safeguards have been put in place. Indeed, it is now well established that FDI flows are encouraged where the country of destination respects civil and political rights, and therefore preserves social and political stability.[7] This is consistent with surveys of managers of transnational corporations, which indicate the importance of such stability for the choice of where to invest in foreign jurisdictions.[8] Therefore, governments whose human rights records are good are rewarded by higher foreign investment flows.[9] This constitutes an incentive for governments to ensure an investment-friendly environment by establishing an adequate legal framework for the benefit of their populations: the attractiveness of jurisdictions whose human rights record is good confers on them an advantage in the competition to attract capital, which is only partially offset in labour-intensive sectors by the fact that, in such jurisdictions, the wages will generally be higher.

---

7 This is the key result of empirical studies performed separately by Dani Rodrik and David Kucera. See D. Rodrik, 'Democracies pay Higher Wages', *Quarterly Journal of Economics*, vol. 114 (1999), 707–738; D. Kucera, 'The Effects of Core Workers' Rights on Labour Costs and Foreign Direct Investment: Evaluating the "Conventional Wisdom"', *IILS Working Paper* No. 130 (2001). These studies and the study mentioned in the following note are cited by the helpful review of the literature made by D.K. Brown, A.V. Deardorff and Robert M. Stern, 'The Effects of Multinational Production on Wages and Working Conditions in Developing Countries', NBER Working Paper No. 9669 (May 2003), available at <http://www.nber.org/papers/w9669> (last consulted on 21 January 2012). For a recent discussion of the various studies having sought to identify correlations or to establish causality links between respect for human rights and attractivity to foreign investment, see M. Sant'Ana, 'Foreign Direct Investment and Human Development: Two Approaches to Assessing Impacts on Human Rights', *Human Rights and International Legal Discourse*, vol. 3, No. 2 (2009), 229–262, esp. 232–248.

8 F. Hatem, *International Investment: Towards the Year 2001*, New York, United Nations, 1997.

9 As pointed out by Brown, Deardorff and Stern, at p. 51 of the working paper cited above, this constitutes one of the most interesting results from the research by David Kucera for the International Labour Organization: 'FDI is attracted to countries with a higher civil liberties index even though labor costs are higher. An increase in the civil-liberties index of one unit (on a 10-point scale), controlling for wages, is associated with a 18.5 percent increase in FDI flows. When the negative impact of increased wages in democracies is factored in, a one-unit increase in the civil-liberties index raises FDI inflows by 14.3 percent. So even though democracies pay higher wages for a given level of worker productivity, they still provide an attractive location for foreign investors.'

Second, the episode illustrates one dilemma that is familiar to all those working at the intersection of foreign investment and human development. There is general agreement that investment should be channelled towards the fulfilment of human rights or, at least, should not lead to violations of such rights. But beyond that minimum standard, where should the public interest be determined? Should investments projects be screened for their contribution to the development of the country as a whole, or to the local communities most directly affected alone? If the latter, is there not a risk that the local communities will capture most benefits – in terms not only of employment opportunities, but also of infrastructure creation and increased fiscal revenues – and that opportunities for redistribution from the richest to the poorest regions will be missed? Should it not be left to the central government, after all, provided it is representative of all components of society, to determine where the appropriate balance should be struck between the local development needs and the needs of the country as a whole? The question of who should determine the public interest is linked to the question of how to avoid the risk that short-term considerations will crowd out the longer-term concern for sustainable development: as this chapter will argue below, the more certain procedural requirements of representativity and accountability are met, the more the choices made by the competent authority should be trusted in principle, and the more they will be immune to challenge.

Third, on the basis of which methodology should the balance be struck between the risks and opportunities, the advantages and liabilities, and the gains and losses that result from the arrival of investment? There are clear limitations to cost–benefit analysis, measuring economic impacts, if the aim is to assess the contribution of FDI to human development. Alternative valuations are available. But two questions emerge. One is how to combine the substantive dimension of such valuations (the type of measurement used) with the procedural dimension (the process through which the pros and cons of FDI projects are assessed). Approaches prioritizing the substantive component cannot be assimilated to approaches prioritizing the procedural dimension: it would be miraculous if the communities participating in shaping investment projects always made choices that were in perfect conformity with the calculations of the experts, based on the measurement tools that they develop. Since the two approaches cannot be considered as perfectly interchangeable, should they be ranked against one another? Or should they be used in combination? It has been suggested above that an inverse relationship should be established between procedural safeguards and substantive requirements – that the more democratic accountability is ensured, the more the choices made by the authorities should be deferred to. How could such a relationship be established in practice? A second question is whether the economic valuation, in and of itself, makes it more difficult for communities consulted in the course of investment projects to reflect upon the reality of their needs and preferences – in other terms, whether economic valuations pre-empt local-level deliberations that take into account the broader range of values that a community may seek to consider in deciding whether or not to welcome a particular investment project.

These are some of the key questions that arise when governments are asked to assess the impacts of investment agreements on the enjoyment of human rights within their jurisdiction, and to provide the communities affected by any particular investment project with a right to be consulted and to have access to remedies where the investment may lead to a violation of their rights. The remainder of this contribution will recall the framework set by international human rights law, in the second section. It will then discuss some of the difficulties involved in the implementation of the framework, focusing in particular on how tradeoffs could be managed, in the typical case where the arrival of FDI creates both winners and losers, and on the relationship between a substantive approach and a procedural approach. A substantive approach is one in which whether or not an investment should take place is decided on the basis of its contribution to human development as measures from a pre-defined scale. A procedural approach, by contrast, gives more weight to the result of deliberative processes within the communities affected. We shall conclude that each of these approaches has weaknesses, and that only by combining the two approaches can we arrive at satisfactory results: it is only through this combination, it will be suggested, that the notion of 'free, prior and informed consent' of the communities affected by the investment project can become both meaningful and workable.

It is against this background that the negotiation and conclusion of investment agreements should be assessed. Two types of agreements should be distinguished, however.[10] First, bilateral or multilateral agreements may be concluded in order to attract investors, by guaranteeing them certain rights.[11] In general, these treaties pertain to admission of investment (defining the conditions of entry of FDI into the country); they protect investors from various forms of expropriation, both direct and indirect (the latter often under the requirement of a 'fair and equitable treatment'); they include guarantees of 'national treatment' (according to which investors enjoy a treatment similar to that enjoyed by the nationals of the host State) and 'most-favoured nation' (according to which they enjoy treatment similar to the best treatment accorded to investors from any other country), as well as provisions allowing the transfer and repatriation of profits (capital transfer provisions); and they have dispute-settlement clauses allowing investors to challenge measures taken by the host State before international arbitral tribunals designated as competent to settle disputes between the investors covered by the treaty and the host State,

---

10 See also *supra*, n. 1.

11 For a more detailed discussion, see Chapter 2 in this volume. And see also R. Dolzer and M. Stevens, *Bilateral Investment Treaties* (The Hague and Boston, Martinus Nijhoff, 1995); or R. Suda, 'The Effect of Bilateral Investment Treaties on Human Rights Enforcement and Realization', in O. De Schutter (ed.), *Transnational Corporations and Human Rights*, Hart Publishing, Oxford and Portland, Oregon, 2006, ch. 3.

established under the rules of the 1965 International Convention on the Settlement of Disputes between States and the nationals of other parties (ICSID)[12] or under the UNCITRAL Arbitral Rules.[13] It is in order to ensure that the negotiation and conclusion of such treaties do not undermine human rights that this author has proposed, in his official capacity as Special Rapporteur on the right to food, the systematic preparation of human rights impact assessments in the course of such negotiations, according to a methodology that was presented at the nineteenth session of the Human Rights Council in March 2012.[14]

Second, project-level investment agreements (often called host government agreements (HGAs)) may be concluded, particularly for larger-scale investment projects that have a long duration, between the individual investor and the host government. The Special Representative of the UN Secretary-General on the issue of human rights and transnational corporations and other business enterprises has proposed a set of Principles for Responsible Contracts to favour the integration of the management of human rights risks in the negotiations between governments and investors;[15] like the above-mentioned methodology on human rights impact assessments, the presentation of these Principles demonstrates the growing interest for bridging the areas of investment and human rights, in part in order to ensure that the race to attract investors will not result in the host State neglecting its duties to protect and fulfil the human rights of its population.

While a number of the requirements set out below relate to individual investment projects, and thus would only be relevant to the negotiation of HGAs, the relationship between these two levels cannot be ignored; in the conclusion of investment treaties, governments should refrain from making commitments that will make it impossible for them to comply with requirements that apply at the level of the individual investment project,[16] for

---

12 575 UNTS 159.
13 The Arbitral Rules adopted by the United Nations Commission on International Trade Law (UNCITRAL) were adopted initially on 28 April 1976; they were revised in 2010. These Rules provide a comprehensive set of procedural rules upon which parties to disputes between States and foreign investors may agree for the conduct of arbitral proceedings.
14 See Guiding Principles on Human Rights Impact Assessments of Trade and Investment Agreements, Report of the Special Rapporteur on the right to food: Addendum, UN Doc. A/HRC/19/59/Add.5 (19 December 2011).
15 Addendum to the Report of the Special Representative of the Secretary-General on the Issue of Human Rights and Transnational Corporations and Other Business Enterprises, J. Ruggie – 'Principles for Responsible Contracts: Integrating the Management of Human Rights Risks into State-Investor Contract Negotiations: Guidance for Negotiators', 25 May 2011, UN Doc. A/HRC/17/31/Add.3.
16 See Guiding Principles on Human Rights Impact Assessments of Trade and Investment Agreements, cited above, Principle 2 ('States must ensure that the conclusion of trade and investment agreements shall not impose obligations inconsistent with their pre-existing international treaty obligations, including those to respect, protect and fulfil human rights').

instance because, by entering into such treaties, they would have created certain 'legitimate expectations' on the part of the investor (such as expectations that the investor will obtain a permit to operate a facility),[17] or because by imposing certain requirements on the investor, they would violate a 'stabilization clause' or an 'economic equilibrium' clause included in a pre-existing investment treaty. In other terms, the freedom of the host government to regulate foreign investment by the conclusion of HGAs, in order to ensure that specific investment projects will contribute to human development and to the fulfilment of human rights, should not be pre-empted by obligations imposed under investment treaties. For this reason, the normative framework set out below relates both to the negotiation and conclusion of investment treaties and to the negotiation and conclusion of HGAs, even though the relationship to investment treaties (as opposed to project-level agreements) may be only indirect.

6.2 The normative framework

This is not the place to review the full range of human rights that could be affected either by the conclusion of an investment treaty, or by a particular investment project.[18] The most frequently invoked human rights in the context of investment projects are the right to adequate food,[19] the right to water[20] –

17 'Legitimate expectations' are expectations on the part of the investor that are reasonable and justifiable in the light of the conduct of the host State (whether consisting in actions or in omissions), and on which the investor is made to rely, 'such that a failure by the host State to honour those expectations could cause the investor (or investment) to suffer damages' (*International Thunderbird Gaming v Mexico*, UNCITRAL, Award, 26 January 2006, para. 147).

18 See, for an overview, Report of the High Commissioner for Human Rights, 'Human Rights, Trade and Investment', UN Doc. E/CN.4/Sub.2/2003/9 (2 July 2003); and see Addendum to the Report of the Special Representative of the Secretary-General on the Issue of Human Rights and Transnational Corporations and Other Business Enterprises, John Ruggie – 'Principles for Responsible Contracts: Integrating the Management of Human Rights Risks into State-Investor Contract Negotiations: Guidance for Negotiators', cited above.

19 The right to adequate food is recognized under Art. 25 of the Universal Declaration of Human Rights (GA Res. 217 A (III), UN Doc. A/810, at 71 (1948)), and under Art. 11 of the International Covenant on Economic, Social and Cultural Rights (adopted on 16 December 1966, G.A. Res. 2200(XXII), UN GAOR, 21st sess., Supp. No. 16, UN Doc. A/6316 (1966), 993 UNTS 3), as interpreted by the Committee on Economic, Social and Cultural Rights (General Comment No. 12: The right to adequate food (1999), UN Doc. E/C.12/1999/5). These prescriptions are complemented by the *Voluntary Guidelines to Support the Progressive Realization of the Right to Adequate Food in the Context of National Food Security* adopted by the Member States of the FAO Council in November 2004, which are a set of recommendations addressed to States for the implementation of the human right to adequate food.

20 Committee on Economic, Social and Cultural Rights, General Comment No. 15 (2002): The right to water (Articles 11 and 12 of the International Covenant on Economic, Social and Cultural Rights), E/C.12/2002/11 of 20 January 2003.

particularly where land is ceded to a foreign investor or where water services are privatized[21] – and the right to health[22] – in order to challenge the environmental consequences of the investment project that may have detrimental impacts on health.[23] In addition, the basic labour rights recognized under the core International Labour Organization (ILO) instruments are often invoked in this context. Labour rights are also protected under general human rights law since a failure to comply with such rights can lead to violations of the rights to work and to an adequate standard of living, or to the right to safe and healthy working conditions, which are recognized under the International Covenant of Economic, Social and Cultural Rights.[24]

Such rights, however, can only be effectively guaranteed and enjoyed in the context of investment projects, if combined with appropriate procedural safeguards. Four safeguards in particular are worth recalling, because of their key role in protecting local communities, and because their implications have not always been well understood. Two of these safeguards stem from the substantive norms of self-determination of peoples and of the right to development. Two others are more strictly procedural in nature: they are the right to information and the right to access to effective remedies.

6.2.1 The right to self-determination and the right to development

The right to self-determination of peoples and, specifically, the right of all peoples freely to dispose of their natural wealth and resources – as stipulated under Article 1 of both 1966 Covenants implementing the Universal Declaration of Human Rights[25] – is one of the most under-rated and under-utilized norms in the international human rights system of protection. If taken seriously, self-determination means that the peoples, not governments alone,

21 For an early study on this topic, that has gained proeminence since, see M. Finger and J. Allouche, *Water Privatization – Trans-National Corporations and the Re-Regulation of the Water Industry*, London, Spon Press, 2002.

22 Committee on Economic, Social and Cultural Rights, *General Comment No. 14: The right to the highest attainable standard of health (Article 12 of the International Covenant on Economic, Social and Cultural Rights)*, (Twenty-second session, 2000), UN Doc. E/C.12/2000/4.

23 See e.g. Analytical Study on the relationship between human rights and the environment, Report of the High Commissioner for Human Rights, UN Doc. A/HRC/19/34 (16 December 2011), para. 67 (recognizing that States may have human rights duties beyond their national territories where transnational corporations over which they may exercise influence contribute to environmental degradation, thus affecting human rights directly or indirectly).

24 International Covenant on Economic, Social and Cultural Rights, cited above, Arts 6 and 11. See also Report of the Special Rapporteur on the right to food, Agribusiness and the right to food, UN doc. A/HRC/13/33 (22 December 2009), paras 13–20.

25 International Covenant on Economic, Social and Cultural Rights, cited above; and International Covenant on Civil and Political Rights (A/RES/21/2200A, 16 December 1966) (999 UNTS 171).

should be making the fundamental choices as to how the resources available should be used: in essence, it is a norm about participatory democracy, particularly in the context of the use, exploitation and allocation of natural resources.

The norm has been invoked, for instance, in order to protect indigenous communities or traditional groups from being deprived of equitable access to the resources on which they depend for their livelihoods. In *Apirana Mahuika et al. v New Zealand*, the Human Rights Committee reads Article 1(2) of the International Covenant on Civil and Political Rights – in conjunction with Article 27 of the Covenant, which recognizes the rights of minorities – as allowing an arrangement about the management of fishing resources, noting that the Maori people 'were given access to a great percentage of the quota, and thus effective possession of fisheries was returned to them', and that the new control structure put in place ensures not only a role for the Maori in safeguarding their interests in fisheries but, in addition, their 'effective control'.[26] The implication would appear to be that these provisions would be violated should any people be deprived of the use they make traditionally of the land and resources on which they rely.[27]

This component of the right to self-determination should not benefit indigenous peoples alone. The requirements applicable to indigenous peoples are now extended to at least certain traditional communities that entertain a similarly 'profound and all-encompassing relationship to their ancestral lands' centred on 'the community as a whole' rather than on the individual: this, the Inter-American Court of Human Rights noted, applies for instance to the Maroon communities living in Suriname, which are not indigenous to the region, but are tribal communities of former slaves that settled in Suriname in the seventeenth and eighteenth centuries.[28]

---

26 Human Rights Committee, *Apirana Mahuika et al. v New Zealand*, Communication No. 547/1993, CCPR/C/70/D/547/1993 (2000), para. 9.7. The Human Rights Committee observed that 'minorities shall not be denied the right, in community with the other members of their group, to enjoy their own culture [which] may consist in a way of life which is closely associated with territory and use of its resources. This may particularly be true of members of indigenous communities constituting a minority': General Comment No. 23: The rights of minorities (Art. 27) (Fiftieth session, 1994), CCPR/C/21Rev.1/Add.5, 4 August 1994, paras 1 and 3.2.

27 A similar conclusion has been derived by the Committee on the Elimination of Racial Discrimination from Article 5(d)(v) of the International Convention on the Elimination of All Forms of Racial Discrimination, which protects the right to property: this requires from States parties that they 'recognize and protect the rights of all indigenous communities to own, develop and control the lands which they traditionally occupy, including water and subsoil resources' (CERD, *Concluding Observations: Guyana*, CERD/C/GUY/CO/14, 4 April 2006, para. 16).

28 *Case of the Moiwana Community v Suriname. Preliminary Objections. Merits, Reparations and Costs*, Judgment of 15 June 2005, Series C No. 124, paras 132–133. See also *Saramaka People v Suriname*, Judgment of 28 November 2007, para. 86 (finding that 'the Court's jurisprudence regarding indigenous peoples' right to property is also applicable to tribal

Indigenous or traditional communities have a special relationship to land. Yet the right to self-determination is recognized to all 'peoples', and its enjoyment should not be made conditional on these peoples being 'indigenous'. Indeed, the clearest illustration of how this relates to the regulation of foreign investors is provided by a case that did not relate, strictly speaking, to indigenous peoples. In Nigeria, local Ogoni communities complained that they were not protected from the negative impacts of the presence of foreign oil companies exploiting the subsoil of the Niger delta in disregard of the consequences on the surroundings. On the basis of a provision of the 1981 African Charter on Human and Peoples' Rights, worded in terms very similar to those of Article 1(2) of the 1966 Covenants – which recognizes the right of all peoples to 'freely dispose of their natural wealth and resources' and prohibits depriving any people from its own means of subsistence[29] – the African Commission on Human and Peoples' Rights affirmed that a State violates its duties under the Charter if it allows private actors, including foreign companies, to 'devastatingly affect the well-being' of the peoples under its jurisdiction.[30] The Commission was explicit on the contribution that Article 21 of the African Charter on Human and Peoples' Rights was expected to make in getting rid of the remnants of colonialism. The origins of that provision, it recalled,

> may be traced to colonialism, during which the human and material resources of Africa were largely exploited for the benefit of outside powers, creating tragedy for Africans themselves, depriving them of their birthright and alienating them from the land. The aftermath of colonial exploitation has left Africa's precious resources and people still vulnerable to foreign

peoples because both share distinct social, cultural, and economic characteristics, including a special relationship with their ancestral territories, that require special measures under international human rights law in order to guarantee their physical and cultural survival').

29 Article 21 of the African Charter on Human and Peoples' Rights (adopted 27 June 1981, OAU Doc. CAB/LEG/67/3 rev. 5, 21 ILM 58 (1982), entered into force Oct. 21, 1986), provides that: '1. All peoples shall freely dispose of their wealth and natural resources. This right shall be exercised in the exclusive interest of the people. In no case shall a people be deprived of it. 2. In case of spoliation the dispossessed people shall have the right to the lawful recovery of its property as well as to an adequate compensation. 3. The free disposal of wealth and natural resources shall be exercised without prejudice to the obligation of promoting international economic co-operation based on mutual respect, equitable exchange and the principles of international law. 4. States Parties to the present Charter shall individually and collectively exercise the right to free disposal of their wealth and natural resources with a view to strengthening African unity and solidarity. 5. States Parties to the present Charter shall undertake to eliminate all forms of foreign economic exploitation particularly that practised by international monopolies so as to enable their peoples to fully benefit from the advantages derived from their national resources.'

30 *The Social and Economic Rights Action Center and the Center for Economic and Social Rights v Nigeria*, African Commission on Human and Peoples' Rights, Comm. No. 155/96 (2001), para. 58. For a comment, see C. Nwobike, 'The African Commission on Human and Peoples' Rights and the Demystification of Second and Third Generation Rights under the African Charter', *African Journal of Legal Studies*, vol. 1 (2005), p. 129.

misappropriation. [In adopting Article 21] the drafters of the Charter obviously wanted to remind African governments of the continent's painful legacy and restore co-operative economic development to its traditional place at the heart of African Society.[31]

The right to development is another norm that may be highly relevant to the regulation of foreign investment in accordance with human rights. The idea of a right to development was first expressed by Kéba M'Baye in his 1972 inaugural lecture to the International Institute for Human Rights.[32] It was then explored in a detailed study authored by Philip Alston for the UN Secretary-General in 1978, prepared at the request of the Commission on Human Rights.[33] The study emphasized that measures adopted at both domestic level and at international level should be mutually supportive and should go hand in hand, and that the realization of the right to development should be based on participation at all levels.[34] In 1986, after five years of discussions within a Working Group established by the Commission on Human Rights,[35] the Declaration on the Right to Development was adopted by the UN General Assembly, defining it as 'an inalienable human right by virtue of which every human person and all peoples are entitled to participate in, contribute to, and enjoy economic, social, cultural and political development, in which all human rights and fundamental freedoms can be fully realized'.[36] Since then, various working groups, task forces and independent experts have been trying to identify ways to overcome obstacles to the right to development, and to define criteria that would allow the measurement of progress in its realization. It is unnecessary here to recount this history in detail.[37] To us, what matters is one key implication of the right to development: that is, the requirement that the revenues from projects that are conducted in the name of 'development' are used for the benefit of the local population, and that the communities affected by the project participate in shaping it.

---

31 Ibid., para. 56.
32 K. M'Baye, *Le droit au développement comme un droit de l'homme*, Leçon inaugurale de la troisième session d'enseignement de l'Institut international des droits de l'homme, 3 July 1972, reproduced in 5 *Revue des droits de l'homme* (1972), p. 503.
33 Commission on Human Rights resolution 4 (XXXIII), adopted on 4 February 1977.
34 The International Dimensions of the Right to Development as a Human Right in Relation with Other Human Rights Based on International Co-Operation, including the Right to Peace, Taking into Account the Requirements of the New International Economic Order and the Fundamental Human Needs, Report of the Secretary-General, UN Doc. E/CN.4/1334, 2 January 1979.
35 Commission on Human Rights Resolution 36 (XXXVII), adopted on 11 March 1981.
36 UN General Assembly, Resolution 41/128 of 4 December 1986 (adopted with only one negative vote (United States), and eight abstentions).
37 For an excellent and well-informed account, by one key actor in this process, see recently S.P. Marks, *The Politics of the Possible. The Way Ahead for the Right to Development*, Dialogue on Globalization, Friedrich Ebert Stiftung, June 2011.

The Declaration on the right to development adopted by the United Nations General Assembly in 1986 expects States to 'formulate appropriate national development policies that aim at the constant improvement of the well-being of the entire population and of all individuals, on the basis of their active, free and meaningful participation in development and in the fair distribution of the benefits resulting therefrom'.[38] It sees development as a process which should benefit 'the entire population and . . . all individuals on the basis of their active, free and meaningful participation in development and in the fair distribution of benefits resulting therefrom', which implies that States ensure the adequate participation of the local communities concerned by investment projects, and that the decision-making process is fully transparent.[39] The revenues gained from these agreements should serve to fulfil the rights of the population, consistent with the duty of States to 'ensure, *inter alia*, equality of opportunity for all in their access to basic resources, education, health services, food, housing, employment and the fair distribution of income'.[40]

The conclusion was drawn by the Working Group on the Right to Development when it noted that the right to development had a direct impact on how FDI should support the fulfilment of the 8th Millennium Development Goal to develop a global partnership for development: that right, it stated,

> implies that foreign direct investment (FDI) should contribute to local and national development in a responsible manner, that is, in ways that are conducive to social development, protect the environment, and respect the rule of law and fiscal obligations in the host countries. The principles underlying the right to development, as mentioned above, further imply that all parties involved, i.e. investors and recipient countries, have responsibilities to ensure that profit considerations do not result in crowding out human rights protection. The impact of FDI should, therefore, be taken into account when evaluating progress in Goal 8 in the context of the right to development.[41]

This argument is further strengthened by the obligation of all States parties to the International Covenant on Economic, Social and Cultural Rights to ensure the progressive realization of the economic and social rights, to the maximum of all available resources, as stated in Article 2(1) of the Covenant: it would be

---

38 Article 2.3.
39 Preamble, para. 2. See also Arts 6.3. and 8.2.
40 Art. 8.1. On the human rights-based economic development which is prescribed by the Declaration on the Right to Development, see M.E. Salomon, *Global Responsibility for Human Rights, World Poverty and the Development of International Law* (Oxford University Press, Oxford, 2007), pp. 129–132.
41 Report of the Working Group on the Right to Development. 7th session (conclusions) E/CN.4/2006/26 (22 February 2006), para. 59.

acting in violation of this obligation if it did not use the revenues made available to move as expeditiously as possible towards that goal.[42]

Invoking the right to development as having to guide the negotiation and conclusion either of investment treaties or of HGAs related to particular projects also has a broader significance, that goes beyond requiring that such instruments do not bring about, or favour, the violation of specific rights. The right to development imposes something more: that the agreement serve the development of the country as a whole, rather than only the specific groups that stand to benefit from its implementation. As such, the right to development brings about a fundamental change of perspective in how HGAs in particular are considered, including concession agreements for the exploitation of certain natural resources, such as minerals or forests. All too often, such agreements are seen as private contracts, in which efficiency is promoted by one party (the State) ceding to another the right to exploit certain resources for which that other party (the investor) disposes of superior knowledge or technology, and for its own profit, against a remuneration that contributes to public revenue and allows the government to discharge certain duties towards its population. But because such agreements are seen as private contracts, they are concluded behind closed doors, and their legitimacy is primarily assessed based on the fact that they suit the interests of both negotiating parties. Instead, once we acknowledge the relevance of the right to development to the negotiation and conclusion of HGAs, the implication is that such agreements should be discussed in open fora, that requirements of public deliberation and transparency that are generally associated with public regulation apply, and that the legitimacy of HGAs should depend on whether they promote the general welfare.[43] It is to these procedural implications that we turn next.

6.2.2 *The right to information and access to remedies*

Although they have procedural implications, in that they imply a requirement to adopt a participatory approach to economic development, the rights of peoples to self-determination and to development primarily assert a substantive standard: they indicate the objectives that development should serve. Other norms are more directly procedural: they serve to define a set of conditions that must be present if participation is to be meaningful, and if governments are to be held accountable to their populations.

---

42 Committee on Economic, Social and Cultural Rights, General Comment No. 12 (1999): The right to adequate food, E/C.12/1999/5, paras 15–16. On the interpretation of this requirement under the Covenant, see further Committee on Economic, Social and Cultural Rights, An Evaluation Of The Obligation To Take Steps To The 'Maximum of Available Resources' Under An Optional Protocol To The Covenant – Statement, UN Doc. E/C. 12/2007/1 (21 September 2007).

43 See in particular N. Miranda, 'Concession Agreements: From Private Contracts to Public Policy', *Yale L.J.*, vol. 107 (2007), p. 510.

Regional human rights bodies have addressed the rights of communities to information on projects that will affect them.[44] For example, after Chile was alleged to have refused to provide certain petitioners with all the information they requested[45] on a forestry company and a deforestation project worth $180 million US dollars project that they considered to be detrimental to the environment and to the sustainable development of the country, the Inter-American Commission on Human Rights took the view that this refusal occurred without the State 'providing any valid justification under Chilean law', in the absence of an effective judicial remedy; in addition, the petitioners 'were not ensured the rights of access to information and to judicial protection, and there were no mechanisms guaranteeing the right of access to public information'. The Inter-American Court of Human Rights agreed. It noted that Article 13 of the American Convention on Human Rights, which guarantees the right to freedom of thought and expression,

> protects the right of the individual to receive such information and the positive obligation of the State to provide it, so that the individual may have access to such information or receive an answer that includes a justification when, for any reason permitted by the Convention, the State is allowed to restrict access to the information in a specific case. The information should be provided without the need to prove direct interest or personal involvement in order to obtain it, except in cases in which a legitimate restriction is applied. The delivery of information to an individual can, in turn, permit it to circulate in society, so that the latter can become acquainted with it, have access to it, and assess it. In this way, the right to freedom of thought and expression includes the protection of the right of access to State-held information . . .[46]

The Court emphasized the relationship between the right of access to information held by the State and democratic accountability:

> [T]he State's actions should be governed by the principles of disclosure and transparency in public administration that enable all persons subject to its jurisdiction to exercise the democratic control of those actions, and so that

---

44 For a discussion, see L.E. Peterson, 'Human Rights and Bilateral Investment Treaties: Mapping the Role of Human Rights Law Within Investor-state Arbitration', *Rights & Democracy* (Ottawa, 2009), p. 42.

45 The request was filed with the Foreign Investment Committee, a public agency tasked with promoting investment and negotiating with foreign investors the conditions of their arrival. Under Chilean law, this Committee is 'the only body authorized, in representation of the State of Chile, to authorize the entry of foreign capital under Decree Law [No. 600] and to establish the terms and conditions of the respective contracts'. It is linked to the President of the Republic through the Ministry of Economy, Development and Reconstruction.

46 *Claude Reyes et al. v Chile*, Judgment of 19 September 2006, Series C No. 151, para. 77.

they can question, investigate and consider whether public functions are being performed adequately. Access to State-held information of public interest can permit participation in public administration through the social control that can be exercised through such access.[47]

As this case makes clear, access to information[48] may be seen as instrumental to the exercise of democratic accountability or, where violations are thought to have occurred, of remedies. Both of these prerogatives, however, are particularly difficult to exercise where they are used in order to reduce the margin of appreciation of the Executive in the negotiation of investment treaties, or when they serve to challenge the consequences of the presence of foreign investors for the local communities affected, in the context of the negotiation of HGAs.

Consider first the case of investment treaties. Such treaties are typically negotiated by the Executive, generally on the basis of model agreements that settle most of the non-essential issues. In practice, there is little or no scrutiny of parliamentary assemblies of such agreements, and no involvement of civil society organizations. It may be argued that the absence of a public debate when such agreements are concluded is in tension with the right of every citizen to take part in the conduct of public affairs, as recognized under the International Covenant on Civil and Political Rights, and that such debate in principle should be conducted by freely elected parliamentary assemblies for approval to ensure that the free expression of the will of the electors will be fully respected.[49] The Declaration on the Right to Development is also explicit on this requirement, since it stipulates that 'States have the right and the duty to formulate appropriate national development policies that aim at the constant improvement of the well-being of the entire population and of all individuals, on the basis of their active, free and meaningful participation in development and in the fair distribution of the benefits resulting therefrom'.[50]

Consider next how most HGAs are negotiated and concluded. In addition to whatever investment treaties may provide, most important investments, particularly in the extractive industry sector, are the subject of investment agreements, negotiated between the foreign investor and the host State government. Such agreements, too, are often concluded outside any form of public scrutiny. Governments often seem to prefer confidentiality, in part because they fear that too much transparency would allow groups of citizens to veto agreements that would be in the interest of the country as a whole (although

---

47 *Claude Reyes et al. v Chile*, op. cit., para. 86.

48 See also Human Rights Committee, General Comment 34. Article 19: freedoms of expression and opinion, UN Doc. CCPR/C/GC/34 (12 Sept. 2011), paras 18 and 19.

49 See Guiding principles on human rights impact assessments of trade and investment agreements, Addendum to the Report by the Special Rapporteur on the right to food to the nineteenth session of the Human Rights Council, UN doc. A/HRC/19/59/Add.5, Principle 1, commentary 1.2. (referring to Art. 25 of the International Covenant on Civil and Political Rights, cited above).

50 Article 2, para. 3.

negatively affecting some groups of citizens), in part – and more generally perhaps – because they prefer to decide how to spend the revenues from the deal which is concluded. Yet, disclosure of the terms of the contract in order to allow for public scrutiny presents a number of advantages. First, being transparent about the negotiations generally strengthens the bargaining position of governments, who could invoke the fact that this would run counter to the expectations of civil society or to those of international donors, in order to refuse to make concessions to the investor.[51] Second, by disclosing the terms of the agreement and ensuring adequate transparency, the State and the investor can reduce suspicion regarding the fairness of the contract terms and guard against unrealistic demands. Conversely, lack of disclosure can contribute to a loss of trust among interested individuals and communities in the project and even between the parties. These are among the reasons why, in proposing a set of Principles on responsible contracts in 2011, the Special Representative of the UN Secretary-General on the issue of human rights and transnational corporations and other business enterprises included a principle on transparency and disclosure of contract terms, according to which 'The contract's terms should be disclosed, and the scope and duration of exceptions to such disclosure should be based on compelling justifications' (Principle 10).[52]

In the absence of adequate scrutiny prior to the conclusion of investment treaties or HGAs, access to remedies *post hoc*, for the communities who are negatively impacted by such agreements once they enter their implementation phase, might be seen as a substitute. Access to effective remedies is a general principle of human rights law, and it is one that is referred to both in the context of human rights impact assessments of investment agreements and in the context of the negotiation of HGAs by the recent attempts by the Human Rights Council Special Procedures to bridge the areas of human rights law and investment law: the Guiding Principles on human rights impact assessments of trade and investment agreements note that, while States have a broad margin of appreciation as to how to assess the compatibility of trade and investment agreements they negotiate with their pre-existing human rights obligations,

---

51 See P. Rosenblum and S. Maples, *Contracts Confidential: Ending Secret Deals in the Extractive Industries*, Washington, DC, Revenue Watch Institute, 2009. Online. Available HTTP <http://www.eisourcebook.org/548_RosenblumContractsConfidentialEndingSecret DealsintheExtractiveIndustry.html> (accessed 25 July 2012); and International Monetary Fund, *Guide on Resource Revenue Transparency*, Washington, DC, 2007, at 14 ('Little by way of strategic advantage thus seems to be lost through publication of contracts. Indeed, it could be argued that the obligation to publish contracts should in fact strengthen the hand of the government in negotiations, since the obligation to disclose the outcome to the legislature and the general public increases pressure on the government to negotiate a good deal').

52 Report of the Special Representative of the Secretary-General on the Issue of Human Rights and Transnational Corporations and Other Business Enterprises, J. Ruggie 'Principles for Responsible Contracts: Integrating the Management of Human Rights Risks into State-Investor Contract Negotiations: Guidance for Negotiators', 25 May 2011, UN Doc. A/HRC/17/31/Add.3 (paras 60–64).

'as the issue [of compatibility] is ultimately a legal one, . . . courts may . . . have a role to play, for instance in hearing claims, based on the conclusions of the human rights impact assessment, as to whether the Executive may sign the agreement or should obtain further improvements, or as to whether it should denounce it';[53] and the Principles for Responsible Contracts note that, while individuals and communities impacted by project activities should have access to effective non-judicial grievance mechanisms, 'such mechanisms should not impede access to remedy through judicial or other non-judicial processes available to individuals and communities impacted by the project'.[54]

However, at this level too, a number of problems arise. Investment treaties protect investors from the adoption of regulations that amount to indirect expropriation, and situations may therefore arise in which the rights of investors are pitted against those of the individuals or communities whose rights are negatively affected by the investment – which is why the Guiding Principles on Business and Human Rights insist that 'States should maintain adequate domestic policy space to meet their human rights obligations when pursuing business-related policy objectives with other States or business enterprises, for instance through investment treaties or contracts'. The Special Representative of the UN Secretary-General on the issue of human rights and transnational corporations and other business enterprises notes in his commentary that:

> Economic agreements concluded by States, either with other States or with business enterprises – such as bilateral investment treaties, free-trade agreements or contracts for investment projects – create economic opportunities for States. But they can also affect the domestic policy space of governments. For example, the terms of international investment agreements may constrain States from fully implementing new human rights legislation, or put them at risk of binding international arbitration if they do so. Therefore, States should ensure that they retain adequate policy and regulatory ability to protect human rights under the terms of such agreements, while providing the necessary investor protection.[55]

53 Guiding principles on human rights impact assessments of trade and investment agreements, Addendum to the Report by the Special Rapporteur on the right to food to the nineteenth session of the Human Rights Council, UN doc. A/HRC/19/59/Add.5, Principle 4, commentary 4.3.

54 Report of the Special Representative of the Secretary-General on the Issue of Human Rights and Transnational Corporations and Other Business Enterprises, J. Ruggie 'Principles for Responsible Contracts: Integrating the Management of Human Rights Risks into State-Investor Contract Negotiations: Guidance for Negotiators', 25 May 2011, UN Doc. A/HRC/17/31/Add.3, para. 55.

55 Report of the Special Representative of the Secretary-General on the Issue of Human Rights and Transnational Corporations and Other Business Enterprises, J. Ruggie Guiding Principles on Business and Human Rights, UN doc. A/HRC/17/31 (21 March 2011), principle 9. The Principles were endorsed by the Human Rights Council in its Resolution 17/4, UN Doc. A/HRC/RES/17/4 (16 June 2011).

Similarly, the Committee on Economic, Social and Cultural Rights has urged that human rights principles and obligations be fully integrated in negotiations related, for instance, to investment treaties.[56] The Sub-commission on Promotion and Protection of Human Rights has asserted the centrality and primacy of human rights obligations in all areas, including international trade and investment.[57]

As also implied by the comment from the Special Representative of the UN Secretary-General on the issue of business and human rights, quoted above, similar problems to those affecting investment treaties restricting the ability of the State to protect human rights may also affect HGAs concluded between the investor and the host State. Such agreements are typically 'internationalized' in that they provide that the law applicable to the investment is not municipal law alone, but either international law (especially the general principles of law as a source of international law[58]), or municipal law 'frozen' at the time the investment agreement is concluded.[59] The purpose of such 'internationalization',

56 See e.g. Statement of the Committee on Economic, Social and Cultural Rights to the Third Ministerial Conference of the World Trade Organization, Seattle, 30 November–3 December 1999 (E/C.12/1999/9); Committee on Economic, Social and Cultural Rights, General Comment No. 12 (1999), *The right to adequate food (Art. 11)*, E/C.12/1999/5, at paras 19 and 36 ('States parties should, in international agreements whenever relevant, ensure that the right to adequate food is given due attention'); Committee on Economic, Social and Cultural Rights, General Comment No. 14 (2000), *The right to the highest attainable standard of health (Article 12 of the International Covenant on Economic, Social and Cultural Rights)*, E/C.12/2000/4 (2000), para. 39 ('In relation to the conclusion of other international agreements, States parties should take steps to ensure that these instruments do not adversely impact upon the right to health'); Committee on Economic, Social and Cultural Rights, General Comment No. 15 (2002), *The right to water (Arts. 11 and 12 of the International Covenant on Economic, Social and Cultural Rights)*, UN Doc. E/C.12/2002/11 (26 November 2002), paras 31 and 35–36 ('States parties should ensure that the right to water is given due attention in international agreements and, to that end, should consider the development of further legal instruments. With regard to the conclusion and implementation of other international and regional agreements, States parties should take steps to ensure that these instruments do not adversely impact upon the right to water. Agreements concerning trade liberalization should not curtail or inhibit a country's capacity to ensure the full realization of the right to water').
57 Sub-Commission on Promotion and Protection of Human Rights, Human Rights as the Primary Objective of Trade, Investment and Financial Policy, UN Doc. E/CN.4/Sub.2/RES/1998/12 (1998); Report of the Sub-Commission on its 50th Sess., UN ESCOR, 50th Sess., at 39, UN Doc. E/CN.4/Sub.2/1998/45 (1998).
58 Statute of the International Court of Justice, Art. 38, para. 1, c.
59 An alternative to either reference to the general principles of law as part of international law or to municipal law as it was at the time of the internationalized contract, is to include in the agreement an 'economic equilibrium' clause ensuring that the investor will be compensated for any economic loss that would result from a regulatory change affecting the investment. See generally for an overview of such clauses and their impact on the ability for the host State to protect human rights, A. Sheppard and A. Crockett, 'Stabilisation Clauses: A Threat to Sustainable Development?', in M. C. Cordonier-Segger, M. Gehring, and A. Newcombe (eds), *Sustainable Development in World Investment Law*, The Hague: Kluwer Law International, 2010, pp. 333–350; and *Stabilization Clauses and*

as implicitly noted by Professor R.-J. Dupuy, acting as the sole arbitrator in the well-known case of *Texaco Overseas Petroleum Co. v Libya*,[60] is essentially to insulate the investor from the risks that would result if the investment were to be subject to the changing municipal law, which the host State – one of the parties to the investment agreement – would be allowed to modify at will. There is a logic to this: a contract that one of the parties can change unilaterally is not binding in fact on that party. But the consequence is that it may be difficult for the groups aggrieved by the particular investment project to file claims against the investor, since the courts may be unwilling or unable to extend the protection of municipal law to the claimants, as this might engage the responsibility of the host State before international arbitral tribunals.[61]

One might argue, of course, that where an investor seeks compensation for the losses inflicted as a result of a measure, whether or not of a regulatory nature, adopted by the host State, that State should be allowed to put forward its human rights obligations – and the rights of the population under its jurisdiction – in order to avoid having to pay compensation. Indeed, it might be said, the 'fair and equitable treatment' owed to the investor should not be defined solely in the interest of the investor, but calls instead for a balancing of the interests involved, including those negatively affected by the investment;[62] and the same requirement is implicit in the notion of arbitrariness that serves to circumscribe prohibited forms of expropriation. It is true of course that the protection of the rights affected by the investment would then risk being made to depend on the State invoking them, as it is the State which is the defending party in State–investor disputes submitted to arbitral tribunals. As noted by Francioni, that not only 'reproduces the paternalistic model of governmental espousal of private claims which does little to advance the individual right of access to justice'; it also would not fit the typical situation, where a government has made a choice – to conclude a particular investment treaty or to allow a particular investment project to move forward – 'against the wishes of special segments of the population'.[63] However, this is, in part, compensated by the increased role that non-governmental organizations acting as *amici curiae* are allowed to play in the adjudicatory process before arbitral tribunals. In addition, unless another law has been designated applicable by the parties, the arbitral

Human Rights. A research project conducted for IFC (International Finance Corporation) and the UN Special Representative of the Secretary-General on business and human rights (by Andrea Shemberg), 11 March 2008.

60 *Journal de Droit international*, vol. 104 (1977), p. 350, translated in 17 ILM 1 (1978).

61 For a detailed discussion, see R. Suda, 'The Effect of Bilateral Investment Treaties on Human Rights Enforcement and Realization', in O. De Schutter (ed.), *Transnational Corporations and Human Rights*, Oxford and Portland: Hart Publishing, 2006, pp. 73–160.

62 F. Francioni, 'Access to Justice, Denial of Justice, and International Investment Law', in P-M. Dupuy, F. Francioni, and E-U. Petersmann (eds), *Human Rights in Investment Law and Arbitration*, Oxford: Oxford University Press, 2009, pp. 63–96, at pp. 72–73.

63 F. Francioni, 'Access to Justice, Denial of Justice, and International Investment Law', op. cit., at 72.

tribunal may have to take into account, as the law applicable to the dispute, not only the investment treaty or the investment agreement concerned, but also other relevant rules of international law.[64] It cannot be excluded, therefore, that international human rights law will be invoked in the context of an investment dispute, even where the respondent government would be unwilling to raise the argument *sua sponte*.

Whether or not such an evolution will occur, bridging the gap between investment law and human rights law, arbitral tribunals in general have not given much weight to this argument. There are exceptions to the rule, of course, to the extent that a 'clean hands' doctrine, denying the investor protection were that investor to act in violation of human rights, has sometimes been alluded to by arbitrators.[65] But the general attitude has been to dismiss arguments based on human rights as irrelevant to investment disputes. This has been the case, at least, when the argument was that the obligations imposed on the host State under investment treaties or HGAs were such that they were an obstacle to that State discharging its duties towards its own population.

For instance, in *Azurix v Argentina,* a US company had obtained for its Argentinean subsidiary ABA a 30-year concession to provide potable water and sewage services in the Province of Buenos Aires, investing about US$550 million in the project. After the Province terminated the concession in 2002, Azurix initiated an ICSID arbitration against Argentina seeking approximately US$600 million in compensation. The Tribunal considered, however, that the actions by the Province had been unreasonable and politicized, leading to violations of the United States–Argentina bilateral investment treaty (BIT). In

64 According to Art. 42.1 of the ICSID Convention: 'The Tribunal shall decide a dispute in accordance with such rules of law as may be agreed by the parties (or in the absence of such agreement) the law of the contacting State party to the dispute (including its rules on the conflict of laws) *and such rules of international law as may be applicable*' (emphasis added). Under Art. 35.1 of the UNCITRAL Arbitration Rules, the Tribunal 'shall apply the law which it determines to be appropriate', and arbitral tribunals consider that 'international law generally applies' (*Eastern Sugar v Czech Republic*, SCC Case No. 088/2004, Partial Award, 27 March 2007, para. 196). Therefore, submission to international arbitral tribunals not only removes the dispute from the sole province of the municipal law applicable in the host State: this 'internationalization' also means that the body of international law rules may apply to the dispute, to the extent that such rules are relevant. As regards the interpretation of investment treaties, this may be justified on the basis of the prescription of Article 32, para. 3, c, of the Vienna Convention on the Law of Treaties, according to which the interpretation of a treaty must take into account 'any relevant rules of international law applicable in the relations between the parties'.
65 See *Phoenix Action v Czech Republic*, ICSID Case No. ARB/06/5, Award, 15 April 2009, para. 78 ('. . . the ICSID Convention's jurisdictional requirements – as well as those of the BIT – cannot be read and interpreted in isolation from public international law, and its general principles. To take an extreme example, nobody would suggest that ICSID protection should be granted to investments made in violation of the most fundamental rules of protection of human rights, like investments made in pursuance of torture or genocide or in support of slavery or trafficking of human organs' (Brigitte Stern, chair of the panel)).

the course of the proceedings, Argentina raised what it presented as 'a conflict between the BIT and human rights treaties that protect consumers' rights', arguing that such a conflict 'must be resolved in favour of human rights because the consumers' public interest must prevail over the private interest of service provider'.[66] The argument was given short thrift by the Tribunal, which noted that it 'fails to understand the incompatibility in the specifics of the instant case. The services to consumers continued to be provided without interruption by ABA during five months after the termination notice and through the new provincial utility after the transfer of service'.[67] In another case, Siemens had been awarded a contract for the setting up and management of a system for the processing of personal data in Argentina, *inter alia*, for immigration control purposes. After the contract was revoked, it filed a claim for compensation. Argentina drew to the Tribunal's attention 'that the constitutional reform of 1994 recognized a number of international instruments on human rights to have constitutional rank' and that 'the human rights so incorporated in the Constitution would be disregarded by recognizing the property rights asserted by the Claimant given the social and economic conditions of Argentina'.[68] The argument was, apparently, that the contract had to be renegotiated, in order for the country to be able to continue to provide basic public services to its citizens. This argument again was set aside by the Tribunal: 'The Tribunal considers that, without the benefit of further elaboration and substantiation by the parties, it is not an argument that, *prima facie*, bears any relationship to the merits of this case.'[69]

At the same time, these cases should certainly not be taken as decisive. In both cases, the conflict between the human rights duties of the State towards its population and its duties towards the investor appeared to be quite weak, and human rights were invoked in conditions that the tribunals concerned, for understandable reasons, could easily dismiss. But another major limitation of this route is that it is not one that is open to the direct victims: the individuals or communities negatively affected by investment projects. The claims of such victims are often barred before domestic courts. And because they have no direct access to investment tribunals, recourse to regional human rights courts has often been shown to be the most effective route. The 2001 case of *The Social and Economic Rights Action Center and the Center for Economic and Social Rights v Nigeria* presented to the African Commission on Human and Peoples' Rights provides one illustration, as we have seen.[70] Another equally well-known

66 *Azurix v Argentina,* ICSID Case No. ARB/01/12, Award, 14 July 2006, para. 254.
67 Ibid., para. 261. See also *Azurix Corp. v Argentine Republic* (ICSID Case No. Arb/01/12), Annulment Proceeding, Decision of the Ad Hoc Committee, Sept. 1, 2009 (rejecting the claim by Argentina that the level of compensation awarded was excessively high).
68 *Siemens v Republic of Argentina*, ICSID Case No. ARB/02/08, Award, 6 February 2007, para. 75.
69 Ibid., para. 79.
70 See above, text corresponding to notes 29–31.

example is the case of *Awas Tingni v Nicaragua*, presented to the Inter-American Court of Human Rights, which resulted in the Nicaraguan government having to annul a logging concession which it has conceded to a foreign company on land that the Awas Tingni community claimed as its ancestral land subject to traditional tenure.[71] These cases are promising, as they demonstrate the willingness of regional human rights bodies to impose on the State a duty to protect human rights even against foreign investors – and whether or not investors claim rights protected under an investment treaty or a HGA concluded by the State.[72] However, reliance on human rights courts does not address satisfactorily the issue of fragmentation of international law: it is only a partial answer to the problem of conflicting obligations imposed on the host State, or to incentives pointing in the opposite direction.

6.3 Implementing the framework: dilemmas in decision-making

The normative framework derived from international human rights law, as has been described above, raises a number of issues that go beyond the question of how it relates to investment law or the question of how the rights to participation or information, or of access to remedies, can be exercised in practice by communities who often lack the effective capacity to do so.[73] Implementing the framework is not only difficult for practical reasons. It also raises a number of questions of principle. Indeed, the recommendations presented to governments in recent years concerning the conciliation of their human rights obligations with the management of FDI is the source of dilemmas that have often been underestimated in discussions concerning the relationship between investment law and human rights law. Two interrelated problems in particular deserve to be mentioned: they are how to manage tradeoffs when the arrival of FDI creates winners as well as losers, and how to reconcile the participation of local communities in determining the conditions according to which investment should be allowed to proceed with other values.

---

71 *Case of Mayana (Sumo) Awas Tingni Community v Nicaragua*, Inter-American Court of Human Rights (ser. C) No. 124 (judgment of 15 June 2005).

72 Indeed, the Inter-American Court of Human Rights has noted that the enforcement of bilateral investment or commercial treaties should always be compatible with the American Convention on Human Rights (signed in San Jose, Costa Rica, 22 November 1969, and entered into force on 18 July 1978, (1969) 9 ILM 101), indicating that the primacy of human rights obligations followed from the special nature of human rights treaties: the American Convention on Human Rights, the Court noted, 'is a multilateral *treaty* on *human rights* that *stands in a class* of its own' (Inter-American Court of Human Rights, *Case of the Sawhoyamaxa Indigenous Community v Paraguay*, Judgment of 29 March 2006, Series C No. 146, para. 140, emphasis in original).

73 See e.g. O. De Schutter and P. Rosenblum, 'Large-scale Investments in Farmland: The Regulatory Challenge', *Yearbook of International Investment Law and Policy*, chap. 14 (2011), pp. 563–610.

The problem of tradeoffs is perhaps the most difficult problem that domestic bodies will face when seeking to reconcile the use of investment agreements and HGAs, providing security to the investor, with the human rights obligations of the host State – including its duty to ensure the right to development. The problem can be simply stated: the arrival of FDI in one country creates a range of employment opportunities, may benefit the local economy by certain linkages, and can bring benefits to the government by the increased tax revenues it will lead to and by the economic growth it will result in. But it may also create a range of negative impacts. Yet, it would be neither realistic nor desirable to allow only investment projects that represent a Pareto-improvement (i.e., in which the situation of no one is worsened as a result). Transition costs are an almost unavoidable part of the arrival of FDI: in the short term at least, and prior to the adoption of compensatory measures, there will therefore be losers. Communities may be deprived ofaccess to the natural resources on which they depend or have their livelihoods disrupted by the investment project,[74] or may even have to be displaced. Workers, both self-employed and employees, may suffer from increased competition on the domestic markets – particularly as FDI is often seen as a means to overcome trade barriers or the costs, including risks linked to currency exchange variations, implied in exporting goods to these markets. How are the benefits and the costs to be evaluated? How can the tradeoff be managed?

6.3.1 Cost–benefit analysis: the economic valuation of pros and cons of investment

Cost–benefit analyses, the classic response to such tradeoff problems, are hardly a suitable means to approach their human rights implications. The problem is not only that cost–benefit analysis substitutes a consequentialist logic for a deontological logic, which may be incompatible with the very significance of fundamental rights as prerogatives that cannot be reduced to their 'value' to the individual, as assessed in monetary terms. Nor is the only problem one of 'incommensurability' (i.e., the difficulty of assessing against one common metric interests as different as the interest of the country as a whole in economic growth, the interest of some members of the local communities in benefiting from the employment opportunities resulting from the arrival of the foreign investor, or the interest of other members of those communities not to lose their access to the natural resources on which they depend).[75] These are real problems that largely serve to explain the scepticism of many towards the reliance on cost–benefit analysis as a means to guide public choices. But other problems

74 See e.g. O. De Schutter, 'The Green Rush: The Race for Farmland and the Rights of Land Users', *Harvard International Law Journal*, vol. 52(2) (2011), pp. 503–559.
75 See, *inter alia*, R. Chang (ed.), *Incommensurability, Incomparability and Practical Reason*, Cambridge, MA: Harvard University Press, 1997.

are more practical in nature: they concern the very feasibility of relying on this method to make the necessary tradeoffs.

First, cost–benefit analysis gives a premium to those who already have the most. It results in this regressive outcome because of the very methods it relies on in order to value the interests (or rights) at stake. The 'revealed preference' approach infers valuations from observable market behaviour. The 'hypothetical markets' method relies on surveys in which people are asked how much they would be willing to pay for a particular benefit, or how much they would be asking in compensation for a particular loss. However, both 'revealed preference' and 'hypothetical markets' methods fail to take into account that the willingness of the individual to pay for a certain advantage is a function, not only of the importance of that advantage to that individual (the extent to which that advantage may contribute to the self-fulfilment of that individual), but also to his or her ability to pay (or the economic necessities and other priorities for the individual with limited resources).[76] In other terms, in such decision-making processes, those who have the highest incomes will in fact exercise a disproportionate influence on the outcome.

Of course, in theory, this could be compensated by adequate transfer mechanisms: for instance, if the better-off persons would be willing to pay 1,000 for a particular industrial plant to be built (for instance, because this will allow them, as highly qualified white-collar workers, to obtain well-paid positions on the plant), and manage to impose a decision in favour of the plant being built against the opposition of the worst-off persons (who would be happy to receive 100 in compensation), a transfer of a sum X (between 100 and 1,000) from the better-off to the worst-off would be Pareto-efficient, improving the position of all without reducing the welfare of any.[77] But that's theory: in practice, particularly in weakly governed jurisdictions, such transfers do not take place, not least because the worst-off segments of the populations are often excluded from political decision-making.

Second, such valuations, whether they are 'contingent valuations' based on surveys or estimates of the 'willingness to pay' in the absence of markets, or whether they are based on the preferences exhibited by economic agents through the choices they make in the market, have been demonstrated to be strongly baseline-dependent, in the sense that the position already occupied by any individual will shape his or her estimation of the value of any regulatory benefits or sacrifices. Richard Thaler, in particular, has highlighted the importance of 'loss aversion' in this regard, by which he referred to the tendency

76 On the difference between actual consent and hypothetical consent and the resulting critique of the willingness-to-pay approaches in cost–benefit analysis, see H. M. Hurd, 'Justifiably Punishing the Justified', *Michigan L. Rev.*, vol. 90 (1992), pp. 2203 ff., at p. 2305; and M. Adler, 'Incommensurability and Cost–Benefit Analysis', *University of Pennsylvania L. Rev.*, vol. 146 (1998), pp. 1371 ff.

77 See R. H. Frank, 'Why Is Cost–Benefit Analysis So Controversial?', *Journal of Legal Studies*, vol. 29 (2000), pp. 913–930.

of agents to attach a greater value to what they risk losing than to what they risk not gaining from any particular policy change – for instance, from the arrival of an investor.[78] The method therefore has a built-in bias in favour of the status quo, or of the preservation of the existing set of entitlements.

At the very least, these weaknesses inherent to cost–benefit analysis justify the position of sceptics who take the view that decisions as to whether the gains from any particular change are sufficiently important to compensate for the losses should not be seen as purely economic valuations based on the methods outlined above.

Of course, an alternative approach would be to allow such decisions to be made by the parties concerned themselves, through negotiations that the State would be facilitating. It is true that in a world in which efficiency in the use of resources was all that mattered, and in which the transaction costs would be equal to zero, there would be strong arguments in favour of resources being allocated through a bargaining process between the parties concerned – for this would lead to the most efficient allocation of resources, and all parties by definition would gain, since they would otherwise not have consented to whichever transfer may have taken place.[79] But in the real world, resources such as land and water are not just economic assets, which should go to the highest bidder because of a presumption that those willing to pay the most will use it most efficiently: for in the real world, such resources are not reducible to their economic value, but access to such resources may also be an element of social citizenship or be constitutive of the identity of the community; those who are ready to pay the most to acquire them may do so for purely speculative purposes, rather than in order to exploit the resources most efficiently; and, most importantly, bargaining processes may be fraught with abuse because of the significant imbalances of power and negotiation skills between the parties.[80] Moreover, economic arguments in favour of a bargaining process in order to allow the parties to discover the most efficient allocation of resources through the process of negotiation presuppose a pre-defined allocation of rights, a 'baseline of pre-existing entitlements', in the jargon of economists, that it is the responsibility of the State to define.

---

78 R. Thaler, 'Toward a Positive Theory of Consumer Choice', *Journal of Economic Behavior & Organization*, vol. 1 (1980), pp. 39–60. See also E. Hoffman and M. L. Spitzer, 'Willingness to Pay vs. Willingness to Accept: Legal and Economic Implications', *Washington University Law Quarterly*, vol. 71 (1993), pp. 59 and ff.; M. Adler, 'Incommensurability and Cost–Benefit Analysis', op. cit., at pp. 1396–1398.

79 See generally R. H. Coase, 'The Problem of Social Cost', *Journal of Law and Economics*, vol. 3 (1960), p. 1.

80 These arguments are relevant, for instance, to discussions concerning titling schemes and the creation of markets for land rights, as a means to allocate access to land: see O. De Schutter, 'The Green Rush: The Race for Farmland and the Rights of Land Users', op. cit., at pp. 526–532.

6.3.2 The procedural approach: the role of participation in managing investment

The Guiding Principles on Human Rights Impact Assessments of Trade and Investments address the question of tradeoffs through a procedural lens. This was considered to represent the most adequate way to combine an approach based on human rights with adequate deference to domestic level decision-making processes: there is no single way to balance advantages and disadvantages across different groups, according to this approach, and the key concern should therefore be that the procedure that was followed in arriving at that balance complies with certain requirements.

Principle 6 of the Guiding Principles states that human rights impact assessments should be used to determine 'both the positive and negative impacts of investment agreements, in order to strike the right balance between competing priorities'.[81] It then formulates a number of conditions, including that (i) the tradeoffs should be decided through open and democratic processes, informed by a human rights impact assessment of the investment agreement;[82] (ii) priorities should involve effective participation of all stakeholders, including the poorest and most vulnerable segments of the population; (iii) however tradeoffs are addressed, they should not result in or exacerbate unequal and discriminatory outcomes, as this would violate the principles of equality and non-discrimination, they should not worsen the economic situation of vulnerable groups, and they should never result in a deprivation of the ability of people to enjoy their basic human rights; (iv) any tradeoff that results in a retrogressive level of protection of a human right should be treated as highly suspect. The document also notes that 'to the fullest extent possible, solutions should be found under which losses and gains are shared across groups, rather

---

81 Guiding Principles on Human Rights Impact Assessments of Trade and Investment Agreements, cited above, at paras 6.1 to 6.7. While these Guiding Principles concern the negotiation and conclusion of investment agreements, including both investment treaties and HGAs, the impacts of the arrival of FDI may be difficult to anticipate at the stage of the conclusion of a treaty facilitating investment flows; in most cases, these impacts can only be addressed when particular investment projects are defined: it is at that level that the problem of tradeoffs will therefore have to be dealt with.

82 Indeed, the more the national or local deliberative processes are open, inclusive and transparent, the more they will be trusted to achieve the right balance between conflicting priorities. The Committee on Economic, Social and Cultural Rights has stated that when assessing whether a State party has taken 'reasonable steps to the maximum of its available resources to achieve progressively the realization of the provisions of the Covenant', as required under Art. 2(1) of the International Covenant on Economic, Social and Cultural Rights, the Committee 'places great importance on transparent and participative decision-making processes at the national level' (Committee on Economic, Social and Cultural Rights, An Evaluation Of The Obligation To Take Steps To The 'Maximum of Available Resources' Under An Optional Protocol To The Covenant – Statement, UN Doc. E/C.12/2007/1, 21 September 2007, para. 11). This illustrates the interplay between the substantive and procedural dimensions implicated in assessing whether investment agreements comply with the requirements of human rights.

than concentrated on one group. This suggests the need to identify mechanisms, such as mitigating measures, ensuring that those benefiting from the agreement will at least in part compensate those who are negatively affected, and that the latter will be protected'.

This approach presents two major advantages: it is grounded in existing human rights law; and it does not pre-empt the outcome of deliberations that should take place at the national and local levels. In practice, however, there are difficulties involved in implementing these recommendations. It is increasingly agreed that investment projects should only be allowed to proceed with appropriate participation of the communities affected. But how to balance the needs of the country as a whole, as determined at the national level, and the needs of the local communities, most directly affected by the arrival of the investment? International human rights law is gradually moving towards imposing a requirement that the communities whose access to natural resources is affected by the investment project give their 'free, prior and informed consent' to the project for it to be allowed to proceed. But under which conditions should a veto power be recognized for the local communities, since this is, in effect, the result of this evolution? Conversely, if a determination is to be made at the national level, without a veto right being recognized for the local communities concerned, how can it be ensured that the rights and interests of these communities will be effectively taken into accounted and, where rights are concerned, fully respected?

Although these questions cannot be addressed in sufficient detail here, it is important to emphasize the complementarity of the processes that take place at the national level (and which determine the investment policy of the country as a whole) and the processes that take place at the local level (involving the local communities directly affected by the arrival of investment). It is clear that decisions cannot be made centrally without ensuring that the rights of the local communities are fully respected, and their interests taken into account: indeed, that is the very purpose both of human rights impact assessments being prepared, and of ensuring that the communities concerned have a right to participate in the decision-making process, to seek and obtain information, and to seek remedies against any decision affecting them. But it should be equally clear that, for local processes to be effective (i.e., for the local communities directly affected by the investment project to be able to truly express their preferences) a national framework for investment is required.

The reason for this is not only that the rights of the local communities should be protected under domestic law in order for these communities to be in a position that allows them to exercise effective bargaining power in their discussions with the investor. It is also that the choices made by one community cannot be analysed or understood in isolation from the choices made by the other communities in the same jurisdiction. Consider two communities, A and B, within the same country, who are both confronted with the question of whether a particular investment project should be encouraged. Suppose that each community is proposed a choice between (i) refusing the investment project, and thus avoiding any risks resulting from the arrival of investment, and (ii) hosting an investment project, from which it would capture certain benefits, but with the attendant risks. In the absence of adequate safeguards against risk, the community will be relatively risk-averse. The choice of each community will therefore go to the least risky option – the first – unless the benefits expected from the investment are valued even higher than the level at which the risk is valued. If, for example, the absence of risk is valued at 1,000, and the benefits to be expected from the arrival of the investor are valued at 500, the choice of the least risky option (i) is perfectly understandable.

But the choice is changed significantly once we incorporate concerns, within each community, that the other community will fare better if the investment goes to that other community. We may indeed presuppose, as seems reasonable, that where an investor comes into a region, this will lead to a 'cluster effect' in which, thanks to a number of spillovers, both upstream (towards suppliers of materials, local workforce and service providers) and downstream (towards retailers and consumers) the region in which the investment is located will be advantaged in comparison to other regions of the same country.[83] This advantage is in part due to the fact that the benefits linked to the arrival of investment *primarily accrue to the region where the investment is located, which gains disproportionately in comparison to the other regions*: for instance, more resources will go to the region where the investment is located, because of the need to create infrastructure in that region; increased incomes in the region concerned lead to higher public revenues from taxes, allowing a better delivery of public services; suppliers of industrial plants created thanks to foreign investment will benefit from technology transfers, allowing them to improve their competitiveness;[84] and the best-qualified workforce will be attracted to the region concerned. We may assign a value to the premium going to the region where such a cluster emerges (thus draining resources from other regions) at, say, 1,200. Part of this premium corresponds to a loss for the region where the investment does not go: we may assign the value of 800 to that loss, which corresponds to a portion

83 Clusters have been defined as 'networks of production of strongly interdependent firms (including specialized suppliers), knowledge producing agents (universities, research institutes, engineering companies), bridging institutions (brokers, consultants) and customers, linked to each other in a value adding production chain' (Joung Hae Seo, *Regional Innovation System and Industrial Cluster: Its Concept, Policy Issues and Implementation Strategies*, paper prepared for the National Workshop on Sub-national Innovation Systems and Technology Capacity Building Policies to Enhance Competitiveness of SMEs, held in Beijing, China, on 27–30 October 2006, p. 5. Online. Available HTTP <www.unescap.org/tid/mtg/siscbp_seo1.pdf> (last consulted 15 March 2012)). Clusters are one phenomenon that, in his well-known 'national diamond', he uses as a theoretical framework to describe the factors that lead to a nation's competitive advantage, M.E. Porter addresses in his book, *The Competitive Advantage of Nations*, New York: Free Press, 1990. See also J. Bröcker, D. Dohse, and R. Soltwedel (eds), *Innovation Clusters and Interregional Competition*, Springer Verlag, 2003.
84 See e.g. J.-P. MacDuffie and S. Helper, 'Creating Lean Suppliers: Diffusing Lean Production through the Supply Chain', *California Management Review*, vol. 39 (4) (1997): 118–52.

of the advantages gained by the region where the investment does do (not all these advantages gained by this region are lost by the other region, although some are – for instance, the more infrastructure built in one region, the less public budgets will allow the building of infrastructure in another region, and the highly qualified workforce migrating to one region is lost by the other).

The existence of such a premium changes the matrix of the choices open to communities A and B. Deciding in isolation, each community, in our scenario, had more reasons to oppose the investment proposed (which was too risky) than to support it; and each therefore would have opted for the status quo (valued, for instance, at 2,000, including 1,000 that represents the value associated with the absence of risk). But now, the two communities are competing with one other. If community A makes the 'safe' choice of not agreeing to the arrival of the investor, but community B in another region of the country does receive the investment, the rewards of community A are equal to 2,000 (the status quo including the absence of risk) minus 800 (the loss from resources it would otherwise be able to preserve if the region receiving the investment were not attracting such resources), with a net total of 1,200. In that scenario, community B did accept the risks associated with the investment, but the costs of such risks are more than compensated by the additional benefits it receives from being the only region to receive investments: if this premium is 1,200 as we have supposed, the situation of community B is 1,000 (status quo reduced by the risk) + 500 (direct benefits from the investor's arrival) + 1,200 (premium going to the region where the cluster emerges as an indirect benefit from the investor's arrival), with a net total of 2,700.

But if each of the communities, not knowing whether the other community will decide to allow the investment to proceed, agrees to the investment, because of its fear that it will otherwise lose out to the other, the situation of each community is that it will take a risk (representing a loss of 1,000 in comparison to the status quo) that is only partially compensated for by the gains from the investment (valued at 500), and this net loss is not offset by the benefits that would accrue from being a 'cluster region' draining resources from the other parts of the country. In this scenario, the net situation of each community will be valued at 1,500, *less than in the absence of any investment in any of the regions concerned*. In other terms, once a specific premium attaches to the fact that one region of the country attracts an investment (such a premium reflecting the fact that this region will be advantaged in comparison to the other regions having made a different choice), we are faced with a classic prisoners' dilemma, in which the choice that is optimal from the individual point of view of each community is not optimal from the collective point of view of both communities (Table 6.1).

This not only shows the kind of problem that can emerge from valuations that are not context-sensitive, and that do not take into account, in particular, how institutions matter and influence upon choices; it also serves to illustrate the difficulty of having communities make choices independently of the choices made by others. It thus highlights the importance of a framework for investment

Table 6.1 Dilemmas in decision-making

		Community B	
		Does not agree to the investment	Agrees to the investment
Community A	Does not agree to the investment	2,000 for each: collectively optimal	2,700 for B 1,200 for A
	Agrees to the investment	1,200 for B 2,700 for A	1,500 for each: collectively sub-optimal

set at the national level, rather than only at the level of each constituent unit within States, in order to ensure that the benefits of investment are maximized and the potential risks or costs minimized. The objective of such a framework should not only be to ensure that each local community may effectively participate in determining the conditions under which the investment may proceed insofar as it is affected; it should also be to ensure that not all the benefits are captured by the local community, but that other parts of the country may reap part of the benefits. Such a framework should be conceived as redistributive: it should not discourage investment, but should promote a more inclusive national economy rather than the formation of 'clusters' of prosperity co-existing with islands of poverty and under-development, thus at the same time removing an incentive for different regions in the country to pursue beggar-thy-neighbour policies that, ultimately, are self-defeating for the population as a whole.

6.4 Conclusion

A number of initiatives have recently been adopted to ensure that international investment works for the benefit of human rights, not only by ensuring that the arrival of investment will not result in human rights violations, but also by placing an important emphasis on the rights of participation and of information, and on access to remedies.[85] This represents significant progress in comparison to approaches that, in the past, simply prioritized the growth in GDP encouraged by the arrival of FDI, or trusted the determinations made by the host government without requiring that certain procedures be followed that improve transparency in decision making and ensure that the rights and interests of the communities affected by the investment will not be sacrificed in the name of attracting investment to the country.

85 See above, text corresponding to notes 11–15.

But considerable problems remain at the level of implementation. Substantive requirements, such as the need to ensure that FDI will contribute to the realization of human rights and to human development, must be combined with procedural requirements of transparency, participation, information, and access to remedies. National-level decision making must be combined with an adequate role for local-level decision making. Only by recognizing the complementarity of these different dimensions will a workable domestic governance framework for investment emerge.

Such a framework should take into account that the substantive requirements imposed on FDI cannot be distinguished from the procedural safeguards that are increasingly imposed: the more transparent, open and participatory the decision-making processes by which investment treaties are negotiated and HGAs concluded, or specific investment projects authorized, the less there will be reasons for courts of other independent bodies to intervene to suspend or block the investment concerned. Similarly, the framework for investment should recognize the complementarity of the setting of priorities at the national level and the need for participation at the local level, by the communities most directly affected. Decisions at the national level must include a careful consideration of the impacts for the local communities: that is the purpose served by human rights impact assessments and the recognition of participatory rights. But conversely, decision-making processes at the local level must be organized taking into account the interdependency of choices made by each community co-existing in the same jurisdiction. This interdependency requires that each community makes a choice concerning the proposed investment without having to fear that it will be made worse off if another community, in another part of the country, makes a different choice: where decisions are taken in a decentralized way, in the absence of a sufficiently robust framework at national level, the risk is that the outcome will be collectively sub-optimal, as each community seeks to attract investors by renouncing the imposition of strong conditions that could maximize the benefits to the local economy while minimizing the negative impacts. President Johnson Sirleaf of Liberia may have been wrong to say that local communities should not create obstacles to the implementation of a policy decided by the central government. But it would be equally naive to suggest that the local communities should decide for themselves what is in their best interests, as if the central government had no role to play in ensuring that investment works for human development.

7 Risk managers or risk promoters?

The impacts of export credit and investment insurance agencies on human development and human rights

Matthias Sant'Ana

7.1 Introduction

Export credit and investment guarantee agencies (ECAs) are government-supported institutions that provide credit or guarantees to firms wishing to export goods or services, or who wish to conduct investment in foreign territories, and who cannot ordinarily obtain them through private institutions. These agencies were originally set up with two overriding goals. First, they were established in order to address failures in the market for trade-related finance. One must bear in mind that these agencies emerged in an economic context that was markedly different from the current one. To the extent that private banks and insurers at the time would not provide loans or guarantees for transactions in which political risk was perceived as too high, or too difficult to estimate, and where prospects of recovery in case of default were either null or dependent on the home state's willingness to espouse private claims through the unwieldy mechanism of diplomatic protection, states found it in their interest to provide export credit and investment guarantee services for those transactions that would not be insured by the private sector. Changing conditions in global economic governance – in particular the strengthening of trade and investment regimes and increased access to private arbitration since the 1980s – greatly improved the position of firms operating on the global markets, and this development could be expected to drive state-supported export credit to an ever more marginal role. To understand why this has not been the case, it is important to note that ECAs have a secondary goal, which is to insulate home-state industries against external risks, such as competitive subsidization of competing foreign firms by their home states, or unexpected contractions of finance in the private market caused, *inter alia*, by financial crises such as that experienced in the core northern economies since 2008.

Though their contribution to the expansion of both trade and investment is considerable, they operate on a relatively narrow set of transaction types, a fact that might go some way to explaining why these agencies are somewhat under-theorized in the field of international human rights law and, to a lesser extent, in that of international economic law. This relative neglect is reason for concern on two principal grounds. First, the manner in which ECAs operate has considerable effects on the capacity of corporations to conduct business, and also on selecting which *types* of investments, or transactions, will be given financial support. For various reasons explored in this chapter, ECAs provide financial support on terms, for reasons, and with a degree of coverage that private risk insurers cannot, or will not, match. This means that it is ECAs, rather than private institutions, that underwrite the riskiest investments, in the most politically and economically unstable regions of the world. Second, ECAs are generally constituted as public entities, or publicly mandated private entities. This would suggest that these agencies could be more easily held accountable – by both national democratic institutions and, to a certain extent, by international monitoring bodies – as compared to other financial institutions operating in the trade finance field.

The importance of trade finance can hardly be exaggerated. Eighty to ninety percent of trade transactions involve some form of credit, insurance or guarantee.[1] In a recent assessment of the impact of the global credit crisis on trade finance, the total value of trade finance arrangements was estimated at US$15.9 trillion, of which roughly a tenth is directly intermediated by ECAs.[2] According to data compiled by the Berne Union (BU), an international association of export credit agencies,[3] exposure of its members for the year 2008 – including short- to long-term export credits, and investment insurance – amounted to nearly US$1.06 trillion. Claims paid in the same period amounted to slightly more than two billion US$, and recoveries to about seven billion.[4] If export credit and insurance are necessary, it is also the case that publicly funded credits are quite *effective* in promoting international trade, with one recent study showing that 'a 10 percent increase in EPA budgets at the mean leads to a 0.6 to 1 percent increase in exports'.[5]

The obvious importance of export credit arrangements explains the considerable efforts, during and after the 2007 to 2009 global financial crisis,

1 M. Auboin, 'Restoring Financial Trade During a Period of Financial Crisis: Stock-Taking of Recent Initiatives', *WTO Staff Working Paper* (ERSD-2009-16), 2009, available at <http://papers.ssrn.com/sol3/papers.cfm?abstract_id=1535309> (accessed 26 March 2012), p. 2. ('Restoring')
2 J.P. Chauffour and M. Malouche (eds), *Trade Finance During the Great Trade Collapse*. Washington DC: World Bank Publications, 2011, p. 4.
3 The Berne Union's mission is to work for cooperation and stability in cross-border trade and to provide a forum for professional exchange among its members. These include 50 governmental and private institutions, as well as the World Bank's Multilateral Investment Guarantee Agency (MIGA). An additional 32 institutions who have yet to meet the Berne Union's membership criteria take part in the Prague Club.
4 Berne Union, *Annual Report 2009 – Celebrating 75 Years of the Berne Union*, London: Berne Union and Exporta Publishing, 2009, p. 89.
5 D. Lederman, M. Olarreaga and L. Payton, 'Export Promotion Agencies Revisited', *World Bank Policy Research Working Paper 5125*, November 2009, at p. 18.

to sustain trade finance. The G-20 meeting in London in 2009 adopted a wide package for injecting additional liquidity and bringing public guarantees in support of $250 billion of trade transactions in 2009 and 2010.[6] Early estimates indicated that the shortfall in trade finance was responsible for approximately 10 to 15 per cent of the fall in world trade.[7] More recent analysis confirms that drying up of trade finance accounted for roughly 10 per cent, though it highlights that the much deeper decline in trade volume and value – in the order of 30 per cent[8] – was due to other factors.[9]

Export credit and investment insurance agencies were first created in the interwar period to address a significant market failure: to provide export credits and insurance to markets not covered by private insurers.[10] They were insurers of last resort, covering risks that could not be properly assessed by capital markets, or providing loans where credit markets considered the business too small, or too risky.[11] As such, they have complemented, rather than competed with, private insurance. Not only did their statutes spell out the complementary nature of the financial services they provide, but developments in international law and policy gradually required them to operate in a manner such as not to distort trade.[12] That ECAs were not considered outright incompatible with trade or investment law is testimony to the fact that the international community recognizes their role in promoting social and economic goals that go considerably beyond narrow commercial interests. These welfare-enhancing goals are, however, traditionally seen from a home state perspective: export

6 M. Auboin, 'Boosting the availability of trade finance in the current crisis: background analysis for a substantial G20 package', *Centre for Economic Policy Research Policy Insight*, No. 35, June 2009, available at <http://www.cepr.org/pubs/policyinsights/PolicyInsight35. pdf> (accessed 26 March 2012), p.6 ('Boosting'), quoting the G-20 communiqué of 2 April 2009, wherein the states pledge to 'take, at the same time, whatever steps . . . to facilitate trade and investment, and, [the G-20] will ensure availability of at least $250 billion over the next two years to support trade finance through export credit and investment agencies and through the MDBs (multilateral development banks).'

7 Ibid.

8 M. Auboin, 'The Challenges of Trade Financing', Commentary, VoxEU.org, London: Centre for Economic Policy Research, 28 January 2009, available at <http://www.voxeu. org/index.php?q=node/2905> (accessed 26 March 2012).

9 I. Asmundson *et al.* 'Trade Finance in the 2008–09 Financial Crisis: Evidence from IMF and BAFT-IFSA Surveys of Banks' in J.P. Chauffour and M. Malouche (eds), *Trade Finance During the Great Trade Collapse*. Washington DC: World Bank Publications, 2011, pp. 89–116, at pp. 97–102 ('Banks attributed both the declines and the increases in the value of trade finance mostly to demand factors. Of these factors, the change in the value of trade was by far the most important, with the rise or fall in commodity prices a distant second').

10 R. Ascari, 'Is Export Credit Agency a Misnomer? The ECA Response to a Changing World', *SACE Working Paper Series*, No. 2 (2007), available at <http://www.sace.it/Gruppo SACE/export/sites/default/download/wpsacen02.pdf> (accessed 26 March 2012), at p. 3.

11 Ibid.

12 See, for an overview, D. Coppens, 'How Much Credit for Export Credit Support Under the SCM Agreement', *Journal of International Economic Law* 12(1), pp. 63–113.

credit support is *acceptable* as long as it does not distort trade, and is *justified* insofar as it allows home states to achieve policy goals such as maintaining a certain level of employment, sustained growth in certain sectors, addressing balance of payment concerns, or levelling the playing field in trade (i.e. countering export credit support by other states). The welfare of foreign states or populations, however, was not one of the policy goals that ECAs were originally designed to fulfil.[13] If the rationale for export credit support was guaranteeing positive externalities *at home*, the question of externalities *in the host state* was not a major consideration.

Medium- to long-term project finance – such as large infrastructure and energy projects – is made possible by the interaction of a number of financial products, originated by multiple actors under different jurisdictions, with widely diverging purposes and characteristics. For instance, the construction of a large dam, or multinational pipeline, requires both stand-alone as well as repeated transactions, occurring over many years, involving transfers between multiple suppliers of goods and services, some of which are within the same corporate entity (intra-firm trade, loans and guarantees between subsidiaries of the same firm), while other involve unrelated enterprises. Both the trade and investment aspects of these operations are financed, insured and re-insured by financial services providers – public and private, national, international and intergovernmental – operating under different jurisdictions, mandates and regulatory regimes. It is, of course, impossible, in this chapter, to assess the discrete impacts of these very different transactions, or the regulatory regimes applicable to them. The analysis, therefore, must focus on the contribution of ECAs to the aggregate outcome, even though this will involve unavoidable simplifications.

This contribution is divided into three parts. It begins with an analysis of national export credit and investment guarantee agencies, highlighting their main organizational features, mandate, economic rationale and legal framework (7.2). The next part analyses the international human rights obligations that apply to capital-exporting states, including the question of their legal duty to cooperate for the promotion of development overseas. The extent of state extraterritorial obligations and the grounds on which their international responsibility can be engaged are also discussed (7.3). The third part assesses the impact of ECA activities in terms of home state human rights obligations (7.4), and the conclusion presents policy proposals for the improvement of the regulation of ECA activities, as well as some observations on the need to envisage such regulation along with the broader issue of private financial services regulation (7.5).

---

13 See J. A. Bohn, Jr., 'Governmental Response to Third World Debt: The Role of the Export-Import Bank', *Stanford Journal of International Law*, 21, 1985, 461–497, at 469 ('Eximbank has no particular mandate to encourage development or to pursue international objectives in furtherance of U.S. foreign policy').

7.2 Export credit and investment insurance agencies

Improving the accountability of ECAs under international law generally, and human rights law in particular, requires a preliminary account of the characteristics of these hybrid institutions, an understanding of their place and role in international trade and investment, and an overview of the international regulatory framework with which states must comply when designing, funding and operating such agencies. However, ECAs are noted for their great diversity, and this has led to considerable misunderstandings about their nature, mandate and function.[14]

7.2.1 *The evolution of form and rationales for ECAs*

Export credit and investment guarantee agencies are quite diversified both in terms of their organizational structure and the degree of control exercised by their home states on their operation. Public control over such entities is crucial in determining the extent to which the actions or omissions of the agency can be attributed to the home state, which in turn determines the availability and nature of the remedies available to potential victims. As will be seen, the fact that an agency 'exercises elements of governmental authority' is crucial to the eventual attribution of responsibility to the state. In order to understand the nature of the business undertaken by ECAs and to identify what traits, if any, distinguish it from private actors in the risk insurance market, it is necessary to discuss the economic and policy rationales behind their operation. With both formal and functional accounts of ECAs, the discussion can then move on to a brief presentation of the impact of such agencies on trade and investment, and of their evolution alongside – and competition with – the private sector insurers and lenders.

7.2.1.1 *Diversity of form*

National export credit and investment guarantee agencies vary in the different aspects of their organizational form and business model.[15] The first aspect is the manner in which they are incorporated under domestic law: some are administrative departments within ministries, some are semi-autonomous public institutions, and still others are private corporations. Of these last, some are totally or partially owned by the state, while others are authorized by law to operate as agents of specific state export credit policies, and do part of their

14 So, as one well-placed observer noted, 'Export credit agencies must deal with a continuing misunderstanding on the part of many – some of which should know better – about their role. Again, export credit agencies are not sources of aid, nor are they sources of united finance. They are not solely, or even primarily vehicles for industrial support or foreign policy'. See, M. Stephens, *The Changing Role of Export Credit Agencies*, Washington DC: International Monetary Fund, 1999, p. 41.

15 Stephens, op. cit., p. 5.

business on their own account, and part on the government's account. What is clear, however, is that all of these agencies, whatever their form under domestic law, can rely on an explicit or implicit governmental guarantee: the backing of the public budget for a substantial part of their transactions. Therefore, even a privately incorporated company, in which the state is not a shareholder, but which carries out transactions as an agent of government-mandated export credit policies, would have the full backing of the state for those obligations assumed on its account.

This 'backing' by the state has two aspects. First, should importers be unable to pay, exporters are sure that an ECA will honour its obligation to cover the defaults, even if this requires transfers from the public budget. The exporter's risk of loss is ultimately assumed by the taxpayer, as occurred during the debt crisis of the 1980s when many export credit insurers faced simultaneous defaults in different countries.[16] A second consequence is that an importer, and its host state, knows that the home state will try to recover its ECA's debts. The diplomatic, political and economic pressure that ECAs could exert through the perceived threat of governmental involvement was one of the main advantages these agencies had when compared to private actors: ECAs had a 'deterrent effect' on defaulting states.[17]

Diversity is also very marked with regard to the types of transactions that ECAs and investment guarantee agencies undertake. Agencies can specialize in only short-term operations, or cover also medium- to long-term transactions. As will be seen later, short-term transactions have been increasingly carried out by private actors, with ECAs focusing their business on medium- and long-term business. They can be exclusively in the business of insurance and issuing guarantees on underlying private loans, or they can lend directly. Some ECAs focus only on trade finance – including not only capital goods, intermediary goods and commodities, but also services – while others also offer guarantees and insurance for investment. Finally, some agencies underwrite only political risk, others only commercial risk, and some do both. As can be seen, the financial products offered are as diverse as the forms that ECAs take, and as with

---

16 See P.E. Comeaux and N.S. Kinsella, 'Reducing Political Risk in Developing Countries: Bilateral Investment Treaties, Stabilization Clauses, and MIGA & OPIC Investment Insurance', *New York Law School Journal of International and Comparative Law* 15, 1994, 1–48.

17 The United States' Overseas Private Investment Corporation (OPIC) had an excellent track record in collecting unpaid importer debt, to the rate of 90 per cent. See, J.M. DeLeonardo, 'Are Public and Private Political Risk Insurance Two of a Kind? Suggestions for a New Direction for Government Coverage', *Virginia Journal of International Law* 45, 2005, 737–787, at p. 744. The same can be said of the US Import-Export Bank which was, during the debt crisis of the 1980s, one of the largest holders of government-to-government debt of all US agencies, see Bohn Jr., op. cit., p. 487. See also Stephens, op. cit., p. 28, noting that one of the distinctive features of export credit and investment insurance was that claims did not necessarily entail losses for the insurers, who 'expect to recover a substantial proportion of the claims they pay . . . and so devote – or should devote – a good deal of time and resources to loss minimization and debt recovery'.

this latter criterion, the *type of transaction* can give rise to different legal consequences under human rights law. It would be much harder to establish, for instance, that a privately incorporated ECA that lends in the short term, on its own account, and is insured by the private sector, could somehow be 'exercising elements of governmental authority', than if the agency were a governmental department, guaranteeing the acquisition of military hardware in a strategically important partner country.[18] Whether or not the conduct of an ECA can be attributed to the State is a question that cannot be answered in the abstract for all agencies, regardless of form, and for all of its transactions.

7.2.1.2 Economic rationale

The simplest model of an international trade transaction would involve an importer paying an exporter in a pre-agreed currency upon receipt of the merchandise. This, of course, involves exporters and importers accepting considerable risks: payment might be withheld even after delivery of goods; or the goods might not be delivered after payment, either because they were lost or because the exporter decided not to honour his word; the currency in which the agreed payment was to be carried out might devalue; war or civil strife might render impossible completion of the deal. One way to reduce risks of non-performance is to have banks in both countries mediate the transaction, as is done with letters of credit. After the importer has placed an order with the exporter, the importer's bank ('I') issues a letter of credit, essentially a promise to pay the exporter upon the presentation of certain documents, and sends it to the exporter's bank ('E'). When the exporter ships the merchandise, it presents E with documents to this effect. Bank E then transmits the documents to I, who pays the value of the letter of credit. With this payment, E can now pay the exporter. Bank I will only release the shipment when it is paid by the importer. This rather circuitous transaction has now reduced some uncertainties: banks operating regularly together will establish trust, and will know the firms on their territory better than foreign banks. But it is still possible that the importer's bank will not be willing or able to effect payment to the exporter's bank. This happens, for instance, when the importer's government sets limits to convertibility of currency, or when the bank becomes illiquid or insolvent. Moreover, importer non-performance is still a possibility, though the risk has now been transferred to the importer's bank.[19]

---

18 This has implications not only for questions of human rights violations linked to a given transaction, but also in other contexts, such as debt restructuring after a sovereign default. Although ECA debt generally gets preferential treatment during debt restructuring, the transaction just described could presumably be treated less favourably than other privately issued trade credit, going through London Club talks, rather than Paris Club negotiations. See M. Auboin, 'International Regulation and Treatment of Trade Finance: What are the Issues?', *WTO Staff Working Paper* (ERSD-2010-09), February 2010, at p. 14. See also Stephens, op. cit., p.42.
19 Stephens, op. cit., p. 7.

Export credit agencies have emerged to reduce or shift these residual risks. They often operate by one of two strategies: extending supplier credit or buyer credit. *Supplier credit* operations involve the ECA providing credit insurance covering the risk that the importer or his bank will not pay. Insurance, and loans, are offered directly to the exporter, or his bank. This is often a short-term transaction (under one year). The other strategy for risk reduction is *buyer credit*, whereby the exporter's bank lends to the importer's bank, and uses the loan to pay the exporter upon proof of performance. The importer's bank must be sure that the importer will pay, or that adequate collateral has been set aside, for it is the bank, and not the importer, who will have to pay the debt to the exporter's bank. Here, the ECA will extend risk insurance to the exporter's bank, to hedge against the risk of non-performance. This type of facility is usually used in mid- to long-term contracts, such as infrastructure and large projects. Because of the long time between the start of operations and completion of the project, ECAs sometimes also extend a separate guarantee to the exporter, to cover the risk that the supply contract is interrupted before completion.[20]

Some export credit agencies also have a role in insuring or issuing guarantees for overseas investment. Some states, such as the United States, have two separate entities.[21] Investment guarantees and insurance can cover both *political* risks – such as currency convertibility and transfer risks, expropriation and political violence – and *commercial* risks – such as non-payment or delayed payment due to insolvency or illiquidity. However, most investment guarantee agencies focus on political risks.

In theory, however, all these operations can be carried out by private actors, without the need for public involvement. This raises two questions. Why have public agencies been created to provide these services? And, even if one admits that there were historical reasons for the development of these institutions, why have they endured despite the tremendous increases in the capacity of private sector financial services? In his seminal work on export credit agencies, Malcolm Stephens identified what he called the 'conventional wisdom' for governmental involvement in the export credit and investment insurance businesses, adducing ten reasons.[22] Hereunder, these reasons will be grouped under four general categories: information incompleteness and asymmetry, government's greater risk-bearing capacity, pursuit of non-commercial policy goals and counter-cyclical credit capacity.

The first reason for government involvement is the fact that private markets could not, or would not, assume the requisite risks involved in overseas

20 Ibid., p. 10. For instance, changing governmental priorities might be to stop, or nationalize a project, denying the exporter the possibility of completing construction, which would preclude the company from drawing on the loan.
21 The Export-Import Bank's business is trade finance and export credits, while the Overseas Private Investment Corporation (OPIC) handles investment insurance.
22 Stephens, op. cit., pp. 29–30.

lending and insurance for the reason that private actors did not have enough information, or that political risks were deemed too uncertain to allow for actuarial analysis and pricing.[23] As compared to states, private insurers were at a distinct disadvantage with respect to the collection, treatment and analysis of information on political conditions in foreign states. By the 1960s, when most OECD (Organization for Economic Cooperation and Development) countries had already established national export credit agencies, the flow of information between states was considerably more segmented than today, and the state's bilateral channels with foreign governments were an extremely privileged source of information and intelligence and an excellent channel of persuasion.[24]

An additional cause for this market failure was the fact that capital markets were considerably smaller, segmented and risk averse. So, on the one hand, exporters and investors could not always expect to raise capital in domestic markets and, on the other hand, they were often too small to be able to access foreign capital markets.[25] Unlike private insurers and banks considering loans, government-run export credit agencies did not have to consider capital and currency requirements, and could absorb even large losses by paying from the public budget and spreading repayment over time. More importantly, governmental agencies could expect 'political coverage' from the government, which put them at a considerable advantage if they had to pursue claims against foreign corporations or governments. This meant that foreign governments treated ECA guaranteed transactions as having a preferential status *de facto*, if not *de jure* (deterrent effect),[26] and that, should a foreign state refuse to pay an ECA debt, the government could pursue claims and recovery through stronger means.[27] The government's greater fiscal capacity also meant that it

23 *Risk* can be assessed on probabilistic terms, if there is enough data on the frequency of the events for which risk is being measured (e.g. the chance that a given number will be rolled on a given die), and if one can price the cost of loss (how much one would lose if the wrong number is rolled). *Uncertainty*, however, refers to events for which no amount of previous events can provide a probability of recurrence (e.g. the chance that a volcano will erupt on any given day). The economic salience of this distinction was first discussed by Frank Knight, of the University of Chicago, in his thesis published in 1921. It is more appropriate, however, to speak of a continuum of uncertainty. On this distinction and its consequences for financial regulation, see A.W. Lo and M.T. Mueller, 'Warning: Physics Envy Can be Hazardous to Your Wealth!', 2010, available at <http://papers.ssrn.com/sol3/papers.cfm?abstract_id=1563882> (accessed 26 March 2012) , p. 9.
24 DeLeonardo, op. cit., p. 743.
25 Ascari, op. cit., p. 3.
26 See Auboin, 2010, op. cit., p. 1, stating that 'Traditionally, trade finance has received preferred treatment on the part of national and international regulators, as well as by international financial agencies in the treatment of trade finance claims, on grounds that trade finance was one of the safest, most collateralized, and self-liquidating forms of trade finance. Preferred treatment of trade finance also reflects the systemic importance of trade, as in sovereign or private defaults a priority is to "treat" expeditiously trade lines of credits to allow for such credit to be restored and trade to flow again.'
27 Stephens, op. cit., p. 28.

could take greater risks in individual transactions, but also bear greater exposure with respect to individual countries.[28] Both risks were certainly too great for the financial industry until the late twentieth century.

A third broad reason for the emergence of public insurance of export credits consists in the pursuit by the state of broader policy goals. The main reason for establishing ECAs was the promotion of exports by the reduction of non-payment risks. Even supposing no information asymmetry existed, though private actors could make a profit from this kind of export credit insurance transaction, they had little incentive to *prefer* this investment over other, possibly more lucrative, transactions. The state, on the other hand, could see the advantage of promoting exports regardless of the transaction's inherent profitability: loss of exports, even if only temporary, could present a state with a number of problems at home. Examples of these are, for instance, the management of unemployment levels and of the balance of payments.[29] If, moreover, the loss of exports were due to another state's subsidization of their own exports, governments would be compelled to provide support – matching other countries' credits – just to 'level the playing field'. Finally, a state's development strategies might require support for specific sectors specializing in higher value products (e.g. aircraft) which depend not only on long-term capital and technology accumulation, but also on considerable economies of scale. Investment sunk over decades could be threatened if other states' export credits could not be matched, thereby damaging nascent or champion industry exports. While private banks and insurers have no duty to consider the effect of their operations on the balance of payments, on the rate of domestic capital accumulation or on unemployment, no government can fail to worry constantly about such issues.

A fourth and final reason why states established such institutions is that during crises, particularly financial ones, credit contraction can stall exports, particularly to emerging economies.[30] In integrated worldwide production chains, this can have devastating 'domino effects': when a country's exports contain a high percentage of components imported from another country, as was the case for Indonesia during the Asian Crisis of the late 1990s,[31] it will be unable to export enough, causing its balance of payments to deteriorate, and affecting other sectors' capacity to secure enough currency to pay foreign currency-denominated debt. As domestic and foreign debtors default, the assets on balance sheets are devalued. This global process of deleveraging requires financial institutions to accumulate good assets to meet capital requirements and operational costs, calling on debtors sooner, and further reducing

28 J.-Y. Wang, M. Mansilla, Y. Kikuchi and S. Choudhury, *Officially Supported Credits in a Changing World*, Washington DC: International Monetary Fund, 2005, p.22.

29 Ibid., at p. 20.

30 A. Thomas, 'Financial Crises and Emerging Market Trade', *IMF Staff Position Note* (SPN/09/04), 11 March 2009.

31 Auboin, 2010, op. cit., p. 14.

liquidity.[32] Reduced liquidity means less tolerance to risk, with loans becoming more expensive and insurance premiums rising. Trade finance is particularly vulnerable to such crises and, in such circumstances, only state-mandated institutions will be in a position to extend credit and avoid a downturn in exports and the underlying domestic economic activity.[33]

7.2.1.3 *Evolution and private sector competition*

The debt crisis of the 1980s had considerable effects on the functioning of world trade and, consequently, on ECAs. These changes proceeded through two channels. On the one hand, the systemic increase in defaults worldwide meant that claims against ECAs increased greatly. On the other hand, the massive scale of developing country sovereign and private defaults presented the world economy with an unprecedented crisis that could not be solved merely by adhering strictly to debt repayment commitments. Even though they did not reduce the net present value of debt,[34] restructurings meant that the prospect of recoverability of ECA claims deteriorated considerably, particularly in the short run.[35] By 1990, total claims were estimated at US$150 billion, only a fragment of which could be recovered by ECAs.[36] Moreover, the crisis ushered a new era in policy thinking, with Thatcherism arguing for the reduction of public deficits, and keeping the government out of any activity that the private sector was willing to undertake,[37] which included, by then, the short-term export credit business.

During the mid-1990s, however, two important developments took place. First, the net cash flow of BU members turned from deficit between 1981 and 1995 to surplus starting in 1996,[38] as the losses inflicted through developing country debt restructuring were recouped. Moreover, non-OECD agencies started to represent an increasing share of export credit worldwide. With the combination of greater competition in short-term export credits, and the improvement of developing country income and creditworthiness, ECAs in developed countries have gradually lost their share of business, as they were

32 International Monetary Fund, *Global Financial Stability Report 2009 – Responding to the Financial Crisis and Measuring System Risks* (Summary Version), April 2009, pp. 5–16.
33 The trade finance gap was estimated at US$25 billion by November 2008, a mere two months after the failure of Lehman Brothers precipitated the global credit crisis. See Coppens, op. cit., p. 69. See also M. Auboin, 'Restoring', op. cit., p.10, stating that 'according to the [IMF-BAFT (Banker's Association for Trade and Finance)] survey, . . . the market gap was well over the $25 billion estimate mentioned above, in fact in the order of $100 billion to $300 billion. This number was also consistent with the amount of letter of credit and other trade bills (such as bankers' acceptances) that market participants were no longer rolled over on the secondary markets'.
34 See Auboin 2010, op. cit., p. 13.
35 Stephens, op. cit., p. 34.
36 Ibid., p. 36.
37 Ibid., p. 32.
38 Wang et al., op. cit., p. 9.

squeezed out of the private market, and could not yet access least-developed country markets.[39] Developed country ECAs still 'filled the gap' in trade finance, but their main business increasingly became that of 'keep[ing] national exporters competitive in global markets by countering foreign government support provided to competitors . . . particularly in sectors with economies of scale and non-competitive market structure, such as aircraft and military equipment'.[40]

Since then two further transformations are of note: the transformations in the scope and reach of private economic activity, and the increased regulation of officially supported export credit. On the first of these transformations, DeLeonardo has argued that the 'old wisdom' on why public sector agencies had an inherent advantage in export credit and investment insurance unravelled in the late 1990s. First, the information asymmetries that existed were considerably reduced: not only do home states actively share intelligence and information on foreign risks with domestic firms, but there has been a proliferation and specialization of private actors in both the information-gathering and risk-rating markets.[41] A second important development is that prospects of private insurance firms recovering against foreign firms or even sovereigns have greatly improved: a growing network of BITs (bilateral investment treaties), the increased recourse to, and better compliance with, investment arbitration, and the gradual erosion, by home state jurisdictions, of sovereign immunities in arguably commercial cases have all contributed to this result. Consequently, private sector actors have been more willing to provide loans and insurance in more countries and on longer terms.[42] Finally, increased understanding and perception of risk after 9/11 has resulted in a broadening of the insurance pool, with more investors and suppliers willing to pay higher premiums, thereby reducing adverse selection.[43]

The second major transformation is the tightening of the international regulatory framework, discussed in more detail below. In brief terms, increased international discipline has focused on two goals: reduced scopes for state subsidization, i.e. the 'squeezing [of] interest rate subsidies out of the system';[44]

---

39 Ibid., p. 19.

40 Ibid., p. 20.

41 To the point where MIGA turned to a coalition of private international risk insurers for statistical and data assistance. See DeLeonardo, op. cit., p. 755. Stephens also argues that private rating and risk assessment agencies, by becoming truly globalized firms, have obtained greater economies of scale – in data collection, processing and analysis – for the simple reason that they do not limit the provision of their services to clients in their home state, as ECAs are required to do. Stephens, op. cit., p. 34.

42 See E. Hayes and A. Cummings, 'Part Two: Political Risk and Insurance – Taming the Risks of Project Finance', *International Financial Law Review* 20, 2001, 17–20, at p. 19.

43 DeLeonardo, op. cit., pp. 751–772. See also A. Khachaturian, '"Are We in Good Hands?" The Adequacy of American and Political Risk Insurance Programs in Fostering International Development', *Connecticut Law Review*, 38, 2006, 1041–1064, at p. 1063.

44 Stephens, op. cit., p. 34.

and the requirement that ECAs break even in the long run (i.e. do not run persistent deficits for protracted periods). Moreover, public pressure has increasingly pushed governments to stop supporting projects with large social and environmental costs through their agencies.[45] Often originating in response to public concern in individual countries,[46] these rising standards are gradually being incorporated under international regulatory frameworks.[47] This has resulted in exporters and investors increasingly preferring to use private insurers and banks, which are seen as more flexible and less demanding in both procedural (screening and monitoring of projects) and substantial ('political' matters such as environmental, labour and social standards) aspects.[48] As investors and exporters turn to private institutions first, ECAs in developed countries have been gradually relegated to the market margins, as insurers of last resort. By the turn of the millennium, twenty underwriters already offered export credit in London alone, with over 85 per cent of short-term export insurance worldwide being offered by private insurers.[49]

These developments have affected project finance in specific ways.[50] The debt crisis of the 1980s showed that the preferred collateral for export credit, sovereign guarantees, was not reliable. Rather than run state enterprises and offer sovereign guarantees, states have increasingly entrusted large infrastructural projects to corporations, and raised capital through foreign direct investment: public utilities have been privatized, and new projects have been tendered through

---

45 One of the early examples of the consideration of host state welfare in project finance was OPIC, which, since its establishment under the Foreign Assistance Act of 1969, took into consideration welfare effects in both the home state (balance of payments and employment) and – since 1985 – the host state (labour rights and environmental protection). See M.B. Perry, 'A Model for Efficient Foreign Aid: The Case for Political Risk Insurance Activities of the Overseas Private Investment Corporation', *Virginia Journal of International Law* 36, 1995, 511–588, at pp. 517 and 522.

46 For a comparative overview of the introduction of labour standards in select export credit and investment insurance agencies, see B. Penfold, 'Labour and Employment Issues in Foreign Direct Investment: Public Support Conditionalities', *International Labour Office Working Paper*, No. 95, pp. 10–22. For an equivalent discussion on the environmental eligibility conditions for ECAs, see M. Knigge, B. Görlach, A.-M. Hamada, C. Nuffort and R.A. Kraemer, 'The Use of Environmental and Social Criteria in Export Credit Agencies' Practices – A Study of Export Credit Agencies' Environmental Guidelines with Reference to the World Commission on Dams', paper commissioned by Deutsche Gesellschaft für Technische Zusammenarbeit GmbH (GTZ), published in 2003 and available at <http:// www.ecologic.de/download/projekte/1800-1849/1809/1809wcd_ecas_en.pdf> (accessed 26 March 2012).

47 See the discussion on the OECD Arrangement below, in section 7.2.2.

48 See Comeaux and Kinsella, op. cit., p. 47; Hayes and Cummings, op. cit., p. 19; Stephens, op. cit., p. 35.

49 Stephens, op. cit., p. 33.

50 For an overview of the general characteristics of project finance, see S. Leader and D.M. Ong, *Global Project Finance, Human Rights and Sustainable Development*, Cambridge: Cambridge University Press, 2011.

open bidding.[51] In project finance, the guarantee is the long-term viability of the project and of its revenue stream, rather than the credibility of any supplier, buyer or insurer. In effect, project finance 'is the financing of a particular economic unit in which the lender is satisfied to look initially to the cash flows and earnings of that economic unit as the source of funds from which a loan will be repaid and to the assets of the economic unit as a collateral for the loan'.[52] With the unprecedented wave of privatizations since the late 1980s, a great number of financial products and strategies have been developed in order to render project finance more flexible, and easier to negotiate.[53] Financing generally consists of two portions: equity and debt capital. Equity investment is usually underwritten by multiple large investors, domestic and foreign, taking large interests each (typically from 20 to 25 per cent). Debt capital is lent by large commercial banks and multilateral agencies, usually obtained through syndicated loans involving multiple banks. These investors jointly establish a corporation under host state law and construct, own and operate the undertaking or facility. Loans are made by this corporation and not by the investors themselves, who do not burden their balance sheets with additional liabilities, preserving their creditworthiness.[54] The elements above explain why this investment technique is so attractive to sponsors: (i) if the project isn't commercially viable, then the lender's only recourse is to take the assets of the foreign corporation (in the form of capital goods, installations, etc.); meanwhile, (ii) the sponsor's credit position in the home state – and therefore its rating – is not compromised. Lenders, however, are particularly keen to ensure project viability, obtaining guarantees against the foreign government and the project corporation, from ECAs and multilateral lending institutions. In effect, observers have noted increased partnerships between private, public and multilateral sectors, with underwriting programmes often involving the World Bank's Multilateral Investment Guarantee Agency (MIGA) as the 'insurer of record' and the participation of other private and public insurers.[55] These risk mitigation techniques are so effective that the credit ratings of a given project are sometimes higher than that of the underlying corporation, or of the state in question.[56]

7.2.2 Regulatory framework

There are essentially two concurrent regulatory frameworks that apply to export credit agencies explicitly. The OECD's *Arrangement on Officially Supported*

---

51 Stephens, op. cit., p. 36. See also N. Nassar, 'Project Finance, Public Utilities and Public Concerns: A Practitioner's Perspective', *Fordham International Law Journal*, 23, 2000, pp. 60–85.
52 Nassar, op. cit., p. 62.
53 Hayes and Cummings, op. cit., p. 19.
54 P. Kundra, 'Looking Beyond the Dabhol Debacle: Examining its Causes and Understanding its Lessons' *Vanderbilt Journal of Transnational Law*, 41, 2008, 907–935, at pp. 909–911.
55 Hayes and Cummings, op. cit., p. 18.
56 Ibid.

Export Credits ('Arrangement') is a 'gentleman's agreement' first adopted in April 1978 to 'provide an orderly use of officially supported export credits' among the participant states.[57] An additional regulatory constraint is imposed by the World Trade Organization's (WTO) *Agreement on Subsidies and Countervailing Measures*,[58] which limits the use of the said subsidies in the trade of goods.

7.2.2.1 The OECD Arrangement

Much of the advantage of having export credit agencies would be nullified if states used them only to subsidize their own exporters, rather than to address a market failure in the trade finance sector. In effect, without some kind of international coordination, ECAs could simply be used by their home states to distort trade in their favour, which would in turn incite, in practice oblige, other states to respond by increasing their own subsidies. This 'war in export subsidies' could be observed during the 1960s and 1970s, when a number of ECAs stimulated exports by practising below-market interest rates.[59] The oil shocks of 1973 and the ensuing debt crisis led a number of governments to contemplate mutual restrictions on export subsidies, which eventually resulted in the 1978 OECD Arrangement. This non-binding agreement started off essentially by setting limits on the permitted terms of export subsidization, but eventually grew into a comprehensive framework, addressing sector-specific issues (civil aircraft, shipbuilding, renewable energy and water projects, nuclear power plants) as well as cross-cutting themes (environmental issues, bribery, mixed credits and debt sustainability). Its purpose was to 'encourage competition among exporters based on the quality and price of goods and services exported rather than on the most favorable officially supported financial terms and conditions'.[60]

The arrangement participants – which include most but not all OECD member states – modify the regulatory framework by consensus, which of course implies that standards evolved gradually and incrementally.[61] Nonetheless, the system is based on three basic principles: (i) commitments to shared subsidization rates[62] and repayment terms; (ii) duties of notification and consultation; and (iii) a 'retaliatory' mechanism consisting in the ability to

---

57 OECD, *Arrangement on Officially Supported Export Credits*, January 2010 Revision [TAD/PG(2010)2], at p. 2.

58 Agreement on Subsidies and Countervailing Measures, 15 April 1994, Marrakesh Agreement Establishing the World Trade Organization, Annex 1A, 1867 UNTS 14.

59 J. K. Levit, 'A Bottom-Up Approach to International Law-Making: A Tale of Three Trade Finance Instruments', *Yale Journal of International Law* 30, 2005, 125–209, at p. 158.

60 OECD Arrangement, Art. 1(b).

61 Levit, op. cit., p. 160.

62 These include the Commercial Interest Reference Rates (CIRRs), the Maximum Repayment Terms (MRTs) and the Minimum Premium Rates (MPRs). See OECD Arrangement Arts 19–22, 11–12 and 24–25, respectively.

'match' offers that depart from the Arrangement terms. The commitments that participants undertake include minimum interest and premium rates and repayment terms linked to rules-based risk assessments for any given country. This has meant that, regardless of a state's financial capacity to provide support to its own exporters, and regardless of its individual assessment of the risk of non-payment by the importer, participant states must charge at least a certain amount of interest, and abide by a maximum schedule of repayment corresponding to a collectively determined rating of the host state's creditworthiness. The second major aspect of the arrangement consists in the duty of participants to notify other participants of any commitments they might be considering entering into, provided that they meet certain threshold criteria.[63] Notification is given to all participants, and can give place to discussions with other participants who would question the application of the arrangements term in a given transaction. If a disagreement cannot be mediated by discussions between participants, the arrangement allows for a participant to 'match' the offer made by a non-complying participant, presumably nullifying any trade-distorting benefit the latter expected to obtain. Non-participants under the OECD arrangement are also given limited information, on a reciprocity basis, on terms and conditions practised. Matching can also take place against non-participants.

The increasing complexity of trade finance, even that practised through official agencies, has led the participants in the Agreement to add understandings and further refine the normative framework applicable to export credit and project finance. This is also due to the OECD's significant work in the area of Official Development Assistance (ODA), which has influenced the way participants approach certain themes. The interaction between export credit and ODA occurs when, for instance, a participant uses 'tied aid' – foreign aid that requires the recipient to spend a certain amount of the donated funds to buy goods and services originating in the donor state – in connection with a development assistance project. In such circumstances, the arrangement contains a 'Checklist of Developmental Quality' that allows one participant to question whether another participant's aid-financed project might have 'a trade motivation for tied aid', i.e. might be disguising export subsidies through highly concessional loans to developing countries.[64] Here, the suspicious state can ask for a 'full Aid Quality Assessment', which will consider how well the proposed project pursues development goals.[65]

---

63 The Arrangement, in Arts 45 through 47, sets out the conditions under which participants are required to give notification. In general, the smaller the value of the transaction, or the higher the amount of concessionality, the later participants can notify their pairs.

64 See Stephens, op. cit., p. 34, suggesting that 'as blanket subsidies were squeezed out, the temptation arose to introduce selective subsidies, largely through the blending of bilateral aid and export credit into so-called mixed-credits'.

65 See Art. 48 of the Arrangement. Annex IX presents a checklist of questions that should be addressed in order to verify whether a project is consistent with the recipient country's

A similar process occurred in the interaction between the Working Party on Export Credits and Credit Guarantees (ECG) and the OECD's Environment Directorate, leading to the incremental adoption of environmental standards, starting in 1998. This process of negotiation resulted in the adoption of the OECD Council *Recommendation on Common Approaches on the Environment and Officially Supported Export Credits* in 2003.[66] The Common Approaches require participants to establish procedures for the screening of all projects with a repayment period superior to two years and value above ten million SDRs.[67] Regardless of the nature of the credit, projects must be classified as high (A), medium (B) or low (C) risk. A full environmental impact assessment is required for Category A projects only,[68] and somewhat lighter assessment is required of Category B projects. In the decision on whether to support the project, participants are required to indicate which conditions are to be fulfilled prior to, during, or after, the conclusion of the project. If conditions are imposed, the participant must provide for monitoring that they are being respected. Finally, participants are asked to report semi-annually on all Category A projects supported, on their compliance with the Common Approaches, and to evaluate the participant's experience with the implementation of the standards contained in them.[69]

development priorities, including criteria such as 'social and distributional analysis' and environmental assessment. The assessment is to be carried out bearing in light of the criteria established by the OECD Development Assistance Committee.

66 OECD, *Council Recommendation on Common Approaches on Environment and Officially Supported Export Credits* [C(2003)236]. The current version was adopted on 12 June 2007 [TAD/ECG(2007)9].

67 Special Drawing Rights, or SDRs, refers to an international reserve asset, created by the IMF in 1969 and calculated from a basket of four key international currencies. In the context used here, it is a simple measure of value. As of 3 August 2012, ten million SDRs are roughly equivalent to $15 million US dollars. See also the IMF factsheet on SDRs. Online. Available HTTP: <http://www.imf.org/external/np/exr/facts/sdr.htm> (accessed 3 August 2012).

68 An illustrative list of Category A projects is appended to the Common Approaches, and includes, among others, thermoelectric power plants, large dams, nuclear fuel production facilities, asbestos extraction and processing, oil refineries, large logging and mining projects, projects in sensitive areas and projects involving the involuntary resettlement of a significant number of affected people.

69 The OECD published a review of member states' practice in 2010, which concludes that 'whilst Members' environmental review systems continue to vary and some Members have little or no experience of dealing with projects with potential adverse environmental impacts, the majority of Members have systems in place for reviewing applications for official support that are broadly compliant with the requirements of the 2007 Recommendation. However, some differences in systems still exist, e.g. with regard to screening applications, reviewing projects for their potential environmental impacts, benchmarking against host and international standards, and making project and environmental impact information publicly available.' OECD Working Party on Export Credits and Credit Guarantees, 'Export Credits and the Environment: 2010 review of members' responses to the survey on the environment and officially supported export credits' (TAD/ECG(2010)10/FINAL), 10 December 2010, p. 2.

The final two areas in which the OECD Arrangement has provided guidelines to participants concern policies against corruption and what can be termed 'debt-sustainability measures'. With regard to corruption, the ECG has elaborated, and the OECD Council has adopted, a *Recommendation on Bribery and Officially Supported Export Credits*, requiring states to adopt a number of measures such as: informing exporters and applicants of the legal consequences of corruption and encouraging them to develop management controls against bribery; demanding they provide declarations to the effect that they or their agents either have not been engaged, or will not engage in bribery; and requiring them to verify and notify if any of the parties to the transactions being envisaged are on publicly available debarment lists. Finally, the issue of the debt burden impact of export credits was first explicitly addressed in a 'Statement of Principles'[70] focusing on the question of 'unproductive loans'. The OECD called upon member states to ensure that 'insofar as official export credits contribute to a country's overall debt burden . . . such credits should not be provided for unproductive expenditure in HIPCs'. The notion of 'unproductive' included 'transactions that are not consistent with [the recipient country]'s poverty reduction and debt-sustainability strategies and do not contribute to their social and/or economic development'. In order to accomplish this, ECG members committed to reporting their transactions to HIPCs and to review them annually. This statement of principles was reviewed in 2007 so as to include countries only eligible for International Development Association (IDA)[71] funds, and also to refer explicitly to the Millennium Development Goals (MDGs) as targets for development. Finally, in 2008 the OECD adopted the *Principles and Guidelines to Promote Sustainable Lending Practices in the Provision of Official Export Credits to Low-Income Countries*,[72] which give greater clarity to the concept of 'sustainable lending', i.e. lending that 'generate[s] net positive economic returns, foster[s] sustainable development by avoiding unproductive expenditures, preserve[s] debt sustainability and support[s] good governance and transparency'.[73] In general terms, the Guidelines and Principles require states to abide by IMF and IDA rules regarding the minimum level of concessionality for loans to low-income countries, to seek assurances from the buyer country that projects meeting a minimum threshold will be 'in line with the country's borrowing and development plans (e.g. consistent with its Poverty Reduction Strategy Paper [PRSP] and/or the budget) following the procedures set forth by the national legislation (e.g. Parliament approval, where required)'.[74]

---

70 *Official Export Credit Support to Heavily Indebted Poor Countries (HIPCS) – Statement of Principles*, adopted 17 July 2001.
71 The International Development Association is the World Bank's specialized branch for the least developed countries, and makes funds available exclusively on highly concessional terms.
72 *Principles and Guidelines to Promote Sustainable Lending Practices in the Provision of Official Export Credits to Low-Income Countries*, adopted 20 February 2008 [TAD/ECG(2008)1].
73 Ibid., para. 3.
74 See para. 4(c). The threshold is that the value be of at least 5 million SDRs, and repayment terms of at least two years.

7.2.2.2 *WTO disciplines*

All of the requirements gradually introduced under the OECD Arrangement's framework are complemented by the disciplines available under WTO law for export subsidies in goods. The *WTO Agreement on Subsidies and Countervailing Measures* ('SCM Agreement') establishes that export subsidies are generally incompatible with WTO law. These are defined as any form of official support[75] – in the form, for example, of loans, grants, guarantees or tax credits – that confers a benefit[76] to the exporter,[77] and that is contingent on either *export performance* or *import substitution*.[78] Export credits fall squarely within this formulation. The original GATT (General Agreement on Tariffs and Trade) agreement did not contain disciplines regarding these subsidies, but states-parties agreed, starting in 1955, on a list of prohibited measures. From these negotiations, and all throughout the next rounds of trade negotiations, the issue of prohibited export credits grew incrementally in precision, and in parallel with the negotiations within the OECD.[79] The SCM Agreement as it now stands contains the above-mentioned definition, and an 'Illustrative List of Export Subsidies,'[80] which contains two provisions focused on ECAs. Item (j) on the List prohibits 'the provision by governments (or special institutions controlled by governments) of export credit guarantee or insurance programmes, of insurance or guarantee programmes against increases in the cost of exported products or of exchange risk programmes, *at premium rates which are inadequate to cover the long-term operating costs and losses of the programmes*' (emphasis added). This is the so-called 'breaking even' requirement: for ECAs to be compatible with WTO discipline, they must practise rates that allow them to be self-sustaining in the long term.

The second provision of interest is item (k), which prohibits 'the grant by governments (or special institutions controlled by and/or acting under the authority of governments) of export credits at rates below those which they actually have to pay for the funds so employed . . . or the payment by them of all or part of the costs incurred by exporters or financial institutions in obtaining credits, in so far as they are used to secure a material advantage in the field of export credit terms'. For ECAs, this entails the prohibition of interest rate subsidization, and forces them to rely on capital market rates rather than the lower public debt (treasury bond) interest rate with which states could, and had, financed ECA credits.[81] Most importantly, however, the second paragraph

---

75 Art. 1.1(a)(1) of the SCM Agreement. 'Support' is based on a cost-to-government standard. See Coppens, op. cit., p. 86.

76 Art. 1.1(b).

77 On the distinction between benefit to the exporter, and benefit to the recipient of the subsidy, see Coppens, op. cit., p. 80.

78 Art. 3.1(a–b) of the SCM Agreement.

79 Coppens, op. cit., pp. 70–75.

80 Annex I to the SCM Agreement.

81 This provision basically tries to nullify the advantage that developed states have in raising funds for ECA credits in the market by issuing low-interest, long maturity treasury bonds.

of this provision allows OECD Arrangement participants to practise the interest provisions of the Arrangement[82] which, as noted above, is an interest rate lower than the prevailing market rates. All ECAs that respect these interest rates will be deemed, in principle, to be in compliance with WTO SCM discipline. This 'safe haven' for ECAs, however does not imply that *any* subsidy complying with OECD Arrangement standards complies, necessarily, with the SCM Agreement.[83]

7.3 Home state human rights obligations

Whether export credit and insurance guarantee agencies can be held accountable for their impact on human development and human rights is a question that requires a number of preliminary problems to be addressed. If by accountability one is referring primarily to responsibility under international law, then two major issues must be clarified from the offset. The first issue is to determine what obligation of international human rights law is breached by the operation of ECAs. The second issue is whether the acts of ECAs can be attributed to their home state under the customary norms on attribution.

On the issue of the obligations potentially breached, the question is whether states – and consequently 'their' ECAs – have an international obligation to promote, or at least not hinder, development (1), or those international human rights which are linked to the concept of human development (2).[84] If such obligations exist with respect to the state, then the question is whether the acts

It also prohibits the state from paying, by other means, the difference between the market rate and the treasury bond rate (otherwise states could instruct ECAs to lend at market rates, but offer interest rate support directly to exporters). The first aspect also tends to neutralize the advantages that states with high credit ratings would have if compared to states with lower credit ratings.

82 Item (k), second paragraph, reads: 'Provided, however, that if a Member is a party to an international undertaking on official export credits to which at least twelve original Members to this Agreement are parties as of 1 January 1979 (or a successor undertaking which has been adopted by those original Members), or if in practice a Member applies the interest rates provisions of the relevant undertaking, *an export credit practice which is in conformity with those provisions shall not be considered an export subsidy prohibited by this Agreement*' (emphasis added).

83 Coppens, op. cit., recalls that 'matching', though allowed under the OECD Arrangement, would be incompatible with the SCM agreement, as decided in the *Canada–Aircraft (Article 21.5 – Brazil) Case* (ibid., at p. 100). He further notes that 'pure cover' (i.e. the provision of insurance or guarantees for third party credits, is not protected under the safe haven, unless the underlying export credit is OECD Arrangement compliant (ibid.). More importantly, however, he notes that although OECD Arrangement-compliant export credits are not prohibited under List item (k), that does not mean that they are permitted under the other SCM Agreement provisions (ibid., pp. 105–109) and could be countervailed if they caused injury to other member states' industries.

84 For a discussion of the concept of development and its link to human rights, see O. De Schutter, J. Wouters, P. De Man, N. Hachez and M. Sant'Ana, 'Foreign Direct Investment, Human Development and Human Rights: Framing the Issues,' *Human Rights and International Legal Discourse*, 3(2), 2009, 137–176, at pp. 149–158.

or omissions of ECAs can be attributed to the state (3). To the extent that these obligations exist and that ECA conduct can be validly attributed to the state, it is then possible to explore the specific grounds for responsibility, and distinguish between two different circumstances of responsibility (4). Before turning to the issue of state obligations, it is useful to recall what the assessment of human development implies, and to identify two possible approaches to accountability.

However one defines development – and there is certainly no overarching consensus on the meaning of the term[85] – there are two general perspectives on how to ensure accountability for development outcomes. One is to focus on the rights of individuals and communities, and to study the manner in which claims can be brought against duty-bearers – individual states or the community of states acting through international organizations. Another way is to look at the reciprocal rights and duties of states, focusing on duties of cooperation and non-interference as well as the principle of self-determination. Here, accountability involves the mechanisms through which states can make claims, or influence each other, in ways conducive to a *development-enabling environment*. In historical terms, the international debate on development swung more strongly towards the latter view from the period of decolonization to the end of the Cold War.[86] Since then, the debate has been characterized by a greater focus on individual and community rights, rather than on the rights of states.[87] This explains why we present two parallel sets of ideas regarding accountability: at a first, broader level, the issue is whether states should, in their mutual relations, proceed in a manner that enhances the capacity of all, and particularly the weakest, to attain growing levels of development. At a second level, we investigate to what extent certain actions by states are so damaging to individuals or communities that they are no longer simply discouraged, but are rather prohibited and sanctioned through the mechanism of international responsibility.

7.3.1 *Is there an obligation to promote (human) development?*

To claim that the promotion of human development is a duty of states would require clear legal sources, the production of which would permit the

---

85 De Schutter et al., op. cit., p. 154.
86 The inherent difficulties of this approach, and the balancing in particular in its connection to the issue of sovereignty over natural resources was discussed in depth in N. Schrijver, *Sovereignty over Natural Resources: Balancing rights and duties*, Cambridge: Cambridge University Press, 1997, chapters 2 and 3.
87 This development is a natural extension of the thawing of political relations since the end of the Cold War, but also of the development of a more comprehensive concept of development – development as the expansion of capabilities – and a greater focus on democratic legitimacy of states and on the role of individual agency in development (as a process and as an outcome). See United Nations Development Programme, *Human Development Report 2000*, Oxford: Oxford University Press, 2000.

identification of rights-holders, duty-bearers and a clearer notion of the content of this duty. This, however, is not a simple matter, for there is still considerable controversy over the interpretation of this duty under international law. The first step is to determine to what extent the international community has defined its reciprocal, multilateral duties of cooperation for development. This is done by assessing the most relevant treaty norms defining the duty of cooperation (1) and by completing the normative lacunae by reference to non-binding, yet widely accepted, instruments and declarations (2). It is then concluded that a duty to 'cause no harm' can be deduced from the different sources of international law (3), and that this standard is clear enough to guide the ulterior discussion on the responsibility of ECAs.

7.3.1.1 Cooperation for development: treaty obligations

The obligation to cooperate for the realization of development is best understood as the sum of multiple, discrete obligations imposed on states in different treaties. The most central source for the obligation is the United Nations Charter, a universally accepted treaty that has primacy over other sources of international obligations. In its preamble, the Charter states that the peoples of the UN, 'determined to promote social progress and better standards of life in larger freedom', will 'employ international machinery for the promotion of the economic and social advancement of all peoples'. The exhortatory language is rendered operative by a number of binding treaty provisions that accomplish one of two things: they either restrict the possibility that states undertake actions that impinge on the self-determination of peoples,[88] or they require states to actively pursue 'co-operation in solving international problems of an economic, social, cultural, or humanitarian character, and in promoting and encouraging respect for human rights and for fundamental freedoms for all without distinction as to race, sex, language, or religion'.[89] Development and human rights, therefore, are seen as essential issues for cooperation among states. If, under Article 1, the goals of respect for self-determination and cooperation are core 'purposes' of the UN, it is in Article 55 of the Charter that the specific means to accomplish them are enumerated. Member states are expected to promote higher standards of living and 'conditions of economic and social progress and development', 'solutions of economic, social . . . and related problems', and 'universal respect for, and observance of, human rights and fundamental freedoms'.[90] There is no suggestion that these obligations of cooperation are limited territorially: all states are jointly and separately held

---

88 Art. 1(2) reads '[The UN's purpose is] to develop friendly relations among nations based on respect for the principle of equal rights and self-determination of peoples'. See United Nations, *Charter of the United Nations*, 24 October 1945, 1 UNTS XVI.
89 Ibid., Art. 1(3).
90 Ibid., Art. 55(1–3).

responsible for the achievement of these purposes, in all states.[91] To a certain extent, this allows the issues of human rights and development to escape from the general presumption that state sovereignty precludes intervention 'in matters which are essentially within the domestic jurisdiction' of states.

As argued by Margot Salomon,[92] Article 55 has been interpreted as founding the normative basis for both the 1948 Universal Declaration on Human Rights and the 1986 Declaration on the Right to Development. Through the Charter, these declarations have achieved a mandatory character, a fact that has received some support in International Court of Justice (ICJ) jurisprudence.[93] We will return to these other instruments below.

Additional sources for a duty to cooperate for development can be seen, albeit in negative form, in both International Covenants on human rights.[94] Common Article 1 of the covenants guarantees the rights of peoples to self-determination, and to the free disposition of their natural wealth and resources.[95] The right to self-determination means that '[peoples] freely determine their political status and freely pursue their economic, social and cultural development'. The entitlement to dispose freely of natural wealth and resources is 'without prejudice to any obligations arising out of international economic cooperation, based upon the principle of mutual benefit, and international law'. These two provisions are deeply embedded in the dynamics of the early post-colonial years, in which the non-aligned countries and the West clashed over the establishment of a New International Economic Order in which the former hoped to rebalance the rules of the global economy.[96] The language, therefore, is somewhat vague and riddled with caveats, as is to be expected given the drafting history of this and other instruments at the time.[97] However, there is little doubt that this provision creates a collective, continuing right of peoples to self-determination,[98] not limited to those under colonization or foreign

---

91 Ibid., Art. 56.
92 M.E. Salomon, *Global Responsibility for Human Rights – World Poverty and the Development of International Law*, Oxford: Oxford University Press, 2007, at p. 67. See also M.E. Salomon, 'International Human Rights Obligations in Context: Structural obstacles and the demands of global justice,' in B.A. Andreassen and S.P. Marks (eds), *Development as a Human Right: Legal, political and economic dimensions*, 2nd edn, Antwerp: Intersentia, 2010, pp. 121–147.
93 Salomon, 2007, op. cit., p. 69.
94 International Covenant on Economic, Social and Cultural Rights, adopted by General Assembly Resolution 2200A (XXI) of 16 December 1966 (UN Doc. A/6316 [1966]), 993 UNTS 3 and International Covenant on Civil and Political Rights, adopted by General Assembly Resolution 2200A (XXI) of 16 December 1966 (UN Doc. A/6316 [1966]), 999 UNTS 171.
95 Art. 1(1–2).
96 See A. Anghie, *Imperialism, Sovereignty and the Making of International Law*, Cambridge: Cambridge University Press, 2004, Chapter 4.
97 See Schrijver, op. cit., pp. 33–113.
98 See M. Nowak, *UN Covenant on Civil and Political Rights – CCPR Commentary*, 2nd Revised Edition, Kehl: Norbert Paul Engel Verlag, e.K., 2005, p. 15.

subjugation.[99] Self-determination contains external (independence) and internal (participatory democracy) dimensions, as well as economic, social and cultural aspects.[100]

Article 2(1) of the International Covenant on Economic, Social and Cultural Rights (ICESCR), which defines the obligations of states with respect to the rights contained in the Covenant, is particularly relevant for our purposes. Each state party 'undertakes to take steps, individually *and through international assistance and co-operation, especially economic and technical*, to the maximum of its available resources, with a view to achieving progressively the full realization of the rights recognized in the present Covenant by all appropriate means, including particularly the adoption of legislative measures'.[101] This provision makes no distinction between developed or developing states, and the Covenant itself does not limit the application of the rights to the state's territory or jurisdiction. This latter omission is particularly relevant in light of the fact that the International Covenant on Civil and Political Rights (ICCPR) does contain a clause limiting the scope of state obligations to individuals 'within its territory and subject to its jurisdiction'.[102] The Committee on Economic, Social and Cultural Rights (CESCR) has interpreted the duty to 'take steps, to the maximum of available resources, through international cooperation' to require developed states to extend assistance so that other states can make progress towards the full realization of the Covenant rights:

> . . . in accordance with Articles 55 and 56 of the Charter of the United Nations, with well-established principles of international law, and with the provisions of the Covenant itself, international cooperation for development and thus for the realization of economic, social and cultural rights is an obligation of all States. *It is particularly incumbent upon those States which are in a position to assist others in this regard.*[103]

Moreover, Article 22 of the ICESCR enables the UN's Economic and Social Council to advise the UN and its specialized agencies on measures they can adopt, within their respective mandates, to further the realization of the Covenant. In order to assist the Council in this task, the CESCR – invited by the Human Rights Commission – adopted a General Comment on international technical assistance measures,[104] in which it elaborates on the role of the UN and its organs and agencies. The Comment notes that the UN had given

99 Ibid., p. 20.
100 Ibid., pp. 22–26.
101 ICCPR, *supra* n. 94., Art. 2.
102 Ibid., Art. 2(1).
103 CESCR, *General comment 3 – The nature of States parties obligations (Art. 2, para. 1)*, adopted 14 December 1990 (UN Document E/1991/23), para. 14 (emphasis added).
104 CESCR, *General comment 2 – International technical assistance measures (Art. 22)*, adopted 2 February 1990 (UN document E/1990/23).

relatively little consideration to the issue of rights, and in particular economic social and cultural rights, in its development activities.[105] Noting that 'many activities undertaken in the name of "development" have subsequently been recognized as ill-conceived and even counter-productive in human rights terms', the Committee suggests that due consideration be given to human rights impact assessment[106] and improved training of UN personnel, and that 'effort should be made, at each phase of a development project, to ensure that the rights contained in the covenants are duly taken into account'.[107] Finally, Article 23 of the Covenant renders explicit that states are expected to achieve the progressive realization of the rights contained in the treaty by 'such methods as the conclusion of conventions, the adoption of recommendations, the furnishing of technical assistance and the holding [of meetings]'. This suggests that treaty-making, and other international coordination measures adopted by states parties, should be conducive to improvement in the realization of Covenant rights, and the adoption of such acts with regressive consequences can, in and of itself, breach the Covenant. In conclusion, it is arguable that there are obligations, under international law, to adopt measures *in favour of*, and in any case *not contrary to*, the economic, social and cultural development of states and their populations. The content, of these obligations, however, is not precisely defined.

7.3.1.2 Completing the normative context: declarations and international conferences

The role of declaratory statements in the formation of customary norms of international law is unsettled. They might be particularly relevant in the context of human rights because the standard rules for finding state practice and *opinio juris* might not be useful. States discuss human rights collectively, not on a bilateral claim and counter-claim manner.[108] It could be, however, that declarations and conference statements are adopted with more ease, and on a wider variety of issues, precisely because the drafters consider themselves not

---

105 Ibid., paras 5 and 8(a). In the latter, the Committee notes 'the failure of each of the first three United Nations Development Decade Strategies to recognize [the] relationship [between rights and development]'.

106 Ibid., para. 8(b), recalling 'the proposal, made by the Secretary-General in a report of 1979 [E/CN.4/1334, para. 314] that a "human rights impact statement" be required to be prepared in connection with all major development cooperation activities'.

107 Ibid., para. 8(d).

108 S. Narula, 'The Right to Food: Holding Global Actors Accountable Under International Law', *Columbia Journal of Transnational Law*, 44, 2006, 691–800, at p. 777–778 (quoting Oscar Schachter, to the effect that the traditional view of state practice and *opinio juris* 'are inappropriate for the formation of custom in the area of human rights, where states do not usually make claims directly on other states and rarely protest one-on-one another state's violations that do not affect their nationals'). See also B. Simma and P. Alston, 'Sources of Human Rights Law: Custom, *Jus Cogens*, and General Principles', *Australian Yearbook of International Law* 12, 1988, 82–108.

to be legally bound by their terms. However that may be, there is little dispute today that some declarations have assumed particular relevance as sources of law because they provide meaning to an underdetermined binding rule. Two declarations adopted by the UN are of special relevance to our subject and illustrate this process of norm formation.

The first of these is the Universal Declaration on Human Rights (UDHR) of 1948, [109] which is widely believed to clarify the human rights that states have pledged to achieve under UN Charter Article 55(a).[110] Though the Charter does not confer rights directly to individuals, it recognizes that individuals have rights under international law, rights the realization of which it is the duty of all states to achieve by 'joint and separate action'. Of the rights proclaimed by the UDHR, two are of particular interest. Article 22 consecrates the right of all persons to the realization 'through national effort and international co-operation' of the economic, social and cultural rights indispensable for their dignity and for the free development of their personality. This exemplifies the rights-based approach to socioeconomic development, whereas Article 28 gives a vivid illustration of a more 'structural' approach by requiring all states to establish a 'social and international order in which the rights and freedoms set forth in this Declaration can be fully realized'. This requirement can hardly be squared with international rules that would allow states or private actors to infringe on the rights of every person to socioeconomic development.

The second source is the Declaration on the Right to Development (DRD) of 1986.[111] As with the UDHR, this Declaration can be understood as an authoritative interpretation of the duty of states to accomplish 'higher standards of living, full employment, and conditions of economic and social progress and development', under Charter Article 55(b). For present purposes, two sets of provisions are particularly relevant. Article 1 defines the concept of development as ensuring that 'every human person and all peoples are entitled to participate in, contribute to, and enjoy economic, social, cultural and political development, in which all human rights and fundamental freedoms can be fully realized'. The second paragraph further requires that development be accomplished in line with the right of all peoples to self-determination and to 'full sovereignty' over natural resources. Article 3 places the 'primary responsibility' for the realization of development on states, requiring them to establish 'national and international conditions favourable to the realization of the right to development'. Furthermore, under Article 3(3), states are required to cooperate in order to eliminate obstacles to development, thereby promoting 'a new international economic order based on sovereign equality, interdependence, mutual interest and co-operation among all States'.

---

109 Universal Declaration of Human Rights, General Assembly Resolution 217A (III), 10 December 1948.
110 See Salomon, 2007, op. cit., pp. 71–75.
111 Declaration on the Right to Development, General Assembly Resolution A/RES/41/128, adopted 4 December 1986, UN Document A/RES/41/53 (1986).

It would be beyond the scope of this chapter to attempt a systematic presentation of the numerous additional sources that could be quoted in support of these basic principles. Numerous World Conferences and other UN Declarations could be relied on to provide evidence of overwhelming support for the notion of development as shared responsibility of the community of states.[112] From the very early development decades, to the post-Cold War World Conferences, all the way to the Millennium Declaration of 2000,[113] these different fora have reinforced the general message of shared responsibility for development. The 2005 World Summit outcome highlighted the structural impediments to autonomous development policies, and the need for preliminary assessment, with particular clarity:

> . . . the increasing interdependence of national economies in a globalizing world and the emergence of rule-based regimes for international economic relations have meant that the space for national economic policy, that is, the scope for domestic policies, especially in the areas of trade, investment and industrial development, is now often framed by international disciplines, commitments and global market considerations. It is for each Government to evaluate the trade-off between the benefits of accepting international rules and commitments and the constraints posed by the loss of policy space. It is particularly important for developing countries, bearing in mind development goals and objectives, that all countries take into account the need for appropriate balance between national policy space and international disciplines and commitments.[114]

These different sources, taken together, and read in the light of the UN Charter, constitute evidence of an increasingly clear normative framework requiring states to cooperate for the achievement of development at home and abroad, and to remove those obstacles to development that originate in the rules that underpin the global economy. This framework grounds both negative obligations – amounting to the prohibition of conduct that institutes or maintains obstacles to development – and the positive, but normatively weak, obligation of cooperating for development, to the extent of the states' capacity to do so.

7.3.1.3 Conclusion: 'Do no harm'?

If the sources discussed above are to be read as suggested, their minimal requirement is that states abstain from knowingly setting obstacles to

---

112 See Salomon, 2007, op. cit., pp. 92–98.
113 United Nations Millennium Declaration, General Assembly Resolution A/RES/55/2, adopted 18 September 2000.
114 2005 World Summit Outcome, General Assembly Resolution A/RES/60/1, adopted 24 October 2005, para. 22(d).

development. This requirement that impact be foreseeable, rather than intended, would seem to be a reasonable compromise: intent would imply a 'penal conception' of accountability, setting the bar too high, whereas dispensing with the requirement of prior knowledge would in practice result in a counter-productive regime of strict liability. The requirement that impact on development be foreseeable, can moreover, be interpreted as imposing the procedural requirement that states undertake assessment of potential consequences of their actions on the development of other states. An appropriate level of due diligence is required. Given that there is little clarity on *both* the measurement of preferred development outcomes and on the foreseeability of impacts, ensuring accountability – at the aggregate level at least – remains elusive. The establishment of the aforementioned procedural requirement moves the debate from resignation with uncertainty, towards a commitment to formulate expectations, perceptions of risk and mitigation policies publicly and prior to any intervention.

7.3.2 *Other international human rights obligations*

If obligations exist to the effect that states must cooperate to create a development-enabling environment, these do not raise issues of interference in the domestic affairs of other states, nor can they be questioned as the illegitimate exercise of extraterritorial jurisdiction. They are merely the collective exercise of consensual policy coordination. They also refer to the improvement of a common regulatory framework under which all states can flourish. This corresponds to an aggregate and structural approach to development. If one looks at development from a rights-based perspective, however, the issues are somewhat different: states are expected to act, or to refrain from acting, on the grounds that the rights of persons within or outside their territory might be violated due to the state's conduct. The practice of human rights courts and monitoring bodies increasingly requires that states take into consideration their duties to respect, protect and fulfil human rights[115] in their territorial and extraterritorial dimensions.[116]

7.3.2.1 *The principle: host state obligation over its own territory*

There is no doubt that, under international law, states have primary responsibility for the realization of human rights within their territory and for

---

115 On this 'tripartite division of obligations', see S. I. Skogly, *Beyond National Borders: States' Human Rights Obligations in International Cooperation*, Antwerp: Intersentia, 2006, pp. 60ff.

116 On this issue, see F. Coomans and M.T. Kamminga (eds), *Extraterritorial application of Human Rights Treaties*, Antwerp: Intersentia, 2004, and M. Gondek, *The Reach of Human Rights in a Globalising World: Extraterritorial Application of Human Rights Treaties*, Antwerp: Intersentia, 2008, in particular Chapter VII.

those persons under their jurisdiction. Even with respect to entitlements of a collective nature, such as the duty of states to cooperate for the development of peoples, this primary role of the state is unquestioned. States must therefore adopt measures that ensure not only that they respect and fulfil the rights of persons subject to their jurisdiction, but also that individuals are protected against rights violations from other non-state actors. The measures to be adopted do not limit themselves to laws or domestic policies, but also include the conduct of states in their international relations. Therefore, it is expected that states, by entering into economic agreements, will previously scrutinize their new commitments in light of prior, or superior, obligations they might have under international law, and in particular those in the field of human rights. This prudential policy of seeking to avoid conflicting obligations during the negotiation and in the interpretation of treaty obligations[117] cannot, however, uniformly avoid the emergence of conflict, in particular because of the open-ended, evolving interpretation of both human rights and international economic law norms. While a state's obligation to protect human rights – such as the right to work or the right to a healthy environment – might require it to enact general legislation to promote higher standards of labour or environmental protection, international investment agreements, or individual host-state agreements, might contain stabilization clauses that in effect deprive the state of the possibility to do precisely that.

When such conflicts arise, and from a purely strategic perspective, states have increasingly strong incentives to comply with the set of obligations that carries the greatest potential for effective sanctions: in general, negative investment arbitration will impose far higher costs on the state than would a regional human rights court. This is not simply because the award itself would impose higher damages, but because of the chilling effect that such decisions can have on the risk perception for other investment in the country. Markets have traditionally been far more tolerant of political and social repression than they have of investor risk. It might be tempting for a state to sacrifice the rights of specific individuals or groups in order to attract investment that is expected to have a net beneficial effect at the national level, even if local welfare effects are negative.

Openness to international trade and investment is also associated with increased vulnerability to external shocks. So even when no regulatory difficulties arise between potentially conflicting obligations during periods of relative stability, a regional or global crisis – often bearing no relation to the host state's policies – can trigger widespread disruption. At this point, a weakened regulatory framework and a reduced fiscal capacity to intervene will aggravate the crisis and its social effects. It is therefore clear that national initiatives to protect human rights and promote development, however

---

117 J. Pauwelyn, *Conflict of Norms in Public International Law – How WTO Law Relates to Other Rules of International Law*, Cambridge: Cambridge University Press, 2003, pp. 237ff.

important, are sometimes perceived as economically impractical and, in some cases, even illicit under rules of international economic law. For this reason, enough latitude in policy must be guaranteed, under international law, for states to pursue their development policies and ensure rights within their borders.[118]

7.3.2.2 Home state obligations

The state of origin of investors is subject to its own human rights obligations under international law, obligations imposed by the Charter on *all* member states – such as the duty to cooperate for development – as well as those specific international human rights obligations that the state has either assumed by the ratification of international treaties, or those it has by virtue of international custom. Every international obligation accepted in this manner creates specific duties of respect, protection and fulfilment. And some of these obligations have extraterritorial dimensions.

The territorial obligations of states in human rights matters require little additional comment: capital-exporting countries are subject to similar legal constraints to capital-importing ones. However, in great measure due to their more advanced, diversified and stable economies, these states are less vulnerable to certain risks, and have substantial capacity – both fiscal and social – to endure the negative effects of crises without severely affecting the enjoyment of rights within their own territory.

The obligation to protect human rights, however, has significant extraterritorial elements. This is not only true in the context of military occupations and the administration of foreign territories,[119] or in the design and implementation of multilateral sanctions in the context of Security Council activities,[120] but especially in the field of development cooperation and with respect to state conduct mediated by international organizations and arrangements. The obligation to protect human rights from non-state threats, in particular, creates an obligation on home states to exercise reasonable measures of precaution to ensure that enterprises incorporated within its territory do not contribute to the violation of human rights abroad.[121] It is

118 N. Hachez and J. Wouters, 'When Rules and Values Collide: How can a Balanced Application of Investor Protection Provisions and Human Rights Be Ensured?', *Human Rights and International Legal Discourse*, 3(2), 2009, 301–344.

119 Gondek, op. cit., pp. 304–316 (referring, *inter alia*, to the ICJ's Advisory opinion on the *Legal Consequences of the Construction of a Wall in the Occupied Palestinian Territories*, for the applicability of economic, social and cultural rights in the occupied territories).

120 Ibid., pp. 340–346.

121 See Office of the High Commissioner for Human Rights, *Guiding Principles on Business and Human Rights – Implementing the United Nations 'protect, respect and remedy' framework*, Geneva: United Nations Publications (HR/PUB/11/04), 2011, Principle 2 ('States should set out clearly the expectation that all business enterprises domiciled in their territory and/or jurisdiction respect human rights throughout their operations.') and commentary.

arguably the case that a similar standard of care is required of the representatives of states acting in international organizations, when they are in a position to block measures that would have detrimental effects on the enjoyment of human rights in third countries.[122]

In summary, states are required to exercise influence on non-state actors by properly regulating multinational corporations operating from their territory, by conditioning public support to these enterprises to adequate standards of human rights due diligence,[123] and by seeking to ensure that the conduct of international organizations of which they are parties is sensitive to the realization of human rights in other countries.

7.3.3 *The question of attribution of conduct to the state*

Under which conditions the acts or omissions of ECAs can be attributed to the state under international law is a crucial stake in the determination of the accountability of these agencies. Under the Articles on Responsibility of States for internationally wrongful acts,[124] attribution of ECA conduct to the state can be envisaged under two different circumstances. Under Article 4, the conduct of any state organ – any person or entity having the status of organ in accordance with internal law – is an act of that state. According to the International Law Commission (ILC) commentaries on Article 4, the reference to state organ extends to organs of government 'of whatever kind or classification, exercising whatever functions and at whatever level in the hierarchy'.[125] This, of course, includes export credit agencies which are part of the public administration. Regarding those agencies which are incorporated under private law, the Articles on Responsibility refer, under Article 5, to the 'conduct of persons or entities exercising elements of governmental authority'.[126] The Commentaries explain that the Article refers to parastatal and former state corporations that have been

---

122 See for instance, Report of the Special Rapporteur on the right to food, Olivier De Schutter (Mission to the World Trade Organization), adopted 4 February 2009 (UN Document A/HRC/10/5/Add.2), para. 50. See also, Report by the Special Rapporteur on the Right to Food, Jean Ziegler, adopted 24 January 2005 (UN Document E/CN.4/2005/47), para. 52.

123 See *Protect, Respect and Remedy: a Framework for Business and Human Rights*, Report of the Special Representative of the Secretary-General on the issue of human rights and transnational corporations and other business enterprises, John Ruggie, adopted 7 April 2008 (UN Doc A/HRC/8/5), paras 56–64.

124 International Law Commission, Draft articles on Responsibility of States for internationally wrongful acts, and commentary, published in *Yearbook of the International Law Commission, 2001*, vol. II, Part Two.

125 Ibid., Commentary to Article 4, para. 6.

126 Ibid., Art. 5, which reads 'The conduct of a person or entity which is not an organ of the State under article 4 but which is empowered by the law of that State to exercise elements of the governmental authority shall be considered an act of the State under international law, provided the person or entity is acting in that capacity in the particular instance.'

privatized but retain certain public or regulatory functions.[127] Thus, the test for attribution is not a *formal*, but rather a *functional* one,[128] as expressed by the ILC:

> The fact that an entity can be classified as public or private according to the criteria of a given legal system, the existence of a greater or lesser State participation in its capital, or, more generally, in the ownership of its assets, the fact that it is not subject to executive control – these are not decisive criteria for the purpose of attribution of the entity's conduct to the State. Instead, Article 5 refers to the true common feature, namely that these entities are empowered, if only to a limited extent or in a specific context, to exercise specified elements of governmental authority.[129]

It is by reference to what the internal law of the state considers to be 'governmental authority', an eminently context-specific notion,[130] that the acts of an entity will be attributed to the state. To the extent that ECAs are underwritten by public funds, can rely on fiscal support from the state, and are accountable – even if not ostensibly – to the public or the government, it is likely that its actions will be attributable to the state.

As other have noted, 'export credit finance and insurance is not inherently a state monopoly.'[131] As discussed above, however, the core function of these agencies *is not* to provide risk insurance *per se*, but rather to provide it (i) under conditions where private institutions are unwilling to do so; and (ii) in the pursuit of domestic policy goals which arguably fall within the traditional scope of 'governmental authority' (i.e. industrial and social policy objectives such as controlling unemployment, defending domestic producers against unfair, subsidized competition from foreign firms, and supporting critical economic sectors). The fact that the state subsidizes the provision of insurance, and potentially backs the transactions of its ECAs – and most notably the risk of foreign non-performance or default – with fiscal support, is only justified

---

127 Ibid., Commentary to Art. 5, para. 1.
128 See K. Keenan, 'Export Credit Agencies and the International Law of Human Rights', Paper prepared for the Special Representative of the United Nations Secretary-General on Business and Human Rights, January 2008, available at <http://198.170.85.29/Halifax-Initiative-Export-Credit-Agencies-Jan-2008.pdf> (accessed 26 March 2012), at p. 2. See also O. Can and S. L. Seck, 'The Legal Obligations with Respect to Human Rights and Credit Export Agencies', paper prepared for ECA-Watch, available at <http://www.halifaxinitiative.org/updir/ECAHRlegalFINAL.pdf> (accessed 26 March 2012), at pp. 6–9.
129 ILC, op. cit., comment to Art. 5, para. 3.
130 Ibid., para. 5, 'Beyond a certain limit, what is regarded as "governmental" depends on the particular society, its history and traditions. Of particular importance will be not just the *content of the powers*, but *the way they are conferred* on an entity, *the purposes* for which they are to be exercised and the *extent to which the entity is accountable* to government for their exercise' (emphasis added).
131 Knigge et al., op. cit., p. 13.

insofar as the purpose of the state intervention is *demonstrably* that of ensuring these domestic policy goals, and 'levelling the playing field', rather than simply distorting trade in its favour. That is why the OECD Arrangement reduces the scope for states engaging in what could otherwise be carried out as a commercial activity by private actors. In practice, the line between an ECA acting in the pursuit of a public mandate that international law considers to fall within 'governmental authority', and its actions as a private insurer, can be blurred. In the case of privately incorporated ECAs, attribution will probably have to be assessed on a case-by-case basis, by an analysis of the nature of the contested transaction.

7.3.4 Grounds for responsibility

There are essentially two manners in which ECA activities, when attributed to the state, could engage its international responsibility. The first involves the ECA failing to carry out required due diligence, thereby aiding or facilitating a violation, by the host state, of human rights obligations. A second hypothesis involves the direct violation of a home state obligation, with the ECA enabling a project that contributes to the violation of human rights in the host state.

7.3.4.1 Aid and assistance to host state unlawful conduct

Article 16 of the Articles on Responsibility establishes that a state which aids or assists another state in the commission of an internationally wrongful act is responsible for that act if it is doing so knowingly, and if the act would be wrongful if committed by it.[132] In practice, this means that the responsibility of the ECA home state can be engaged if it supports a project or investment, when the host is negligent in its obligation to protect human rights in its own territory. If, in these circumstances, the home and host state share the same obligations under international law (i.e. if the conduct, if carried by the assisting state, would have been a breach of its own international human rights duties – the act of assistance, of providing financial means for the illicit conduct, can engage the responsibility of the ECA home state). The test would seem to be two-pronged: whether the state had knowledge of the likelihood of wrongful conduct,[133] and whether there was intent to facilitate the occurrence of the

---

132 ILC, op. cit., Art. 16 reads: 'A State which aids or assists another State in the commission of an internationally wrongful act by the latter is internationally responsible for doing so if: (a) that State does so with knowledge of the circumstances of the internationally wrongful act; and (b) the act would be internationally wrongful if committed by that State.'

133 Ibid., Commentary to Art. 16, para. 4 reads: 'A State providing material or financial assistance or aid to another State does not normally assume the risk that its assistance or aid may be used to carry out an internationally wrongful act. If the assisting or aiding State is unaware of the circumstances in which its aid or assistance is intended to be used by the other State, it bears no international responsibility.'

wrongful act.[134] Though the ILC explicitly envisages a state incurring responsibility for 'provid[ing] material aid to a State that uses the aid to commit human rights violations',[135] the requirement of intent makes it harder to found responsibility based on mere financial aid.[136] However, given the increasing use of *ex ante* impact assessments of large projects, and given the high impacts of such investment projects, the requirements of knowledge and intent could be met if, for instance, mitigation policies prescribed by the impact assessment were not carried out faithfully, or were not even required by the ECA as a condition for disbursements, or the payment of guarantees. Both preliminary risk assessment and the systematic monitoring of compliance with socio-environmental and human rights conditions are therefore crucial in ensuring that project finance is accountable.

7.3.4.2 *Home state wrongful conduct*

A second ground for responsibility of the state involves the breach, by ECA activities, of the home state's own obligations to protect human rights. As discussed previously, every state has an obligation under the UN Charter to cooperate for development, including the obligation to abstain from measures that would entail regression in the realization of the right to development and of other human rights. Additionally, states have extraterritorial obligations under human rights treaties, and most notably the duty to regulate the conduct of non-state actors over which they have influence, so that their conduct does not lead to the violation of human rights abroad. As public entities, ECAs can contribute to this process by screening the projects they might guarantee, putting particular emphasis on investor and exporter human rights due diligence obligations. An ECA can require, for instance, that those seeking insurance commit themselves to presenting assessments of possible negative impacts prior to investment, and continuous reporting after the investment has been initiated. Furthermore, it could condition the payment of claims to the full respect of social, environmental and human rights conditions, giving investors a strong incentive to comply with project commitments scrupulously. In its role as enabler of foreign investment and international trade, and as insurer of last resort, the ECA is in a particularly fruitful position to exert pressure on prospective clients to integrate human rights and development considerations into their project design and implementation.

134 Ibid., para. 5.
135 Ibid., para. 9.
136 This point seems to have been overlooked by the Independent Expert on the effects of foreign debt on the enjoyment of human rights, when he fails to include the intent requirement in his assessment of accomplice responsibility. Cephas Lumina, *Report of the Independent Expert on the effects of foreign debt and other related international financial obligations of States on the full enjoyment of all human rights, particularly economic, social and cultural rights* (A/66/271), 5 August 2011, para. 52.

Human rights treaties require not only that states adopt measures to protect the rights of individuals from unlawful infringements by non-state actors, but also demands that efficient remedies be put in place to ensure that those whose rights have been violated can seek redress.[137] Failure to provide such a redress mechanism can itself lead to a violation, by the state, of its obligations under international human rights law. Therefore, states should ensure that ECAs be subject to accountability within the home state, possibly before domestic courts, and also that these agencies embed redress mechanisms in the projects they finance, allowing for affected populations to communicate grievances to the agency, or to a delegated authority within the host country.

7.4 An assessment of development and human rights impacts of ECAs

In line with the author's previous work on the impact of FDI (foreign direct investment) on human development,[138] this section discusses the potential impacts of ECA-supported credits, insurance and guarantees at two different levels. In a first step, the aggregate, national-level impacts are briefly addressed (1). The next step consists in the evaluation of effects at the project level, and their contribution to human development (2).

7.4.1 Macro-level aspects

The simplest way to characterize ECA contribution to national aggregates is to think of its activities as allowing investment and trade to take place in environments and under conditions that market operators would consider too risky for themselves. Therefore, ECAs allow an increase of total investment, but select riskier projects and countries. Though not all of this is due to the inherent political difficulties of operating in the host state – private financial actors must consider the twin imperatives of meeting capital requirements and of diversifying the portfolio of investments to spread the risk – it is reasonable to conclude that a considerable amount of investment would not take place if governments did not step in to offer guarantees to their exporters and investors.

When an ECA supports a project or transaction, it is underwriting the inflow of foreign currency into the host state, and guaranteeing it against the risk of non-convertibility. The creditors in the agency home state expect that the importer, or the project operator, will not only be commercially viable, but will also be able to acquire currency in order to repay foreign loans. Though trade finance, and in particular short-term trade credit, is generally self-liquidating and low risk, the medium- and long-term transactions that constitute the

---

137 OHCHR, op. cit., Principle 25 and Commentary.
138 M. Sant'Ana, 'Foreign Direct Investment and Human Development: Two Approaches to Assessing Human Rights Impacts', *Human Rights and International Legal Discourse* 3(2), 2009, 229–262.

ECA's core business are a different matter. For instance, infrastructure projects, such as telecommunications, energy or water provision services, often involve contracts in foreign currency, but have revenue streams in domestic currency.[139] When a currency devaluation affects the country, BITs or host state agreements might require that tariffs be adjusted upwards, which of course is an unpopular policy with consumers. In cases such as the privatization of the water supply in Argentina,[140] this puts states in a difficult position: the state must either increase prices, facing internal opposition and reducing access to an indispensable resource, or freeze tariff rates and be challenged by foreign investors through investment arbitration.[141] In the past, with a monetary system based on pegged currencies, foreign exchange shortages leading to balance of payment difficulties meant that the state would suspend convertibility. This would be typically considered to fall within political risk insurance, covered by ECAs. However, as monetary markets integrate and floating exchange has now become the norm, foreign exchange shortages lead to depreciation of national currency, normally classified as commercial risks. Though commercial risk insurance coverage in the short term is carried out mostly by private actors, currency depreciation can have considerable effects on project viability.[142] Widespread capital market liberalization has also meant that steep fluctuations of national currency are more frequent. In case a serious devaluation occurs, importers with foreign currency-denominated debt will have greater risk of default or insolvency, which in turn might put pressure on states to either assume part of buyer, project, or bank debt, or establish exchange rate protections for them.[143] In such infrastructure projects, FDI means that the state must commit a substantial portion of its foreign reserves to repayment of private debt held by foreign investors. If it fails to do so, not only will the resulting balance of payment difficulties affect the entire economy – and particularly the capacity to acquire vital imports – but it might precipitate a debt crisis.[144]

Some commentators have pointed out the strong link between trade finance and debt,[145] and, as seen above, the OECD considers that ECAs have a significant role to play in ensuring that credit facilities extended to least-developed

---

139 Stephens, op. cit., p. 36.
140 See International Centre for Human Rights and Democratic Development, *Human Rights Impact Assessments for Foreign Investment Projects – Learning from Community Experiences in the Philippines, Tibet, the Democratic Republic of Congo, Argentina, and Peru*, 2007, available at <http://epe.lac-bac.gc.ca/100/200/301/intl_centre_human_rights/human_rights_impact-e/E84-21-2007E.pdf> (accessed 6 August 2012).
141 This was the object of the International Centre for the Settlement of Investment Disputes (ICSID) arbitration, in *Aguas Cordobesas S.A., Suez, and Sociedad General de Aguas de Barcelona S.A. v Argentine Republic* (ICSID Case No. ARB/03/18), which ended in a settlement.
142 Stephens, op. cit., pp. 43–44.
143 Ibid., pp. 37–38.
144 Lumina, op. cit., paras 11–17.
145 See, for instance, Auboin, 2010, op. cit., p. 8, and Bohn, op. cit., p. 487.

countries do not worsen a country's debt sustainability situation. The OECD emphasis on screening out 'unproductive credits', discussed previously, focuses on the idea that only investment that can produce a sustained stream of revenue or that considerably multiplies the capacity of states to service their debt should be promoted. Under the OECD arrangement this results in a bifurcated system: for the least developed countries, investments that cannot be justified as productive and safe have to be funded on a highly concessional basis, whereas self-sustaining projects could benefit from standard ECA facilities.

This is particularly relevant in periods of crisis. Since the Basel Committee on Banking Supervision (BCBS) reviewed its criteria for assessing the risk of trade finance in the Basel II framework on 'international convergence of capital measurement and capital standards', trade finance has been rated as more risky than under Basel I. This has meant that, during financial crises, the availability of trade finance has decreased disproportionately.[146] When private sector creditors and insurers retract from the market, ECAs are asked to fill the trade finance gap as a matter of urgency, which precludes thoughtful consideration of the impact that this new debt might have on the country's debt sustainability in the longer term. Furthermore, involvement of multilateral agencies and ECAs often gives *de facto* preferred creditor status to guaranteed loans and investments, which also suggests that developing countries will be less able to restructure their debt.[147]

7.4.2 *Project level aspects*

Investment projects funded by ECAs can have important nationwide effects, as when the provision of public goods such as water or electricity becomes costlier in order to satisfy the conditions imposed by host-state agreements or BITs. But projects with a large physical footprint also have important local-level impacts including, *inter alia*, the forced evictions of native populations, denial of access to vital means of production or pollution of natural resources, harsh labour conditions or deterioration of health. The crucial issue, therefore, is to ensure that negative impacts that can be foreseen are effectively considered in the design and management of projects.

In a study of labour and employment issues in FDI, Bonnie Penfold noted that of the 25 publicly held agencies offering overseas investment insurance reviewed by the study, only four required labour or employment-related standards of their clients.[148] The standards against which the screening of projects was to be made involved, in the case of the US Overseas Private Investment Corporation (OPIC), the rights to organize and bargain collectively, a minimum age for labour, prohibition of forced labour and acceptable conditions of work. Labour standards were assessed by asking potential investors

146 Auboin, 2010, op. cit., p. 8.
147 Hayes and Cummings, op. cit., p. 17.
148 Penfold, op. cit., p. 11.

to explain how labour relations were integrated into the project, and to answer precise questions on the status of workers in the project envisaged. Misrepresentations and failure to disclose information could lead to cancellation of insurance. Though this might be an interesting approach to ensuring accountability for labour standards violations, the fact that few public insurers have included such conditions in their screening processes suggests that the issue is still in its infancy.

A similar type of study, focusing on environmental criteria in ECA-supported projects,[149] assessed the environmental conditions required by nine OECD-member ECAs in relation to large dam projects, using the World Commission on Dams framework of analysis. It notes, first, that environmental and social standards were the exception until the late 1990s. Currently, however, these conditions have been integrated into all of the nine ECAs assessed, though the methods and depth of their integration into the project design process varies considerably. In terms of screening, all ECAs use questionnaires supplied with applications for support, and on this basis categorize projects according to their risk. In accordance with OECD Arrangement rules, a full environmental assessment is required only in the highest risk category. Small or short-term projects are often exempted from screening procedures. The requirement that mitigation measures designed to reduce impact be monitored has also increasingly been included in loan agreements, establishing covenants and imposing reporting requirements. Reporting is usually done by the project sponsor, though some ECAs are starting to use third-party monitoring. Failure in the reporting duties and in the implementation of mitigation measures can result, in most cases, in withdrawal of coverage. However, the study confirms that this sanction has hardly ever been used by the agencies. Transparency and disclosure policies of ECAs have traditionally been a contentious question due to the conflicting demands of ECA public mandate and client confidentiality. The trend observed in the study, however, has been towards more disclosure, in a more timely and accessible manner. Finally, the issue of public participation remains elusive, although ECAs have in general tended to require that sponsors undertake consultations with affected communities, generally as part of environmental impact assessment.[150]

There is no systematic requirement to assess the impact of projects on human rights standards. Some ECAs, such as the US OPIC, the Swiss ERG and the British ECGD do assess projects in terms of their coherence with the state's other international policies, such as the promotion of sustainable development, human rights and good governance. However, unlike social or environmental standards, these criteria are not subject to specific questionnaires that must be submitted by exporters or investors applying for insurance. Given that ECAs are not obliged to disclose the full reasoning behind each lending or insurance

---

149 Knigge et al., op. cit.
150 See OECD Working Party on Export Credits and Credit Guarantees, op. cit.

decision, it is difficult to see how vague references to international policy objectives will affect the consideration of any specific application for insurance coverage. At best this serves the purpose of enabling an ECA to refuse projects where it is otherwise undecided on their ultimate impacts.

One of the difficulties in ensuring accountability for the negative impacts of ECAs on human development and human rights is the difficulty of apportioning blame in a context where multiple actors are involved, and where the ECA's own contribution to the day-to-day operation of the project is relatively marginal. This might be a general problem of the accountability of financial institutions.[151] The Office of the Compliance Advisor Ombudsman of the International Finance Corporation (IFC) (and MIGA), in reviewing financial sector activities of the IFC, observed that 'financial sector projects are less known to and less understood by affected communities because disclosure provisions required in the financial markets in which IFC operate are less transparent, and the structures and instruments used by IFC to support private sector development through financial intermediaries and other instruments are complex'.[152] In those cases where it can be clearly established that ECA involvement was decisive for the project's initiation, one could more easily claim that it holds particular responsibility for the violations that might follow from that project. It is only through increased scrutiny of ECA compliance with due diligence requirements that pressure will be brought to bear: it is the failure to exercise a duty of care, rather than direct contribution to violations, that will be the object of accountability.

7.5 Improving the quality of FDI through better regulation of ECAs?

Though individual institutions may vary, export credit agencies have overall become more regulated in the last decade – via the OECD Arrangement, the WTO discipline or by national governments – and have been required to consider a growing number of issues in making decisions on supporting specific projects. This is a positive development: as any other provider of a public good, it is important that ECAs be subject to clear rules of accountability and responsive to the concerns of home and host societies. At the same time, it is possible that by imposing different, and at times contradictory, requirements on these agencies states might be leading them into a dead end. First, their very existence is predicated on the idea that there is a market failure in the field of insurance, and that state involvement is therefore necessary. Thus ECAs are accepted as long as they do not run persistent deficits, and that the terms they

---

151 M. Dowell-Jones and D. Kinley, 'The Monster Under the Bed: Financial Services and the Ruggie Framework' in R. Mares (ed), *The UN Guiding Principles on Business and Human Rights – Foundations and Implementation*, Leiden: Martinus Nijhoff, 2011.
152 IFC Compliance Advisor Ombudsman, 'IFC's Investment Projects in the Financial Sector', *Appraisal Report* C-R1-Y11-F135, 27 June 2011, p. 1.

offer to their clients are relatively close to OECD-agreed rates. Their role is expected to diminish as private insurance markets develop better capacity and coverage. Pushed to the margins of the market, these agencies specialize in 'hard cases', which reduces opportunities to spread risk. Because of adverse selection, ECAs are exposed to a greater risk of facing non-performance by importers, and – particularly in times of crisis – this might lead to the losses being assumed by the taxpayer. Moreover, public concern is increasingly pushing governments to structure their agencies so as to take into consideration additional criteria of eligibility, such as respect for social and environmental standards. Increasing the due diligence obligations of ECAs without imposing comparable constraints on their private sector competitors who, moreover, are unburdened by 'political considerations' or concern over the welfare of national exporters, shifts the risks of investment insurance from the moderately accountable public sphere to the still unaccountable private sphere.

Further regulation – such as the requirement of human rights impact assessment – without imposing comparable costs on private competitors will tend to exacerbate this trend. This would not be, in itself, problematic. If private markets could offer the same or better terms to investors and exporters, it might be more effective to channel the public funds allocated to ECAs today to other institutions, particularly those involved with development cooperation *directly*. At present, ECAs wear multiple hats: they support domestic exporters, but also support the government's foreign policy goals, such as development; they must remain strictly complementary to the private insurance market, but at the same time must fill the trade finance gap in times of crisis. In carrying out these disparate missions the agencies regularly frustrate different constituencies. An exclusive focus on ensuring the accountability of government-supported financial actors is misplaced: there cannot be an overall improvement in the quality of trade and investment insurance without a commitment by states to regulate both public and private actors. It is the export credit and insurance guarantee industry as a whole that should be the object of specific due diligence requirements.

This is even clearer when one considers that ECAs are only marginally responsible for the credit itself. Eighty-five per cent of trade finance is carried out by private actors. As insurers, ECAs *enable* other lenders to provide funds for projects. It is arguable that ECA due diligence obligations are distinct from those of the investor, and from those of the lender. From an accountability perspective, claims against ECAs are less likely to succeed because of their remoteness from the causally relevant facts: harm caused by the operation of a firm in the 'real economy' is made possible by private loans, themselves made possible by public guarantees. The line between 'making credit available' and making it marginally 'cheaper' is at times difficult to discern. Accordingly, apportioning the responsibility for negative impacts can be difficult, in practice. A common framework of regulation, stipulating the different degrees of due diligence required, might be the best way to preserve the specific character of private and public actors in this area.

Another general conclusion from the preceding discussions is that ECAs' role in project and trade finance must be assessed simultaneously in terms of local and national impacts. While screening projects and categorizing them in terms of risk, due attention must be given not only to the commercial viability of the project or loan, but also to the burdens that the transaction will impose, during its life-cycle, to the national economy as a whole. Special attention should be given to the issue of repayments of loans made in foreign currency. This question has already been integrated, although somewhat loosely, in the OECD Arrangement. In poorer countries, it might be preferable to extend loans in domestic (host-state) currency, but this will, of course, considerably reduce the incentives for private lender involvement: sovereign and multilateral lenders might therefore consider providing credit with a greater degree of concessionality.

With respect to the screening of projects eligible for official support, the current process of integrating social and environmental concerns into project design must be reinforced and made more systematic and participatory, in line with general principles of human rights law. Ideally, ECAs should explicitly rely on third-party guidelines – such as the World Bank's operational policies or OECD DAC standards – or develop their own publicly available standards for project finance. Adherence to these guidelines and standards would not only show commitment to best practice, but also provide clearer benchmarks against which project performance could be measured. Grievance mechanisms should be included so as to provide a venue for affected populations to voice their concerns regarding specific projects, thereby providing ECA management with a broader range of stakeholder opinion.

States should mandate their ECAs to include human rights considerations in the selection of projects to support. This should be done by clarifying the agency's own human rights policy, and by requiring that sponsors and lenders provide information on the expected human rights implications of projects for which they seek public support. This should include, at a minimum, the description of the expected risks to human rights, the measures adopted to prevent potential rights violations by the project or its local partners, the mechanisms put in place to monitor compliance with social, environmental and human rights conditions, and the remedies available to individuals who might consider that their rights have been violated, or that mitigation policies have not been faithfully adhered to. Failure to disclose relevant information on human rights, social and environmental issues, as well as non-compliance with agreed conditions, should result in loss of coverage by the investor or lender.

Screening and monitoring would have their usefulness diminished if ECAs were not subject to comprehensive disclosure obligations. Giving due regard to commercially sensitive client information, ECAs should publicize, in a timely manner, the results of their assessments of the human rights, social and environmental risks to which a project is exposed. They should make clear on what basis these assessments influenced the decision to grant support, and should make public the conditions and mitigation obligations they have attached to the loan or guarantee. Monitoring activities should also be made public, allowing affected populations to examine whether the project sponsors are submitting adequate and complete information, and to assess whether the ECA is effectively requiring compliance with its conditions and mitigation policies.

The availability of remedies should be an important consideration in the design of project loans and guarantees. The ECAs should require the projects they support to afford public participation and grievance mechanisms to affected populations. These mechanisms should allow individuals and groups to challenge adherence by the project sponsor to the loan conditions and mitigation policies, and to bring new or emerging issues to the attention of management and foreign supporters. Moreover, individuals should have the possibility of appealing directly to the ECA when a sponsor fails to design or effectively provide such grievance mechanisms.

7.6 References

A. Anghie, *Imperialism, Sovereignty and the Making of International Law*, Cambridge: Cambridge University Press, 2004.

R. Ascari, 'Is Export Credit Agency a Misnomer? The ECA Response to a Changing World', *SACE Working Paper Series*, No. 2, 2007, available at <http://www.sace.it/GruppoSACE/export/sites/default/download/wpsacen02.pdf> (accessed 26 March 2012).

I. Asmundson et al. 'Trade Finance in the 2008–09 Financial Crisis: Evidence from IMF and BAFT-IFSA Surveys of Banks' in J.P. Chauffour and M. Malouche (eds), *Trade Finance During the Great Trade Collapse*. Washington DC: World Bank Publications, 2011, pp. 89–116.

M. Auboin, 'The Challenges of Trade Financing', Commentary, VoxEU.org, London: Centre for Economic Policy Research, 28 January 2009, available at <http://www.voxeu.org/index.php?q=node/2905> (accessed 26 March 2012).

M. Auboin, 'Restoring Financial Trade During a Period of Financial Crisis: Stock-Taking of Recent Initiatives', *WTO Staff Working Paper* (ERSD-2009-16), available at <http://papers.ssrn.com/ sol3/papers.cfm?abstract_ id=1535309> (accessed 26 March 2012).

M. Auboin, 'Boosting the Availability of Trade Finance in the Current Crisis: Background Analysis for a Substantial G20 Package', *Centre for Economic Policy Research Policy Insight*, No. 35, June 2009, available at <http://www.cepr.org/pubs/policyinsights/PolicyInsight35.pdf> (accessed 26 March 2012).

M. Auboin, 'International Regulation and Treatment of Trade Finance: What are the Issues?', *WTO Staff Working Paper* (ERSD-2010-09), February 2010

Berne Union, *Annual Report 2009 – Celebrating 75 Years of the Berne Union*, London: Berne Union and Exporta Publishing, 2009

O. Can and S. L. Seck, 'The Legal Obligations with Respect to Human Rights and Credit Export Agencies', paper prepared for ECA-Watch, available at <http://www.halifaxinitiative.org/updir/ECAHRlegalFINAL.pdf> (accessed 26 March 2012).

J.P. Chauffour and M. Malouche (eds), *Trade Finance During the Great Trade Collapse*, Washington DC: World Bank Publications, 2011.

P.E. Comeaux and N.S. Kinsella, 'Reducing Political Risk in Developing Countries: Bilateral Investment Treaties, Stabilization Clauses, and MIGA & OPIC Investment Insurance', *New York Law School Journal of International and Comparative Law* 15, 1994, 1–48.

F. Coomans and M.T. Kamminga (eds), *Extraterritorial Application of Human Rights Treaties*, Antwerp: Intersentia, 2004.

D. Coppens, 'How Much Credit for Export Credit Support Under the SCM Agreement', *Journal of International Economic Law* 12(1), 2009, 63–113.

J. M. DeLeonardo, 'Are Public and Private Political Risk Insurance Two of a Kind? Suggestions for a New Direction for Government Coverage', *Virginia Journal of International Law* 45, 2005, 737–787.

O. De Schutter, J. Wouters, P. De Man, N. Hachez and M. Sant'Ana, 'Foreign Direct Investment, Human Development and Human Rights: Framing the Issues,' *Human Rights and International Legal Discourse*, 3(2), 2009, 137–176, at pp. 149–158.

M. Dowell-Jones and D. Kinley, 'The Monster Under the Bed: Financial Services and the Ruggie Framework' in R. Mares (ed.), *The UN Guiding Principles on Business and Human Rights: Foundations and Implementation*, Leiden: Martinus Nijhoff, forthcoming.

M. Gondek, *The Reach of Human Rights in a Globalising World: Extraterritorial Application of Human Rights Treaties*, Antwerp: Intersentia, 2008.

N. Hachez and J. Wouters, 'When Rules and Values Collide: How Can a Balanced Application of Investor Protection Provisions and Human Rights be Ensured?', *Human Rights and International Legal Discourse*, 3(2), 2009, 301–344.

E. Hayes and A. Cummings, 'Part Two: Political Risk and Insurance – Taming the Risks of Project Finance', *International Financial Law Review* 20, 2001, 17–20.

International Centre for Human Rights and Democratic Development, *Human Rights Impact Assessments for Foreign Investment Projects: Learning from Community Experiences in the Philippines, Tibet, the Democratic Republic of Congo, Argentina, and Peru*, 2007, available at <http://epe.lac-bac.gc.ca/100/200/301/intl_centre_human_rights/human_rights_impact-e/E84-21-2007E.pdf> (accessed 6 August 2012).

International Monetary Fund, *Global Financial Stability Report 2009 – Responding to the Financial Crisis and Measuring System Risks* (Summary Version), April 2009.

K. Keenan, 'Export Credit Agencies and the International Law of Human Rights', Paper prepared for the Special Representative of the United Nations Secretary-General on Business and Human Rights, January 2008, available at <http://198.170.85.29/Halifax-Initiative-Export-Credit-Agencies-Jan-2008.pdf> (accessed 26 March 2010).

A. Khachaturian, '"Are We in Good Hands?" The Adequacy of American and Political Risk Insurance Programs in Fostering International Development,' *Connecticut Law Review*, 38, 2006, 1041–1064.

M. Knigge, B. Görlach, A.-M. Hamada, C. Nuffort and R.A. Kraemer, 'The Use of Environmental and Social Criteria in Export Credit Agencies' Practices – A Study of Export Credit Agencies' Environmental Guidelines with Reference to the World Commission on Dams', paper commissioned by Deutsche Gesellschaft für Technische Zusammenarbeit GmbH (GTZ), published in 2003 and available at <http://www.ecologic.de/download/projekte/1800-1849/1809/1809wcd_ecas_en.pdf> (accessed 26 March 2012).

P. Kundra, 'Looking Beyond the Dabhol Debacle: Examining its Causes and Understanding its Lessons' *Vanderbilt Journal of Transnational Law*, 41, 2008, 907–935.

S. Leader and D.M. Ong, *Global Project Finance, Human Rights and Sustainable Development*, Cambridge: Cambridge University Press, 2011.

D. Lederman, M. Olarreaga and L. Payton, 'Export Promotion Agencies Revisited', *World Bank Policy Research Working Paper 5125*, November 2009.

J.K. Levit, 'A Bottom-Up Approach to International Law-Making: A Tale of Three Trade Finance Instruments', *Yale Journal of International Law* 30, 2005, 125–209.

A.W. Lo and M.T. Mueller, 'Warning: Physics Envy Can be Hazardous to Your Wealth!', 2010, available at <http://papers.ssrn.com/sol3/papers.cfm?abstract_id=1563882> (accessed 26 March 2012)

S. Narula, 'The Right to Food: Holding Global Actors Accountable Under International Law', *Columbia Journal of Transnational Law*, 44, 2006, 691–800.

N. Nassar, 'Project Finance, Public Utilities and Public Concerns: A Practitioner's Perspective', *Fordham International Law Journal*, 23, 2000, 60–85.

M. Nowak, *UN Covenant on Civil and Political Rights: CCPR Commentary*, 2nd Revised Edition, Kehl: Norbert Paul Engel Verlag, e.K., 2005.

Office of the High Commissioner for Human Rights, *Guiding Principles on Business and Human Rights – Implementing the United Nations 'protect, respect and remedy' framework*, Geneva: United Nations Publications (HR/PUB/11/04), 2011.

J. Pauwelyn, *Conflict of Norms in Public International Law: How WTO Law Relates to Other Rules of International Law*, Cambridge: Cambridge University Press, 2003.

B. Penfold, 'Labour and Employment Issues in Foreign Direct Investment: Public Support Conditionalities', *International Labour Office Working Paper*, No. 95.

M.B. Perry, 'A Model for Efficient Foreign Aid: The Case for Political Risk Insurance Activities of the Overseas Private Investment Corporation', *Virginia Journal of International Law* 36, 1995, 511–588.

M.E. Salomon, *Global Responsibility for Human Rights: World Poverty and the Development of International Law*, Oxford: Oxford University Press, 2007.

M.E. Salomon, 'International Human Rights Obligations in Context: Structural obstacles and the demands of global justice,' in B.A. Andreassen and S.P. Marks (eds), *Development as a Human Right: Legal, Political and Economic Dimensions*, 2nd edn, Antwerp: Intersentia, 2010, pp. 121–147.

M. Sant'Ana, 'Foreign Direct Investment and Human Development: Two Approaches to Assessing Human Rights Impacts', *Human Rights and International Legal Discourse* 3(2), 2009, 229–262.

N. Schrijver, *Sovereignty over Natural Resources: Balancing Rights and Duties*, Cambridge: Cambridge University Press, 1997.

B. Simma and P. Alston, 'Sources of Human Rights Law: Custom, *Jus Cogens*, and General Principles', *Australian Yearbook of International Law* 12, 1988, 82–108.

S.I. Skogly, *Beyond National Borders: States' Human Rights Obligations in International Cooperation*, Antwerp: Intersentia, 2006.

M. Stephens, *The Changing Role of Export Credit Agencies*, Washington DC: International Monetary Fund, 1999.

A. Thomas, 'Financial Crises and Emerging Market Trade', *IMF Staff Position Note* (SPN/09/04), 11 March 2009.

United Nations Development Programme, *Human Development Report 2000*, Oxford: Oxford University Press, 2000.

J.-Y. Wang, M. Mansilla, Y. Kikuchi and S. Choudhury, *Officially Supported Credits in a Changing World*, Washington DC: International Monetary Fund, 2005.

8 Improving the framework of negotiations on international investment agreements

Philip De Man and Jan Wouters

8.1 Introduction

The present framework of international investment agreements (IIAs) is primarily composed of bilateral investment treaties (BITs) and regional economic integration agreements with investment chapters (REIAs). They are complemented by a small number of multilateral conventions, which are mainly limited to regulating trade-related matters and formal aspects of the investment regime.[1] This complex maze of investment agreements and the balance reflected therein between the needs and concerns of developed and developing countries is the outcome of a long and still ongoing process of economic negotiations. International investment negotiations are unique in that they bring together a wide range of players with largely opposing views on issues that are strongly interrelated with other economic matters. The inherently volatile nature of investment negotiations is further exacerbated by the fact that the needs and interests of the same set of players can be realized

---

1 For an overview of the history and composition of the present IIA framework, see K.J. Vandevelde, 'A brief history of international investment agreements', *University of California Davis Journal of International Law and Policy*, 2005–2006, vol. 12, pp. 157–94; V. Mosoti, 'Bilateral investment treaties and the possibility of a Multilateral Framework on Investment at the WTO: Are poor economies caught in between?', *Northwestern Journal of International Law and Business*, 2005–2006, vol. 26, pp. 108–16; R. Dattu, 'A journey from Havana to Paris: The fifty-year quest for the elusive multilateral agreement on investment', *Fordham International Law Journal*, 2000–2001, vol. 24, pp. 275–316; R. Leal-Arcas, 'The multilateralization of international investment law', *North Carolina Journal of International Law and Commercial Regulation*, 2009, vol. 35, pp. 51–70; J.W. Salacuse and N.P. Sullivan, 'Do BITs really work? An evaluation of bilateral investment treaties and their grand bargain', *Harvard International Law Journal*, 2005, vol. 46, pp. 68–75. See also J. Wouters, P. De Man and L. Chanet, 'The long and winding road of international investment agreements. Toward a coherent framework for reconciling the interests of developed and developing countries?', *Human Rights and International Legal Discourse*, 2009, vol. 3, pp. 263–300. See further the annual reports on recent developments in international investment agreements by the United Nations Conference on Trade and Development (UNCTAD) and the 1996 UNCTAD compendium of multilateral, regional, regional integration, bilateral and non-governmental international investment instruments (3 volumes). Online. Available HTTP: <http://unctad.org> (accessed 2 August 2012).

at multiple and partially overlapping levels and venues. While these characteristics compound the generalization of the outcome of investment talks, they underscore the importance of the process of negotiation itself. Any analysis of the means to strengthen consideration of the needs of developing countries in the international investment framework should therefore first assess whether and how the framework of negotiations on IIAs itself can be improved.

Recent discussions at the Working Group on the Relationship between Trade and Investment (WGTI) of the World Trade Organization (WTO) have underscored the importance of installing a proper negotiation framework to accurately reflect developing countries' sustainable development goals in investment agreements.[2] An elaborate investment framework has already been installed at the bilateral and regional level. However, as it has failed to deflect sufficient flows of foreign direct investment (FDI) to the world's poorest economies, it should be examined whether the negotiation dynamics at the multilateral level could allow for a more balanced IIA framework. The WTO has acknowledged that the choice of improving the negotiations on IIAs in essence amounts to the following policy choice:

> [D]o [States] continue to approach the FDI issue as they have until now, that is bilaterally, regionally and plurilaterally, and on an ad hoc basis in sectoral and other specific WTO agreements; or do they seek to integrate such arrangements into a comprehensive and global framework that recognizes the close linkages between trade and investment, assures the compatibility of investment and trade rules and, most of all, takes into account in a balanced way the interests of all the members of the WTO – developed, developing and least-developed alike [*sic*]. Only a multilateral negotiation in the WTO, when appropriate, can provide such a global and balanced framework.[3]

2 The deliberations at the WTGI did not amount to proper negotiations on a multilateral framework on investment, as the Doha Ministerial Declaration explicitly stated that 'negotiations will [only] take place after the Fifth Session of the Ministerial Conference on the basis of a decision to be taken, by explicit consensus, at that session on modalities of negotiations'. Such a consensus was never reached. See Doha Ministerial Declaration, WT/MIN(01)/DEC/1, 14 November 2001, para. 20. Online. Available HTTP: <http://www.wto.org/english/thewto_e/minist_e/min01_e/mindecl_e.htm> (accessed 13 March 2012).

3 WTO, *Annual report 1996. Special topic: Trade and foreign direct investment*, Geneva: WTO Publications, 1996, p. 59. These two options are also put forward in A.V. Ganesan, 'Developing countries and a possible multilateral framework on investment: Strategic options', *Transnational Corporations*, 1998, vol. 7(2), pp. 10–1; M.A. Srur, 'The international investment regime: Towards evolutionary bilateral and regional investment treaties?', *Manchester Journal of International Economic Law*, 2004, vol. 1, pp. 55–7; B. Hoekman and K. Saggi, 'Multilateral disciplines for investment-related policies?', World Bank Policy Research Working Paper No. 2138, June 1999, p. 20. Online. Available HTTP: <http://ideas.repec.org/p/wbk/wbrwps/2138.html> (accessed 13 March 2012).

In order to make an informed decision on the preferred alternative and the most appropriate negotiating means of achieving it, the present chapter will assess the case for initiating deliberations on a multilateral framework on investment (MFI) from the perspective of developing countries, taking into account their assent to a bilateral regime that mainly caters to the needs of foreign investors. To this end, the chapter will, first, outline the general political and economic dynamics that guide international investment negotiations in a globalized world (Section 8.2). This section will end with a brief overview of specific recommendations to improve the negotiation position of developing countries, which are mainly situated at the multilateral level. Based on the insights gained from this analysis, an attempt will be undertaken to explain the ambivalent attitude of developing countries to international investment negotiations at the bilateral and multilateral level. This will allow identifying the main reasons for the opposition of developing countries to negotiating an MFI as a means of pursuing their development goals, despite the obvious failure of the present regime to fulfil this aim (Section 8.3). After singling out the main sources of opposition to multilateral negotiations from developing countries, the following section of the chapter will attempt to determine whether these substantive arguments are valid and sufficient reasons to further postpone multilateral investment negotiations, particularly in light of the improved negotiation position of developing countries at the global scene (Section 8.4). This section will also take into account the closely related question of which forum is suited best to accommodate the interests of developing countries. Finally, in addition to the preceding formal considerations, the chapter will also aim to identify a limited number of substantive aspects that could be tackled in multilateral investment negotiations so as to improve the development balance of the current IIA regime (Section 8.5).

Throughout the chapter, it will be argued that a case can be made for the negotiation of an MFI, though this strongly depends on the timing of the initiative, the procedure to be followed and the substantive issue to be tackled during the discussions. The one-sidedness of the current international investment regime clearly illustrates that the negotiation dynamics at the bilateral level are insufficient to bring about a balanced outcome that adequately reflects the development needs of poor capital-importing economies. At the same time, recent attempts have shown that broad and ambitious multilateral negotiations may be premature given the lack of incentives for concessions in the investment realm on the part of both developed and developing countries. Furthermore, developing countries already experience significant difficulties in implementing their existing trade-related investment obligations at the multilateral level. Therefore, any suggestions for improvement of the international investment negotiation framework at the multilateral level should be incremental in nature. Each step in the process should provide for reciprocal benefits between developed and developing countries and duly take into account the situation of the pre-existing bilateral investment regime.

8.2 The negotiation of international investment agreements

Over time, international economic negotiations have become increasingly complex. They tackle ever more issues with mounting technicality and bring together a growing number of players at overlapping levels and in multiple fora.[4] Unlike problems in the realm of international politics, economic issues are integrated into an entire regime that can typically be split into several components, placed into different contexts and linked with other topics. This endows the parties involved with plenty of room to manoeuvre by trading off concessions in various fields.[5] Parallel negotiations on overlapping issues are increasingly common.[6] At the same time, the heightened visibility of broad international economic negotiations and the increased stakes of intertwined economic discussions markedly reduce the flexibility of the negotiating partners involved. It is clear that the wide diffusion of power[7] across multiple actors and issues renders any generalized statement on the outcome of international economic negotiations both impossible and nugatory, the process of negotiating itself remaining of utmost importance.[8] Nowhere is this more evident than in the tangled framework of negotiations on IIAs, which mobilize all combinations of developed and developing countries at the bilateral, regional, plurilateral and multilateral level on a wide range of issues.

8.2.1 *Plurality of issues: linkage and tradeoff opportunities*

A first set of issues that is often considered in combination with investment is that of trade-related matters. It is commonly acknowledged that trade and investment economically act as complements rather than substitutes. They reinforce each other substantially, most notably through the mechanism of intra-firm trade flows between the various divisions of multinational enterprises, which double as the primary sources of FDI.[9] The economic linkage between

---

4 A. Landau, 'Analyzing international economic negotiations: Towards a synthesis of approaches', *International Negotiation*, 2000, vol. 5, pp. 1–19.

5 See in general on this issue B. Spector and I.W. Zartman (eds), *Getting it done: Post-agreement negotiation and international regimes*, Washington DC: United States Institute of Peace Press, 2003.

6 See F.O. Hampson, *Multilateral negotiations: Lessons from arms control, trade and the environment*, Baltimore: Johns Hopkins University Press, 1995, p. 348.

7 Term coined in J.P. Singh, 'Weak powers and globalism: The impact of plurality on weak-strong negotiations in the international economy', *International Negotiation*, 2000, vol. 5, p. 451.

8 See in general J.S. Odell, 'From London to Bretton Woods: Sources of change in bargaining strategies and outcomes', *Journal of Public Policy*, 1990, vol. 8, pp. 287–315.

9 See WTO, *supra* note 3, pp. 44 and 52–5. See also R.E. Caves, *Multinational enterprise and economic analysis*, Cambridge: Cambridge University Press, 2007, pp. 29–67; J.H. Dunning and S. Lundan, *Multinational enterprises and the global economy*, London: Edward Elgar, 2008; J.M. Kline and R.D. Ludema, 'Building a multilateral framework for investment:

both issues is legally reflected in a rising number of regional economic integration agreements that address investment alongside trade and in the initiation of multilateral investment negotiations at the forum of international trade organizations, such as the WTO.[10] Investment negotiations are often linked with non-trade issues as well, such as labour and environment, so as to facilitate tradeoffs across different fields. Indeed, parallel negotiations on related issues have sometimes been specifically suggested as a remedy to resolve deadlocks in stalemated discussions on investment.[11]

It should be stressed, however, that the close economic connection between trade and investment by no means implies that negotiation experiences with the former should dictate deliberations on the latter.[12] Trade and investment negotiations differ in some key respects, most importantly as regards the reciprocal nature of the respective processes.[13] Trade negotiations bring together countries that are driven by similar objectives and result in relations that by definition are characterized by a certain level of reciprocity. To be sure, sectoral differentiation and conditional carve-outs may alter the balance between the negotiating partners, yet the fundamental dynamics of the process are guided by an intrinsic mutuality in rights and obligations. The economic relationship between FDI home and host countries is different in that it brings to the table countries with inherently opposite goals.[14] An increasing number of South–South IIAs notwithstanding,[15] bilateral and, especially, multilateral

Comparing the development of trade and investment accords', *Transnational Corporations*, 1997, vol. 6(3), p. 9; P. Gugler and J. Chaisse, 'Foreign investment issues and WTO law: Dealing with fragmentation while waiting for a multilateral framework', in J. Chaisse and T. Balmelli (eds), *Essays on the future of the World Trade Organization: Policies and legal issues*, Geneva: Edis, 2008, p. 137; B. Hoekman and K. Saggi, *supra* note 3, p. 18.

10 For data on the proliferation of regional agreements addressing investment and trade, see UNCTAD, *Investment Provisions in Economic Integration Agreements*, New York and Geneva: United Nations, 2006, pp. 13–53.

11 B. Schwartz, 'The Doha Round and investment: Lessons from Chapter 11 of NAFTA', in T. Weiler (ed.), *NAFTA investment law and arbitration: Past issues, current practice, future prospects*, Ardsley: Transnational Publishers, 2004, pp. 450–2; B. Martin, 'An environmental remedy to paralyzed negotiations for a multilateral foreign direct investment agreement', *Golden Gate University Environmental Law Journal*, 2007, vol. 1, pp. 209–66.

12 For a concise overview of the history of international trade agreements, starting with the 1860 Cobden–Chevalier treaty between the United Kingdom and France, and its relevance for investment agreements, see J.M. Kline and R.D. Ludema, *supra* note 9, pp. 1–21; G.R. Winham, 'The evolution of the world trading system – The economic and policy context', in D. Bethlehem, D. McRae, R. Neufeld and I. Van Damme (eds), *International trade law*, Oxford: Oxford University Press, 2009, pp. 9–13; J.H. Jackson, 'The evolution of the world trading system – The legal and institutional context', ibid., pp. 31–53.

13 B. Dymond and M. Hart, 'The Doha investment negotiations: Whither or wither', *Journal of World Investment and Trade*, 2004, vol. 5, pp. 274–5; J.M. Kline and R.D. Ludema, *supra* note 9, p. 15.

14 B. Dymond and M. Hart, *supra* note 13, p. 276.

15 Several theories have been offered to explain this evolution without affecting the validity of the contentions made here. As such, developing countries may conclude IIAs among each other because of political considerations or because a common third-party investor

negotiations on investment typically pitch developed capital-exporting and developing capital-importing countries against each other. In theory, the *quid pro quo* negotiated in these agreements resides in the fact that countries party to the treaty mutually agree to offer the same standards for foreign investors wishing to invest in their State.[16] In practice, however, the negotiation process between both sides amounts to a bid to reconcile the investment protection and liberalization requirements of the former with the regulatory demands of the latter. Indeed, the rise of several economies in transition notwithstanding, investment flows in the current economy are highly skewed as developed countries continue to be the primary source and destination of most of the world's capital whereas developing countries on the whole remain net importers of FDI.[17] The specific dynamics of investment negotiations between capital-importing and capital-exporting countries thus do not allow for a *quid pro quo* to come about when they are limited to investment protection and liberalization issues alone.[18] Other provisions catering to the regulatory and development needs of developing host countries should thus be introduced, yet the one-sidedness of most BITs currently in force shows that the potential for a balanced outcome of investment negotiations is rather limited, at least at the bilateral level.

The economic reality underlying international investment negotiations thus appears to warrant the introduction of additional issues in order to better balance the scales between the countries involved. However, conjugating investment with unrelated topics does not necessarily facilitate the negotiation process. Issue linkage acts as a two-edged sword that can cut both ways.[19] It is

wishes to improve capital flexibility between both capital-importing countries. See Z. Elkins, A.T. Guzman and B. Simmons, 'Competing for capital: The diffusion of bilateral investment treaties, 1960-2000', *University of Illinois Law Review*, 2008, pp. 299–301. Developing countries are also often actively sponsored to conclude IIAs among each other by UNCTAD and leading developed countries: see, for example, the UNCTAD report on the Ronde de négociations d'accords bilatéraux de promotion et de protection des investissements pour les pays francophones d'Afrique, held 2–6 February 2004 in Brussels. Online. Available HTTP: <http://www.unctad.org/sections/dite_pcbb/docs/dite_pcbb_ias0027_en.pdf> (accessed 13 March 2012).

16 R. Neufeld, 'Trade and investment', in D. Bethlehem, D. McRae, R. Neufeld and I. Van Damme (eds), *supra* note 12, p. 620.

17 See the data in UNCTAD, *Development and globalization: Facts and figures*, New York and Geneva: United Nations, 2004, p. 32. The scales were temporarily balanced by the recent global financial crisis, which hit the developed countries first and hardest, and resulted in a steep decline in FDI inflows among these countries of 29 per cent in 2008 and 2009. Initially, the FDI flows to developing countries and economies in transition kept rising, although the numbers dropped in these countries as well from the second half of 2008. See UNCTAD, *World investment report 2009. Transnational corporations, agricultural production and development*, New York and Geneva: United Nations, 2009, pp. 3–40.

18 In this sense also J. Faundez, 'Beyond bilateral investment treaties', Paper presented at the APEC workshop on bilateral and regional investment rules/agreements, May 2002, p. 155. Online. Available HTTP: <http://www.apec.org> (accessed 13 March 2012).

19 B. Hoekman and K. Saggi, *supra* note 3, p. 23.

liable to complicate discussions by introducing topics that either toughen the positions of the countries involved on the original issue under consideration or call into question the aptitude of the initial negotiation forum. For example, it is likely that the bargaining tactic of explicitly linking investment with agriculture at the WTO by the European Union, Switzerland, Japan and the Republic of Korea, i.e. parties with highly protective agriculture markets, ultimately proved counterproductive to the case of negotiations on an MFI.[20] One should therefore not wholly discard the option of using intra-investment trade-offs and issue linkages as a means of negotiating the needs of the economically weaker, capital-importing States in international agreements. As will be argued in subsequent sections of this chapter, various substantive rights and obligations of parties to investment negotiations can be offset against each other so as to reach a balanced agreement that takes into account the interests of all countries concerned.[21] The multilateral level will be suggested as the most appropriate avenue for this approach, even though the balancing act at this level is severely impeded by the existence of a partially overlapping patchwork of asymmetric agreements at the bilateral level.[22]

A number of other factors further complicate the negotiation of international investment treaties when compared to trade agreements. Additional impediments mainly flow from the political sensitivity and the intrusive nature of investment measures and the difficulties that arise when trying to quantify their influence on the host economy.[23] Provisions in international trade agreements typically produce effects of an economic nature for an identifiable set of transactions between given trading partners, the value of which is therefore, at least in theory, not too difficult to appraise. The situation is different for investment agreements, however. Due to the recent drop in official development assistance and the increased reliance of developing countries on FDI flows as a means of spurring sustainable development, agreements imposing investment protection and liberalization obligations considerably limit the capacity of host countries to pursue national goals of establishing an enabling domestic regulatory framework. As such, IIAs affect a wide range of issues vital to a large group of people, thus explaining why developing countries are often reluctant to make concessions in investment negotiations. The inherent difficulties in quantifying the effects of investment measures only add to this intransigence. The oft-repeated call during investment discussions for more information through further studies should thus not necessarily be seen as a

---

20 P. Sauvé, 'Multilateral rules on investment: Is forward movement possible?', *Journal of International Economic Law*, 2006, vol. 9, pp. 340–1.

21 See further Section 8.5 of this chapter.

22 See further Section 8.4 of this chapter.

23 J. Kurtz, 'A general investment agreement in the WTO? Lessons from Chapter 11 of NAFTA and the OECD Multilateral Agreement on Investment', *University of Pennsylvania Journal of International Economic Law*, vol. 23, 2002, vol. 23, pp. 724–32; S. Young and A.T. Tavares, 'Multilateral rules on FDI: Do we need them? Will we get them? A developing country perspective', *Transnational Corporations*, 2004, vol. 13(1), p. 8.

deliberate tactic on the part of capital-importing countries to stall the proceedings, but as a legitimate query for increased technical assistance. This will allow developing countries to make more informed decisions on the obligations they undertake.[24]

8.2.2 Plurality of actors: fragmentation and sources of bargaining power

A second aspect of the power diffusion that further complicates the conclusion of IIAs relates to the increased number of actors with divergent interests that have to be taken on board during the negotiations.[25] In this context, it becomes clear that addressing the legitimate development needs and regulatory concerns of certain capital-importing developing countries is only part of the process of creating a permissive context for successful investment negotiations.[26] As noted previously, the expanding scope and visibility of international economic negotiations in recent years has drawn the attention of a large number of players in the international investment field, ranging from international organizations and national parliaments to non-governmental organizations (NGOs), environmentalists, consumer groups and the media. The diffusion of power in this respect is most notable at the multilateral level, where the high stakes, scope and visibility draw most attention, thus offering a potential explanation for the particular difficulties encountered in concluding IIAs at this level.[27] It is important to understand that the requirement of inclusiveness in international investment negotiations goes beyond the mere procedural observation made time and again after the failed attempts of the Organization for Economic Co-operation and Development (OECD) to conclude a Multilateral Agreement on Investment (MAI), when it was duly noted that developing countries as well as representatives of civil society should be consulted during the proceedings.[28] A truly integrated approach implies actively pursuing the

---

24 See also B. Bora and M. Graham, 'Investment and the Doha development agenda', in E.-U. Petersmann (ed.), *Reforming the world trading system: Legitimacy, efficiency and democratic governance*, Oxford: Oxford University Press, 2005, pp. 350–2; UNCTAD, *International investment agreements: Trends and emerging issues*, New York and Geneva: United Nations, 2006, pp. 70–1.

25 On the diffusion of authority from States to other actors in the investment system, see T.-H. Cheng, 'Power, authority and international investment law', *American University International Law Review*, 2004–2005, vol. 20, pp. 465–520.

26 J. Kurtz, *supra* note 23, pp. 714 and 788–9.

27 For a more detailed examination of the paradoxical approach of developing countries to bilateral and multilateral investment negotiations, see Section 8.3 of this chapter.

28 See in general UNCTAD, *Lessons from the MAI*, New York and Geneva: United Nations, 1999; C. Schittecatte, 'The politics of the MAI: On the social opposition of the MAI and its role in the demise of the negotiations', *Journal of World Investment*, 2000, vol. 1, pp. 329–56; M.W. Sikkel, 'How to establish a multilateral framework for investment?', in E.C. Nieuwenhuys and M.M.T.A. Brus (eds), *Multilateral regulation of investment*, Boston: Kluwer, 2001, pp. 176–9; N.J. Schrijver, 'A multilateral investment agreement from a

integration of the interests of all players likely to be affected by the investment agreement.[29]

The wide reach of this substantive interpretation of the requirement of an integrated approach to investment negotiations is perhaps most often overlooked in negotiating parties' relations with relevant players at the domestic level. Governments recognizing the ineffectiveness of certain performance requirements or the costly distortive effects of investment incentives may well be inclined to liberalize certain sectors of their domestic industry were it not for the political impediments they face due to the strong opposition of their business community. International agreements pursuing liberalization will only be able to help national governments overcome such opposition by inserting topics on the negotiation agenda that are of interest to the relevant domestic groups so as to induce them to support the planned reforms.[30] The 1948 Charter of the International Trade Organization (ITO) as well as the OECD MAI talks floundered, *inter alia*, because they failed to gain the support of multinational enterprises because the provisions that were initially inserted to serve their interests were substantially watered down.[31] To be sure, while the development needs of the poorest and weakest economies of our world may be far more pressing than the economic interests of a conglomerate of wealthy transnational corporations, a sweeping approach that attempts to remedy the one-sided nature of the existing IIA network by largely ignoring the wishes of those players that most strongly dominate the trade and investment flows will not be conducive to the successful conclusion of any international

North-South perspective', ibid., pp. 29–32; P. Read, 'International investment in the WTO: Prospects and challenges in the shadow of MAI', *Bond Law Review*, 1999, vol. 11, pp. 369–75; P.T. Muchlinski, 'The rise and fall of the Multilateral Agreement on Investment: Where now?', *International Lawyer*, 2000, vol. 34, pp. 1050–3. See further the joint statement by 565 NGOs opposing the MAI. Online. Available HTTP: <http://www.twnside.org.sg/title/565-cn.htm> (accessed 13 March 2012); Resolution of the European Parliament containing recommendations to the Commission on negotiations in the framework of the OECD on a multilateral agreement on investments (MAI), *OJ C* 104, 11 March 1998, pp. 143–8; Report of the Standing Committee on Foreign Affairs and International Trade, Sub-Committee on International Trade, Trade Disputes and Investment, *Canada and the Multilateral Agreement on Investment*, Report of Canada's House of Commons Committee, Ottawa, December 1997 (List of recommendations). Online. Available HTTP: <http://www2.parl.gc.ca/HousePublications/Publication.aspx?DocId=1031512&Language=E&Mode=1&Parl=36&Ses=1> (accessed 13 March 2012).

29 A. Beviglia Zampetti and T. Frederiksson, 'The development dimension of investment negotiations in the WTO: Challenges and opportunities', *Journal of World Investment*, 2003, vol. 4, p. 421.

30 B. Hoekman and K. Saggi, *supra* note 3, pp. 7–8.

31 For more on the failure of the MAI talks, see the documents referred to *supra* note 30. On the opposition of the (US) business community to the ITO Charter, see P.B. Christy III, 'Negotiating investment in the GATT: A call for functionalism', *Michigan Journal of International Law*, 1990–1991, vol. 12, pp. 773–5; R. McCulloch and R. Owen, 'Linking negotiations on trade and foreign direct investment', in C.P. Kindleberger and D.B. Audretsch (eds), *The multinational corporation in the 1980s*, MIT Press: 1983, p. 350.

investment negotiation.[32] Conversely, an approach that receives the broad support of key domestic players will substantially increase the bargaining power of negotiation partners. When faced with a strong market-driven approach by developed countries, developing countries as well should mobilize their domestic private sector to actively contribute to the positive formulation of an investment negotiation agenda that more fully reflects their views and interests.[33] The technical assistance capabilities of developing countries' private sectors is a particularly potent but as yet untapped source of bargaining power for the traditionally weaker States, which could contribute to reaching more equitable and hence more durable investment agreements.

The level of integration and mobilization of the commercial intelligence networks of a State as well as its capacity to enrol the international civil society in a strong coalition are but two of the various factors that are typically identified as sources of bargaining power in international investment negotiations.[34] The negotiation position of a developing host country in particular is furthermore determined by its development needs and motivation to attract FDI, the level and internal division of its sovereign decision-making authority, the political will, energy and dedication to implement an established political programme and, most importantly, by such economic determinants as the size of its domestic market and the value of its natural resources.[35] The roots of a government's bargaining position thus to a large extent mirror the traditional determinants of a host country's capacity to attract FDI.[36] A developing nation with a sizeable domestic market and an abundance of low-cost skilled professionals will still be able to attract capital even in the absence of an international agreement protecting and liberalizing foreign investment in that country. The ability to walk away from negotiations is the ultimate source of bargaining power.[37] For a host country, this essentially hinges on the intrinsic attractiveness of its national economy as

---

32 See also B.N. Zeiler-Kligman, 'Preaching against the choir: An examination of the influence of multinational enterprises on the negotiation of investment rules at the World Trade Organization', *Whitehead Journal of Diplomacy and International Relations*, 2006, vol. 7, pp. 118–19.

33 See M. Mashayekhi and M. Gibbs, 'Lessons from the Uruguay Round negotiations on investment', *Journal of World Trade*, 1999, vol. 33, p. 12.

34 See in general, J. Braithwaite and P. Drahos, *Global business regulation*, Cambridge: Cambridge University Press, 2000, pp. 475–506.

35 F.M. Abbott, 'Bargaining power and strategy in the foreign investment process: A current Andean code analysis', *Syracuse Journal of International Law and Commerce*, 1975, vol. 3, pp. 325–8; P. Drahos, 'When the weak bargain with the strong: Negotiations in the World Trade Organization', *International Negotiation*, 2003, vol. 8, pp. 82–4; A. Landau, *supra* note 4, pp. 10–3.

36 For an overview of host country determinants of FDI, see UNCTAD, *World investment report 2003. FDI policies for development: National and international perspectives*, Geneva: United Nations, 2003, p. 85 (Table III.1). See also A. Beviglia Zampetti and T. Frederiksson, *supra* note 29, pp. 406–14.

37 A. Landau, *supra* note 4, p. 12.

a destination for FDI and the alternatives to which it can turn as a substitute for any given discussion.

The strong preponderance of economic determinants for guiding FDI flows that remain by and large unaffected by the existence of international rules is frequently raised as an argument against the need for spending much effort on negotiating an MFI.[38] While the impact of international investment agreements on capital flows is indeed heavily disputed,[39] this is rather an argument against IIAs in general that fails to explain why countries should resist the conclusion of a multilateral investment treaty while at the same time vigorously pursuing BITs. Furthermore, this critique is also undermined by the observation that many factors influencing the bargaining position and the economic attractiveness of a host country are dependent on the substance of international engagements previously taken up by the government in question. As such, the ability of many developing countries to credibly and effectively oppose limitations on their regulatory freedom in a multilateral framework is severely restricted by the protection and liberalization requirements laid down in the pre-existing web of BITs.[40] The efficacy of sovereign authority as a source of bargaining power and as a means of creating an enabling economic environment depends on the extent to which this authority has been preserved by previous engagements.[41]

The impact of the internal division of decision-making authority on the bargaining power of negotiation parties is most obvious when observing the relationship between the European Union and its Member States in multilateral

---

38 This point was raised emphatically during the WGTI discussions: see the summary of the discussions in the Report (1998) of the WGTI to the General Council, WT/WGTI/2, 8 December 1998, paras 195–6 (WGTI Report (1998)); WGTI Report on the Meeting of 1 and 2 October 1998 – Note by the Secretariat, WT/WGTI/M/6, 3 November 1998, para. 69. All documents of the WGTI are available at the website of the WTO: <http://www.wto.org/english/tratop_e/invest_e/invest_e.htm> (accessed 13 March 2012). The same point was made in UNCTAD, *supra* note 36, pp. 85–9; B. Hoekman and K. Saggi, *supra* note 3, p. 21.

39 On the inconclusive nature of the impact of IIAs on FDI flows, economic growth and human development, see L. Colens, M. Maertens and J. Swinnen, 'Foreign direct investment as an engine for economic growth and human development: A review of the arguments and empirical evidence', *Human Rights and International Legal Discourse*, 2009, vol. 3, pp. 177–228; P. Nunnenkamp and J. Spatz, 'FDI and economic growth in developing economies: how relevant are host-economy and industry characteristics', *Transnational Corporations*, 2004, vol. 13(3), pp. 52–86; M. Hallward-Driemeier, 'Do bilateral investment treaties attract FDI? Only a bit . . . and they could bite', World Bank Policy Research Working Paper No. 3121, June 2003. Online. Available HTTP: <http://ideas.repec.org/p/wbk/wbrwps/3121.html> (accessed 13 March 2012). Compare E. Neumayer and L. Spess, 'Do bilateral investment treaties increase foreign direct investment to developing countries?', *World Development*, 2005, vol. 33, pp. 1567–82; J.W. Salacuse and N.P. Sullivan, *supra* note 1, pp. 67–130.

40 This is the main tenet of the argument advanced in V. Mosoti, *supra* note 1, pp. 95–138.

41 For more on the impact of the phenomenon of parallel negotiations at different levels on the conclusion of specific investment agreements, see the following section of this chapter.

investment negotiations. It has been argued that the domestic ratification procedures and the lack of a strong and clear negotiating mandate for the European Community before the entry into force of the Lisbon Treaty severely hampered coordination among EU Member States during the discussions on the OECD MAI.[42] The ultimate decision of France to withdraw from the MAI negotiations in October 1998 seems to support this theory.[43] At the very least, it bolstered support for the call in the European Parliament's resolution to '[bring FDI issues] within the sphere of responsibilities of the EU as an integral part of the common commercial policy in the foreseeable future'.[44] In reply to this emphatic plea, Article 206 of the Treaty on the Functioning of the European Union (TFEU) now proclaims that 'the Union shall contribute, in the common interest, to the harmonious development of world trade, the progressive abolition of restrictions on international trade and on foreign direct investment, and the lowering of customs and other barriers'. Article 207(1) of the TFEU expressly lists FDI as an integral part of the Union's common commercial policy (CCP).[45] Moreover, EU competence in this area is exclusive,[46] implying that only the Union may legislate and adopt legally binding acts, the Member States being able to do so themselves only if so empowered by the Union or for the implementation of Union acts.[47] Accordingly, the EU shall also have exclusive competence to negotiate and conclude international agreements covering investment measures, insofar as their conclusion is provided for in a legislative act of the Union or is necessary to enable the Union to exercise its internal competence, or in so far as its conclusion may affect common rules or alter their scope.[48] Interestingly, the TFEU no longer contains the provision of

---

42 J.F. Morin and G. Gagné, 'What can best explain the prevalence of bilateralism in the investment regime?', *International Journal of Political Economy*, 2007, vol. 36, p. 62.

43 C. Schittecatte, *supra* note 28, p. 350. See the 15 October 1998 edition of *L'Humanité* for an account of the debate surrounding the withdrawal of France from the MAI. Online. Available HTTP: <http://www.humanite.fr/node/317548> (accessed 2 August 2012).

44 Resolution of the European Parliament containing recommendations to the Commission on negotiations in the framework of the OECD on a multilateral agreement on investments (MAI), *supra* note 28, para. I.8.

45 Article 207(1) TFEU provides that '[t]he common commercial policy shall be based on uniform principles, particularly with regard to changes in tariff rates, the conclusion of tariff and trade agreements relating to trade in goods and services, and the commercial aspects of intellectual property, foreign direct investment, the achievement of uniformity in measures of liberalisation, export policy and measures to protect trade such as those to be taken in the event of dumping or subsidies. The common commercial policy shall be conducted in the context of the principles and objectives of the Union's external action.' Corresponding provisions were laid down in Arts. III-314 and III-315 of the European Constitution.

46 Art. 3(1)(e) TFEU provides that the Union shall have exclusive competence in the area of the common commercial policy.

47 Art. 2(1) TFEU.

48 Art. 3(2) TFEU. Art. 207(6) in this respect clarifies that '[t]he exercise of the competences conferred by this Article in the field of the common commercial policy shall not affect the delimitation of competences between the Union and the Member States, and shall not lead

the former Treaty establishing the European Community (TEC), stipulating that the external powers of the Union with respect to the CCP 'shall not affect the right of the Member States to maintain and conclude agreements with third countries or international organizations in so far as such agreements comply with Community law and other relevant international agreements'.[49] The impact of EU law on the ability of the Union's Member States to separately negotiate and conclude investment treaties is further bolstered by a recent series of judgments of the European Court of Justice (ECJ) instituted by the European Commission against Austria, Sweden and Finland.[50] In all three cases, the ECJ held that a clause granting the free transfer, in freely convertible currency, of payments connected with an investment codified in a string of BITs concluded by the aforementioned Member States with the United States was incompatible with the powers of the Council under the EC Treaty to adopt unilateral measures restricting the free movement of capital and of payments.[51]

The ECJ judgments rebuking EU Member States for not having removed the incompatibilities between their BITs with third countries and certain provisions of Union law highlight a particular problem concerning investment agreement negotiations that has arisen due to the recent transfer of competence on investment to the EU after Lisbon. If the Commission holds the exclusive competence to negotiate treaties on behalf of the Union and its Member States, the latter are to refrain from any such initiatives, even for the purpose of addressing alleged incompatibilities between their existing BITs and EU law. Article 2(1) of the TFEU requires that Member States be expressly empowered by the Union in order to (re)negotiate their own investment treaties with third countries. In the meantime, however, BITs concluded by Member States before the entry into force of the Lisbon Treaty remain fully valid under public

---

to harmonization of legislative or regulatory provisions of the Member States in so far as the Treaties exclude such harmonization'. Compare previous Art. 133(6) TEC.

49 Art. 133 (5)(4) TEC. See A. Dimopoulos, 'The Common Commercial Policy after Lisbon: Establishing Parallelism between Internal and External Economic Policy?', *Croatian Yearbook of International Law*, 2008, vol. 4, p. 125.

50 ECJ, Case C-205/06 *Commission v Austria* [2009] ECR I-1301; ECJ, Case C-249/06 *Commission v Sweden* [2009] ECR I-1335; ECJ, Case C-118/07, *Commission v Finland* [2009] ECR I-10889. See C.-H. Wu, 'Foreign direct investment as common commercial policy: EU external economic competence after Lisbon', in P.J. Cardwell (ed.), *EU external relations law and policy in the post-Lisbon era*, The Hague: TMC Asser, 2012, pp. 383–7; N. Lavranos, 'Commission v. Austria; Commission v. Sweden [notes]', *American Journal of International Law*, 2009, vol. 103, pp. 716–22. On the possibility of conflicts between intra-EU BITs and EU law, see H. Wehland, 'Intra-EU investment agreements and arbitration: Is European Community law an obstacle?', *International and Comparative Law Quarterly*, 2009, vol. 58, pp. 297–320; M. Wierzbowski and A. Gubrynowicz, 'Conflicts of norms stemming from intra-EU BITS and EU legal obligations: Some remarks on possible solutions', in C. Binder, U. Kriebaum, A. Reinisch and S. Wittich (eds), *International investment law for the 21st century: Essays in honour of Christoph Schreuer*, Oxford: Oxford University Press, 2009, pp. 544–60.

51 Arts. 57(2), 59 and 60(1) TEC.

246 Foreign Direct Investment and Human Development

international law, even though they may give rise to internal disputes under EU law. It follows that, until the patchwork of Member States' BITs with third countries is replaced by an encompassing framework of IIAs negotiated by the Commission on the basis of a comprehensive Union policy on investment, legal uncertainty will flourish unless contained by the timely adoption of transitional measures. As the Lisbon Treaty lacked any explicit transitional provisions on this point, the Commission has taken it upon itself to develop a draft regulatory framework, which, however, has attracted its fair share of criticism.[52]

The Commission's draft regulation, which was accompanied by the communication 'Towards a comprehensive European international investment policy',[53] sets out to establish the terms, conditions and procedure under which Member States can be authorized to maintain, amend or conclude, respectively, existing or new BITs with third countries.[54] Agreements already concluded by Member States before the adoption of the draft regulation will, considering their continuing validity under public international law, be authorized to remain in force or to enter into force, yet only if their existence is notified in time to the Commission.[55] On this occasion, the Commission will review the notified agreements for their compatibility with Union law, the likelihood of overlaps with an agreement of the Union in force with the corresponding third country and their potential for constituting an obstacle to the development and implementation of the EU CCP.[56] If one of these conditions is not met, the authorization will be withdrawn, after proper consultations with the Member State concerned.[57] Under the same conditions, a Member State may be authorized by the Commission to open formal negotiations for amending an existing BIT or for concluding a new BIT with a third country.[58] As part of this authorization procedure, the Commission may require that 'appropriate clauses' be included in the negotiations. Moreover, the relevant Member State must keep the Commission informed of the progress and results of the

---

52 Commission proposal for a regulation of the European Parliament and of the Council establishing transitional arrangements for bilateral investment agreements between Member States and third countries, COM(2010) 344 final, 7 July 2010 ('Draft Regulation'). For a discussion of the Commission proposal, see S. Woolcock and J. Kleinheisterkamp, 'The EU approach to international investment policy after the Lisbon Treaty', study for the European Parliament, October 2012, pp. 14–51 and 53–70. Online. Available HTTP: <http://www.europarl.europa.eu/committees/en/studies.html> (accessed 16 March 2012); C.-H. Wu, *supra* note 50, pp. 389–390. See also the Report of the European Parliament Committee on International Trade on the Commission proposal, A7-0148/2011, 14 April 2011.
53 Communication from the Commission to the Council, the European Parliament, the European Economic and Social Committee and the Committee of the Regions, COM(2010) 343 final, 7 July 2010.
54 Art. 1 Draft Regulation.
55 Arts. 2–3 Draft Regulation.
56 Art. 5 Draft Regulation.
57 Art. 6 Draft Regulation.
58 Arts. 7–11 Draft Regulation.

negotiations and should tolerate the Commission as an active participant in the negotiations, if so requested.[59] All the while, the Member States are sternly reminded, with reference to the ECJ judgments against Austria, Sweden and Finland, of their obligation to take all necessary measures to eliminate incompatibilities, where they exist, with the law of the Union.[60]

The Commission proposal, which has yet to be adopted, has been criticized mainly for giving overly broad discretionary powers to the Commission through the proposed authorization procedure, hence paradoxically frustrating the basic goal of the regulation, i.e. enhancing legal certainty during the period of transition between the entry into force of the Lisbon Treaty and the elaboration of a broad-based EU investment policy.[61] Indeed, the Commission itself has stressed that the regulation and accompanying communication are merely the 'first steps' in the development of a European international investment policy.[62] The fact that one of the criteria for authorizing Member States to commence negotiations on BITs with third countries refers to their compatibility with a European investment policy that is still very much in the making has been strongly denounced.[63] Nevertheless, if adopted, the proposed regulation, despite its shortcomings, could improve legal certainty concerning BIT negotiations to some extent. Importantly, it would avoid a scenario in which third countries could take the unclear status of their BITs with EU Member States under Union law as a pretext to escape their obligations towards European investors or to gain leverage in (re)negotiations with their individual Member State partners with respect to the Commission.[64] At the same time, however, the mechanism provided by the draft regulation allowing the Commission to withdraw a previously granted authorization to a Member State to renegotiate a high-standard BIT with a third country might be interpreted by the latter as a signal to aim for a less stringent regime when negotiating with the EU.[65] Yet again, it could be argued just as well that a Union unrestrained by a credible threat of its individual Member States to pull out of the negotiations would force the Commission to more concessions, thus paradoxically reducing its bargaining power.[66]

---

59 Arts. 9–10 Draft Regulation.
60 Ninth recital of the Draft Regulation. The Report of the European Parliament, *supra* note 52, recommends deleting this particular recital.
61 Similar denunciations were voiced concerning the ECJ siding with the Commission in its judgments against Austria, Sweden and Finland: see C.-H. Wu, *supra* note 50, p. 386; P. Koutrakos, 'Case C-205/06, Commission v. Austria, judgment of the Court (Grand Chamber) of 3 March 2009; Case C-249/06, Commission v. Sweden, judgment of the Court (Grand Chamber) of 3 March 2009', *Common Market Law Review*, 2009, vol. 46, p. 2067.
62 Commission Communication, *supra* note 53, p. 2.
63 Report of the European Parliament, *supra* note 52, p. 18.
64 See S. Woolcock and J. Kleinheisterkamp, *supra* note 52, pp. 54–9.
65 Ibid., p. 69.
66 Compare A. Landau, *supra* note 4, p. 16.

Whatever transitional arrangements are ultimately adopted, and whatever their effect, it can hardly be doubted that the very elevation of FDI to an exclusive EU competence through inclusion in the CCP has given more clout to the negotiation position of the European Commission. This is reflected in the Commission's stated aim of future actions on investment 'to deliver better results as a Union than the results that have been or could have been obtained by the Member States individually'.[67] General negotiation theories indeed imply that a region speaking with one voice on the basis of a common investment policy is stronger than when acting as a loose conglomerate of players with differing interests. Recent experiences of the Commission in its trade and investment negotiations with third-country regional blocs would appear to confirm this view. Before the entry into force of the Lisbon Treaty, the Member States had already authorized the Commission to commence so-called 'region-to-region' negotiations on a free trade agreement incorporating investment provisions with seven countries of the Association of Southeast Asian Nations (ASEAN). Progress was slow, however, due to the strongly differing negotiation objectives among the various ASEAN partners. The Member States of the EU therefore empowered the Commission to start negotiations with individual ASEAN countries, starting with Singapore and Malaysia in 2010. Relatively speaking, these region-to-country negotiations have fared remarkably well and should be finalised in the coming months.[68] The ASEAN experience shows that the negotiation position of the EU is stronger when it can act as a bloc, allowing the Commission to set the terms for discussion and to change the negotiation conditions and forum as it fits best for the Union. The negotiation tactic of the Commission for future Free Trade Agreements (FTAs) with third countries has been strongly influenced by the ASEAN chapter:

> The Commission initially pursued a region-to-region approach in several FTA negotiations as a first-best option because of the advantages it brings for EU exporters and partner country industries and consumers. If successful, a region-to-region FTA provides EU industry with access to a large market based on consistent conditions and enhances intra-regional trade at the partner's end. The Commission continues to pursue this approach, for instance in the case of the Mercosur and [Gulf Cooperation Council] negotiations. However, in other negotiations, the regional counterparts sometimes represent groups that are substantially less

67 Commission Communication, *supra* note 53, p. 6.
68 European Commission Staff Working Document, Report on progress achieved on the Global Europe Strategy, 2006–2010, SEC(2010) 1268/2, November 2010, p. 8. See also the speech by the European Commissioner for Trade, Karel De Gucht, 'EU-ASEAN: An efficient machine for the next 45 years' at the conference 'ASEAN at 45: Regional Hopes, Global Clout', Brussels, 19 June 2012. Online. Available HTTP: <http://europa.eu/rapid/pressReleasesAction.do?reference=SPEECH/12/462&format=HTML&aged=0&language=EN&guiLanguage=en> (accessed 8 August 2012).

integrated than the EU. Internal coordination and agreement on common positions among members is a constant challenge. Complex intra-group dynamics can lower the level of ambition as negotiating partners settle for the lowest common denominator. In these cases, a bilateral approach can often yield better results. This led the Commission to conclude bilateral trade deals with some Latin American countries and to re-launch negotiations with ASEAN countries on a one-to-one basis, starting with Singapore. By aiming for consistency in each bilateral FTA, a subsequent consolidation of bilateral deals at the regional level remains possible and indeed desired.[69]

Until a veritable comprehensive European international investment policy has been developed, the benefits to be reaped from the enhanced Commission negotiation position will necessarily remain incompletely realized. The lack of a well-developed investment prong of the Union's CCP will offer third country partners ample ammunition during their dealings with the Commission, as opposed to when negotiating with individual EU Member States that have amassed decades of experience in BIT negotiations and have a well-aligned investment policy. One of the main points of discussion regarding a future EU investment policy concerns the replication of the Member State BIT provisions on investor–state dispute settlement at the Union level. Moreover, there is still legal uncertainty as to what exactly falls under the notion of 'foreign direct investment' in Article 207 of the TFEU, hence severely obscuring the scope of the investment competences of the Union. Preliminary assessments of the rather limited scope of the FDI notion appear to indicate that the Commission, despite the 'exclusive' nature of its investment competences, might still have to negotiate alongside its Member States to conclude comprehensive investment agreements that have a reach comparable to the current high-standard BITs of the latter.[70] Further, within the Union itself, opposition against the exercise of the Commission's 'exclusive' negotiation powers might persist among Member States for fear of having their national interests disregarded for the greater European good.[71] The potentially mixed nature of EU negotiations offers ample opportunity for individual Member States to hold back progress at the Union level, potentially cancelling out the benefits that the Union might gain from cementing its FDI competences in the CCP.

---

69 Ibid., p. 23.
70 See S. Woolcock and J. Kleinheisterkamp, *supra* note 52, pp. 12–3; C.-H. Wu, *supra* note 50, pp. 398–9. For a detailed analysis of the scope of FDI competences under the European Constitution and the Treaty of Lisbon, see J. Ceyssens, 'Towards a Common Foreign Investment Policy? – Foreign Investment in the European Constitution', *Legal Issues of Economic Integration*, 2005, vol. 32, pp. 272–90; A. Dimopoulos, *supra* note 49; J. Karl, 'The competence for foreign direct investment: New powers for the European Union?', *Journal of World Investment and Trade*, 2004, vol. 5, pp. 429–39. See further J. Wouters, P. De Man and L. Chanet, *supra* note 1, pp. 292–9.
71 S. Woolcock and J. Kleinheisterkamp, *supra* note 52, p. 15.

8.2.3 Improving the negotiation position of developing countries

The trend of power diffusion in international economic negotiations has increased the sets of options and strategies that are available to negotiation partners, in particular at the multilateral level. Coercive and confrontational power play by governments is slowly being replaced with pragmatism.[72] This evolution does not appear to have been to the detriment of developing countries, who in the past decades have succeeded in blocking or at least reducing the scope of several far-reaching and intrusive proposals on investment introduced by the United States, the European Union, Canada and Japan in the context of GATT (General Agreement on Tariffs and Trade) and WTO negotiation rounds. The decision to negotiate services on a separate track from goods, with a clear development focus, the resulting General Agreement on Trade in Services (GATS) and the limited scope of the Agreement on Trade-Related Investment Measures (TRIMs) all give a clear indication of the rising bargaining power of developing countries during the Uruguay Round.[73]

It is tempting to attribute the relative degree of success of developing countries in the framework of the GATT and the WTO to the numerical majority they have attained in these organizations since the mid-1980s.[74] Success in negotiations does not merely depend on the ability to outnumber the opposing party, however. In practice, their large and unwieldy number may very well weaken the relative position of developing countries in investment negotiations, for a number of reasons.[75] First, the requirement of decision-making by consensus introduced in GATT 1947 and maintained in the agreement establishing the WTO to a large extent nullifies the potential of the numerical majority factor for developing countries.[76] There is little advantage

72 J.P. Singh, *supra* note 7, pp. 451–2.

73 M. Mashayekhi and M. Gibbs, *supra* note 33, pp. 4–10. For more on the Uruguay Round negotiations from the perspective of developing countries, see J.P. Singh, 'The evolution of national interest: New issues and North-South negotiations during the Uruguay Round', in J.S. Odell (ed.), *Negotiating trade: Developing countries in the WTO and NAFTA*, Cambridge: Cambridge University Press, 2006, pp. 41–84.

74 For more on the evolution of the membership and the participation of developing countries in the GATT and the WTO, see J.S. Odell, *supra* note 8; B.M. Hoekman and M.M. Kostecki, *The political economy of the world trading system: The WTO and beyond*, Oxford: Oxford University Press, 2001, pp. 393–410. The WTO explicitly recognizes that the majority of its members qualify for the criteria of developing and least-developed countries: WTO, *Who are the developing countries in the WTO?* Online. Available HTTP: <http://www.wto.org/english/tratop_e/devel_e/d1who_e.htm> (accessed 13 March 2012).

75 P. Drahos, *supra* note 35, pp. 85–7.

76 Article IX.1 of the Agreement establishing the World Trade Organization (WTO Agreement) provides that '[t]he WTO shall continue the practice of decision-making by consensus followed under GATT 1947. Except as otherwise provided, where a decision cannot be arrived at by consensus, the matter at issue shall be decided by voting' (footnote omitted). The consensus requirement is fulfilled 'if no Member, present at the meeting when the decision is taken, formally objects to the proposed decision'. The WTO

in gathering a large coalition of like-minded States if one headstrong country can obstruct the entire proceedings. Second, and more importantly, the moniker 'developing country' as used by the United Nations is ill-defined and lumps together a wide variety of States that often have few common characteristics apart from a shared level of material well-being that is lower than that of their developed counterparts. Major economic determinants for attracting FDI, such as market size and natural resources, vary widely among the large group of developing countries and so does the need among these countries to conclude an international investment agreement.[77] As mentioned earlier, developing countries with an attractive economic climate such as India, China and Indonesia can afford to remain rather intransigent during investment negotiations as they would not necessarily be worse off if no deal could be reached that is in line with their demands.[78] Conversely, least-developed countries that are unable to attract foreign investors on the basis of their economic situation alone should logically be more inclined to concede to the demands of their developed negotiation partners so as to boost their investment climate through legal means.[79] To complicate matters further, some developing countries are no longer solely importers of capital, thus calling into doubt the once tenable equation of capital-exporting/capital-importing countries and developed/developing countries.

Since most developing countries do not have a strong economic starting position and cannot effectively rely on the power of numbers to defend their interests on the international stage, their best chances of turning the tables at investment negotiations to their advantage is by resorting to a series of tactics and strategies that might indirectly improve their bargaining power. Many recommendations and suggestions to this effect have been put forward in academic literature. However, most of these are not specifically tailored to the idiosyncrasies of international economic negotiations and are generally available to all parties gathered at the negotiation table, be they developed or developing countries. The following therefore focuses on the two most important strategies that may be of particular use to developing countries in investment negotiations. First of all, it stands to reason that the needs and interests of developing countries will only be reflected in international negotiations if they are formally

Agreement is available online at <http://www.wto.org/english/docs_e/legal_e/04-wto. pdf> (accessed 13 March 2012).

77 A.V. Ganesan, *supra* note 3, pp. 33–5.

78 India is among the most ardent opponents of a multilateral agreement on investment, notwithstanding the many bilateral and regional treaties it has concluded in this area in recent years. For a more detailed account of the position of India in investment negotiations, see the country's submissions to the WTO WGTI (*infra* notes 107, 125, 213 and 216). See further J. Chaisse, D. Chakraborty and A. Guha, 'India's multilayered FDI regulation: Between resistance to multilateral negotiations and unilateral proactivism', in J. Chaisse and P. Gugler (eds), *Expansion of trade and foreign direct investment in Asia – Strategic and policy challenges*, London: Routledge, 2009, pp. 240–68.

79 A.V. Ganesan, *supra* note 3, p. 34.

included in the process from the start so as to be able to positively influence the contents of the negotiation agenda.[80] The absence of developing countries as formal negotiation partners is obviously a severe impediment to reaching a balanced agreement, as is apparent from the MAI experience. Second, the proactive participation of developing countries should also be guaranteed during the actual negotiations. This necessitates the formation of strong coalitions between like-minded developing countries through which they can defend their views on certain key issues by formulating counterproposals to positions defended by parties with opposing views.[81] Finally, more reactive and opportunistic tactics, which are less relevant in this context, include the exploitation of temporal breaches in the cordon of economically powerful States.[82] In addition, one should also keep in mind the strategies mentioned earlier in this chapter, which include, one may recall, issue linkage and tradeoffs, the mobilization of domestic commercial intelligence networks and the enrolment of the international civil society into a single coalition.

In the end, what is most vital for developing countries in investment negotiations is to translate their numerical superiority into a potent source of additional bargaining power by transforming the current heterogeneous amalgamate of States, united only in their opposition to further encroachment on their sovereignty, into a cohesive bloc exhibiting strong leadership, intensive monitoring capacity and avid participation and cooperation from all governments concerned.[83] This will allow them to positively influence the agenda of investment negotiations and defend well-informed positions on pre-negotiated key issues in order to counter propositions antithetical to their interests put forward by their economically stronger opponents. A positive approach guided by these rules of thumb will ideally obviate the need for more confrontational and counterproductive tactics, thus heightening chances of

---

80 The need for a proactive strategy by developing countries in investment negotiations is particularly stressed in R.H. Thomas, 'The need for a Southern African Development Community response to proposals for a Multilateral Agreement on Investment', *World Competition*, 1998, vol. 21, pp. 85–106. See further J.P. Singh, *supra* note 7, pp. 471–73, referring to D.C. Bennet and K.E. Sharpe, 'Agenda setting and bargaining power: The Mexican State versus transnational automobile corporations', *World Politics*, 1979, vol. 32, pp. 57–89.
81 M. Mashayekhi and M. Gibbs, *supra* note 33, pp. 3 and 12–3.
82 E. Benvenisti and G.W. Downs, 'The empire's new clothes: Political economy and the fragmentation of international law', *Stanford Law Review*, 2007–2008, vol. 60, pp. 620–1.
83 An example of a well-organized group of developing countries that resisted caving in to the demands of developed countries was the so-called Cairns Group of agricultural exporters at the Uruguay Round. For more on the Cairns Group and the importance of formalizing group life at the WTO as a means of strengthening the position of developing countries during negotiations, see P. Drahos, *supra* note 35, pp. 88–103; R.A. Higgott and A.F. Cooper, 'Middle power leadership and coalition building: Australia, the Cairns Group and the Uruguay Round of trade negotiations', *International Organization*, 1990, vol. 44, pp. 589–632; J. Whalley, *What can the developing countries infer from the Uruguay Round models for future negotiations*, New York: United Nations, 2000.

reaching a balanced treaty that reflects the interests of developed and developing countries alike, be they net importers or exporters of capital.

The increased complexity of international economic negotiations described above has most definitely added to the options of the governments involved to pursue their interests, making it all the harder to make any generalized statements on the outcome of any particular proceeding. This is further exacerbated by the fragmentation of the international investment landscape.[84] It has been argued that powerful developed countries have consciously pursued a policy of fragmentation of international investment law in the past decades in order to consolidate their position in a rapidly changing globalized economy to counter the rise of developing countries at the multilateral stage.[85] They have done so by relying on a number of strategies, the most important of which are avoiding negotiations on broad, comprehensive agreements in favour of a large number of narrow, functionally defined treaties and shifting to alternative levels or venues when the initiative negotiation forum is perceived as being too responsive to the interest of weaker States.[86] As such, the frustration of the United States at the collapse of the MAI negotiations may help to explain the dramatic increase in BITs that took place in the late 1990s and its apparent lack of interest in initiating discussions on a multilateral investment framework at the WTO.[87] However, it fails to account for the observation that developed countries are typically the most ardent supporters of a comprehensive MAI, while many a developing country remains averse to the idea. The following section will therefore turn to the dynamics of parallel investment negotiations with a view to determining the appropriate level and venue for negotiating improvements to the existing IIA framework.

8.3 Multi-level bargaining: tackling the investment paradox

Throughout the years, most developing countries have consistently opposed starting negotiations on a comprehensive MFI while at the same time vigorously supporting the conclusion of investment treaties with more intrusive provisions at the bilateral level, both with developed and with other developing countries.[88] The most striking example of this strong predisposition to

---

84 On the fragmented state of international investment law and possible remedies to counter this trend, see P. Gugler and J. Chaisse, *supra* note 9; A. van Aaken, 'Fragmentation of international law: The case of international investment law', *Finnish Yearbook of International Law*, 2006, vol. 17, pp. 91–130.

85 E. Benvenisti and G.W. Downs, *supra* note 82, pp. 599–600 and 610–19.

86 Other strategies include the formulation of agreements in the context of infrequently convened multilateral negotiations and consciously avoiding the creation of a powerful and independent bureaucracy or judiciary.

87 J.W. Salacuse and N.P. Sullivan, *supra* note 1, pp. 75–8.

88 See R. Dozler, 'New foundations of the law of expropriation of alien property', *American Journal of International Law*, 1981, vol. 75, p. 567; M. Sornarajah, *The international law on*

bilateralism is India, which since the liberalization of its economic policies on trade and investment in 1991 through the conclusion of several BITs and REIAs has nevertheless continued its staunch opposition to a codification of the same provisions at the multilateral level.[89] This was once again demonstrated at the recent discussions in the WTO Working Group on the Relationship between Trade and Investment. Explaining the ambivalent attitude of developing countries toward discussions on investment at different levels can help to reveal the main concerns of these countries and hence reveal possible means of improving the international negotiation framework of IIAs.

Before embarking on an assessment of the most intellectually appealing theories that have been proffered in legal and political literature, two clarifications are in order. First, it has already been implied that theories questioning the need for concluding IIAs *as such*, without differentiating between the level at which they are negotiated, should be discarded wholly since they cannot satisfactorily explain why developing countries should resist only the negotiation of *multilateral* rules on investment. Statements recalling the lack of empirical evidence for the influence of investment treaties on the flow of FDI can therefore not be taken into account as valid objections to concluding an MFI.[90] Second, the so-called enlightenment theory is generally considered untenable as well.[91] According to this hypothesis, developing countries have gradually come to realize that their initial opposition to binding investment rules does not serve their own interests, thus spurring them into negotiating investment agreements to further their own goals. While it is true that the general attitude of the developing world toward FDI has altered fundamentally since the 1970s, this evolution in itself cannot explain why these countries keep resisting negotiating multilateral rules that *at the same time* are being codified in far more intrusive BITs. Furthermore, one would expect developing countries to communicate this sudden change of heart at the same forum where they so fiercely resisted the codification of investment norms, i.e. at the multilateral rather than the bilateral level.[92]

The economic dynamics of international economic negotiations as set out in the previous section already provide us with a number of potential explanations for the paradoxical behaviour of developing countries observed in investment negotiations. First, the noted asymmetry in bargaining power between developed and developing countries is arguably greater in a bilateral setting

foreign investment, Cambridge: Cambridge University Press, 2010, pp. 211–12; S.W. Schill, *The multilateralization of international investment law*, Cambridge: Cambridge University Press, 2009, pp. 23–64.

89 See J. Chaisse, D. Chakraborty and A. Guha, *supra* note 78, pp. 240–68.

90 This argument is advanced in S. Young and A.T. Tavares, *supra* note 23, pp. 18–19.

91 A.T. Guzman, 'Why LDCs sign treaties that hurt them: Explaining the popularity of bilateral investment treaties', *Virginia Journal of International Law*, 1997–1998, vol. 38, pp. 667–8; J.F. Morin and G. Gagné, *supra* note 42, p. 54.

92 See A.T. Guzman, *supra* note 91, pp. 667–9 for a refutation of the enlightenment theory and other related theories commonly suggested in legal literature.

than in a multilateral context, which might explain why weaker States have signed into heavily one-sided BITs while at the same time opposing the codification of similar rules at a global level.[93] The subsequent rounds of negotiations and discussions on investment matters at Uruguay, the OECD and Doha seem to support this theory in that developing countries indeed appear capable of mounting a relatively coherent opposition to developed countries, which, in a multilateral setting, turn out less unified than their shared goals of investment protection and liberalization might suggest.[94] The continued opposition of many developing countries to the negotiation of an MFI is somewhat baffling, however, in light of the existing network of intrusive BITs. Given the far-reaching nature of the provisions in these agreements, one might expect developing countries to be rather supportive of switching negotiations to a level and forum where their bargaining power can be increased through coalitions in order to remedy the bilateral inequities. In reality, however, it is the developed countries that most ardently strive for multilateral negotiations on investment.

A second theory that has already been hinted at therefore links the investment paradox to the impact of domestic players on the positions of their governments at international negotiations. This hypothesis contends that the diffusion of power across international and national actors particularly complicates the proceedings of multilateral negotiations as opposed to bilateral talks since the increased visibility of the former makes them more vulnerable to attacks from civil society.[95] This is evidenced by the tumultuous events surrounding the OECD MAI deliberations and the 1999 WTO ministerial meeting in Seattle. Protests by NGOs and other pressure groups can easily force nationally elected negotiating partners in a heavily mediatized multilateral setting to derogate from provisions that have since long been incorporated in BITs. This, in turn, will cause the business community to lose interest in multilateral investment negotiations as well, as they are unlikely to result in standards that can rival the provisions of pre-existing bilateral treaties, which already to a large extent cater to the needs of investors.[96] This explanation is particularly appealing in

---

93 This explanation is raised in J.W. Salacuse, 'Towards a global treaty for investment protection? Lessons from the failure of OECD's MAI', in N. Horn and S. Kroll (eds), *Arbitrating foreign investment disputes: Procedural and substantive legal aspects*, New York: Kluwer, 2004, p. 75; P. Sauvé, *supra* note 20, p. 342. See also S.W. Schill, *supra* note 88, pp. 88–9, who at the same time criticizes an overly simplistic hegemonic approach to the investment paradox.

94 The main issues that divided the US, the EU and Canada during the MAI negotiations were the controversy surrounding the US Helms-Burton Act on the recovery of claims concerning property owned in Cuba by American nationals, a provision excepting regional economic integration organizations (REIOs) such as the EU from the scope of the MAI's non-discrimination clauses and the regulatory exception for promoting cultural and linguistic diversity, which mainly France and Canada insisted upon. See P.T. Muchlinski, *supra* note 28, pp. 1046–8.

95 J.F. Morin and G. Gagné, *supra* note 42, pp. 62–4.

96 K. Kennedy, 'A WTO agreement on investment: A solution in search of a problem?', *University of Pennsylvania Journal of International Economic Law*, 2003, vol. 24, p. 85;

that it suggests that the failure of the most recent multilateral negotiations on investment at the OECD and the WTO may not necessarily be due to the traditional opposition between developed/capital-exporting and developing/capital-importing countries but can be attributed to external factors that are more easily remedied than deep-rooted differences of opinion on key investment issues.[97]

It is likely, however, that more fundamental dynamics are at work in creating and sustaining the investment paradox than the mere influence of domestic players on their governments. A more forceful explanation of the eagerness of developing countries to engage in bilateral talks while withstanding multilateral negotiations is offered by the competitive theory of BIT diffusion.[98] This theory suggests that, when pitched against developed negotiation partners in a bilateral setting, a prisoner's dilemma kicks in that brings developing countries to agree to intrusive provisions in BITs in order to gain a competitive advantage over other developing countries that have a similar economic profile. Conversely, no such dynamics are at work at the multilateral level, as collective negotiations by definition result in comparable conditions for all developing countries. As such, this could explain why developing countries resist multilateral investment negotiations even though it appears in their interest to depart from the bilateral level. The competitive theory has been criticized for overestimating the effect of IIAs on the flow of investment.[99] Empirical evidence has shown that some developing countries succeed in attracting FDI in the absence of BITs while others avidly take up bilateral commitments without being able to alter capital flows in their advantage,[100] thereby underscoring that it is the economic fundamentals of a host country rather than the IIAs concluded by it that determine the movement of investment.[101] This finding does not invalidate the competitive theory as such, however, since the applicability of the hypothesis is expressly limited to the treaty-negotiation behaviour of host countries that are closely substitutable venues for investment, thereby to a large extent eliminating the distortive effect of economic fundamentals.[102] The competitive theory thus offers a powerful explanation for the paradoxical behaviour of developing countries at different levels of investment

UNCTAD, *Lessons from the MAI*, *supra* note 28, p. 24; E.M. Graham, *Global corporations and national governments*, Washington DC: Institute for International Economics, 1996, p. 89; *id.*, *Fighting the wrong enemy: Antiglobal activists and multinational enterprises*, Washington DC: Institute for International Economics, 2000, p. 192.

97 In this sense also S.W. Schill, *supra* note 88, p. 63.

98 See A.T. Guzman, *supra* note 91, pp. 639–88; Z. Elkins, A.T. Guzman, B. Simmons, *supra* note 15, pp. 265–304.

99 J.F. Morin and G. Gagné, *supra* note 42, pp. 58–9.

100 L.E. Peterson, 'Bilateral investment treaties and development policy-making', International Institute for Sustainable Development, November 2004. Online. Available HTTP: <www.iisd.org/pdf/2004/trade_bits.pdf> (accessed 13 March 2012).

101 See references *supra* note 38.

102 Z. Elkins, A.T. Guzman and B. Simmons, *supra* note 15, pp. 281–2.

negotiations, while allowing for sufficient differentiation among these countries on the basis of their varying economic fundamentals.

The theory does not explain, however, why some weak developing countries with a similar economic profile that have concluded BITs would nevertheless also be inclined to support the commencement of negotiations of a multilateral investment framework. During the discussions at the WGTI, for example, it became clear that developing countries such as Chinese Taipei, Hong Kong, Chile, Costa Rica and Turkey supported investment negotiations in the WTO, while stronger developing countries such as China, India and Brazil continued to oppose them.[103] If IIAs indeed matter less to economically stronger host countries, it would stand to reason that these countries should exhibit less paradoxical behaviour than their weaker counterparts in negotiating IIAs. This does not seem to be the case. It would therefore appear that a final explanation for a developing country's attitude in investment negotiations is to be found in the value it attaches to retaining the necessary regulatory power for directing FDI flowing into its economy towards certain sectors in order to attain specific development goals, regardless of whether this capital is obtained through IIAs or the intrinsic attractiveness of its economy. Powerful host countries such as India and China would therefore oppose the negotiation of an MFI despite having concluded manifold BITs because they believe the latter agreements pose less of a threat to their regulatory sovereignty.

The perceived flexibility bilateral talks offer to the mutual negotiating partners does indeed appear to be a crucial element in explaining the widespread surge in BITs and the lack of progress at the multilateral level.[104] The advantages of bilateralism for catering to the specific needs of developing countries were stressed on numerous occasions by India during the recent WGTI discussions:

> Developing countries need to retain the ability to screen and channel FDI in tune with their domestic interests and priorities. Bilateral investment treaties have been favoured the world over for precisely the flexibility they provide to the host country while at the same time extending necessary protection to foreign investors.[105]

---

103 P. Sauvé, *supra* note 20, p. 331.

104 J.F. Morin and G. Gagné, *supra* note 42, pp. 64–9. The flexibility of BITs is also stressed as an important asset in UNCTAD, *Trends in international investment agreements: An overview*, New York and Geneva: United Nations, 1999, pp. 46–7.

105 See the following communications of India to the WTO WGTI: WT/WGTI/W/148, 7 October 2002, para. 5; WT/WGTI/W/150, 7 October 2002, para. 12. See also WGTI Report (1998), para. 186 ('an important advantage of bilateral investment treaties was that they could be tailored to the specific circumstances of the parties concerned and could address specific concerns, such as development issues'); Report (2000) of the WGTI to the General Council, WT/WGTI/4, 27 November 2000, para. 44 (WGTI Report (2000)).

Developed countries as well would seem to benefit significantly from the dynamics of bilateral negotiations, although the argument is more equivocal in this case. Bilateral talks allow strong economic players to more carefully select and screen their contracting partners while the increased asymmetry grants them more leverage to impose broader security exceptions on countries that, while potentially important economic consorts, do not necessarily rank as political or military allies.[106] The heated discussions at the OECD resulting in lengthy catalogues of exceptions to the fundamental principle of national treatment in the aborted MAI reaffirmed that even among developed countries the need for flexibility in investment relations remains high on the agenda.[107] Furthermore, the currently prevalent system of sequential bilateralism also allows for an adaptive evolution of investment agreements in reaction to a rapidly changing political and economic context.[108] The importance of such flexibility has been clearly demonstrated by the sobering experience of the North American Free Trade Agreement (NAFTA).[109] A series of high-profile arbitration cases brought against the United States and Canada under the NAFTA dispute-settlement provisions made it apparent that, like developing countries, developed host countries are not immune to the impact of creeping IIA provisions on their sovereign power to take certain measures to protect the environment and other sustainable development goals.[110] The three NAFTA members responded to these panel decisions by issuing an interpretative note clarifying the scope and meaning of a number of provisions in the free trade agreement, albeit without resolving the most pressing issue of balancing the protection of sovereignty and the need to sanction regulatory takings.[111] In a further reaction to these events Canada revised its model BIT in 2003 in order to 'reflect and incorporate the results of its growing experience with the implementation and operation of the investment chapter of the

---

106 China–US BIT negotiations provide a good example: see C. Congyan, 'China–US BIT negotiations and the future of investment treaty regime: A grand bilateral bargain with multilateral implications', *Journal of International Economic Law*, 2009, vol. 12, pp. 457–506. See further Z. Drabek, 'A Multilateral Agreement on Investment: Convincing the sceptics', WTO Staff Working Paper ERAD-98-05, June 1998, pp. 6–8. Online. Available HTTP: <http://www.wto.org/english/res_e/reser_e/ae9805_e.htm> (accessed 13 March 2012).

107 See the last version of the MAI draft at <http://www1.oecd.org/daf/mai/pdf/ng/ng987r1e.pdf> (accessed 13 March 2012).

108 J.F. Morin and G. Gagné, *supra* note 42, p. 68.

109 J. Kurtz, *supra* note 23, pp. 732–56.

110 See, among other cases, NAFTA Arbitration, *S.D. Meyers, Inc. v Government of Canada*, ILM, 2001, vol. 40, p. 1408; NAFTA Arbitration, *Methanex v United States*, ILM, 2005, vol. 44, p. 1345.

111 Notes of interpretation of certain Chapter 11 provisions issued by the NAFTA Free Trade Commission on 31 July 2001. Online. Available HTTP: <http://www.international.gc.ca/trade-agreements-accords-commerciaux/disp-diff/nafta-interpr.aspx?lang=en> (accessed 13 March 2012).

NAFTA'.[112] The United States for its part adopted a new model BIT as well,[113] which is currently being further revised following campaign pledges by President Barack Obama to 'ensure that foreign investor rights are strictly limited and will fully exempt any law or regulation written to protect public safety or promote the public interest'.[114] It is highly doubtful that such rectifying steps could have been taken equally swiftly in the context of an MAI.

The above evolution may well account for the noted surge in the number of BITs that are currently being renegotiated by developed countries.[115] However, it does not dovetail with the observation that developed countries have concluded fewer BITs in general in recent years while initiating proceedings at the multilateral level more forcefully than ever. Two fundamental questions arise in this context. First, if all developed countries acknowledge the importance of flexibility in bilateral talks, as do their developing partners, is there really a pressing need for embarking on universal negotiations? The United States, traditionally a staunch supporter of universal rules on investment, has already shown itself less than enthusiastic about an MFI at the WTO, thus possibly signalling a wish to return to the bilateral level. However, the American approach may also be explained by the particular choice of venue and the relatively strong development focus of the WGTI mandate rather than by any real lack of interest in an MFI as such. Secondly, if the views of developed and developing countries are indeed converging ever more closely as a result of the increased recognition of the need for regulatory freedom, why, then, have discussions at the WGTI failed to give way to fully fledged negotiations on multilateral investment rules? These observations ultimately raise the question of whether an improvement of the negotiation context of IIAs should take place at the bilateral or multilateral level. What is the added value of an MFI in this respect? What is the appropriate forum for improving the international investment negotiation framework and what substantive provisions should be discussed? These issues will be tackled in the following two sections of this chapter.

112 Statement by Canada's Department of Foreign Affairs and International Trade. Online. Available HTTP: <http://www.international.gc.ca/trade-agreements-accords-commerciaux/agr-acc/fipa-apie/index.aspx> (accessed 13 March 2012).

113 Online. Available HTTP: <http://www.state.gov/documents/organization/117601.pdf> (accessed 13 March 2012).

114 D. Vis-Dunbar, 'United States reviews its model bilateral investment treaty', *Investment Treaty News*, 5 June 2009. Online. Available HTTP: <http://www.investmenttreatynews.org/cms/news/archive/2009/06/05/united-states-reviews-its-model-bilateral-investment-treaty.aspx> (accessed 13 March 2012).

115 See UNCTAD, *Recent developments in international investment agreements (2007–June 2008)*, New York and Geneva: United Nations, 2008, p. 5; *id.*, *Recent developments in international investment agreements (2008–June 2009)*, New York and Geneva: United Nations, 2009, pp. 5–6. This trend is reinforced by the actions of EU Member States to amend their BITs in conformity with former Art. 307 TEC (current Art. 351 TFEU). See *supra*.

8.4 The case for negotiating a multilateral framework on investment

Positions on the need for negotiations on an MFI differ widely among governments and do not run neatly along the lines of the developed, capital-exporting countries versus developing, capital-importing countries axis. As the discussions in the WGTI revealed, the main opponents to commencing formal negotiations on an MFI in the framework of the WTO were such large developing countries as India, China, Indonesia and Brazil, joined in their opposition mainly by Malaysia, the Philippines and Thailand. The United States also exhibited lukewarm support at best for what they feared would be negotiations resulting in a low-standard treaty that would fail to engender significant enthusiasm in its domestic business society.[116] Outspoken support for multilateral investment negotiations came from the European Union, Canada and Japan, whose submissions were backed by such diverse developing countries as Chile, Chinese Taipei, Costa Rica, Hong Kong, the Republic of Korea and Turkey. In the end, the diverging views of the main players in the debate could not be reconciled, as is clear from the observations in the closing paragraphs of the final report of the WGTI to the WTO General Council in 2003: while some noted that, after seven years of discussions and exchanging views, 'the point has been reached where further progress could be made only be moving beyond the analytical phase of work and entering into a negotiating phase', others maintained that further analysis and discussion was needed before such a decision could be taken, as 'the Working Group's deliberations had revealed [that] the extent to which the substance, implications and rationale of a prospective multilateral investment framework were still unclear'.[117] Finally, some delegations explicitly noted that their contributions and interventions in the WGTI 'were made without prejudice to their position with regard to the need for a multilateral framework on investment in the WTO'.[118] Tactical considerations in view of a strategic tradeoff with concessions on agriculture notwithstanding, one should take to heart these submissions to the WGTI as they are the most recent authoritative statements on the issue of multilateral investment negotiations.

Academics as well seem to be unable to agree on the future course of action for improving the current IIA framework. Some authors assert that the need for spending valuable resources on negotiating an MFI is obviated by the existence of an expansive patchwork of BITs and REIAs that should be

---

116 P. Sauvé, *supra* note 20, p. 330. This clearly reflects the American experience with previous multilateral initiatives on investment, ranging from the stillborn ITO Charter to the compromise that is the TRIMs Agreement and the failed MAI. See also J. Kurtz, *supra* note 23, p. 774.

117 Report (2003) of the WGTI to the General Council, WT/WGTI/7, 11 July 2003, para. 56 and para. 58 (WGTI Report (2003)).

118 Ibid., para. 55.

interpreted as a *de facto* multilateral treaty.[119] Others argue that there would be little added value to starting negotiations on a new global agreement on investment in light of the existing IIAs and that the current trend of bilateralism should be intensified to ensure universal coverage of international relations on investment through BITs.[120] Still others contend that such universal coverage has already been reached as most BIT provisions have reached the status of either customary international law or of general principles of law pursuant to Article 38 of the Statute of the International Court of Justice.[121] When one approaches the case for an MFI from the perspective of furthering the interests of developing countries through the negotiation of IIAs, however, most authors agree that some form of progress at the multilateral level is the only viable approach.[122]

8.4.1 *The flexibility argument*

Throughout the discussions in the WTO working group on trade and investment, a great many arguments were raised both opposing and supporting the commencement of negotiations of an MFI. The submissions and interventions reflected in the 1998 report of the WGTI especially centred on the question of the need for multilateral negotiations on an issue that was already covered by an impressive network of bilateral treaties. It is not within the ambit of the present chapter to recount every argument for or against an MFI raised in the context of the WGTI discussions. Many of these arguments amount to statements of fact that are of less relevance to the question addressed here and the reader is referred to the respective reports of the working group for a comprehensive account of these claims and assertions.[123] The focus in this

---

119 S.W. Schill, *supra* note 88.
120 M.A. Srur, *supra* note 3, pp. 74–5.
121 J.W. Salacuse and N.P. Sullivan, *supra* note 1, pp. 112–15; P. Read, *supra* note 28, p. 362. See also A. Gunawardana, 'The inception and growth of bilateral investment promotion and protection treaties', *American Society of International Law Proceedings*, 1992, p. 550; J. Faundez, *supra* note 18, pp. 154–5; V. Mosoti, *supra* note 1, pp. 132–3.
122 See, *inter alia*, J.W. Salacuse, 'Towards a new treaty framework for direct foreign investment', *Journal of Air Law and Commerce*, 1984–1985, vol. 50, pp. 1005–10; R.H. Thomas, *supra* note 80, pp. 92–3 and 105; E. Chalamish, 'The future of bilateral investment treaties: A *de facto* multilateral agreement?', *Brooklyn Journal of International Law*, 2009, vol. 34, p. 353; B. Bora and M. Graham, *supra* note 24, pp. 341–5; E. Benvenisti and G.W. Downs, *supra* note 82, pp. 625–31; P. Drahos, *supra* note 35, pp. 80–1. For more details on the substantive content of such an agreement, see Section 8.5 of this chapter.
123 See in particular the summaries of the discussions in WGTI Report (1998), paras 145–52; Report (1999) of the WGTI to the General Council, WT/WGTI/3, 22 October 1999, paras 72–7 (WGTI Report (1999)); Report (2001) of the WGTI to the General Council, WT/WGTI/5, 8 October 2001, paras 9–12. See also India's communication WT/WGTI/W/86 of 22 June 2000. For a general overview of arguments for and against MFI negotiations, see H. Fridh and O. Jensen, 'Multilateral or bilateral investment negotiations: Where can developing countries make themselves heard?', CUTS Briefing Paper No. 9, 2002, p. 5. Online. Available HTTP: <http://www.cuts-international.org/

section will be on those arguments that best reflect the most pressing concerns and needs of developing countries, taking into account the reality of international economic negotiations as related previously. This will allow us to make pointed observations on how to steer negotiations in the direction of a more development-friendly IIA framework.

The previous sections on the dynamics of international investment negotiations and possible explanations for the paradoxical behaviour of developing countries in multi-level bargaining suggested that the main reason why developing countries would oppose discussions on a binding MFI was the perceived lack of flexibility spelled by such an agreement. The discussions at the WGTI strongly support this hypothesis. Indeed, statements by developing countries arguing the importance of a flexible framework on investment for pursuing domestic development policies dominated much of the initial stages of the debate. In essence, the argument made by the developing countries most hostile to multilateral investment negotiations was the following. The existence of an investment agreement is not an important determinant of investment decisions by foreign corporations. A sound, sustainable macroeconomic and financial environment is far more important for attaining a country's development goals than simply attracting FDI. Therefore, a multilateral agreement that curtails a host country's regulatory freedom would not serve its development needs.[124] Put differently, '[w]ithout sufficient domestic capabilities, FDI and foreign technology seldom [permeate] the productive system of the national economy. Selective and judicious interventions by governments [are] therefore considered necessary.'[125]

In light of these arguments, it was asserted that,

> to substantiate the argument that the establishment of a multilateral framework on investment would entail significant benefits, especially when compared with existing bilateral investment agreements, it would need to be shown that such a framework would provide for the same degree of flexibility as bilateral investment agreements for countries to pursue development objectives while attracting foreign investment.[126]

From a political point of view, the case for flexibility through bilateral talks over multilateral negotiations is strong in theory, in that it allows governments to selectively improve diplomatic ties with key regional and international partners through direct interaction and cooperation. In practice, however, the

---

ccier_publications.htm> (accessed 15 March 2012); Z. Drabek, *supra* note 106; B. Dymond and M. Hart, *supra* note 13.

124 WGTI Report (1998), paras 195–6.

125 Ibid., para. 196. Broadly similar arguments are reflected in WGTI Report (2000), paras 73 and 77; Report (2002) of the WGTI to the General Council, WT/WGTI/6, 9 December 2002, para. 9 (WGTI Report (2002)).

126 WGTI Report (1998), para. 209.

potential political and economic advantages of bilateralism are negated by the reality of a saturated network of BITs with a highly similar content. Even though a detailed comparison of the BITs concluded by a wide variety of countries reveals several important nuances in the specific formulation of various provisions, which, as various rounds of negotiation on multilateral investment rules have eminently demonstrated, cannot be ignored in a global context, it is difficult to argue that these differences are a reflection of the wishes of the developing country partners, if only for reasons of increased asymmetry in bilateral relations. Furthermore, keeping in mind the failure of the MAI, proponents of a multilateral investment treaty have already settled to the idea that a comprehensive global investment agreement reflecting the high standards of the existing BIT regime is an unrealistic objective. Incidentally, one of the reasons why the MAI negotiations met with such strong opposition from civil society and the developing world was the apparent inability of the agreement to assuage the concerns of the impact of investment rules on the freedom of governments to regulate key areas of domestic policy.[127] The final draft agreement, however, did not substantially depart from the existing model BITs of many developed countries, leading to a lack of interest from the business community and some of the main original supporters of a multilateral treaty on investment. In turn, the failure of the MAI discussions inspired the United States to more vehemently pursue its liberalization commitments at the bilateral level. It follows that, if the provisions of BITs are truly deemed to safeguard sufficient regulatory freedom for host countries, then it is rather unclear why a multilateral treaty that in essence reflects the substance of these provisions would provoke such a strong reaction. This becomes all the more puzzling in the context of the discussions on the WTO MFI, which from the outset took a more balanced, pro-development approach than the MAI. The NAFTA arbitration experience further supports the contention that a future MFI will not pose more stringent limits on the freedom of host countries than the current generation of BITs.

The only reason why developing countries would thus remain opposed to universal investment rules in the name of flexibility is because they would fear that a treaty of equal application to all host countries would deprive them of their competitive edge by limiting their flexibility to redirect investment flows from their closest rivals. It should be kept in mind that investment provisions are most likely to produce competitive effects between countries that find themselves in similar situations. Seen from this perspective, however, the flexibility argument contradicts other reasons often stated in opposition to multilateral rules on investment. Indeed, the theoretical possibility of negotiating different rules with different partners offered in bilateral talks appears to be negated by the basic idea of similarity underlying the theories of authors referred to above, who assert that no valuable resources should be

---

127 See the documents referred to *supra* note 28.

wasted on negotiations for an MFI since the existing web of BITs should be interpreted as a *de facto* global treaty on investment or amounts to customary international law with respect to general principles of law. The multilateralization argument asserts that,

> [t]o a large extent, the regime established by bilateral investment treaties . . . approximates a truly multilateral system which is based on a single multilateral treaty. It is based on rather uniform general principles and disposes of a compliance mechanism that ensures their implementation. While the argument is not that all BITs are identical, one can observe a significant convergence on the level of the texts of the treaties that is complemented by various mechanisms that mitigate differences in scope and wording, including MFN clauses, the possibility of corporate structuring, and the modes of treaty interpretation and application by arbitral tribunals.[128]

The principle of non-discrimination as reflected in the most-favoured nations treatment provisions codified in nearly all modern BITs in particular makes the argument of bilateral flexibility hard to sustain. Not only do MFN clauses significantly cap a host country's freedom to negotiate exceptions and other specificities for attaining development goals in current bilateral talks, they also make it noticeably more difficult to deviate from previous engagements in future negotiations, even if they occur between two close political and economic partners.[129]

The importance of the ubiquitous requirement of non-discrimination in countering the concerns of the developing countries in their opposition to an MFI was also recognized by the governments of the developed countries, who, in response to the flexibility argument advanced during the WGTI discussions, argued that,

> it appeared that underlying these points was a concern regarding the implications of multilateral rules for the ability of countries to regulate economic activities. This concern was valid and shared by all countries but did not constitute an argument against the benefits of establishing collective disciplines regarding the exercise of regulatory authority in certain areas. Regulatory sovereignty was adequately protected by the principle of non-discriminatory treatment of foreign investment.[130]

Finally, it has already been argued that there are good reasons to assume that the dynamics of competition have resulted in the conclusion of BITs that place stricter limitations on developing host countries' regulatory sovereignty than

128 S.W. Schill, *supra* note 88, p. 368.
129 Ibid., pp. 195–6.
130 WGTI Report (1998), para. 197.

they would have accepted if the pitfalls of the prisoner's dilemma had been avoided through the pursuit of multilateral negotiations. In this light, the competitive reflex among developing countries thus becomes a further element that restricts these countries' room to manoeuvre in bilateral bargaining. Moreover, as most competition occurs among countries with similar economic fundamentals and with close geographic proximity, the plea for flexibility becomes a particularly untenable argument against multilateral rules considering the fact that the same countries that oppose such rules are increasingly entering into comprehensive regional economic integration agreements containing investment chapters.

This is not to say that the goal of flexibility in itself is not a valuable objective of investment negotiations in general or that maintaining a certain level of regulatory freedom would not be of a nature to contribute to meeting the development objectives of poor economies. On the contrary, the importance of retaining a certain level of flexibility in economic regulations became apparent in the reactions of governments all over the world to limiting the effects of the recent financial turmoil, and the validity of a strict investment regime in developing countries was recognized by the IMF and the World Bank in the aftermath of the Asian capital crisis in the late 1990s.[131] The point that is being made, however, stresses that it is not necessarily true that bilateral negotiations are inherently more flexible in producing outcomes that cater to the development needs of host countries than multilateral talks, due to the pre-existing patchwork of bilateral and regional investment agreements which significantly cap developing countries' room to manoeuvre in asymmetric bilateral deliberations. In light of these observations, and given the apparent incapacity of the present bilateral regime to redirect investment flows so as to contribute to the development goals of the world's poorest economies, the question remains whether postponing negotiations on a multilateral investment agreement can still be considered a viable option.

8.4.2 A case for multilateral investment negotiations?

It has been argued that the need for retaining a certain level of sovereignty for directing the influx of FDI does not make a convincing case against multilateral negotiations because the specificities of the existing bilateral regime already to a large extent cap this flexibility. This does not necessarily imply, however, that the undeniably multilateral characteristics of the present BIT framework would completely obviate the need for installing a more formal MFI. A further assessment of the case for and against a multilateral investment agreement is needed.

Arguments raised in favour of a multilateral investment treaty typically focus on the formal aspects of the negotiation process and the architectural

---

131 J. Chaisse, D. Chakraborty and A. Guha, *supra* note 78, p. 241. See also WGTI Report (1999), paras 8–17.

advantages resulting from a comprehensive universal agreement.[132] First, it has already been held that the negotiation position of developing countries with a weaker economic starting position than their developed contracting partners can be significantly enhanced at the multilateral level. While it is true that the actualization of this potential to a large degree depends on the formation of strong coalitions that take a proactive approach to setting the agenda and defending unified positions on key issues of consensus, the very nature of multilateral negotiations allows for better opportunities to rectify the asymmetries in two-player talks that are often compounded by competitive impulses.

A second, more fundamental argument supportive of an MFI takes into account the broader structural and architectural implications of concluding a comprehensive and universal agreement on investment. The existing IIA framework is composed of an impressive number of overlapping bilateral and regional treaties, with substantive provisions that often differ in small but important respects. The result is a confusing patchwork of IIAs with incomplete geographic coverage, the enforcement of which is undermined by manifold opportunities for forum shopping and the risk of obtaining mutually inconsistent arbitral decisions. It is often contended that replacing such a vast, complex network of IIAs with a single comprehensive MFI would significantly enhance the stability, efficiency and transparency of the existing IIA framework. First, a multilateral investment agreement would provide stability for foreign investors by locking in what might otherwise amount to a mere momentary trend in liberalization and protection, thus shielding them from sudden changes.[133] This increased level of economic and political stability would, in turn, facilitate compliance by foreign investors with the host country regime in place. Second, although the negotiation of individual BITs is arguably less time-consuming and costly than the entire process of multilateral discussions among a plenitude of countries with differing objectives, the costs of negotiating and periodically reviewing a single MAI would ultimately be much lower than the transaction costs associated with the negotiation, monitoring and implementation of the current patchwork of IIAs. This prospect of increased efficiency should particularly appeal to developing host countries, whose infrastructures are often thought to be too weak to implement their international investment obligations.[134] Finally, the intrinsic transparency and enhanced

132 See, *inter alia*, R. Leal-Arcas, *supra* note 1, pp. 121–6.
133 K. Vandevelde, 'Sustainable liberalism and the international investment regime', *Michigan Journal of International Law*, 1997–1998, vol. 19, pp. 390 and 398; P. Read, *supra* note 28, p. 387; S. Young and A.T. Tavares, *supra* note 23, p. 9; E.M. Graham, 'Direct investment and the future agenda of the World Trade Organization', in J.J. Schott (ed.), *The world trading system: Challenges ahead*, Washington DC: Institute for International Economics, 1996, p. 208.
134 See M. Khor, 'The WTO, the post-Doha agenda and the future of the trade system: A development perspective', Paper presented at the WTO on behalf of the Third World Network, May 2002. Online. Available HTTP: <http://www.twnside.org.sg/title/mkadb.htm> (accessed 13 March 2012).

consistency of a multilateral investment treaty would likely defuse conflicts between governments, reduce distortions in FDI flows and improve the allocation of resources so as to allow a more equitable and efficient distribution of capital that would mainly benefit poor economies.[135]

The empirical sustainability of the latter claims in support of an MFI is unclear and the debate surrounding the issue is redolent of the discussion on the capacity of BITs to enhance FDI flows to developing countries. Some authors assert that the only benefits to be gained from establishing multilateral investment rules are of a political rather than economic nature,[136] while other studies have come to the exactly opposite conclusion.[137] Irrespective of how this discussion would eventually be settled – if it can indeed be authoritatively decided – the aforementioned arguments in favour of a global investment agreement all have to be qualified in that their ultimate value hinges on the implied assumption of supplanting the existing network of IIAs by a single all-encompassing instrument on investment. The practicability of such a feat is highly dubious, however, if only for the enormous administrative challenge the simultaneous handling of over 2,000 BITs with varying scope and coverage would pose for the governments involved. This undertaking is further compounded by the prevalent practice of tacitly renewing modern BITs on their expiry date unless explicitly denounced with a one-year advance notification after an initial period of ten years.[138] The apparent preference of developing countries for a bilateral approach would also seem to relegate a unification of the international legal investment framework through the establishment of a formal MFI to the distant future. Furthermore, previous efforts at negotiating a multilateral investment framework have clearly shown that an MFI codifying the high liberalization and protection standards of many modern BITs is unattainable. It is therefore unlikely that developed countries would agree to the substitution of their bilateral networks by a single IIA if

135 See WGTI Report (1998), para. 187; WGTI Report (1999), para. 76.
136 P. Nunnenkamp, 'FDI for development? Assessing the case for a multilateral investment agreement from the perspective of developing countries', *Journal of World Investment*, 2003, vol. 4, pp. 586–8 and 590–2 and studies referenced.
137 S. Young and A.T. Tavares, *supra* note 23, arguing the economic case for an MFI by referring to studies documented in UNCTAD, *World Investment Report 1996. Investment, trade and international policy arrangements*, Geneva: United Nations, 1996; E.M. Graham, *Global corporations and national governments*, *supra* note 96; T.L. Brewer and S. Young, *The multilateral investment system and multinational enterprises*, Oxford: Oxford University Press, 2000; P. Sauvé and C. Wilkie, 'Investment liberalization in the GATS', in P. Sauvé and R.M. Stern (eds), *GATS 2000. New directions in services trade liberalization*, Washington DC: Brookings Institution, 2000, pp. 331–63; S. Young and T.L. Brewer, 'Overview and public policy reflections', in T.L. Brewer, S. Young and S.E. Guisinger (eds), *The new economic analysis of multinationals: An agenda for management, policy and research*, Cheltenham: Edward Elgar, 2003, pp. 249–74.
138 UNCTAD, *The REIO Exception in MFN Treatment Clauses*, Geneva and New York: United Nations, 2004, p. 57.

that would mean scaling back the treatment of their investors abroad.[139] Indeed, during the discussions in the WGTI the proponents of a WTO MFI frequently observed that,

> while the creation of multilateral rules on investment was desirable, this did not mean that multilateral rules should replace bilateral investment agreements. Rather, multilateral investment rules and bilateral investment agreements could be complementary and mutually reinforcing.[140]

The complementary nature of a future multilateral investment agreement implies that whether the establishment of an MFI will enhance the predictability, transparency and consistency of the current IIA framework will mainly depend on how the relationship with the existing bilateral, regional and multilateral investment rules is handled in the negotiations. This means that the cost–benefit analysis of a multilateral investment treaty has to take into account the substantive content of its projected provisions and the interrelated issue of the negotiation forum.[141] Multilateral investment rules will only command the support of all countries if they add value over existing instruments, otherwise the lack of incentives will undermine all negotiation efforts.[142]

The integrated reality of the modern globalized economy has been identified as a crucial factor in determining the negotiation dynamics on investment issues. The interrelated nature of investment and other elements of the international economic regime offer many opportunities for issue linkage as an important means of facilitating negotiations. In light of the increasingly recognized complementarity between trade and investment and the rising importance of FDI in general, the existence of a strong universal trade regime is therefore frequently suggested as a major reason for establishing a parallel MFI. As such, the EU has argued that '[t]rade and investment are inextricably linked and should therefore be dealt with in a more integrated way. . . . As the process towards world-wide trade liberalization and rule-making trade has moved significantly forward, therefore, so should multilateral liberalization and protection of investment.'[143] The negotiation opportunities offered by possible tradeoffs between matters of investment and trade may explain the wide success of regional economic integration agreements in recent years when compared to the relative decline in investment-specific BITs. The need for a

---

139 See also P. Nunnenkamp, *supra* note 136, p. 587.
140 WGTI Report (1998), para. 208. See also WGTI Report (1999), para. 76; WGTI Report (2000), para. 74. See also R. Leal-Arcas, *supra* note 1, p. 135.
141 A.V. Ganesan, *supra* note 3, p. 17.
142 P. Sauvé, *supra* note 20, p. 350.
143 European Union Agenda, 'Exploring the issue relating to trade and investment', December 2000. Online. Available HTTP: <http://www.wto.org/trade_resources/quotes/mts/investment.htm> (accessed 13 March 2012).

holistic and inclusive approach has also most definitely inspired the decision to move deliberations on an MFI from the OECD to the WTO.

It is commonly acknowledged that States view international organizations as strategic instruments for advancing their own interests.[144] They will therefore aim to institute negotiations at the forum that is best in line with their needs and which allows them to maximize their bargaining power, through both procedural tactics and substantive measures. The history of the past sixty years clearly reflects an opportunistic power-based approach to multilateral investment negotiations.[145] After the failure to establish the International Trade Organization as the third pillar of the Bretton Woods system, and after the Havana Charter was rejected by the United States, the developed countries turned to bilateral negotiations to safeguard the protection of their investors in developing countries, in particular through the so-called Hull rule on prompt, adequate and effective compensation for expropriation.[146] When the number of developing countries was multiplied by the wave of decolonization in the 1960s, these countries used their newly gained numerical majority at the United Nations to challenge the Hull rule in the General Assembly by voting for resolutions on a New International Economic Order, stressing the principle of national sovereignty over natural resources.[147] In the meantime, the World Bank proved a successful forum for the negotiation of various procedural rules on investment, resulting in the establishment of the International Centre for the Settlement of Investment Disputes (ICSID)[148] and the Multilateral Investment Guarantee Agency (MIGA).[149] Substantive multilateral investment rules remained elusive and the negotiation difficulties in this context eventually

---

144 N. Bayne, 'What governments want from international economic institutions and how they get it', *Government and Opposition*, 1997, vol. 32, pp. 361–79.

145 For an account of the regime-shifting behaviour of States in investment negotiations, see E. Smythe, 'Your place or mine? States, international organizations and the negotiation of investment rules', *Transnational Corporations*, 1998, vol. 7(3), pp. 85–119. See also H. Fridh and O. Jensen, *supra* note 123; A.V. Ganesan, *supra* note 3, pp. 27–32.

146 See Exchange of Letters between US Secretary of State Cordell Hull and Mexican Minister of Foreign Relations Eduardo Hay, reprinted in *American Journal of International Law Supplement*, 1938, vol. 32, p. 181. For more on the Hull rule and compensation for investment expropriation, see T.W. Wälde and B. Sabahi, 'Compensation, damages, and valuation', in P.T. Muchlinski, F. Ortino and C.H. Schreuer (eds), *The Oxford handbook of international investment law*, Oxford: Oxford University Press, 2008, pp. 1049–124, in particular pp. 1068–9.

147 See UNGA Resolutions 3201 (S-VI) and 3202 (S-VI) of 1 May 1974 containing the Declaration and the Programme of Action on the Establishment of a New International Economic Order.

148 Established by the Convention on the settlement of investment disputes between States and nationals of other States, adopted on 18 March 1965. Online. Available HTTP: <http://icsid.worldbank.org/ICSID/ICSID/DocumentsMain.jsp> (accessed 13 March 2012).

149 Established by the Convention establishing the Multilateral Investment Guarantee Agency, adopted on 11 October 1985. Online. Available HTTP: <http://www.miga.org/documents/miga_convention_november_2010.pdf> (accessed 8 August 2012).

spurred a move to the GATT in the 1980s in what amounted to a first bid to reconcile trade and investment rules. By this time, however, the numerical superiority of the developing world was also reflected in the composition of the GATT membership, which severely compounded the discussions for those countries striving for further liberalization of capital movement at the multilateral scene. Disillusioned with the compromissory nature of the GATS and TRIMs Agreement bargained during the Uruguay Round, the developed countries therefore moved the discussions on investment to the OECD. It soon became clear, however, that the exclusion of the main addressees of multilateral investment rules at the OECD would severely mortgage the practical value of any agreement concluded at this international organization. A final switch therefore identified the WTO as the new forum for deliberations on an MFI in 1996.[150]

The WTO presents itself as an appropriate venue for reaching an MAI that can balance the interests of both developed and developing countries. On the one hand, the inclusive nature of the membership, the provisions for special and differential treatment of LDCs and the enhanced means of participation of civil society in the proceedings of the organization[151] make the WTO a particularly appealing forum for defending the interests of developing countries.[152] While it is true that these countries have frequently opposed the negotiation of new investment rules at this organization on the ground of disillusionment with the realization of the expected benefits of the GATS and TRIMs Agreement,[153] the very process of negotiation of these agreements during the Uruguay Round has nevertheless demonstrated the promising potential of this venue. The potential for improving the WTO as an international organization does not preclude it from currently being the most appropriate venue where developing countries can make themselves heard by their developed contracting partners. Moreover, it has been argued previously that developing countries can turn their numerical majority in the WTO into a potent source of bargaining power if they can succeed in building strong coalitions. At the same time, the goal and composition of the WTO is not so unbalanced as to *prima facie* deter either the group of developed or developing countries from negotiating at this organization, as opposed to the OECD or the United Nations Conference on Trade and Development (UNCTAD).

Indeed, the characteristics of the WTO also appear to cater to the needs of the leading economies for reaching a balanced MFI. During the discussions on

---

150 Singapore Ministerial Declaration, WT/MIN(96)/DEC, 13 December 1996, para. 20. Online. Available HTTP: <http://www.wto.org/english/thewto_e/minist_e/min96_e/wtodec_e.htm> (accessed 13 March 2012).

151 See the WTO Guidelines for arrangements on relations with Non-Governmental Organizations, WT/L/162, 18 July 1996.

152 Also in this sense: A.V. Ganesan, *supra* note 3, pp. 30–2; R.H. Thomas, *supra* note 80, pp. 92–3 and 105; B.N. Zeiler-Kligman, *supra* note 32; E. Benvenisti and G.W. Downs, *supra* note 82, pp. 625–31; E. Chalamish, *supra* note 122, pp. 311–2.

153 See M. Khor, *supra* note 134.

the MAI, the Canadian Minister of International Trade designated the WTO the 'ultimate home' of an MFI while half of the other OECD Member States at least did not express any opposition to such a forum switch.[154] While the United States does not strongly favour the WTO for strategic reasons, its participation in the WGTI deliberations revealed that it was willing to compromise on the venue if this would mean reaching a multilateral agreement that reflected its interests. The European Union in particular has always been adamant in its preference for the WTO as the appropriate investment venue, presumably because of the stronger coordinating role of the European Commission at this organization as opposed to the OECD, which is largely dominated by the EU Member States, as the proceedings of the MAI negotiations have demonstrated.[155] It should be noted, however, that the EU's unflinching support for a WTO MFI was largely inspired by the linkage opportunities the Doha agenda presented between investment and agriculture. The failure to reach any substantive tradeoffs in this respect has severely tainted the Union's preference for the WTO. Hence, after it became clear that Singapore issues, including investment, would not be addressed at the WTO Doha round, the EU proceeded to adopt a more opportunistic approach, continuously supporting a multilateral solution at the WTO in its official statements yet simultaneously lifting the *de facto* moratorium on negotiating new FTAs with key economic partners.[156] The 2006 Commission communication *Global Europe: Competing in the World* set forth a number of criteria for identifying choice third countries with which the Commission, if necessary empowered by the Member States before the entry into force of the TFEU, should commence negotiating broad free trade agreements, incorporating therein the highest investment standards practically achievable.[157] As such, negotiations were successfully launched in 2007 between the EU and South Korea, resulting in an FTA that has provisionally been applied since 1 July 2011.[158] The EU–Korea FTA is commonly characterized as embodying the most comprehensive investment provisions of all EU free trade agreements to date and it is considered a benchmark for future EU FTA negotiations.[159] Other notable FTA efforts addressing a wide range of investment issues include ongoing negotiations between the Commission and India

---

154 E. Smythe, *supra* note 145, pp. 85–6.
155 The European Commission has played an active part in the WGTI discussions by making submissions on all key issues discussed in the working group.
156 Communication from the Commission to the Council, the European Parliament, the European Economic and Social Committee and the Committee of the Regions, Global Europe: Competing in the World, COM(2006) 567 final, 4 October 2006, pp. 8–9; Global Europe Strategy Progress Report, *supra* note 68, p. 3.
157 Ibid., p. 9.
158 Notice concerning the provisional application of the Free Trade Agreement between the European Union and its Member States, of the one part, and the Republic of Korea, of the other part, *OJ* L 168, 28 June 2011, p. 1.
159 Global Europe Strategy Progress Report, *supra* note 68, pp. 6–7; C.-H. Wu, *supra* note 50, p. 395.

(ongoing on the basis of a negotiation schedule lining up a number of technical and potential ministerial meetings for the remainder of 2012), a number of ASEAN Member States (*supra*), Canada (last round in October 2011), Mercosur (last round in March 2012, next round scheduled for October 2012), the Gulf Cooperation Council (suspended in December 2008), Russia (with little progress) and the European Neighbourhood, including, most recently, Moldova and Georgia (launched in December 2011) and Armenia (launched in February 2012).[160]

The Union's intent to insert ambitious investment chapters in FTAs as a new negotiation strategy, foreshadowed by the Commission's Global Europe strategy, was clearly made apparent through the adoption by the Council in 2006 of its 'Minimum Platform on Investment for EU Free Trade Agreements', in which it outlined a standardized negotiation proposal advising the Commission on ongoing and future FTA negotiations with third countries concerning trade and investment.[161] Hence, the Union's current post-Lisbon strategy concerning the negotiation of investment agreements can be categorized as a three-pronged approach, ranging from the short-term incremental insertion of investment chapters in free trade agreements, via the negotiation of bilateral and regional investment agreements, to the long-term goal of reaching consensus on a comprehensive multilateral investment treaty:

> In the **short term**, the prospects for realizing the integration of investment into the common commercial policy arise in ongoing trade negotiations, where the Union has so far only focused on market access for investors. The latest generation of competitiveness-driven Free Trade Agreements (FTAs) is precisely inspired by the objective of unleashing the economic potential of the world's important growth markets to EU trade and investment. The Union has an interest in broadening the scope of negotiations to the complete investment area. . . . In the **short to medium term**, the Union should also consider under which circumstances it may be desirable to pursue stand-alone investment agreements [referring to China and Russia in particular]. . . . Should a comprehensive, across-the-board, investment agreement with a country, or a set of countries, prove impossible or

160 The Commission website on trade <http://ec.europa.eu/trade/creating-opportunities/bilateral-relations> (accessed 3 August 2012) provides updates on the most recent developments in these negotiations. For a periodically updated state of play, see European Commission, 'Overview of FTA and other trade negotiations', last updated 25 July 2012. Online. Available HTTP: <http://trade.ec.europa.eu/doclib/docs/2006/december/tradoc_118238.pdf> (accessed 8 August 2012)

161 Council Doc. 15375/06, 27 November 2006; more recently, Council Doc. 7242/09, 9 March 2009. Both documents are subject to limited availability. See A. De Mestral, 'Is a Model EU BIT possible – or even desirable?', in K.P. Sauvant *et al.* (eds), *FDI perspectives. Issues in international investment*, January 2011, p. 73. Online. Available HTTP: <http://www.vcc.columbia.edu/files/vale/content/PerspectivesEbook.pdf> (accessed 16 March 2012).

inadvisable in the foreseeable future, sectoral agreements may be an option whose desirability, feasibility and possible impact would be further assessed. These sectoral negotiations should be based on the principles set out in this Communication and remain in line with further developments of the common investment policy. In the same vein, the feasibility of a multilateral initiative could be further considered in the long term.[162]

While the Commission's negotiation strategy particularly stresses a region-to-country approach, based on a rigorous selection of third countries and an individually tailored approach to the negotiation process with each key economic partner,[163] the EU nevertheless never loses sight of its ultimate goal of brokering a comprehensive multilateral investment treaty at the WTO – even if this goal is relegated to the long term. The Global Europe strategy unequivocally states that '[t]here will be no European retreat from multilateralism. We stand by our commitment to multilateralism and are prepared to pay, reasonably, to keep the system thriving.'[164] Though recognizing that the suspension of the Doha negotiations was a 'missed opportunity', the Commission reaffirmed its commitment to the WTO and emphasized that it was 'working hard to resume negotiations as soon as circumstances in other countries allow'.[165] In a 2010 follow-up document to its 2006 communication, the Commission repeated this firm commitment to multilateralism, immediately qualifying it, however, by again highlighting the skirmishes that hampered progress at the WTO Doha round.[166]

Whether the increased FDI competences of the European Union after Lisbon will have an impact on the Commission's preference for the WTO as an investment forum remains unclear. Arguably, the impact of the inclusion of FDI in the exclusive EU common commercial policy on the negotiation position of the Commission at the multilateral level will remain limited, as the Commission was already empowered to negotiate on behalf of all EU Member States in light of its WTO membership.[167] As previously discussed, however, the exclusive competence might add substantial clout to the powers of the Commission to negotiate favourable region-to-country free trade agreements with a number of rising economic powers, as is evidenced by a recent surge in bilateral negotiations on trade and investment (*supra*). It follows from the bifurcated approach adopted in the 2006 Global Strategy, however, that

---

162 Commission Communication, *supra* note 53, p. 7 (emphasis in original, footnote omitted). See also Global Europe Strategy, *supra* note 156, p. 12.

163 Global Europe Strategy, *supra* note 156, p. 10; Commission Communication, *supra* note 53, p. 6.

164 Global Europe Strategy, *supra* note 156, p. 8. See also p. 12: 'The principal substantive means of achieving our goals remains through the system of multilateral negotiation. That is why Europe remains strongly committed to multilateralism.'

165 Ibid.

166 Global Europe Strategy Progress Report, *supra* note 68, pp. 4–5.

167 C.-H. Wu, *supra* note 50, p. 393.

such an increased focus on bilateral investment-related FTAs should not necessarily be to the detriment of the EU's multilateral commitment. Both approaches should be seen as separate strategies striving towards the same goal: 'The EU's top priority will be to ensure that any new FTAs, including our own, serve as a stepping stone, not a stumbling block, for multilateral liberalization.'[168]

In the end, the prospect of a broad, integrated and inclusive investment agreement at the WTO remains the principal reason for developed countries in favour of increased investment liberalization to retain their commitment to MFI negotiations at the WTO. The active participation of developing countries is an absolute prerequisite for multilateral negotiations to result in a balanced investment treaty. For without the presence of those host countries most protective of their domestic industries, there is no incentive for developed countries to make any concessions either.[169] Furthermore, the WTO has already successfully concluded several agreements that either directly address the relationship between investment and trade, like the GATS and TRIMs Agreement, or that may serve as a source of inspiration for certain provisions of a future MFI, such as the Agreement on Subsidies and Countervailing Measures (ASCM). The GATS in particular has been identified as a valuable starting point for furthering multilateral investment negotiations, both by delegations at the WGTI and in academic literature.[170] At the very least, the scope of the agreement on trade in services offers manifold opportunities for issue linkages. First, mode 3 of the GATS applies to investment by defining trade in services as the supply of a service by a service supplier of one Member through commercial presence in the territory of any other Member.[171] Second, the GATS also covers the movement of natural persons between the territory of two Members in mode 4. Excepting goods, the GATS agreement thus takes a comprehensive approach to regulating transboundary economic flows, albeit in a rather limited and sometimes haphazard manner. The coverage of labour movement in particular offers promising potential for further deepening the mutual liberalization commitments of developed and developing countries through the GATS.[172]

While the possibility of adopting a holistic, integrated approach to investment thus argues for the WTO as the appropriate venue for initiating multilateral negotiations, it should be recalled that the prospect of successfully

---

168 Global Europe Strategy, *supra* note 156, p. 8: 'Many issues, including investment, . . . which remain outside the WTO *at this time* can be addressed through FTAs' (emphasis added).

169 In this sense also E. Smythe, *supra* note 145, p. 112; E.M. Burt, 'Developing countries and the framework for negotiation on foreign direct investment in the World Trade Organization', *American University Journal of International Law and Policy*, 1997, vol. 12, p. 1049.

170 See *infra*.

171 Art. I (2)(c) GATS.

172 This option is further explored in the next section of this chapter.

concluding a single comprehensive multilateral investment agreement with high standards that would supplant the present IIA regime is highly unlikely. Given its complementary nature, negotiations on an MFI should therefore only be initiated if it can provide added value to all parties involved when compared to the existing network of bilateral and regional agreements. Furthermore, an MFI should be reconciled with the existing multilateral rules on investment in the framework of the WTO. Finally, it has been argued that the need for retaining a certain measure of regulatory flexibility is vital for both developing and developed countries. This further militates against initiating negotiations on a far-reaching and detailed MFI. It follows from the foregoing considerations that a balanced and durable MAI can only be attained through a cautious and incremental *de minimis* approach that is based on reciprocal commitments.[173] This implies favouring an approach that (a) focuses on issues that prove not too divisive; (b) allows for significant *quid pro quo* bargains that cannot be realized at the bilateral level, either within or outside the investment framework; and/ or (c) builds on accepted multilateral rules on investment. It will be argued that this gradualist approach fits well with the WTO as a *de facto* regime of permanent negotiation.[174]

8.5 Building blocks for a balanced MFI

8.5.1 Discussions at the WTO WGTI

In trying to identify the substantive negotiation building blocks for a qualified approach to a multilateral investment framework, the productive discussions held in the WTO working group on trade and investment from 1997 to 2003 should prove particularly instructive for a number of reasons. First, it has been argued in the previous section that, in spite of the recent failure, the WTO may well be the only feasible forum for holding inclusive negotiations on a balanced and coherent MFI. Second, the composition of the WGTI reflects a diverse membership gathering the main capital-importing and capital-exporting economies in a thorough discussion on a wide variety of issues with a clear development focus. Finally, the written submissions and oral statements made by delegations during the deliberations at the working group are among the most recent and authoritative clarifications of the viewpoints of their respective governments and should therefore be given due attention. The discussions have also revealed a number of alternative solutions to improving the negotiation

---

173 A gradual approach to multilateral investment rules was already advocated in P.M. Goldberg and C.P. Kindleberger, 'Toward a GATT for investment: A proposal for supervision of the international corporation', *Law and Policy in International Business*, 1970, vol. 2, p. 322. See also D. Julius, 'International direct investment: Strengthening the policy regime', in P.B. Kenen (ed.), *Managing the world economy: Fifty years after Bretton Woods*, Washington DC: Institute for International Economics, 1994, p. 274.

174 Term suggested in G.R. Winham, *supra* note 12, p. 25.

framework of IIAs which have been further elaborated upon in academic literature.

The balanced nature of the mandate of the WGTI is clear from the Doha Ministerial Declaration, which recognized,

> the case for a multilateral framework to secure transparent, stable and predictable conditions for long-term cross-border investment, particularly foreign direct investment, that will contribute to the expansion of trade, and the need for enhanced technical assistance and capacity-building in this area. . . . Any framework should reflect in a balanced manner the interests of home and host countries, and take due account of the development policies and objectives of host governments as well as their right to regulate in the public interest.[175]

After it was established at the 1996 WTO Ministerial Conference in Singapore, discussions at the WGTI in its first year mainly focused on general statements on the nature of the work to be pursued under the mandate contained in the Singapore Ministerial Declaration. In light of the submissions and statements made by the delegations, a checklist of issues suggested for study was prepared by the Chairman, which guided the organization of the work of the WGTI until the 2001 Doha Ministerial Conference.[176] The checklist grouped the items of discussion under four main headings, all of which were thoroughly debated by the participating delegations: (1) implications of the relationship between trade and investment for development and economic growth; (2) the economic relationship between trade and investment; (3) stocktaking and analysis of existing international instruments and activities regarding trade and investment; and (4) other issues such as the identification of common features, differences, overlaps, conflicts and gaps in existing international instruments and a discussion of the advantages and disadvantages of entering into bilateral, regional and multilateral rules on investment, including from a development perspective.[177]

These initial discussions resulted in the identification of the following seven main issues to be clarified by the working group in its final years of deliberation after the Doha Ministerial Conference:

> scope and definition; transparency; non-discrimination; modalities for pre-establishment commitments based on a GATS-type, positive list approach;

---

175 Doha Ministerial Declaration, *supra* note 2, para. 20 and para. 22. This is a clear departure from the strong liberalization agenda of the OECD and the Free Trade Area of the Americas (FTAA).

176 Report (1997) of the WGTI to the General Council, WT/WGTI/1, 25 November 1997, para. 3.

177 See the WGTI Report on the Meeting of 2 and 3 June 1997 – Note by the Secretariat, WT/WGTI/M/1, 2 July 1997, Annex 1.

development provisions; exceptions and balance-of-payments safeguards; consultation and the settlement of disputes between members.[178]

The following sections will analyse the discussions of the working group based on the comments made by key delegations on issues covered during the exchange of views on the seven issues listed for further clarification in the Doha Declaration, against the backdrop of the general debate on the items included in the checklist for further study. This will allow us to give a focused account of the most recent WGTI deliberations with a view to identifying the main items for possible inclusion in a *de minimis* multilateral investment agreement at the WTO, fully taking into account the concerns expressed by developing countries in the general discussions during the first years of the debate at the WGTI.[179]

8.5.2 Specific issues for consideration in multilateral negotiations

8.5.2.1 Transparency and capacity building

During the discussions at the WGTI, a main argument raised by delegations opposing the commencement of formal negotiations on a WTO MFI was the lack of empirical evidence that IIAs in general and a multilateral framework in particular could increase FDI flows to developing countries. Indeed, it was mentioned previously that the main factor for attracting, absorbing and directing FDI toward specific development goals is the economic infrastructure of a host country rather than the investment treaties it has concluded.[180] The inconclusive nature of the case for economic benefits of a global investment treaty notwithstanding, it follows from the foregoing that a crucial element in overturning opposition to multilateral investment negotiations would be to

---

178 Doha Ministerial Declaration, *supra* note 2, para. 22.

179 A full overview of the discussions on the seven items identified in the Doha Declaration can be found in the last two reports of the WGTI to the WTO General Council: WGTI Report (2002) and WGTI Report (2003). For an abbreviated account of these deliberations, see T.H. Moran, 'The relationship between trade, foreign direct investment, and development: New evidence, strategy, and tactics under the Doha development agenda negotiations', Paper prepared for the Asian Development Bank's Study on regional integration and trade: Emerging policy issues for selected developing member countries, September 2002, pp. 17–32. Online. Available HTTP: <citeseerx.ist.psu. edu> (accessed 13 March 2012); B. Bora and M. Graham, *supra* note 24, pp. 345–50; P. Sauvé, *supra* note 20, pp. 4–9. Compare these seven items with the twelve elements identified for further discussion by the Working Group on Investment of the Free Trade Area of the Americas: see R. Echandi, 'Bringing investment to the aegis of the multilateral trading system: Steps taken in the context of the FTAA Negotiation Group on Investment', in M. Bronckers and R. Quick (eds), *New directions in international economic law: Essays in honour of John H. Jackson*, 2000, The Hague: Kluwer, pp. 402–11. The negotiations of the FTAA did not result in a multilateral investment agreement.

180 See *supra*.

focus the debate on a multilateral investment treaty on the need for creating a legal framework that strengthens the infrastructure of host country economies and increases the transparency of the domestic regulatory regime. Such an MFI would create an enabling FDI framework that allows the economic fundamentals of host economies to more clearly manifest themselves without infringing the regulatory autonomy of developing countries while also contributing to meeting their development goals. The inherently transparent nature of universally applicable rules makes a multilateral agreement the method of choice for negotiating commitments on enhancing the economic infrastructure of host countries.[181]

Discussions in the WGTI expressly noted that the best way to maximize the benefits of FDI was through the adoption of measures of a generic nature aimed at improving the overall regulatory and economic environment of host countries.[182] Many delegations recognized the importance of transparency in this respect and issued repeated calls for a barebones approach to multilateral negotiations that remained limited to less contentious issues, among which transparency and technical assistance figured prominently.[183] Other factors also argue for negotiating an MFI of limited scope that focuses on transparency and capacity building. First, the concept of securing a transparent framework for foreign investment was emphasized in the Doha Declaration. Second, several WTO Members cited national surveys during the WGTI debate suggesting that increased transparency in national and international investment rules was a main objective of their business communities. An MFI that focuses on transparency would therefore likely receive the necessary support of important domestic players, avoiding the pitfalls of earlier multilateral negotiation rounds on investment. Furthermore, transparency obligations do not figure prominently in most existing IIAs. This institutional gap in the bilateral and regional framework could thus usefully be filled by a multilateral treaty.[184] Finally, several WTO agreements already contain provisions imposing transparency obligations that might also be relevant for investment regulation.[185] Article III of GATS was specifically mentioned in this regard as a potential source of inspiration for MFI rules on transparency.[186]

---

181 WGTI Report on the Meeting of 8 December 1997, WT/WGTI/M/3, 10 February 1998, para. 23.
182 WGTI Report (1998), para. 41.
183 Report on the Meeting of 8 June 2000 – Note by the Secretariat, WT/WGTI/M/11, 24 July 2000, para. 51. See also the WGTI Report on the Meeting of 22 and 23 March 1999 – Note by the Secretariat, WT/WGTI/M/8, 11 May 1999, para. 72. The importance of capacity-building technical cooperation is also underscored in UNCTAD, *supra* note 24, pp. 71–2.
184 WGTI Report (2002), para. 37.
185 For a full overview and classification of these provisions, see WGTI Report (2000), paras 68–70.
186 Article III(1) GATS states that '[e]ach Member shall publish promptly and, except in emergency situations, at the latest by the time of their entry into force, all relevant

Investment talks that focus on the rather uncontroversial and as of yet largely unregulated issue of transparency would thus provide a promising starting point for meaningful negotiations on an MFI.[187] The issue could divert the attention of delegations from more contentious and divisive issues such as investment protection and liberalization commitments, which in any case are already touched upon in a plenitude of bilateral and regional arrangements. The detailed level of discussion and the closely converging views on transparency in the final two reports of the WGTI already suggest that it should not be too difficult to reach consensus on the matter in future negotiations.[188] Indeed, the rather technical issue of transparency offers much potential for a mutually advantageous improvement of the overall economic environment of developing countries that would benefit both foreign investors and capital-importing countries. Nevertheless, while delegations did not contradict the significant advantages of enhanced transparency provisions for developing countries,

> some expressed concerns that the administrative costs of possible obligations could outweigh any benefits in terms of attracting foreign investors. . . . It was [therefore] suggested that a multilateral framework should include clear and detailed provisions for linking the implementation of transparency obligations and procedural reform to technical assistance and capacity building.[189]

The need of developing and least-developed countries for enhanced support for technical assistance and capacity building was recognized in the Doha Ministerial Declaration (para. 20). The view was widely shared among WGTI delegations that the WTO, in cooperation with UNCTAD and other international organizations, should concentrate on assisting developing countries to (1) prepare for issue-specific discussions and possible future multilateral negotiations on investment; (2) implement existing WTO rules; and (3) build the human and institutional capacities of their domestic

---

measures of general application which pertain to or affect the operation of this Agreement. International agreements pertaining to or affecting trade in services to which a Member is a signatory shall also be published'. Article X GATT 1994 was also referred to during discussions.

187 See also A. Beviglia Zampetti and T. Frederiksson, *supra* note 29, p. 434; T.H. Moran, *supra* note 179, pp. 18–21 and 39. Sauvé also identifies transparency as arguably the only issue that could easily be anchored within an MFI, yet is wary of the enforceability of such provisions in the WTO context: P. Sauvé, *supra* note 20, p. 345; *id.*, 'Scaling back ambitions on investment rule-making at the WTO', *Journal of World Investment*, 2001, vol. 2, p. 536. The importance of capacity building and transparency in the framework of the WGTI is also stressed in A. Mukerji, 'The WTO debate on trade and investment and the "development dimension"', *Journal of World Investment*, 2001, vol. 2, pp. 749 and 754.

188 WGTI Report (2002), paras 37–50; WGTI Report (2003), paras 22–27.

189 WGTI Report (2002), para. 49.

economies.[190] The first element of the capacity-building programme suggested by the WTO mirrors the recommendations made earlier in this chapter aiming to improve the bargaining power of developing countries in multilateral negotiations, while the second prong serves to remedy some of the concerns these countries have voiced about the WTO as a forum for MFI negotiations. Finally, the third area of assistance aims to improve the general economic infrastructure of host countries as a durable means of ensuring that FDI flows take root in poor countries.

Proactive long-term measures on technical assistance and capacity building are preferable to the inclusion of separate special and differential treatment provisions for developing countries and LDCs in an MFI. The WTO agreements traditionally provide for such treatment by allowing, *inter alia*, extended implementation periods for countries that do not rank among developed economies.[191] The Doha Declaration also emphasizes 'the special development, trade and financial needs of developing and least-developed countries . . . as an integral part of any [multilateral investment] framework' (para. 22). While it is not disputed that these needs are real, it is doubtful they would be served by an MFI that in essence creates a distinct investment regime for developing countries. Differential treatment in the context of IIAs would ultimately be to the detriment of the intended beneficiaries. Excepting developing countries from the scope of multilateral commitments would send a negative signal to potential investors and would create a more favourable regime for foreign investment in developed than in developing countries. This would obviously run counter to the objectives of a balanced multilateral investment treaty.[192] Home country commitments under the guise of technical assistance and capacity building are therefore a preferable, more sustainable means of improving the investment climate in developing countries. Moreover, the increased attractiveness of developing countries as a destination for FDI would ideally reintroduce a modicum of reciprocity in the effects of an expected further liberalization of capital movement, which traditionally favours developed countries as the primary sources of FDI.[193]

8.5.2.2 Investment liberalization

Apart from a small minority of recent investment agreements mainly concluded at the instigation of the United States, most IIAs do not provide for non-

---

190 WGTI Report (2002), para. 9. The European Community in particular stressed the need for technical assistance and capacity building for developing countries in a separate submission: see Communication of the European Community and its Member States on technical assistance and capacity building related to foreign direct investment, WT/WGTI/W/102, 29 May 2001.

191 Art. 5(2) TRIMs.

192 B. Dymond and M. Hart, *supra* note 13, pp. 281–2; J.M. Kline and R.D. Ludema, *supra* note 9, p. 17.

193 A. Beviglia Zampetti and T. Frederiksson, *supra* note 29, pp. 427–8.

discriminatory treatment of foreign investors at the pre-establishment phase.[194] Unhindered market access has therefore been identified as an important area where complementary multilateral rules on investment could deliver considerable added value to capital-exporting countries by filling a major gap in existing liberalization commitments.[195] The unfettered application of national and most-favoured nation treatment to all stages of the lifecycle of FDI was the main goal pursued by developed countries in most of the previous multilateral rounds of investment negotiations. As such, the OECD mandate for negotiating an MAI was predominantly aimed at achieving an agreement that would

> go beyond existing commitments to achieve a high standard of liberalisation covering both the establishment and post-establishment phase with broad obligations on national treatment, standstill, roll-back, non-discrimination/ MFN, and transparency, and apply disciplines to areas of liberalisation not satisfactorily covered by the present OECD instruments.[196]

The discussions at the WTO WGTI revealed that most developed countries still maintain a strong demand for greater liberalization commitments by host countries and it is likely that no consensus on a substantive MFI can be reached without progressive market access commitments. While the discussions in the working group did not amount to an explicit agreement on the issue, a GATS-type positive-list approach to pre-establishment liberalization appeared the most viable solution, in particular as it had already been singled out for specific deliberations in the Doha Declaration.[197] Nevertheless, developing countries were at pains to stress that the imperfections of the globalized market necessitated maintaining domestic policies that imposed distortive investment measures such as performance requirements and incentives in order to maximize the benefits of FDI for host country economies and development goals.[198]

Performance requirements encompass a wide variety of measures ranging from mandatory technology transfers and restrictions on industrial property ownership to employment and trade-balancing requirements.[199] They are typically imposed by developing countries in order to stimulate the growth of

---

194 UNCTAD, *Bilateral investment treaties 1995–2006: Trends in investment rulemaking*, New York and Geneva: United Nations, 2007, pp. 21–6.

195 R. Echandi, *supra* note 179, pp. 395–7 and 412–13.

196 Report by the Committee on International Investment and Multinational Enterprises (CIME) and the Committee on Capital Movements and Invisible Transactions (CMIT), *A multilateral agreement on investment*, May 1995. Online. Available HTTP: <http://training. itcilo.it/actrav_cdrom1/english/global/blokit/mairap95.htm> (accessed 13 March 2012).

197 Paragraph 22 of the Declaration expressly listed the GATS-type approach as one of the seven issues for further consideration for inclusion in a future MFI.

198 WGTI Report (1998), para. 42.

199 For a comprehensive overview of the various types of performance requirements, see UNCTAD, *supra* note 137, pp. 177–9.

their domestic economy by diverting foreign investments to certain pre-determined sectors and industries. Investment incentives on the other hand are offered by developing and developed countries alike, depending on the type of incentive, as a means of attracting increased FDI flows. Developed countries can afford to offer candidate-investors unconditional *a priori* incentives in the form of cash grants while resource constraints generally limit the options of developing countries to less attractive fiscal incentives, which are furthermore often made conditional upon the acceptance of certain performance requirements.[200] Apart from engendering unfair competition between countries at different levels of development, the practice of investment incentives also risks pitching developing countries against each other in a deleterious race to the bottom to compensate for weak economic fundamentals. If no obvious market failures exist then investment incentives may well amount to pure transfers of limited resources from the host country to foreign investors and result in the distortion of international trade flows.[201]

Empirical evidence of the distortive effects of investment incentives is inconclusive, however. Some studies have demonstrated that offering fiscal incentives to inward FDI fails to be effective once the impact of the economic fundamentals of the host country are taken into account,[202] while other surveys suggest that incentives do affect locational decisions of foreign investors if all other determinants are equal.[203] The equivocal case for investment incentives has led some authors to question the need for regulating the matter at the multilateral level. It has been argued that, if incentives are ineffective, they fail to be distortive, while effective locational incentives should not be prohibited as they may help to ensure the efficient redirection of FDI towards locations where it is valued most.[204] However, this argument disregards the development needs of host countries that are not in a position to incentivize foreign investors and fails to take into account the negative impact of locational incentive competition on developing countries.

The competitive theory has been identified as one of the main hypotheses for explaining the paradoxical behaviour of developing countries at the bilateral and multilateral level. It follows that a main rationale for commencing

200 See in general UNCTAD, *Incentives and foreign direct investment*, Geneva and New York: United Nations, 1996; *id.*, *Incentives*, New York and Geneva: United Nations, 2004. See also the WGTI Report on the impact of investment incentives and performance requirements on international trade – Note by the Secretariat, WT/WGTI/W/56, 30 September 1998.
201 A. Beviglia Zampetti and T. Frederiksson, *supra* note 29, pp. 432–4 and 441–2.
202 See, *inter alia*, the study in R.E. Caves, *supra* note 9.
203 S. Guisinger *et al.*, *Investment incentives and performance requirements*, New York: Praeger, 1985; M. Devreux and R. Griffiths, 'Taxes and the location of production: Evidence from a panel of US States', *Journal of Public Economics*, 1998, vol. 68, pp. 335–67; J.R. Hines, 'Altered States: Taxes and the location of FDI in America', *American Economic Review*, 1996, vol. 86, pp. 1076–94.
204 B. Hoekman and K. Saggi, *supra* note 3, pp. 11–13.

negotiations on a proper multilateral investment framework lies in tackling the harmful effects of incentive competition among developing countries at the bilateral level.[205] Indeed, several delegations at the WGTI recognized the perverse effects of incentive competition between developing countries as resembling 'a prisoner's dilemma in which only cooperation among participants provided a mutually beneficial solution',[206] adding that 'restraint on the use of incentives was difficult to achieve in a unilateral or bilateral context'.[207] Further discussions revealed a number of potential solutions to resolve this dilemma at the multilateral level. First, it was noted that, since many developing countries offer extensive incentives in order to counter the repelling effects of performance requirements, the first-best solution was to prohibit both the incentive and the regulatory distortion.[208] As the existence of market imperfections did not allow for such an ideal approach, however, it was suggested that a more appropriate response was 'to strengthen the institutional and administrative capacity of governments to administer incentives effectively rather than to prohibit incentives'.[209] It was added that it might be useful to explore criteria to differentiate objectionable from non-objectionable incentives akin to the categorization suggested in the ASCM.[210] This might be linked with proposals to expand the TRIMs Agreement as a means to discipline a more substantial list of performance requirements.[211]

205 In this sense also A.V. Ganesan, *supra* note 3, pp. 23–4; R.H. Thomas, *supra* note 80, p. 105; B. Schwartz, *supra* note 11, pp. 460–1; E. Chalamish, *supra* note 122, p. 320.
206 WGTI Report on the Meeting of 1 and 2 October 1998, *supra* note 38, para. 11.
207 Ibid., paras 12–13 and para. 15.
208 Working Group on the Relationship between Trade and Investment – Report on the Meeting of 30 and 31 March 1998, WT/WGTI/M/4, 5 June 1998, para. 22. This solution is also suggested in S. Young and A.T. Tavares, *supra* note 23, p. 9; S. Young and T.L. Brewer, *supra* note 137; T.H. Moran, *Foreign direct investment and development*, Washington DC: Institute for International Economics, 1998.
209 WGTI Report on the Meeting of 1 and 2 October 1998, *supra* note 38, para. 14.
210 WGTI Report (1998), para. 92 and para. 99; WGTI Report (1999), para. 43. See also the WGTI Report on the Meeting of 22 and 23 March 1999, *supra* note 183, paras 30–31 and para. 38; WGTI Report on the Meeting of 3 June 1999 – Note by the Secretariat, WT/WGTI/M/9, 19 July 1999, paras 17–19.
211 Expansion of the illustrative list of performance requirements in the TRIMs Agreement and application of the ASCM to investment have been mentioned as likely approaches to multilateral investment negotiations in, *inter alia*, P. Read, *supra* note 28, pp. 398–400; A. Mukerji, *supra* note 187, pp. 757–8; T.H. Moran, *supra* note 179, pp. 15–17; R. Dattu, *supra* note 1, p. 314; P. Sauvé, *supra* note 187, pp. 531–3; M. Mashayekhi and M. Gibbs, *supra* note 33, pp. 3–4; R. Edwards and S. Lester, 'Towards a more comprehensive World Trade Organization Agreement on Trade Related Investment Measures', *Stanford Journal of International Law*, 1997, vol. 33, p. 169; E.M. Burt, *supra* note 169, pp. 1059–61. This last author also notes that India argued at the WGTI that the working group only had the authority to discuss the TRIMs Agreement (pp. 1051–1052). However, M.A. Srur (*supra* note 3, pp. 66–7) warns against overly optimistic assessments of the TRIMs Agreement as an appropriate starting point for MFI negotiations, given the criticisms that have been voiced against the treaty. P.B. Christy III (*supra* note 31, pp. 796–8) also argues against expanding the TRIMs.

The call for strengthening the economic fundamentals of host countries in order to limit the distortive effects of investment incentives ties in with the above argument favouring capacity building and technical assistance as a means of achieving a more durable and mutually beneficial improvement to the investment climate of developing countries. In any event, a multilateral solution that allows a controlled balance of investment incentives and performance requirements rather than disciplining both without exception is more likely to receive the support of developing countries, who continue to stress the importance of such distortive practices as a means of supporting their development goals. Furthermore, the widespread use of incentives among developed countries and their exclusion from most BITs, from NAFTA and from the negotiation agenda at the MAI appears to confirm that these countries are not ready to discuss the complete elimination of investment incentives either.[212] This is not to say that these distortive practices should not be addressed in an MFI, however, as it has been argued that developing countries can only overcome their deleterious competition at the multilateral stage. Moreover, the fact that developed countries appear more successful in using incentives to attract investment while performance requirements are more prevalent among developing countries indicates that there is room to negotiate a reciprocal tradeoff on these issues which can only be reached at the multilateral scene.[213] This intra-investment issue linkage may then be complemented by tradeoffs outside the realm of capital movement.

8.5.2.3 *Linking capital and labour movement*

An issue linkage that has received little attention in the discussions at the WTO working group on trade and investment, yet offers promising potential for reconciling the demands of developed and developing countries, is that of a tradeoff between capital liberalization and labour movement. The issue figured prominently in the submissions of India to the WGTI, where it was held that,

> while trade concerns itself with delivery of economic goods, investment involves their production. Along with money, material and machinery, labour as a factor of production would need to be equally considered. If other factors of global production are liberalized, can restrictions on mobility of labour be conducive to mutual supportiveness of trade and investment, or to economic growth and development? The extensive

---

212 Compare B. Hoekman and K. Saggi, 'Multilateral disciplines and national investment policies', in B. Hoekman, A. Mattoo and Ph. English (eds), *Development, trade and the WTO: A handbook*, Washington DC: World Bank, 2002, p. 445. While the draft MAI contained an expanded list of prohibited performance requirements, the related issue of incentives was explicitly postponed for discussion after the MAI was adopted.
213 J. Kurtz, *supra* note 23, p. 732.

debate on free mobility of capital may have to be supplemented by an equally extensive study on free mobility of labour. If cheap labour is an important determinant of investment decisions, and results in higher profitability for investors which can be ploughed back into the home country economy, it may be, at the least, equitable to augment host country economies by returns from a mobile labour working in the investors' home country.[214]

The position of India confirms that the movement of labour as a production factor alongside capital is of particular interest to developing countries, as they have a considerable comparative advantage in this area.[215] The negotiation of this issue could thus be usefully linked to the FDI liberalization demands of the developed countries. From both a legal and an economic point of view, the case for multilateral rules on the free movement of people is no weaker than the case for free movement of capital, considering the potential global welfare gains of increased immigration flows and the lack of universal rules on the matter.[216] In light of the importance attached to the movement of personnel by India, the staunchest opponent to multilateral rules on FDI flows, the option of conducting parallel negotiations on both issues should thus be given considerable thought.[217]

To be sure, the free movement of people is already covered to some extent in mode 4 of the GATS. The practical applicability of the relevant provisions to developing countries is very limited, however, as they only pertain to the temporary entry of managerial and other categories of high-level personnel. If the free movement of people is to become a veritable bargaining chip for developing countries in the face of capital liberalization claims by their developed negotiation partners, the GATS provisions should be extended to cover lower-level labour forces as well. Such an expansion was not part of the Doha investment agenda, however, thus fuelling the intransigence of key developing countries such as India.

214 Communication from India on the relationship between trade, investment and development, WT/WGTI/W/72, 13 April 1999, para. 3. See further communications WT/WGTI/W/39, 4 June 1998 and WT/WGTI/W/86, 22 June 2000. For more on India's position on the linkage between the movement of capital and the movement of labour, see J. Chaisse, D. Chakraborty and A. Guha, *supra* note 78, pp. 240–68.

215 J. Kurtz, *supra* note 23, pp. 776–7 and 781.

216 B. Hoekman and K. Saggi, *supra* note 3, p. 18; M. Trebilcock, 'The law and economics of immigration policy', *American Law and Economics Review*, 2003, vol. 5, pp. 271–317; M.J. Trebilcock and R. Howse, *The regulation of international trade*, London: Routledge, 2005, pp. 611–36.

217 Das is more sceptical of this negotiation strategy: see S.P. Das, 'An Indian perspective on WTO rules on foreign direct investment', in A. Mattoo and R.M. Stern (eds), *India and the WTO*, Washington DC: The World Bank and Oxford University Press, 2003, pp. 141–68.

8.5.2.4 Relationship between an MFI and the existing IIA framework: dispute settlement

One of the main dissatisfactions of the proponents of an MFI with the existing bilateral investment regime is the inherent risk of inconsistency and confusion that may arise from the interpretation of a multitude of slightly varying provisions in a large number of investment treaties of limited application.[218] To some extent these substantive differences may be reconciled by codifying clearly defined universal rules in a multilateral investment agreement. Indeed, the NAFTA experience seems to indicate that more closely circumscribed provisions may go a long way in mitigating the risks of uncoordinated judicial activism.[219] Nevertheless, the intrinsic possibility of forum shopping in an IIA framework where nationality is progressively losing its relevance as a tying factor militates for further measures to enhance the consistency of the international investment regime. These measures may take the form of an MFI that is submitted to a single dispute settlement mechanism in order to reduce the likelihood of mutually incompatible arbitral decisions. To the extent the WTO is accepted as the appropriate venue for negotiating an MFI, it appears likely that the WTO Understanding on rules and procedures governing the settlement of disputes (DSU) will be made applicable.[220] Indeed, one of the main reasons for adopting a multilateral approach to investment in the framework of the WTO was the possibility of employing the existing DSU in investment disputes.[221]

However, the WTO DSU differs in some key respects from the many BIT provisions on the resolution of investment conflicts.[222] A comprehensive MFI containing substantive provisions also covered at the bilateral level should thus provide a means of reconciling both dispute-settlement mechanisms. The DSU adopted at the Uruguay Round is primarily aimed at the authoritative settlement of disputes among governments by bringing the responsible State into compliance with its obligations towards other WTO Members without requiring retrospective relief in the form of damages.[223] Compensatory awards are only available in case the immediate withdrawal of the relevant trade measure is impracticable and only as a temporary measure pending the withdrawal of the measure that is found to be inconsistent with a covered WTO agreement.[224] On the other hand, BITs typically allow private investors to directly bring claims against the host country government under the rules of

---

218 See, for example, the mutually incompatible decisions in the conflict between Lauder and CME against the Czech Republic: T.-H. Cheng, *supra* note 25, pp. 482–4.

219 This is the main tenet of the argument raised in J. Kurtz, *supra* note 23.

220 Annex 2 of the WTO Agreement.

221 WGTI Report (2002), para. 144.

222 On the negotiation history of the DSU, see J.H. Jackson, *supra* note 12, pp. 45–50. See also J.C. Hartigan (ed.), *Trade disputes and the dispute settlement understanding of the WTO: An interdisciplinary assessment*, Bingley: Emerald, 2009.

223 V. Mosoti, *supra* note 1, pp. 124–7.

224 Article 3(7) DSU.

ICSID or UNCITRAL with a view to receiving monetary compensation for a perceived violation of their rights under the IIA regime. Case law has shown that pecuniary damages are a particularly useful remedy for investment violations, which typically take the form of direct expropriation or regulatory takings. It has therefore been argued that the BIT regime is more attuned to the specific needs of an investment framework.[225]

The settlement of disputes among parties to a future multilateral investment treaty received only scarce attention during the discussions at the WTO WGTI and remained relatively uncontroversial. What few submissions were made on the subject argued that

> any prospective investment agreement should be anchored firmly in the procedures, rules and structures of the WTO dispute settlement system. . . . If the objective was to secure a 'transparent, stable and predictable framework' for investment, it would be counterproductive – and unnecessarily confusing – to establish a separate system for settling disputes among parties to a prospective multilateral investment framework. Also, to the extent that existing WTO agreements such as the GATS and the TRIMS Agreement included investment-related provisions, the WTO provisions on dispute settlement were already applicable to investment.[226]

It seems highly unlikely that the conclusion of a future MFI under the auspices of the WTO would result in the introduction of BIT-specific dispute-settlement characteristics in the DSU. The architectural overhaul and political sensitivities that the inclusion of compensatory awards in investor-to-State proceedings in the framework of the WTO would entail are rather drastic.[227] At the same time, such an overhaul appears unnecessary if the scope of multilateral investment negotiations would remain limited to the discussion of a *de minimis* MFI as suggested in the present chapter. It should be kept in mind that a multilateral investment treaty would not supplant the existing IIA regime as a codification of the high BIT standards at the global level seems unlikely. Investors' claims for compensation arising from direct and indirect expropriation would thus likely remain subject to arbitral review pursuant to the proceedings of ICSID and UNCITRAL, obviating the need to alter the WTO DSU rules in this respect. The quest for increased consistency in the interpretation of bilateral investment rules may alternatively be achieved through the instalment of an appellate body akin to the mechanism in the WTO DSU, although this option

---

225 J.M. Kline and R.D. Ludema, *supra* note 9, pp. 19–20.

226 WGTI Report (2002), para. 143.

227 R. Neufeld, *supra* note 16, pp. 642–3. See also B. Mercurio, 'Why compensation cannot replace trade retaliation in the WTO dispute settlement understanding', *World Trade Review*, 2009, vol. 8, pp. 315–38. Some authors still argue for the inclusion of investor–State dispute settlement in the context of a WTO MFI: R. Leal-Arcas, *supra* note 1, pp. 133–4; J. Kurtz, *supra* note 23, p. 739.

poses many problems of its own as well.[228] Moreover, excluding investors' standing in dispute settlement proceedings against host countries is likely to be to the benefit of developing countries, which often struggle in finding the necessary resources to defend themselves properly against more potent multinational enterprises. The inclusion of BIT-like rights for investors in dispute proceedings against host countries was one of the many features of the MAI that was fiercely opposed by civil society. The high costs of litigation for developing countries may furthermore be tempered by avoiding arbitration proceedings through the application of the WTO model of good offices, conciliation and mediation.[229] Developed countries' enthusiasm for unbridled investor-to-State dispute settlement has also been tempered by the NAFTA experience. Admittedly, concerns have been raised over the scope of cross-retaliation and cross-compensation in the trade area in the case of investment-related disputes if the WTO DSU were to be applied to a future MFI.[230] However, the WTO dispute-settlement mechanism already applies to the investment provisions contained in the GATS and TRIMs Agreement. Experience with these treaties indicates that the possibility of cross-retaliation in the WTO to the detriment of developing countries is largely theoretical.

8.5.2.5 Relationship between an MFI and existing WTO rules: the GATS

A future multilateral agreement on investment will not only have to fit in with the existing IIAs at the bilateral and regional level. In order to realize the goal of an improved architectural basis for regulating trade and investment, negotiations on an MFI will also need to settle the relationship with the current WTO rules on investment that are covered mainly in the ASCM, the TRIMs Agreement and GATS. The option of expanding the coverage of the first two agreements was hinted at in the previous sections on investment liberalization and has been suggested by many authors and delegations as a useful starting point for multilateral investment talks.[231] However, their limited scope, the difficulties encountered in particular during the negotiations on the compromissory TRIMs Agreement and the largely untested applicability of the ASCM provisions on investment measures somewhat restrict the practicability of an approach based on the expansion of these treaties.

On the other hand, the possibility of building on the GATS as an intermediate step in further expanding the multilateral investment framework was raised ever more prominently as the discussions at the WTO WGTI

---

228   See D.A. Gantz, 'An appellate mechanism for review of arbitral decisions in investor-State disputes: Prospects and challenges', *Vanderbilt Journal of Transnational Law*, 2006, vol. 39, pp. 39–76.
229   WGTI Report (2002), para. 145.
230   UNCTAD, *supra* note 36, pp. 95–6. See Article 22 DSU on the possibility of cross-retaliation.
231   *Supra* notes 213–14.

progressed.[232] The example of a GATS-type positive-list approach had already been mentioned expressly in the Doha description of the mandate of the WGTI, and subsequent discussions in the working group on the subject were thorough and productive, without, of course, resolving every controversy on the subject. In any event, the previous sections have highlighted several features of the GATS that point to its usefulness as a means of reconciling the needs and concerns of both developed and developing countries.

First, it was noted that one of the main reasons why developed countries pursued negotiations on a multilateral investment treaty was the prospect of furthering liberalization in capital flows. Recent developments of the globalized economy have brought to light the increased importance of market access in the service sector. As a result, most barriers and restrictions on investment flows in developing countries can be found in the provision of services.[233] To a large extent the potential gains of multilateral rules on investment for developed countries can thus be realized by expanding the existing WTO rules on trade in services codified in the GATS.[234] Second, WGTI discussions clearly show that the positive-list system of progressive liberalization as foreseen in the GATS is much preferred by developing countries as opposed to the top-down approach adopted in most BITs and the MAI draft.[235] A cautious bottom-up take on pre-establishment liberalization in services could thus cater to the needs of developed countries while taking into account the calls for respecting the regulatory sovereignty of developing host countries. Indeed, the most fervent MFI proponents at the WTO all tabled submissions that endorsed a GATS-like approach as a flexible means of regulating pre-establishment investment commitments.[236] Third, it has been suggested that concessions by developing

---

232 See in particular the communication by the Republic of Korea on the General Agreement on Trade in Services (GATS) and its implications for an investment agreement, WT/WGTI/W/96, 6 March 2001. For an academic appraisal of this option, see M. Roy, 'Implications for the GATS of negotiations on a multilateral investment framework: Potential synergies and pitfalls', *Journal of World Investment*, 2003, vol. 4, pp. 963–86; B. Dymond and M. Hart, *supra* note 13, pp. 283–5; P. Sauvé and C. Wilkie, *supra* note 137, pp. 331–63; P. Gugler and J. Chaisse, *supra* note 9, pp. 166–8; A. Beviglia Zampetti and T. Frederiksson, *supra* note 29, pp. 437–9.

233 See UNCTAD, *World investment report 2004: The shift towards services*, New York and Geneva: United Nations, 2004; *id., Measuring restrictions on FDI in services in developing countries and transition economies*, New York and Geneva: United Nations, 2006. The long lists of reservations in Chapter 11 of NAFTA and the draft MAI overwhelmingly apply to the services sector.

234 B. Hoekman and K. Saggi, *supra* note 3, pp. 3, 8 and 22 ('we conclude that priority should be given to continuing the process of multilateral trade liberalization, focusing attention as far as investment (establishment) policies are concerned in sectors where FDI is critical as a mode to contest markets, *i.e.* services').

235 See the summary of the discussions and possible means of reconciling the various positions on the subject in WGTI Report (2002), paras 106–21 and the communications of the Members referred to in these paragraphs.

236 See the 27 June 2002 communications by the European Community, the Republic of Korea and Japan, respectively: WT/WGTI/W/121, para. 20; WT/WGTI/W/123, para. 27; WT/WGTI/W/125, para. 18.

countries in the area of pre-establishment capital liberalization may need to be matched by similar concessions by their developed negotiating partners in the field of labour movement. Once more, the GATS provides a useful starting point for further liberalization in this field as mode 4 of the agreement already covers the movement of certain categories of key personnel. Finally, building on existing WTO rules that are already subjected to the DSU markedly facilitates the regulation of an MFI dispute settlement mechanism.

Apart from identifying the GATS as a possible source of inspiration for a future MFI, the relationship between the two agreements was not addressed comprehensively at the WGTI.[237] It was not until the final year of deliberations before the discontinuation of the investment debate that the issue was explicitly broached in a number of communications from Japan.[238] The submissions of the Japanese government and the statements by other delegations in the ensuing discussion suggested three possible modalities for regulating the interaction between the GATS and a future MFI: (1) exclude services from the coverage of the MFI; (2) include services in the MFI, thereby necessitating changes to the GATS in order to avoid conflicts and inconsistencies; and (3) have the MFI apply to both goods and services but limiting its application to services to rules that go beyond the provisions of the GATS.[239] A detailed assessment of these modalities is beyond the scope of the present chapter as the implications of the relationship between an MFI and the existing WTO agreements require a thorough assessment of the entire WTO structure. Suffice it to mention that any renegotiation of WTO rules pertaining to investment in services will have to respect the carefully crafted compromise between developed and developing countries in the different modes of the GATS. As the Doha experience has shown, such an exercise cannot be undertaken successfully without a sufficiently broad mandate that allows flexibility on a wide variety of issues, ranging from capital and labour liberalization to dispute settlement.

8.6 Conclusion

The present chapter has aimed to assess the most practical and efficient means of improving the framework of negotiations on IIAs so as to reach a balanced outcome that better reflects the needs and interests of the developing world. In so doing, however, it has been stressed that the relevance of IIAs in attracting FDI, be it for development purposes or other goals, is to be seen as merely a part of the overall efforts of a host country to make its economic climate more appealing to foreign investors. From a sustainable development perspective, investment negotiations should ideally be tailored to the conclusion of IIAs that allow the economic fundamentals of a host country to fully manifest themselves in a durable manner, rather than provide *ad hoc* exceptions and

---

237 For a detailed discussion of this relationship, see M. Roy, *supra* note 232.
238 WT/WGTI/W/156, 8 April 2003 and WT/WGTI/W158, 11 April 2003.
239 WGTI Report (2003), para. 52.

limitations for developing countries to creeping protection and liberalization obligations. A multilateral framework on investment of limited scope that focuses on transparency measures and technical assistance would likely be less controversial, easier to negotiate and more complementary to the existing IIA framework than an attempt to replicate the high standards of present BITs in a single global treaty.

Technical assistance and capacity-building commitments by home countries can be mutually beneficial for both developed and developing countries as a prospering market in the latter will increase the export options of the former. At the same time, the existence of an elaborate network of BITs that already to a large extent reflects the wishes of foreign investors implies that there is little incentive for capital-exporting countries to unilaterally concede to the sustainable development needs of poor host countries in multilateral negotiations. Moreover, the limited scope of an MFI restricted to technical measures may fail to raise the necessary support to expend resources on costly multilateral deliberations. The option should thus be considered to broaden the ambit of MFI negotiations to include such intra-investment tradeoffs as pre-establishment liberalization commitments in the service sector by introducing further disciplines on the use of incentives and performance requirements. Earlier experiences show that such a move would likely meet with much opposition from all parties involved, yet it is clear that the negotiation dynamics at the bilateral level necessitate multilateral progress on these issues. Furthermore, if multilateral provisions on progressive investment liberalization can be linked with home country commitments to strengthen the economic infrastructure of host countries, an MFI might prove more acceptable to some of the traditionally recalcitrant developing countries. Alternatively, consideration should be given to linking investment negotiations with parallel deliberations on other economic issues that are of primary interest to capital-importing countries, such as the free movement of personnel.

Recent WTO discussions at the WGTI reveal that the GATS may well provide a useful starting point for such an exercise, although one should of course be wary of disturbing the precarious equilibrium negotiated in this agreement by initiating additional multilateral investment deliberations. Premature and overly ambitious multilateral negotiations that fail to consider the relationship with existing investment rules pose a serious risk of nullifying what little progress has been made on this front in the past couple of decades. On the other hand, headstrong opponents of multilateral investment negotiations should recognize that a pragmatic approach to multilateral investment negotiations that incentivizes both capital-importing and capital-exporting countries by offering mutually beneficial prospects of a durably strengthened host country economy is a case well worth pursuing that could rectify many of the existing imbalances in the current IIA framework.

9 The role of development banks

The European Investment Bank's substantive and procedural accountability principles with regard to human rights, social and environmental concerns*

Nicolas Hachez and Jan Wouters

9.1 Introduction

This chapter examines the principles of accountability applied by the European Investment Bank (EIB) in comparison with those of other multilateral lending institutions (MLIs).[1] Compared to other MLIs, rather little has been written on the EIB, the European Union (EU)'s long-standing MLI, though it is the world's major MLI in terms of lending activity.[2] Until recently the EIB was criticized for its weak accountability standards, though it now seems to be engaged in reform so as to improve its practices on this account. After a brief presentation of the EIB, its mandate and institutional design, we analyse and appraise its substantive and procedural accountability principles and practices. Our appraisal specifically takes into account the fact that the EIB forms part of the EU legal order and the opportunities this may offer to achieve and set best practices with regard to its accountability.

* This chapter is reprinted—with slight adaptations—from N. Hachez and J. Wouters, 'A Responsible Lender? The European Investment Bank's Environmental, Social and Human Rights Accountability', *Common Market Law Review*, 49, 2012, 47–95. The authors are grateful to Dr. Margot Salomon, Ms. Alison McDonnell, and the anonymous reviewers of the *Common Market Law Review*, whose suggestions and comments helped greatly improve this piece. The authors also thank the editorial board and the publisher of the *Common Market Law Review* for graciously agreeing to the reproduction of this article in this volume.
1 We define MLIs as (organs of) international organisations incorporated as banks providing finance solutions (through e.g. loans or loan guarantees) to public or private institutions for investment in development projects.
2 See C. Wright, 'European Investment Bank: Promoting Sustainable Development, "Where Appropriate"', Study for CEE Bankwatch Network, 2007, p. 55. Online. Available HTTP <http://www.bankwatch.org/documents/EIB_where_appropriate.pdf> (accessed 24 July 2012).

9.2 Multilateral lending institutions, their impact and accountability

As powerful development actors with considerable influence on the realization of large-scale investment projects such as infrastructure projects (e.g. building of roads, schools, hospitals, dams) or industrial projects for the exploitation of natural resources (e.g. pipelines, mining, oil drilling), MLIs have a potentially huge impact on living conditions in the areas where the projects they finance are carried out. Through financing, they contribute to the development of recipient countries, by providing capital and technical assistance, under conditions which would not be available otherwise. It is clear that MLIs are a great asset for promoting worldwide development. Conversely, the investment projects financed by MLIs may also carry negative externalities requiring careful oversight. Such projects sometimes involve the resettlement of local populations, the transformation of indigenous lands, deforestation, pollution, employment of workers for heavy tasks, and at times, cooperation with entities that have a poor record for democracy and human rights. This impact, as well as the leverage that MLIs possess – through loan conditionality – to curb the negative aspects of investment projects, has led certain actors to demand increased accountability for MLIs' financing practices under the headings of human rights, and of social and environmental concern. Such demands were spurred by the revelation that certain projects had harmed local populations and the environment.

Accountability is our key word. We define it as a set of principles and procedures under which an actor accounts for the impact of its actions – as a governing entity or more generally as a power wielder – on the individuals, groups or interests that it governs or affects. Accountability is a universally recognized governance principle applicable to every institution of a public nature to ensure the latter's abidance by the democratic standards of our times.[3] We focus on accountability for human rights, social and environmental impacts, and towards stakeholders that are external to the entity in question ('the public').[4] Such an accountability relationship to external stakeholders has been incrementally operationalized by MLIs in the last two decades. In order to meet external accountability demands, MLIs have since the early 1990s been putting in place accountability schemes accessible to stakeholders impacted from human rights, social or environmental points of view. Such schemes contain substantive and

---

3 A. Wolf, 'Symposium on Accountability in Public Administration: Reconciling Democracy, Efficiency and Ethics – Introduction', *International Review of Administrative Sciences* 66, 2000, 16.

4 On the distinction between 'internal' accountability (shareholder model), i.e. between an institution and its constituencies (e.g. the EIB and its shareholders) and 'external' accountability (stakeholder model), owed by an institution to the wider public, and in particular to the people affected by its activities, see R. Keohane, 'Global Governance and Democratic Accountability', in D. Held and M. Koenig-Archibugi (eds), *Taming Globalization: Frontiers of Governance*, Cambridge: Polity Press, 2003, p. 130.

procedural sets of norms.[5] *Substantive accountability norms* are the material human rights, social and environmental rules, principles and standards by which MLIs are bound or to which they commit. They set ground rules for the projects that MLIs finance. In theory, each project applying for financing must be screened against, and comply with, such ground rules before receiving finance. *Procedural accountability norms* refer to procedures that ensure that the substantive norms are applied in the MLI's activities and that call the organization to account in cases where they were not. Such procedural norms are of a prospective or retrospective nature. Prospective procedures refer to those mechanisms through which MLIs seek to *take into account*, i.e. collect and input, stakeholder views, preferences and interests in policies or operational decisions (principle of responsiveness, i.e. participation). Retrospective procedures are those mechanisms through which MLIs *render account* for their failure to abide by applicable substantive norms, by disciplining faulty agents and tracking down dysfunctions and by providing redress to victims.

9.3 The EIB: a lone star in the EU universe

9.3.1 *Institutional status of the EIB*

Present in the European Treaties since 1957, the EIB is a somewhat strange object in the EU galaxy.[6] The Treaties did not classify it under any sort of institutional category, and therefore the EIB must *a contrario* be seen as neither an EU 'institution',[7] an EU 'agency' nor an EU 'advisory body'. The EIB is therefore to be classified in the remaining category of EU organs, as a 'body'.[8] Bodies normally form an integral part of the EU institutional set-up,[9] and as such are subject to the Treaties, including the Charter of Fundamental Rights. However, the EIB is endowed – for the purpose of conducting its banking activities – with an international legal personality distinct from that of the Union itself (Article 308(1) of the Treaty on the Functioning of the European Union (TFEU)).[10] It is also organized as an autonomous corporate structure

---

5 See E. Suzuki and S. Nanwani, 'Responsibility of International Organizations: the Accountability Mechanisms of Multilateral Development Banks', *Michigan Journal of International Law* 27, 2005–2006, 203 ff.

6 See generally D. R. Dunnett, 'The European Investment Bank: Autonomous Instrument of Common Policy?', *Common Market Law Review* 31, 1994, 721.

7 See Art. 13(1) of the Treaty on European Union.

8 The EIB is unequivocally designated as such in the case law of the ECJ. An early case is ECJ, Case 110/75, *Mills v European Investment Bank*, [1976], ECR p 955. Recently, see General Court, Case T-461/08, *Evropaïki Dynamiki v EIB* [2011] not yet published in the ECR, para. 46. See also K. Lenaerts and P. Van Nuffel, *European Union Law*, London: Sweet & Maxwell, 2011, p. 552.

9 See European Union, 'EU Institutions and other Bodies'. Online. Available HTTP <http://europa.eu/about-eu/institutions-bodies/index_en.htm> (accessed 24 July 2012).

10 Dunnett, op. cit., p. 732. Within EU Member States, see Art. 26 of the EIB Statute, annexed as the fifth Protocol to the Treaties, and C.D.C. Spirou, *La Banque Européenne*

whose shareholders are the EU Member States, and is governed by a specific Statute laid down in Protocol No. 5 to the Treaties. And indeed, the European Court of Justice (ECJ) has found that the EIB's status as a financial institution justifies that it may to some extent operate 'independently' from the rest of the EU order, as it stated that '[i]n order to perform the tasks assigned to it by . . . the Treaty the [EIB] must be able to act in complete independence on the financial markets, like any other bank'.[11]

However, according to Article 1 of its Statute, the EIB 'shall perform its functions and carry on its activities in accordance with the provisions of the Treaties and of this Statute'. It has been argued,[12] and so judged by the ECJ, that the EIB's distinct legal personality and large 'degree of operational and institutional autonomy does however not mean that it is totally separated from the Communities and exempt from every rule of Community law. It is clear in particular from Article 130 of the Treaty [now Article 309 TFEU] that the Bank is intended to contribute towards the attainment of the Community's objectives and by virtue of the Treaty forms part of the framework of the Community.'[13] The 'independence' of the EIB from the EU order would rather seek to protect it from interference by other EU organs 'in the management of its affairs, in particular in the sphere of financial operations',[14] and must be qualified from a public accountability perspective. This chapter attempts to make sense, from an accountability point of view, of the ambiguous nature of the EIB both as an EU body and as an independent financial institution.

9.3.2 The EIB's multi-faceted mandate

Article 309 of the TFEU defines the 'task of the EIB' as follows:

> [T]o contribute, by having recourse to the capital market and utilising its own resources, to the balanced and steady development of the internal market in the interest of the Union. For this purpose the Bank shall, operating on a non-profit-making basis, grant loans and give guarantees which facilitate the financing of the following projects in all sectors of the economy:
>
> (a) projects for developing less-developed regions;
> (b) projects for modernising or converting undertakings or for developing fresh activities called for by the establishment or

---

d'Investissement – Aspects juridiques des ses Opérations de Financement, Lausanne: Université de Lausanne, 1989, pp. 41 ff.
11 ECJ, Case 85/86, *Commission v Board of Governors*, [1988] ECR 1988, 1281, para. 28.
12 See Opinion of Advocate General Mancini in Case 85/86, *Commission v Board of Governors* [1988] ECR 1988, p. 1281, para. 12.
13 ECJ, Case 85/86, op. cit., para. 29. See also L. Amoyel, 'Mainstreaming Human Rights in the European Investment Bank', *Baltic Yearbook of International Law* 3, 2003, p. 257.
14 ECJ, Case C-15/00, *Commission v EIB* [2003] ECR 2003 p. I-07281, para. 102.

functioning of the internal market, where these projects are of such a size or nature that they cannot be entirely financed by the various means available in the individual Member States;

(c) projects of common interest to several Member States which are of such a size or nature that they cannot be entirely financed by the various means available in the individual Member States.

In carrying out its task, the Bank shall facilitate the financing of investment programmes in conjunction with assistance from the Structural Funds and other Union Financial Instruments.

Article 309 refers only to activities to be carried out inside the Union, although the EIB's activities encompass both an intra-EU as well as an extra-EU dimension.[15] The EIB's historical, intra-EU role made it an instrument of economic, social and territorial cohesion of the Union. More precisely, the EIB is programmed for 'promot[ing] [the EU's] overall harmonious development', in particular by 'reducing disparities between the levels of development of the various regions and the backwardness of the least favoured regions'.[16] However, the mandate of the EIB also extends outside the EU,[17] in the framework of the Union's external relations policies, in particular development cooperation.[18] This implies striving to fulfil the EU external relations objectives listed in Article21 TFEU, among which feature human rights, as well as the protection of the environment.[19] Accordingly, Article 209 TFEU calls upon the EIB to contribute to implementing the Union's development cooperation policies. The role of the EIB in this ambit was recognized by the EU and the Member States in the 'European Consensus on Development'.[20] The EIB has been carrying out extra-EU activities since 1963, and in order not to affect the EIB's credit standing as a result of extra-EU operations, the Union's budget now guarantees EIB loans made in 'eligible' countries against political and sovereign

---

15 The proportion of projects funded by the EIB is still hugely in favour of intra-EU projects (in a proportion of about nine-tenths. See EIB, 'Projects Financed'. Online. Available HTTP <http://www.eib.org/projects/loans/index.htm> (accessed 24 July 2012).
16 See Arts 174 and 175 TFEU.
17 See Art. 16(1) Statute providing that the EIB may grant finance outside the territory of EU Member States, although this requires a vote at a qualified majority by the Board of Governors.
18 See ECJ, Case C-155/07, *Parliament v Council* [2008] ECR 2008 p. I-8103, paras 57 ff.
19 See Decision of the European Parliament and of the Council of 25 October 2011 granting an EU Guarantee to the European Investment Bank against Losses under Loans and Loan Guarantees for Projects Outside the Union and repealing Decision no. 633/2009/EC, 1080/2011/EU, *OJ L* 280, 27/10/2011, pp. 1–16 (hereinafter the 'External Mandate'), recital 20 and Art. 3(2), citing Art. 21 TFEU.
20 European Consensus on Development: Joint declaration by the Council and the representatives of the governments of the Member States meeting within the Council, the European Parliament and the Commission on the development policy of the European Union entitled 'The European Consensus on Development', *OJ C* 46, 24/2/2006, para. 119.

risks. This guarantee mechanism, commonly referred to as the EIB's 'External Mandate',[21] identifies policy objectives which the EIB should pursue in the eligible countries. Geographically, the External Mandate covers Pre-Accession countries; Neighbourhood and Partnership Countries; Asian and Latin American countries; and South Africa. Cooperation with the ACP (African, Caribbean and Pacific) Countries and Overseas Countries and Territories (OCT) is directly covered by the Cotonou Agreement[22] and the Overseas Association Decision.[23] The EIB's External Mandate must create synergies with the EU external relations policies and its various funds.[24] The EU institutions oversee the External Mandate as the Commission must report annually on it to the Parliament and the Council.[25]

The increasing complexity of the EIB's mandate has been criticized as blurring its real role in intra- and extra-EU development, and as challenging its capacity to pursue both its banking objectives and the EU's various policies. From a *sui generis* instrument of economic planning within the Union, the EIB would have evolved into a financial arm implementing an increasingly heterogeneous range of internal and external policies, always arguably 'in the interest of the Union'.[26] For example, as a response to the current economic crisis, the Commission requested the EIB to provide funds and programmes as part of its 'European Economic Recovery Plan'.[27] The EIB accordingly increased its lending volume by 30 per cent (15 billion Euros) for the period from 2009 to 2010, for the following objectives: support for SMEs (small and medium enterprises) and mid-cap companies; energy, climate change and infrastructure; and convergence lending to poorer regions.[28] Some non-governmental organizations (NGOs) criticized these measures, in particular the support to SMEs through 'global loans' (see below), as lacking transparency and accountability.[29]

---

21 See the External Mandate, op. cit.
22 Partnership Agreement between the Members of the African, Caribbean and Pacific Group of States of the One Part, and the European Community and Its Member States, of the Other Part, done at Cotonou, on 23 June 2000, *OJ* L 317/3, 15/12/2000. See particularly Art. 31, para. 5; Art. 76, para. 1(d), and generally Annexes I and II of the Agreement.
23 Council Decision of 27 November 2001 on the association of the overseas countries and territories with the European Community, 2001/822/EC, *OJ L* 314, 30/11/2001, pp. 1–77.
24 See External Mandate, op. cit., recitals 27–28.
25 Ibid., Art. 11.
26 This vague phrase was used, sometimes uncritically, to justify all sorts of additions to the EIB's mandate. See Dunnett, op. cit., pp. 721–727.
27 See European Commission, 'A European Recovery Plan', 26/11/2008, COM(2008) 800 final, p. 7.
28 See EIB, 'The Bank promoting European objectives – EIB anti-crisis measures', Briefing Note No. 01, 9/3/2009. Online. Available HTTP <http://www.eib.org/attachments/general/events/briefing2009_01_anti_crisis_en.pdf> (accessed 24 July 2012).
29 See Counter Balance, 'The EIB and the economic crisis', 28/8/2009. Online. Available HTTP <http://www.counterbalance-eib.org/?p=301> (accessed 24 July 2012); and

Also, the expansion of the EIB's mandate constrains its staff resources, which raises doubts as to its ability to make truly informed decisions, notably about the human rights, social and environmental impacts of every investment project,[30] even though an 'Environment and Social Office' (ESO), composed of specialists in environmental, social and climate change issues, was created in 2009. The ESO develops the EIB's policies on these issues and advises the Projects Directorate in assessing projects along these lines.[31] Still, the Mid-Term Review of the EIB's External Mandate for 2007 to 2013 (the 'Mid-Term Review'), carried out by a 'Steering Committee of Wise Persons',[32] recommended that the External Mandate of the EIB be 'streamlined' and refocused on sectors in which the EIB can make a difference, such as climate change mitigation, infrastructure work, or SME support.[33] Accordingly, the External Mandate was amended in late 2011, and enjoins the Commission and the European External Action Service to develop country- or region-specific 'operational guidelines' to ensure that the EIB action is in line with the EU external relations policies.[34] The 2011 External Mandate also contains a 2 billion euro guarantee for climate change mitigation projects, which creates a two-pronged External Mandate, with the 'General Mandate' and the 'Climate Change Mandate'.[35] Moreover, the External Mandate urges the EIB to 'consider

I. Besedova, 'Missing in action – The winners, the losers and the unknowns of the European Investment Bank's anti-crisis SME offensive in central and eastern Europe', CEE Bankwatch Network, 10/2010. Online. Available HTTP <http://bankwatch.org/publications/missing-action-winners-losers-and-unknowns-european-investment-banks-anti-crisis-sme-of> (accessed 24 July 2012).

30 European Commission, 'Report from the Commission to the European Parliament and the Council on the Mid-Term Review of the External Mandate of the EIB', 21/4/2010, COM(2010) 173 final, p. 10 (concluding notably that 'a broadening and increasingly ambitious EU external agenda points to the need for increased policy coherence . . .'). See also A. Wilks, 'Corporate welfare and development deceptions – Why the European Investment Bank is failing to deliver outside the EU', Study for Counter Balance, 2/2010. Online. Available HTTP <http://www.counterbalance-eib.org/wp-content/uploads/2011/01/SReport-EN-web.pdf> (accessed 24 July 2012).

31 See EIB, 'EIB's Environment and Social Office. Online. Available HTTP <http://www.eib.org/projects/news/eibs-environment-and-social-office.htm?lang=-en> (accessed 24 July 2012).

32 Chaired by former IMF Managing Director Michel Camdessus. See European Investment Bank, 'European Investment Bank's External Mandate 2007–2013 Mid-Term Review', 2/2010 (hereinafter the 'Mid-Term Review'). Online. Available HTTP <http://www.eib. org/attachments/documents/eib_external_mandate_2007-2013_mid-term_review.pdf> (accessed 24 July 2012). This Mid-Term Review was mandated by Art. 9 of the previous External Mandate Decision (Decision of the European Parliament and of the Council of 13 July 2009 granting a Community Guarantee to the European Investment Bank against Losses under Loans and Loan Guarantees for Projects Outside the Community, 633/2009/EC, OJ L 190, 22/7/2009, pp. 1–10, hereinafter the 'Previous External Mandate').

33 Mid-Term review, op. cit., pp. 11–13.

34 External Mandate, op. cit., Arts 6 and 8.

35 See the External Mandate, op. cit., Art. 2.

increasing its activity in support of health and infrastructure'.[36] In any event, the increasingly large and complex scope of EIB missions has implications for its accountability, with more people and places potentially impacted by its activities.

9.3.3 The EIB's lending activities

In light of its mandate, the EIB defines itself as a 'policy-driven public bank'[37] whose objective is to attain the EU's policy objectives.[38] In practice, this is achieved through (long-term) loans and loan guarantees (Article 309 TFEU and 16 Statute) for public or private investment projects (Article 19 Statute).[39] The EIB also borrows and invests on capital markets to finance itself (Articles 20 and 21 Statute). The EIB grants finance 'to the extent that other funds are not available elsewhere on reasonable terms' (Article 16(1) Statute), and that other sources of financing are also used (Article 16(2) Statute) for at least 50 per cent of the investment costs of a project.[40] In addition, loans are made 'conditional either on a guarantee from the Member State in whose territory the investment will be carried out or on other adequate guarantees, or on the financial strength of the debtor' (Article 16(3) Statute).

The EIB has set substantive priorities for its finance activities, differentiated between intra-[41] and extra-EU activities.[42] Such priorities derive from the EU policy objectives and, for out-of-EU loans, are enumerated in the External Mandate itself.[43] In this regard, coordination with EU institutions, agencies and funds is taking place to ensure synergies between EIB and EU policies.[44]

---

36 Ibid., Art. 3, para. 4.
37 See item 'What is the EIB?' in the EIB's FAQs. Online. Available HTTP <http://www.eib.org/infocentre/faq/index.htm> (accessed 24 July 2012).
38 See how the EIB plans to support EU policies in EIB, 'Corporate Operational Plan 2011–2013' (hereinafter the 'Corporate Operational Plan'). Online. Available HTTP <http://www.eib.org/attachments/strategies/cop_2011_en.pdf> (accessed 24 July 2012).
39 The EIB actually offers a variegated portfolio of products (see EIB, 'Products: Lending, blending and advising'. Online. Available HTTP <http://www.eib.org/products/>, accessed 24 July 2012). 'Facilities' were set up in order to implement various EU policies pertaining to a certain region or to a certain topic. See e.g. the 'Facility for Euro-Mediterranean Investment and Partnership (FEMIP)', grouping all EIB activities in that region (see EIB, 'Facility for Euro-Mediterranean Investment and Partnership (FEMIP)'. Online. Available HTTP <http://www.eib.org/projects/regions/med/index.htm>, accessed 24 July 2012).
40 See EIB, 'Project Loans'. Online. Available HTTP <http://www.eib.org/products/loans/index.htm> (accessed 24 July 2012).
41 See Corporate Operational Plan, op. cit., Introduction.
42 Ibid.
43 Contrary to the Previous External Mandate (op. cit.), for which such objectives were described in the recitals, the current External Mandate lists its objectives in the text of the decision itself (op. cit., Art. 3).
44 See EIB, 'EU Institutions'. Online. Available HTTP <http://www.eib.org/about/partners/cooperation/index.htm> (accessed 24 July 2012). See also Council Regulation (EC)

Cooperation with other MLIs is also in order (Article 14 Statute).[45] The EIB operates on a non-profit-making basis, and its income should be adjusted to market conditions and enable the EIB to meet its obligations, cover its expenses, and build a reserve fund (Article 17 Statute). The EIB grants loans and guarantees alongside financing provided by other EU instruments such as the Structural and Cohesion Funds or, outside the EU, the numerous external relations instruments.[46] The EIB also conducts several 'Joint Actions' with private institutions, with EC and national institutions, or with other MLIs,[47] with which increased cooperation is encouraged by the External Mandate and the Mid-Term Review.[48]

Finally, in 1994, a new instrument was created alongside the EIB: the European Investment Fund (EIF).[49] The EIF is a self-standing investment fund providing financial intermediaries with products and solutions more specifically targeted at SMEs within the EU, the (potential) candidate and EFTA (European Free Trade Association) countries. A public–private partnership, the EIF is owned by the EIB, the Commission, and a number of other public and private institutions. The EIB and the EIF together form the EIB Group.[50]

9.3.4 The EIB's organizational framework

The EIB's peculiar organizational framework allows it to operate independently as a normal bank as much as possible. The Member States are the EIB's shareholders, and contribute to the capital in proportion to their economic weight (GDP) at the time of accession.[51] The EIB's organs are the Board of

---

No. 1083/2006 of 11 July 2006 laying down general provisions on the European Regional Development Fund, the European Social Fund and the Cohesion Fund, *OJ* L 210/25, 31/7/2006.

45 See also Art. 9 External Mandate (op. cit.) and e.g. the Memorandum of Understanding between the European Commission, the European Investment Bank together with the European Investment Fund, and the European Bank for Reconstruction and Development in respect of Development outside the EU, 1/3/2011. Online. Available HTTP <http://www.ebrd.com/pages/news/press/2011/110301.shtml> (accessed 24 July 2012); or with regard to collaboration with the International Finance Corporation, see IFC, 'Western Europe'. Online. Available HTTP <http://www.ifc.org/ifcext/westeurope.nsf/Content/EIB> (accessed 24 July 2012).

46 Such as the Instrument for Pre-Accession Assistance, the European Neighbourhood and Partnership Instrument, the Development Cooperation Instrument, or the Instrument for Stability.

47 Corporate Operational Plan, op. cit., p. 7.

48 See External Mandate, op. cit., recitals 22, 36 and 37, and Mid-Term Review, op. cit., pp. 31–37.

49 See generally <http://www.eif.org/> (accessed 24 July 2012).

50 See the Statutes of the European Investment Fund, adopted on 14/6/1994, last amended 30/11/2007, *OJ* C 225, 10/08/2001.

51 As at 1 April 2010, the Bank's subscribed capital amounted to more than EUR 232bn. See EIB, 'Shareholders'. Online. Available HTTP <http://www.eib.org/about/structure/shareholders/index.htm> (accessed 24 July 2012).

Governors, the Board of Directors, the Management Committee (exercising management functions), and the Audit Committee (for control purposes).

The Board of Governors is the highest organ of the EIB, and is composed of 27 Governors (one per shareholder), who are the Ministers designated by the Member States (generally Finance Ministers: see Article 7(1) Statute). It 'lay[s] down general directives for the credit policy of the Bank, in accordance with the Union's objectives' and ensures that they are implemented (Article 7(2) Statute). It sets the principles applicable to the finance operations decided by the Board of Directors (see below). It approves the Board of Directors' annual report and the financial statements, and may decide modifications of capital (Article 7(3) Statute).

The Board of Directors comprises 28 principal members, one appointed by each Member State, and one by the Commission,[52] and 18 alternate directors (Article 11(1) and (2) Statute).[53] The Board may also co-opt non-voting expert members with expertise in the EIB's fields of activity (Article 11(4) Statute and Article 16 Rules of Procedure[54]). The Board of Directors makes the finance decisions, and 'lay[s] down the terms and conditions constituting the general framework for the Bank's financing, guarantee and borrowing operations, in particular by approving the criteria for the fixing of interest rates, commission and other charges' (Article 18 Rules of Procedure, and Article 9(1) Statute). It also approves the financing and guarantees operations[55] and authorizes borrowing operations (Article 18 Rules of Procedure). These operational decisions are normally made after proposals from the Management Committee (see below). More generally, the Board of Directors ensures 'that the Bank is properly run in accordance with the Treaty, the Statute, the directives laid down by the Board of Governors and the other texts governing the Bank's activity in the performance of its task under the Treaty' (Article 9(1) Statute and Article 18 para. 2 Rules of Procedure). It sets the EIB's management policy, ensures consistency among EIB policies, and oversees its financial equilibrium, etc. (Article 18 Rules of Procedure). In all those tasks, the Board of Directors largely relies on proposals and initiatives from the Management Committee, to which it may delegate some of its functions (Article 9(1) Statute).

---

52 The DG Economic and Financial Affairs (ECFIN) represents the Commission in the EIB Board. See EC Economic and Social Affairs, 'Coordination with the European Investment Bank'. Online. Available HTTP <http://ec.europa.eu/economy_finance/financial_operations/coordination/eib/index_en.htm> (accessed 24 July 2012).

53 Large shareholders may appoint more alternates than smaller ones.

54 EIB, 'Rules of Procedure of the European Investment Bank', 25/4/2012 (hereinafter the 'Rules of Procedure'). Online. Available HTTP <http://www.eib.org/attachments/general/rulesofprocedure_en.pdf> (accessed 23 July 2012).

55 Under Art. 19 Statute a system of checks and balances requires that opinions from the relevant Member State, the Commission and the Management Committee be sought prior to project approval. If the Commission or the Management Committee gives a negative opinion, the Board's decision must be unanimous to grant finance. If both the Commission and the Management Committee give negative opinions, the Board may not grant finance.

The Management Committee conducts the daily business of the EIB. It is composed of a President (who presides without vote over the Board of Directors: Article 9(2) Statute) and eight Vice-Presidents (Article 11(8) Statute). Its main task is to administer the EIB and to prepare the Board of Directors' financing and borrowing decisions (Article 11(3) Statute).[56] The staff of the EIB is under the authority of the President of the Management Committee (Article 11(7) Statute), who adopts organization and operation rules for the Bank's departments, including staff rules (Article 23 Rules of Procedure).

Contrary to most other MLIs' voting patterns, voting power is not entirely aligned with capital weight at the EIB.[57] Decisions must be adopted at a double majority, both of the members of the Board and of the amount of capital (the majority can be simple or qualified; Article 8 Statute). The same sort of regime applies to the Board of Directors, even though decisions at a simple majority only require one-third of the votes representing one-half of the capital (Article 12 Statute). Therefore, at least in the Board of Governors, voting rules act as safeguards against unilateral decisions made by large shareholders, while barring measures lacking their support. However, for out-of-EU EIB decisions, beneficiary countries have no vote at all, contrary to the usual rules of regional development banks.[58] Therefore, what is relatively egalitarian and progressive inside the EU is also quite conservative in excluding beneficiary countries from decisions on projects located outside the EU.

Finally, the EIB has a control organ, the Audit Committee, which verifies that 'the activities of the Bank conform to best banking practice', and that its operations have been conducted and its books kept properly. It also audits the EIB accounts (Article 12(1) and 12(2) Statute).

9.4 Principles of accountability and the EIB

A study of the principles governing the accountability of the EIB is of great importance for a number of reasons. First, the EIB is the largest multilateral lending institution, in terms of the volume of its loans (see above, section 9.3.1). In 2010, it disbursed 57.5 billion euro in loans and its volume of loan

---

56 Under Art. 11(4) Statute the Management Committee acts 'by a majority when delivering opinions on proposals for raising loans or granting of finance, in particular in the form of loans and guarantees'.

57 For a comparative analysis of voting rules in Regional Development Banks, see E.R. Carrasco, W. Carrington and HJ. Lee, 'Governance and Accountability: The Regional Development Banks', 27 *Boston University International Law Journal* 1 (2009); J.W. Head, 'For Richer or for Poorer: Assessing the Criticisms Directed at the Multilateral Development Banks', *University of Kansas Law Review* 52, 2003–2004, 267 and 299.

58 MLIs often distinguish between 'beneficiary' Member States and the others. Still, beneficiary countries usually get a vote in lending decisions, which is not the case at the EIB for out-of-EU loans. See e.g. Agreement Establishing the Asian Development Bank, done at Manila on 4/12/1965, in force 22/8/1966, Art. 1, which limits lending to 'developing member countries in the region'. That status is determined by the Board of Governors (Art. 28(4)), in which all members have (weighted) votes (Arts 27 and 33).

signatures was 71.8 billion.[59] Thus EIB funding makes a great number of investments possible. However, the EIB's financial intervention alone does not entirely reflect its impact on investment conditions. As it usually only lends money alongside other institutions, its contribution must also be analysed in terms of its 'leverage', i.e. the extent to which EIB involvement in a project induces other actors to come on board. A 2009 study showed that for every euro lent by the EIB within the EU in 2006 (an average of 3.6) was made available from elsewhere for the project.[60] The EIB's impact is additionally increased by its expanding geographic reach, now coupled with the EU's external relations policies. This impact is also enhanced by the nature of the financed projects (infrastructure, energy, exploitation of natural resources, etc.[61]), which are typically the source of important positive and negative externalities.[62] This powerful position alone warrants a strong accountability review. In this regard, large private financing institutions have recently taken important steps to upgrade their accountability practices as a result of growing external scrutiny.[63]

Another element justifies our paying attention to the EIB's accountability. The EIB is a public institution, governed and capitalized by public entities. It is also 'a policy-driven bank', and is mandated to implement EU policies. It is fundamentally a political organ[64] claiming to act in the public interest – in other words, a government agency. This impacts investment conditions in two respects. First, the EIB may not finance projects which do not espouse EU policy objectives. Second, the EIB's political objectives influence the behaviour of actors connected with projects. This influence may be official/legal, using conditionality in finance contracts, or more diffuse, in that (public or private)

59 See EIB, 'Annual Report 2010 – Volume II: Financial Report', p. 29. Online. Available HTTP <http://www.eib.org/attachments/general/reports/fr2010en.pdf> (accessed 24 July 2012). In 2011, loan signatures decreased to 61 billion, marking 'a gradual return to normal lending levels after reaching record heights in 2008, 2009 and 2010 in response to the financial crisis'. See EIB, 'Financial Report 2011', p. 16. Online. Available HTTP <http://www.eib.org/attachments/general/reports/fr2011en.pdf> (accessed 25 July 2012).

60 N. Robinson, 'The European Investment Bank: The EU's Neglected Institution', *Journal of Common Market Studies* 47, 2009, 656. The EIB claims that its historical leverage is 'five times the Bank's financing'. See EIB, 'EIB Directors approve anti-crisis measures', 16/12/2008. Online. Available HTTP <http://www.eib.org/about/press/2008/2008-159-eib-directors-approve-anti-crisis-measures-for-2009-2010.htm> (accessed 24 July 2012).

61 See the breakdown by sector. Online. Available HTTP <http://www.eib.org/projects/loans/sectors/index.htm> (accessed 24 July 2012).

62 These effects are described as 'non-financial leverage'. See Robinson, op. cit., p. 663.

63 See e.g. the 'Equator Principles' (Online. Available HTTP <http://www.equator-principles.com/>, accessed 24 July 2012), a Code of Conduct (inspired by the IFC's social and environmental 'Performance Standards'), endorsed by more than 60 high-profile private banks and financial institutions which voluntarily commit to follow them in project finance activities.

64 Contrary to the IBRD, which is prevented by its Charter from intervening, via its financial activities, in the political affairs of its borrowers. See IBRD Articles of Agreement, done at Bretton Woods on 22/7/1944, effective 27/12/1945, last amended 16/2/1989, Art. IV, Section 10.

actors seeking EIB financing will be inclined to mirror the EIB's policy lines in order to receive financing.[65] Given the above, modern democratic governance standards require that the EIB be accountable, to the extent of its impact, for the design and consequences of its lending policies.[66] In the next sections we analyse and evaluate the principles governing the accountability of the EIB, from a substantive and procedural point of view.

9.4.1 Substantive accountability principles

Accountability implies that conduct will be assessed against certain standards. In this respect, effective accountability for issues as complex and high-profile as human and social rights or the environment requires a firm normative background. This section addresses the substantive human rights, social and environmental norms against which the conduct of the EIB is supposedly benchmarked, as a result either of applicable binding rules or of voluntary commitments made by the EIB itself.

9.4.1.1 In search of an effective substantive accountability framework

Generally, MLIs are self-standing international organizations governed by a 'Charter Treaty'. These charters establish the MLI's terms of reference, and confer on it relative autonomy vis-à-vis the international legal order at large, as most charters give one of their internal organs competence about charter interpretation.[67] Also, MLI charters are usually vague or silent as to what norms govern other issues than the purely financial aspects of their operations. This created speculation concerning the relationship of MLI activities with international norms such as human rights, or international environmental law. Except for *jus cogens*, customary international law, and the rules of particular international law which they have adhered to,[68] MLIs have tended to downplay the relevance of those legal regimes for their activities, at least until recently.

---

65 See Robinson, op. cit., p. 667. Some authors encourage MLIs to use this leverage to foster laudable goals, such as corporate social responsibility. See A. Vives, 'The Role of Multilateral Development Institutions in Fostering Corporate Social Responsibility', *Development* 47, 2004, 45.

66 In this regard, the Mid-Term Review (op. cit., p. 37) recommends that out-of-EU EIB activities be revised, so as to be 'fully accountable as a public institution, and focus on tangible benefits and positive impact for the final project beneficiaries; [and so as to] strengthen the consultation process with local civil society'.

67 See J. W. Head, 'Law and Policy in International Financial Institutions: The Changing Role of Law in the IMF and the Multilateral Development Banks', *Kansas Journal of Law and Public Policy* 17, 2007–2008, 208–210 and 219. The tendency of MLIs to expand the reach of their activities beyond their intended mandate through wide charter interpretations was criticized as 'mission creep' by some authors. See Head, 'For Richer or for Poorer', op. cit., p. 265.

68 See analogically S. I. Skogly, *The Human Rights Obligations of the World Bank and the International Monetary Fund*, London and Sydney: Cavendish Publishing, 2001, pp. 80 ff.

Some MLIs, such as the World Bank, tend to regard their position in respect of such international legal norms as one of promotion rather than one of obligation.[69] Schemes of accountability and internal policies based on those norms, where they exist, remain largely voluntary and stem more from a sense of political accountability in regard to sensitive issues than from a conviction to be bound by hard 'legal' obligations.[70]

As indicated above, the EIB is less of a self-standing institution than the usual MLI: it is embedded in the EU legal order (albeit with a distinctive status), which contains hard human rights, social and environmental norms backed with effective enforcement and remedies. To what extent does this elaborate legal framework act as a body of substantive accountability principles for the EIB?

9.4.1.2 The EU legal order

The EIB is bound by its Statute and the Treaties, from which its existence and mandate derive. Article 1 of the Statute makes this explicit.[71] The EIB must act in accordance with the Treaties,[72] including with respect to human rights (notably the Charter of Fundamental Rights), social rights and policy, and the environment.[73] When acting outside the EU, the EIB is consequently bound by Treaty provisions on external relations (Part 5 TFEU), especially those on development cooperation,[74] on which the External Mandate is based.[75] This arguably requires that the EIB comply and take account of relevant international law and initiatives.[76]

Many programmatic provisions of the Treaties, i.e. 'primary' EU law, are implemented by EU legislation. What is the relationship of the EIB with secondary EU law? The ECJ has emphasized that the EIB's particular status does not remove it entirely from the EU legal order. The EIB is naturally

---

69 Also, regarding the IMF, see P. Schmitt, 'The Accountability of the International Monetary Fund for Human Rights Violations', in J. Wouters, E. Brems, S. Smis and P. Schmitt (eds), *Accountability for Human Rights Violations by International Organisations*, Antwerp and Oxford: Intersentia, 2010, p. 431.

70 See, *inter alia*, K. De Feyter, 'Self-Regulation', in W. Van Genugten, P. Hunt and S. Matthews (eds), *World Bank, IMF and Human Rights*, Nijmegen: Wolf Legal Publishers, 2003, p. 79.

71 Art. 1 of the EIB Statute notably reads as follows: '[the EIB] shall perform its functions and carry on its activities in accordance with the provisions of the Treaties and of this Statute.'

72 See Spirou, op. cit., p. 161: 'la BEI n'est pas une institution proprement dite de la Communauté, mais . . . sa mission se situe toute entière dans le cadre du Traité.'

73 See e.g. Arts 151 ff. TFEU (on social standards), Arts 190 ff. TFEU (on the environment).

74 See Art. 209(3) TFEU.

75 ECJ, Case C-155/07, op. cit.

76 Art. 208(2) TFEU: The Union 'shall comply with the commitments and take account of the objectives [it] approved in the context of the United Nations and other competent international organizations'.

subject to the secondary legal rules which are *applicable to it*, in the sense that it can be considered a *direct addressee* of such rules. Examples of such rules having been deemed legally binding on the EIB by the ECJ include rules applicable to the EU institutions' staff,[77] rules about income tax on staff wages,[78] the rules concerning the powers of OLAF (the European Anti-Fraud Office) to combat fraud and investigate in this connection,[79] general principles of labour law,[80] and rules on public procurement.[81] It can also be argued that the EIB is bound by the EU legislations[82] (or EU agreements such as the Cotonou Agreement) assigning it special mandates outside the EU.[83]

The trickier question concerns the status of those rules of EU legislation of which the EIB cannot be considered a direct addressee and which are not *applicable* to the EIB but are nonetheless *relevant* to its activities. As an instrument of EU policies, the EIB must arguably place the body of EU human and social rights and environmental legislation at the centre of its activities. This, however, leaves open the question of the EIB's obligations with regard to those 'relevant' legislations when granting finance to investment projects. When secondary law provisions are not formally applicable to the EIB, if the EIB decides to grant finance to a project which is at odds with those provisions, the 'legality' (i.e. abidance to norms) of such a decision by the EIB in relation to those provisions is not *stricto sensu* at stake.[84] Still, as an EU body, the EIB arguably has a general obligation not to undermine EU legislation, though the latter as such may not be applicable to it. The activities of the EIB must be conducted *with due regard for* EU legislation.[85] In case it were to grant finance to a project violating EU law provisions, the EIB would rather breach its obligation of due regard than violate those provisions directly. The justification for the obligation of due regard arguably lies in Articles 209 and 309 TFEU, enjoining the EIB to pursue the interests of the Union, which are embedded into EU legislation. This conclusion is also supported by the EIB policy to use EU law as social and environmental standards, even when not formally applicable.

The obligation of due regard may receive different practical applications. Obviously, the EIB may not impose conditions on a borrower which would oblige the latter to violate its obligations at EU law, but it should also craft its conditionality requirements so as to foster the borrower's compliance with EU

---

77 See ECJ, Case 110/75, op. cit.; Case C-499/99 P, *EIB v Hautem* [2001] ECR 2001, p. I-6733, paras 90–96.

78 See Case 85/86, op. cit.

79 See ECJ, Case C-15/00, op. cit., paras 95 ff.

80 See CFI, Case T-192/99, *Dunnett et al. v EIB* [2001] ECR 2001 p. II-00813, paras 95 ff.

81 General Court, Case T-461/08, op. cit.

82 See External Mandate, op. cit., esp. recital 21 and Art. 7, enjoining the EIB to assess the development-related aspects of projects, including on environmental, social, and human rights counts.

83 ECJ, Case C-370/89, *SGEEM & Etroy v EIB* [1992], ECR 1992, p. I-06211, para. 30.

84 Dunnett, op. cit., pp. 752–753.

85 Ibid., p. 753.

policies.[86] Likewise, the EIB may not finance projects which violate EU law and should conduct reasonable control as to this.[87] However, the strict rules on delegation of powers regarding compliance with EU law applicable to EU 'agencies' do not concern the EIB, since its powers do not derive from an act of delegation, but from primary law.[88] In conclusion, EU primary and, up to a point, secondary rules may constitute a normative framework for the EIB. However, their capacity to act as substantive accountability principles for EIB activities is qualified by the EIB's independence and wide margin of appreciation in its operations. Alleged deviations from EU law resulting from EIB activities should be manifest before it can be accused of crossing the limits of its discretion.[89]

9.4.1.3 Statements of principles

In light of the unclear status of international law for MLI activities, and in response to increasing accountability demands from civil society, MLIs have started to design internal codes of conduct equipped with grievance mechanisms, developing so-called 'best practices' in MLI accountability. Over the years, the EIB kept a low profile and asserted its autonomy towards the EU legal order.[90] As indicated above, it is unclear to what extent the Union *acquis* applies *per se* to EIB operations, and, as a result, what traction or influence EU human rights, social and environmental rules may have on the EIB's lending activities.[91] The EIB also started to adopt 'statements of principles', aiming to spell out the environmental and social standards and practices which it commits to apply in the course of its lending operations.[92] It did so partly under pressure from the

---

86 Head, 'Law and Policy in International Financial Institutions', op. cit., p. 213.

87 See Decision of the European Ombudsman on complaint 1807/2006/MHZ against the EIB, 17/12/2007. Online. Available HTTP <http://www.ombudsman.europa.eu/cases/home.faces> (accessed 24 July 2012).

88 S. Griller, 'Everything under Control? The "Way Forward" for European Agencies in the Footsteps of the Meroni Doctrine', *European Law Review* 35, 2010, 8.

89 Finance decisions indeed require balancing conflicting norms and interests. See L. Amoyel, op. cit., p. 269.

90 See C. Amicucci, 'The European Investment Bank', in *Budgeting for the Future. Building Another Europe – European Economic Policies from a Civil Society Perspective*, Rome; Sbilanciamoci!, 2008, p. 199. Online. Available http <http://www.tni.org/sites/www.tni.org/files/download/buildinganothereurope.pdf> (accessed 24 July 2012). A coalition of NGOs – Counter Balance – was, however, formed in 2007 to monitor and 'challenge' the EIB on development and sustainability grounds: see <http://www.counterbalance-eib.org/> (accessed 24 July 2012).

91 See EIB, 'The EIB Statement of Social and Environmental Standards and Practices', 2009 (hereinafter the 'Statement'). Online. Available HTTP <http://www.eib.org/attachments/strategies/eib_statement_esps_en.pdf> (accessed 24 July 2012). See para. 10, p. 6: 'The Bank is . . . bound by EU law and committed to promoting EU policy objectives.' It is unclear, though, how the 'bindingness' of EU law is operationalized and enforced in finance decisions.

92 The EIB adopted its first set of environmental principles in 1996 (Statement, op. cit., para. 6, p. 6).

EU institutions, in particular the European Parliament,[93] and from civil society, and perhaps also because the implementation of EU development policies raises explicit human rights, social and environmental concerns. Accordingly, the External Mandate expressly provides, since 2011, that '[t]he EIB's own rules and procedures shall include the necessary provisions on assessment of environmental and social impact of projects and of aspects related to human rights to ensure that only projects that are economically, financially, environmentally and socially sustainable are supported under [the External Mandate]'.[94]

The EIB has adopted a multi-tiered structure of instruments addressing social and environmental standards. At the top of the pyramid are broad statements of principles, the most prominent of which are the 2006 European Principles for the Environment, to which the EIB committed along with four other European development banks.[95] The Principles reflect a common approach to project finance, based on the environmental principles contained in the EU Treaties, as well as in EU legislation. Accordingly, the signatory banks will only finance projects which comply with the environmental rules, principles and standards enshrined in the EU Treaties, in EU legislation and in multilateral environmental agreements. Outside the EU, such rules, principles and standards will be applied 'subject to local conditions'. A second over-arching statement of principles is the EIB Group's 2005 'Statement on Corporate Social Responsibility'. It states the EIB's view of sound business and its adherence to the triple bottom line, which must be applied transparently and accountably to all lending operations and in setting the EIB's lending priorities.[96]

A second tier of social and environmental principles is constituted by the 'EIB Statement of Environmental and Social Principles and Standards',[97] the last version of which was released in 2009. It describes the environmental and social principles to be applied by EIB staff and informs external stakeholders

---

93 The European Parliament closely oversees the EIB, and has passed several resolutions concerning it (see Amoyel, op. cit., pp. 266–267). See e.g. European Parliament, 'Resolution of 6/5/2010 on the European Investment Bank's annual report for 2008', 2009/2166(INI). On EIB social and environmental standards, see 'Resolution on EIB annual report for 2005', 15/2/2007, 2006/2269(INI), paras 22 and 23.

94 External Mandate, op. cit., Art. 7(1).

95 See the May 2006 'European Principles for the Environment', and the EPE Banks' Declaration. Online. Available HTTP <http://www.coebank.org/upload/infocentre/Brochure/en/EPE_Declaration.pdf> (accessed 24 July 2012). The EPE banks are the Council of Europe Bank (CED); the European Bank for Reconstruction and Development (EBRD); the European Investment Bank (EIB); the Nordic Environment Finance Corporation (NEFCO); and the Nordic Investment Bank (NIB).

96 EIB Group, 'Statement on Corporate Social Responsibility', May 2005, p. 3 (hereinafter the 'CSR Statement'). Online. Available HTTP <http://www.bei.org/attachments/strategies/statement_csr_en.pdf> (accessed 24 July 2012).

97 Ibid.

of the EIB's requirements.[98] Yet it is unclear to what extent it 'binds' the EIB from an accountability perspective. The Statement states that it 'must be applied by the staff of the EIB in all its operations', without further elaboration.[99] The Statement reaffirms the concern of the EIB for introducing environmental and social considerations[100] in its lending activities and identifies the substantive principles and standards used to that effect. In this regard, the EIB establishes that its primary frames of reference are EU law and policies, notably the sixth Environmental Action Programme of the EU,[101] the EU Sustainable Development Strategy[102] and the EU Consensus on Development.[103] In terms of implementation, the EIB will specifically target projects 'that contribute directly to environmental sustainability and social well-being in support of sustainable development'.[104] These projects are part of the EIB's environmental lending priorities.[105] On the other hand, the EIB ensures that all financed projects – even if not part of the environmental priorities – meet 'environmental and social acceptability' with regard to the relevant standards.[106] The EIB's policy also has a dynamic and managerial aspect: projects must include a management component to mitigate risks deriving from socially and environmentally sensitive activities.[107] In other words, for each project, the EIB

---

98 Ibid., para. 9, p. 6.

99 No mention of the Statement or of any attention to social or environmental issues is made in the Staff Regulations (see EIB, 'Staff Regulations of the European Investment Bank', 20/4/1960, last revised 1/1/2009. Online. Available HTTP <http://www.eib.org/attachments/general/eib_staff_regulations_2009_en.pdf>, accessed 24 July 2012) or in the 'Staff Code of Conduct' (1/8/2006. Online. Available HTTP <http://www.eib.org/attachments/thematic/code_conduct_staff_en.pdf>, accessed 24 July 2012), though one may expect that employees must apply the employer's policies in their professional activity.

100 Which the EIB claims that it derives from the principle of sustainable development enshrined in EU policies (Statement, op. cit., paras 8 and 10, p. 6).

101 See Decision No. 1600/2002/EC of the European Parliament and of the Council of 22 July 2002 laying down the Sixth Community Environment Action Programme, *OJ* L 242, 10/9/2002, e.g. Art. 7(2)

102 Council of the European Union, Renewed EU Sustainable Development Strategy, 26/6/2006, 10917/06, urging (p. 21) the EIB to 'assess its lending against . . . the Millennium Development Goals and sustainable development'. Online. Available HTTP <http://register.consilium.europa.eu/pdf/en/06/st10/st10917.en06.pdf> (accessed 24 July 2012).

103 Ibid.

104 Statement, op. cit., preamble, para. 1.

105 See Corporate Operational Plan, op. cit.; EIB, 'Environmental and Social Practices Handbook', 24/2/2010, p. 11 (hereinafter the 'Handbook'). Online. Available HTTP <http://www.eib.org/attachments/thematic/environmental_and_social_practices_handbook.pdf> (accessed 24 July 2012). See also generally European Commission, 'The Sixth Environment Action Programme of the European Community 2002–2012'. Online. Available HTTP <http://ec.europa.eu/environment/newprg/intro.htm> (accessed 24 July 2012).

106 Statement, op. cit., p. 10.

107 Ibid., para. 4, p. 10.

seeks to increase environmental and social benefits, and decrease environmental and social costs.[108]

The Statement lists the sources of the EIB's environmental and social principles and standards: the over-arching environmental principles contained in the Treaty; the fundamental human rights referred to in the EU Charter; relevant EU environmental and social legislations; internationally recognized and sector-specific good environmental and social practices; and a minimum set of social standards, 'in line with the requirements of the multilateral development banks, consistent with those identified in the Charter'.[109] The Statement requires that all the projects the EIB finances within the EU comply with the relevant environmental principles contained in international conventions incorporated in EU law,[110] in the Treaties[111] and in EU secondary law,[112] notably concerning environmental impact assessments (EIAs). Within the EU such principles are binding on project promoters, but the EIB reserves the right to set higher standards where appropriate.[113] Outside the EU, the EIB also uses EU law standards as benchmarks,[114] even if they are more stringent than those applicable in the national legislation. Application of EU standards is, however, subject to practical feasibility and project promoters must justify derogations.[115]

The EIB applies a 'human rights-based approach' to social issues, focusing on the standards contained in the Charter of Fundamental Rights as well as on

---

108 Ibid., pp. 11 ff.
109 Ibid., para. 8, p. 7.
110 See ibid., paras 36–38, p. 16. 'Phased compliance' is allowed in enlargement countries subject to certain conditions and justification of the project promoter.
111 Such as the integration principle (Art. 6 TFEU), and that of aiming at a high level of environmental protection based on the precautionary principle (Art. 95(3) and 174(2) TFEU). Statement, op. cit., para. 23, p. 13,
112 Emission standards and 'ambient' standards are discussed (Statement, op. cit., paras 33–34, pp. 15–16.), and compiled in the 'Sourcebook on EU Environmental Law', Study prepared for the EPE Banks, 19/12/2008. Online. Available HTTP <http://www.eib.org/attachments/strategies/sourcebook_on_eu_environmental_law_en.pdf> (accessed 24 July 2012).
113 Statement, op. cit., para. 18, p. 8.
114 Ibid, para. 20, p. 8: 'Within the EU, the EIB assumes that EU environmental and social law has been correctly transposed into national law and that national law is being enforced by the responsible authorities. EIB due diligence focuses particularly on countries and/or specific laws where there is evidence to suggest these assumptions may be false.' Principles contained in bilateral and partnership agreements concluded with the EU in its external relations also apply. Ibid., para. 19, p. 8.
115 See ibid. para. 40, p. 17: 'for a variety of reasons, including institutional capacity, technological capability, availability of investment funds and consumer ability and willingness to pay, for a particular project the immediate achievement of EU requirements may not be practical and, in some cases, may not be desirable. When the case arises, it is incumbent on the promoter to provide an acceptable justification to the Bank for a deviation from EU standards, within the framework of the environmental and social principles and standards set out in the Statement. In such cases, provision should be made for a phased approach to higher standards.'

'international good practices'.[116] Remarkably, the Statement does not explicitly refer to international *legal norms* such as the International Labour Organization (ILO) Conventions, though it mentions such instruments in passing.[117] The Statement logically implies that EU legal requirements must be met by projects funded inside the EU and assumes they will be enforced by national authorities, but it is less adamant on the benchmarking of out-of-EU projects against EU social requirements. Despite the existence of a 'Sourcebook of EU Social Law',[118] the normative references are quite vague, and are chiefly to the 'Guidance Notes' that the EIB established on social issues (see below), and to MLI best practices.[119] The Statement briefly discusses its approach to involuntary resettlement, indigenous people and other vulnerable groups, ILO Core Labour Standards, and Occupational Health and Safety.[120] These short and general discussions concerning a limited range of social issues may, however, not be said to set 'standards' as such.

The third tier of the EIB's set of substantive accountability principles seeks to clarify the concrete operation of social and environmental standards in the EIB's lending activities. What the EIB calls its 'operational frame-work for integrating environment and social issues into EIB financing' is contained in its 'Environmental and Social Practices Handbook' (the 'Handbook'),[121] the last version of which is dated February 2010. The Handbook restates the environmental and social principles and standards applied by the EIB, in a more exhaustive and precise way than the Statement, as well as the fact that all projects are – in principle – supposed to comply with them.[122] It also lists a number of accountability 'safeguards' of a more procedural nature.[123]

The Handbook then describes how these standards are applied throughout the life of the project, from its consideration for financing to its approval, launch and monitoring. Projects undergo a pre-appraisal and an appraisal phase regarding social and environmental issues prior to approval, and continued monitoring thereafter. At the pre-appraisal stage they are screened against social and environmental risks (notably to identify applicable substantive standards[124]), and categorized according to their various environmental and

---

116 Ibid., para. 46, p. 17.
117 Ibid., paras 53–54, pp. 18–19, citing the ILO Core Labour Standards or the UN Declaration on the Rights of Indigenous Peoples.
118 See Handbook, op. cit., para. 22, p. 16 and 'Sourcebook on EU Social Law – Prepared by Christopher Wright, University of Oslo, for the European Investment Bank', 4 October 2010, available from the EIB Information Desk (infodesk@eib.org) upon request, and on file with the authors.
119 Statement, op. cit., para. 49, p. 18.
120 Ibid., paras 51 ff., pp. 18–19. The Statement also discusses standards regarding cultural heritage (paras 56 ff.); consultation, participation and public disclosure (paras 59 ff., see *infra*); biological diversity (paras 67 ff.); and climate change (paras 75 ff.).
121 Handbook, op. cit., p. 9.
122 See ibid., pp. 16–17.
123 See e.g. ibid., p. 17, Table B.
124 E.g. the EU law requirement of an Environmental Impact Assessment (EIA). Handbook, op. cit., p. 30.

social impacts.[125] The pre-appraisal phase also includes obtaining the advice of the Commission.[126] The ensuing appraisal phase then enquires into whether and under what conditions projects may be approved.[127] During that phase, the EIB reviews the results of the EIAs (if one was required under relevant EU law[128]) and of the Social Impact Assessments (as established under the Social Assessment Guidance Notes[129]). It also checks compliance with other relevant legal requirements (such as compliance with the biodiversity norms contained in the Birds and Habitat Directives) and a number of other elements.[130] All this information then yields an 'Environmental and Social Impact Rating' reflecting the degree of social and environmental risk (low, moderate or high) associated with the project. The rating must be supported by stated reasons[131] and is included in the Appraisal Report, along with proposed environmental and social conditions and monitoring requirements to be included in the finance contract.[132] Based on the non-binding[133] Appraisal Report, the Board of Directors makes the final decision on approval or rejection.[134]

These sets of substantive environmental and social standards have been criticized by external observers. Although the EIB's requirement of compliance with EU law where it applies (i.e. within the EU) must be approved, the strength of the reference to EU law as a benchmark for out-of-EU projects is

125 Ibid., pp. 22 ff.
126 See 'Art. 19 procedure', above note 56, and Handbook, op. cit., p. 32. DG ECFIN is responsible for contacts with the EIB, and has set up the 'Groupe Interservice BEI' (GIB). The GIB prepares collegiate opinions on behalf of the Commission regarding the compliance with EU rules and policies of financing requests (see EC, 'Coordination with the European Investment Bank'. Online. Available HTTP <http://ec.europa.eu/economy_finance/financial_operations/coordination/eib/index_en.htm>, accessed 24 July 2012).
127 See generally EIB, 'Appraisal'. Online. Available HTTP <http://www.eib.org/projects/cycle/appraisal/index.htm> (accessed 24 July 2012).
128 See Handbook, op. cit., pp. 38 ff.
129 The Guidance Notes are found in Annex 13 to the Handbook, and relate to involuntary resettlement, labour, vulnerable groups, community health and safety, and community participation. See also the Social Impact Assessment procedure, based on the Guidance Notes, in the Handbook, op. cit., pp. 52 ff.
130 See a summary of the Environmental and Social Assessment in the Appraisal Phase (Handbook, op. cit., pp. 40–41). The assessment varies with the type of loan applied for. Other elements to be assessed relate to climate change (pp. 50 ff. of the Handbook), to the Environmental and Social capacity of the promoter (pp. 54 ff.), to public consultation and participation (pp. 55 ff.), and to disclosure of information (pp. 56 ff.).
131 Along four categories: A (acceptable with positive or neutral residual impacts – low risk); B (acceptable with minor negative residual impacts – low or moderate risk); C (acceptable with major negative residual impacts – moderate or high risk); and D (not acceptable – high risks). D-rated projects are normally 'screened out' at the end of the pre-appraisal stage. See Handbook, op. cit., pp. 58–61.
132 Ibid., p. 70. See the points covered in the report in EIB, 'The Project Cycle at the European Investment Bank', 12/7/2001, pp. 4–5. Online. Available HTTP <http://www.eib.org/attachments/strategies/cycle_en.pdf> (accessed 24 July 2012).
133 See, however, the checks and balances included in Art. 19 Statute (see above note 55).
134 Handbook, op. cit., p. 60.

less convincing, in particular outside (potential) candidate countries, where EU standards are only applied 'if practical and feasible' (or, in critics' words: 'where appropriate'[135]), with very vague conditions for derogation.[136] The open-endedness of the additional international environmental and social norms and standards which the EIB applies[137] is also a cause of concern. In addition, the appraisal of environmental issues at the EIB relies greatly on EIAs when they are required by relevant EU rules. The responsibility for EIAs falls to the project promoter (which may create conflicts of interest) and the EIB staff is suspected of doing little cross-examination.[138] To summarize, the above suggests that, to a significant extent, the EIB's principles, standards and operational policies do not constitute a firm substantive accountability framework containing clear-cut performance standards which the EIB binds itself to *apply* in relation to all projects it finances. Rather, they look like an indicative list of potentially relevant elements which the EIB will *consider* in making its finance decisions. An opposite remark can also be made regarding the general use of EU standards as benchmarks for projects outside the EU. Should this be pushed too far, the EIB risks appearing paternalistic or somewhat imperialist in applying EU law beyond its jurisdiction.

Criticism has also arisen in respect of social standards. Social aspects of projects within the EU are covered by the national authorities' application of EU law. For projects outside the EU, the EIB is developing a 'Results Measurement (REM) Framework' for appraising whether projects are consistent with the EIB's mandate, objectives, policies and standards.[139] In respect of social issues specifically, the Statement indicates that '[t]he EIB restricts its financing to projects that respect human rights and comply with EIB social standards, based on the principles of the Charter of the Fundamental Rights of the European Union and international good practices.'[140] The benchmark for this commitment is the 'EU social *acquis*, i.e. the body of laws, principles, policy objectives, declarations, resolutions and international agreements defining the social policy of the EU',[141] which are substantiated in an 'EIB Reference

---

135 See Wright, op. cit. However, national legislation and international conventions ratified by the host country must always be complied with. (Statement, op. cit., para. 39, p. 16).
136 Handbook, op. cit., p. 40.
137 The Statement lists examples (op. cit., para. 43, p. 17): Recommendations of the World Commission on Dams; findings and recommendations of the Extractive Industry Review; the rules of the Extractive Industry Transparency Initiative; FSC principles, EMAS Scheme. The Equator Principles are not listed, though the EIB is prepared to work on that basis 'in case of co-financing'. See ibid., para. 23, p. 9.
138 See Wilks, op. cit., p. 20, and Decision of the European Ombudsman closing his inquiry into complaint 244/2006/(BM)JMA against the EIB, 4/5/2009. Online. Available HTTP <http://www.ombudsman.europa.eu/cases/home.faces> (accessed 24 July 2012).
139 On the Results Measurement (REM) Framework, see EIB, 'Measuring development results'. Online. Available HTTP <http://www.eib.org/attachments/country/eib_rem_results_en.pdf> (accessed 23 July 2012).
140 Statement, op. cit., para. 46, p. 17.
141 Handbook, op. cit., p. 16, and fn. 7.

Book on EU Social Legislation'[142] and in EIB Social Assessment Guidance Notes. The Guidance Notes are five short documents specifying the standards and requirements of the EIB with regard to (i) involuntary resettlement; (ii) the rights and interests of vulnerable groups; (iii) labour standards; (iv) occupational and community health and safety; and (v) public consultation and participation in project preparation.[143] These Guidance Notes provide a framework to EIB staff for appraising projects in regard of social issues.[144] They have been criticized for their 'lack of clarity, consistency and comprehensiveness',[145] but are being revised (Guidance Notes on vulnerable groups and on public consultation and participation are still in progress). Guidance Notes are organized in reference to EIB appraisal procedures and contain references to applicable international norms, standards and EU legislation. However, they are guidelines addressed to EIB staff for preparing Appraisal Reports, but arguably do not constitute firm substantive commitments binding the EIB.

Arguably, more social issues than the five identified in the Guidance Notes can arise in relation to a project. The EIB acknowledges this,[146] but no specific standard or guidance note is available in such case. Additionally, the EIB lacks a self-standing human rights policy.[147] The EIB repeatedly refers to the Charter and claims that it will not finance projects violating human rights[148] or located in countries declared 'off limits' for human rights motives by the European Council.[149] Despite this 'precautionary' stance, the External Mandate nevertheless makes 'eligible' a number of countries known for their poor human rights record or situation of armed conflict, such as Afghanistan, Libya, Iraq, Syria or Cambodia. Moreover, a country such as Belarus may become eligible upon decision of the Commission, based 'on an overall political assessment, including aspects related to the democracy, human rights and fundamental freedoms'.[150]

Human rights considerations are therefore weakly embedded into the EIB's appraisal and monitoring process,[151] as human rights impact assessments are not mainstreamed in practice. A credible EIB human rights policy could,

---

142 See 'Sourcebook on EU Social Law', op. cit.

143 See Annex 13 of Handbook, op. cit.

144 In this regard, all Guidance Notes contain a checklist of relevant elements to be verified.

145 See Wright, op. cit., pp. 51–52.

146 According to the Handbook (op. cit., p. 52), such issues 'may relate . . . to governance, transparency and capacity issues; conflict potential and sensitivity related to access to resources or allocation of project benefits; exacerbated inequalities; and complex institutional environments and social dynamics'.

147 Wright, op. cit., p. 27.

148 See e.g. EIB, 'Corporate Social Responsibility Report 2011, p. 36. Online. Available HTTP <http://www.eib.org/attachments/general/reports/crr2011_en.pdf> (accessed 25 July 2012).

149 See Statement, op. cit., para. 46, p. 17.

150 See External Mandate, op. cit., recital 10, Art. 4, and Annexes II and III.

151 Mid-Term Review, op. cit., pp. 15–16.

however, make a significant difference, e.g. for human rights in business.[152] In response to this criticism, and in light of the widely recognized UN-endorsed 'protect, respect and remedy' business and human rights framework,[153] the EIB has clarified that its 'approach to human rights is focused on respect for environmental, social and economic rights in direct link with EIB-financed projects'. It is reviewing its social standards and operational practices to align them with the framework.[154] Finally, an accountability gap exists for 'Global Loans', i.e. loans made to other institutions for financing investment projects pursuing certain objectives.[155] In such cases, environmental and social appraisals are the responsibility of the intermediary institution, and EIB safeguards are *de facto* bypassed.[156]

In conclusion, where EU law is not binding, i.e. outside the EU, the EIB environmental and social standards for projects are deficient[157] and do not constitute a firm substantive benchmark for assessing EIB action. As a remedy, authors suggested the setting up of a definite list of 'no-go' areas or sectors.[158] And indeed, the EIB now publishes an indicative list of 'activities excluded from EIB lending'.[159] The list is general, but it specifically excludes munitions and weapons, as well as military/police equipment or infrastructure. Observers have, moreover, noted that the EIB's environmental and social standards and its operational practices are rather descriptive and hardly operative. They are

---

152 In this regard, see the discussion on the role of Export Credit Agencies in UN Human Rights Council, 'Protect, Respect and Remedy: a Framework for Business and Human Rights – Report of the Special Representative of the Secretary-General on the Issue of Human Rights and Transnational Corporations and Other Business Enterprises, John Ruggie', 7/4/2008, A/HRC/8/5, paras 39–41.

153 Ibid.

154 See EIB, 'The EIB approach to human rights'. Online. Available HTTP <http://www.eib.org/about/news/business-and-human-rights.htm> (accessed 24 July 2012).

155 Handbook, op. cit., p. 44.

156 See Wilks, op. cit., p. 25. Global Loans are used in the framework of the EIB's contribution to the Commission's crisis recovery plan (see above) to support to SMEs. See Counter Balance, 'European Investment Bank and the economic crisis', op. cit., p. 4, noting that intermediary institutions 'will be responsible for evaluating each loan application submitted by an SME. For most operations, it will be entirely up to the intermediary bank to decide whether or not to grant a loan to the SME'. The External Mandate (op. cit., recital 19), however, contains the following hortatory language: 'Where appropriate, through its cooperation with those intermediary institutions, the EIB should request that their clients' projects be checked against criteria in line with Union development goals so as to provide added value.'

157 According to CSO reports, a number of dysfunctional projects tend to corroborate this. See, e.g. the numerous reports published by the NGO 'Counter Balance'. Online. Available HTTP <http://www.counterbalance-eib.org/?cat=3> (accessed 24 July 2012).

158 Like the IFC's exclusion list. Online. Available HTTP <http://www1.ifc.org/wps/wcm/connect/Topics_Ext_Content/IFC_External_Corporate_Site/IFC+Sustainability/Sustainability+Framework/IFC+Exclusion+List/> (accessed 24 July 2012). See Wilks, op. cit., p. 23.

159 EIB, 'Excluded Activities'. Online. Available HTTP <http://www.eib.org/attachments/documents/excluded_activities_2012_en.pdf> (accessed 24 July 2012).

more an 'aid to project preparation' for staff than real social safeguards engaging the EIB.[160] Likewise, the ESO (see above), composed of experts in social and environmental issues, plays a support and advice role at the margins of the project cycle, and has no power to oppose the financing of a project. Accordingly, the Mid-Term Review pointed out deficiencies in the application of the standards and recommended that the 'due diligence process' and the project monitoring be strengthened, notably in respect of social standards.[161] Causes for all this may be the EIB's limited staff resources,[162] but also the fact that generally it seems to value the volume of the money lent rather than the quality of the projects financed. Staff are in this regard insufficiently trained to assess the non-financial aspects of projects,[163] and are incentivized – via bonuses – based only on the volume of loans extended.[164] Therefore, if the EIB is to really support EU external policies, including the promotion of sustainable development, current practices should be profoundly revised.[165] As a first step in that direction, the External Mandate has included since 2011 an obligation for the EIB to appraise and monitor the social, environmental and human rights aspects of projects (Article 7). Notably, it provides for the development by the EIB of 'performance indicators in relation to development, environmental and human rights aspects of projects' (Article 6.2), on which it will have to report on a yearly basis (Article 7.3). Additionally, it urges the EIB to devote sufficient human and financial resources to external activities (recital 35). In conclusion, though the EIB's lending volume exceeds that of other MLIs, its substantive accountability standards seem off the mark compared to MLIs' best practices, this in several respects ranging from the clarity and comprehensiveness of the applicable standards to their binding and operational character.[166]

9.4.2 Procedural accountability principles

In this section we analyse three procedural principles that are instrumental in operationalizing accountability relationships between authorities or power

---

160 T. Griffiths, 'Making the Grade: A survey of IFI social policies, international development standards and the policies of the European Investment Bank (EIB)', 31/12/2006, p. 32. Online. Available HTTP <http://www.forestpeoples.org/sites/fpp/files/publication/2010/08/eibifipoliciesbankwatchdec06eng.pdf> (accessed 24 July 2012).

161 Mid-Term Review, op. cit., pp. 16 and 24.

162 The Mid-Term Review points out in this regard that '[c]ompared to other IFIs, the EIB present the highest ratio in terms of lending volume per staff member.' Ibid., p. 26. See also Wilks, op. cit., p. 12.

163 Mid-Term Review, op. cit., p. 15.

164 See Wilks, op. cit., p. 12.

165 Mid-Term Review, op. cit., p. 26.

166 See e.g. the EBRD's 'performance requirements' in its 'Environmental and Social Policy', May 2008. Online. Available HTTP <http://www.ebrd.com/downloads/about/sustainability/2008policy.pdf> (accessed 24 July 2012), or the World Bank's 'operational and safeguard policies', contained in its 'Operational Manual' (see World Bank, 'Operational Manual', last version 20/10/2011. Online. Available HTTP <http://go.worldbank.org/DZDZ9038D0>, accessed 24 July 2012). For a comparison see Wright, op. cit.

wielders and their public or external stakeholders. Procedural principles are necessary to ensure that an entity acts in conformity with the substantive principles it is bound to follow. The three principles are transparency, participation and remedies.

9.4.2.1 A meta-principle: transparency

We define transparency as the degree of access of the public to information concerning an institution, person or entity. Transparency acts as an enabler of accountability.[167] Lack of transparency hinders the activation of accountability channels,[168] as stakeholders are not aware of the relevant facts and practices.[169] Democratic accountability requires that governing entities adopt an active policy of openness towards their stakeholders, through disclosure of information and documents.[170] The degree of openness or transparency of a person or entity is a function of four variables: the fullness of the disclosed information (i.e. what is disclosed or kept confidential); its accessibility (location, language, cost, etc.); its timeliness (before or after relevant decisions, etc.); and the existence and quality of a recourse to dissatisfied information-seekers.[171]

Transparency is one of the EU's fundamental governance principles as per Articles 1 TEU and 15 TFEU. In relation to it, however, the EIB struggles with the intricacies of its dual nature: a bank on the one hand, requiring client confidentiality; and an EU body on the other, demanding accountability to the public.[172] The EIB's special transparency regime (Article 15, para. 3 TFEU) arguably recognizes this duality, as it states that the institutions' general transparency regime and the citizens' right of access to documents only apply to the EIB 'when exercising [its] administrative tasks'. While this notion – added by the Lisbon Treaty – is quite elusive, it might be suspected to leave out the documents of the EIB acting as a bank *per se*, especially finance contracts. It is difficult to assess what impact this may have on the applicability to the EIB of EU law regarding access to documents. As a matter of international law, the Aarhus Convention on public transparency and participation regarding

---

167 See T. N. Hale and A.-M. Slaughter, 'Transparency: Possibilities and Limitations', *The Fletcher Forum of World Affairs* 30, 2006, 153.

168 On this notion of accountability 'channels', see, among many other sources, R. Mulgan, *Holding Power to Account: Accountability in Modern Democracy*, Basingstoke: Palgrave MacMillan, 2003; in the EU context see C. Harlow, *Accountability in the European Union*, Oxford: Oxford University Press, 2002.

169 Stiglitz argues that transparency reduces information asymmetries, and the risk of abuse or mismanagement. (J. Stiglitz, 'Transparency in Government', in *The Right to Tell – The Role of Mass Media in Economic Development*, Washington D.C.: WBI Development Studies, 2002, pp. 28–29.)

170 Ibid., pp. 29–31.

171 P. J. Nelson, 'Transparency Mechanisms at the Multilateral Development Banks', *World Development* 29, 2001, 1836.

172 See Amoyel, op. cit., p. 270, characterizing the EIB's position as 'dichotomous'.

environmental matters[173] encompasses EIB acts, and therefore the EU Regulation implementing the Aarhus Convention (the 'Aarhus Regulation')[174] applies to the EIB. Its Article 3 extends to the EIB the scope of Regulation 1049/2001 regarding public access to the documents of the EU Institutions[175] for what regards 'environmental information'.[176] For acts containing other sorts of information, it is clear from its title that Regulation 1049/2001 only applies to European Parliament, Council and Commission documents and not to the EIB.[177] However, given the new Article 15(3) TFEU, it seems that the Regulation could be amended so as to include EIB documents, but only as they concern its 'administrative tasks'.

In any event, the EIB has long adopted a 'Transparency Policy', its last version in February 2010,[178] which recognizes that the EIB is a bank *and a public institution* and that it must therefore be accountable to EU citizens and other stakeholders, owing them transparency on its operations.[179] In this respect, the EIB views transparency as 'an environment in which the objectives of policies, its legal, institutional, and economic framework, policy decisions and their rationale, and the terms of EIB accountability, are provided to the public in a comprehensive, accessible and timely manner'.[180] Operational decisions, such as project-related decisions, are excluded from this definition, which only addresses 'policies'.

---

173 Regulation (EC) No. 1367/2006 of the European Parliament and of the Council of 6 September 2006 on the application of the provisions of the Aarhus Convention on Access to Information, Public Participation in Decision-making and Access to Justice in Environmental Matters to Community Institutions and Bodies, *OJ* L 264/13, 25/9/2006.

174 See UNECE Convention on Access to Information, Public Participation in Decision-making and Access to Justice in Environmental Matters, done in Aarhus on 25/61998, effective 30/10/2001.

175 Regulation (EC) No. 1049/2001 of the European Parliament and of the Council of 30 May 2001 regarding public access to European Parliament, Council and Commission documents, *OJ* L 145/43, 31/5/2001.

176 See EIB, 'Access to Environmental Information', 28/6/2007. Online. Available HTTP <http://www.eib.org/projects/documents/access_to_information.htm>; and 'EIB applies the Aarhus Regulation on public access to environmental information'. Online. Available HTTP <http://www.eib.org/about/news/eib-applies-the-aarhus-regulation-on-public-access-to-environmental-information.htm> (both accessed 24 July 2012).

177 The EIB held this position against a complaint before the European Ombudsman for refusing to disclose a loan contract not containing environmental information. See Decision of the European Ombudsman closing his inquiry into complaint 2145/2009/RT against the EIB, 12/3/2010, para. 11. Online. Available HTTP <http://www.ombudsman.europa.eu/cases/home.faces> (accessed 24 July 2012).

178 EIB, 'The EIB Transparency Policy', 2/2/2010 (hereinafter 'Transparency Policy'). Online. Available HTTP <http://www.eib.org/attachments/strategies/transparency_policy_en.pdf> (accessed 24 July 2012).

179 Ibid, point i.2, p. 4.

180 Ibid., point i.5, p. 4.

Being an EU public body,[181] the EIB finds the source of its transparency policy in the EU Treaties and legislation. Complementing the provisions of the Treaties applicable to the EIB,[182] the Transparency Policy is designed so as to 'take account of and comply with' the regulation concerning public access to institutions' documents[183] and the principles of the European Transparency Initiative,[184] the Aarhus Regulation, and the regulation concerning the protection of personal data.[185] Importantly, the Transparency Policy states that, in the case of discrepancy between it and the applicable EU legislation or the Aarhus Convention, the latter two will prevail.[186] The primary transparency principle at the EIB is that all information shall in principle be disclosed upon request or by publication[187] (presumption of disclosure) in a non-discriminatory manner and without privileged treatment,[188] unless there is a 'compelling reason' for non-disclosure.[189] The 'compelling reasons' accounting for exceptions to the general disclosure regime are exposed in the Transparency Policy, and most importantly include the protection of: the public interest, as regards international relations or the financial, monetary or economic policy of the EU, its institutions and bodies or a Member State; privacy and the integrity of the individual, in particular in accordance with EU legislation regarding the protection of personal data; commercial interests of a natural or legal person; intellectual property; court proceedings and legal advice; and the purpose of inspections, investigations and

181 Ibid., point ii.7, p. 5.
182 See Art. 1 TEU, and Art. 15 TFEU, on openness of the institutions, and Art. 6 TEU on democracy.
183 Regulation (EC) No. 1049/2001, op. cit.
184 See European Commission, 'Green Paper – European Transparency Initiative', 3/5/2006, COM(2006) 194 final. Generally Online. Available HTTP <http://ec.europa.eu/transparency/eti/index_en.htm#1> (accessed 24 July 2012).
185 Regulation (EC) No. 45/2001 of the European Parliament and of the Council of 18 December 2000 on the protection of individuals with regard to the processing of personal data by the Community institutions and bodies and on the free movement of such data, *OJ* L 8/1, 12/1/2001.
186 On all this, see Transparency Policy, op. cit., point ii.8, p. 5.
187 Ibid., point 4.1.2, p. 16. The EIB publishes the 'documents that are of general public interest, which could interest a large number of stakeholders and/or members of the public'. A list of such documents is included in Annex 1 to the Policy (p. 22) and concerns mostly general documents on the policies, standards and practices of the EIB. Exceptions to disclosure are only valid as long as justified and at most 30 years (point 4.1.4, p. 16). The archives of the EIB, some up until 1980, are available at the European University Institute (Florence). Online. Available HTTP <http://www.eib.org/infocentre/publications/archives/index.htm> (accessed 24 July 2012).
188 Also, see Transparency Policy, op. cit., point 5.1.3, p. 9: the Bank applies a language regime taking account of the public's needs. The EIB's statutory documents and key documents with a particular importance for the public are available in all EU languages. Others are in at least English, French and German with possible translations.
189 Ibid., point 5, p. 9.

audits.[190] In particular, the EIB is mindful to preserve the degree of confidentiality required by the commercial interests of its clients, particularly its private clients.[191] Concretely, the EIB has, in principle, refused to disclose, for example, the finance contracts it signs with its clients, for reasons ranging from professional secrecy under Article 339 TFEU to the 'professional ethics, rules and practices of the banking sector'.[192] The EIB has also been somewhat reluctant to disclose documents related to finance contracts, such as appraisal or monitoring reports, on the grounds that they concern 'the professional evaluation and opinions forming part of the EIB's internal decision-making process'.[193]

The policy, however, states that the EIB must interpret exceptions to access to environmental information restrictively,[194] but, as the above indicates, exceptions are rather open-ended, leaving room for interpretation.[195] Any denial of access must be stated,[196] and the exceptions are largely copied from the applicable EU regulations. The extensive case law from the ECJ on the matter may provide interpretative guidance.[197] In case the EIB refuses to disclose information, a confirmatory application may be filed, or a complaint to the Complaints Mechanism (see below). Information requests must normally be handled within fifteen working days, unless an extension is necessary for reasons of language or complexity.[198] A reasonable fee may additionally be charged.[199]

Though they are not perfect,[200] the EIB's transparency practices generally compare well with those of other MLIs.[201] Two issues in particular merit

---

190 Ibid., point 5.2.2. and 5.2.3, pp. 9–10. The last four reasons being trumped by 'an overriding public interest', normally presumed for emissions into the environment (ibid., point 5.2.3, p. 10)

191 Ibid., point 5.2.8, p. 10. Other exceptions exist, notably as regards the Bank's own borrowing activities.

192 See Decision of the European Ombudsman on complaint 948/2006/BU against the EIB, 28/9/2007 (Online. Available HTTP <http://www.ombudsman.europa.eu/cases/home. faces>, accessed 24 July 2012), against a decision of the EIB not to disclose a finance contract with the Slovak Republic, on the grounds that 'as in any banking relationship, the Finance Contract was considered confidential in the interest of the consumer'.

193 Decision of the European Ombudsman on complaint 1807/2006/MHZ, op. cit. The EIB ended up disclosing the documents, and its decisions were here made on the basis of a former version of its rules on access to documents.

194 Transparency Policy, op. cit., point 5.2.6, p. 10.

195 One World Trust, 'EIB Accountability Profile', 9/12/2008. Online. Available HTTP <http://www.oneworldtrust.org/index.php?option=com_docman&task=cat_view& gid=81&Itemid=55> (accessed 24 July 2012).

196 Transparency Policy, op. cit., point 5.2.11, p. 10 and point 4.5.10, p. 18.

197 The European Ombudsman often refers to such case law in information disclosure cases.

198 Transparency Policy, op. cit., point 4.5.5, p. 17.

199 Ibid., point 4.5.13, p. 18.

200 See European Parliament, 'Resolution of 29 March 2012 on the European Investment Bank (EIB) – Annual Report 2010' (2011/2186(INI)), esp. paras. 16, 59, 62, 63.

201 The One World Trust ranks the EIB first among Intergovernmental Organizations with regard to transparency. On the World Bank, see B. Jenkins, 'The World Bank's

examination. First, the EIB's disclosure practices during a project's appraisal, i.e. before the Board of Directors' approval and the signature of the contract, are problematic, as the 'Proposal from the Management Committee to the Board of Directors', that is, the assessment as to whether and why a project should be financed, is not released prior to its approval.[202] After approval, public sector project proposals are disclosed on request. For private sector projects, 'information designated by the Bank's private sector counterparts as confidential cannot be disclosed'.[203] The EIB publishes a list of the projects on its website at least three weeks prior to a Board decision,[204] with 'project summaries'. The focus in those summaries is placed on environmental and social issues.[205] All public projects are listed, as well as all private sector projects responding to a call for tender in the Official Journal, and/or which required an EIA. Publication of private projects may be dispensed with to protect certain commercial interests.[206] Where an EIA is required, the project promoter must prepare a non-technical summary (NTS), and an environmental impact statement (EIS) in a language accessible to the local public. The promoter must publicize these documents, and the EIB provides, if possible, a link to them in the Projects List.[207]

Such a policy may defeat the accountability-enabling function of transparency. If only summary information is released shortly before approval, and if 'sensitive' projects may escape disclosure for commercial reasons, stakeholders will not be able to call the EIB to account before the project is on track, which resembles a policy of *fait accompli*.[208] But accountability is also prospective and entails that an institution should 'take account' of stakeholders' interests and preferences when acting.[209] In this regard, the absent or incomplete information disclosure

New Access to Information Policy – Conceptual Leap with Limits', Study for the Bank Information Center and the Global Transparency Initiative, March 2010. Online. Available <http://www.bicusa.org/en/Document.102097.aspx> (accessed 24 July 2012).

202 Transparency Policy, op. cit., point 4.3.1, p. 16.
203 Ibid.
204 The list is called the 'project pipeline' (EIB, 'Projects to be financed'. Online. Available HTTP <http://www.eib.org/projects/pipeline/index.htm>, accessed 24 July 2012). Regarding the completeness of those summaries, in comparison to those of, e.g., the EBRD, an NGO writes: 'If you open at random a project description page on the website of the [EBRD], and then do the same on the EIB's website, it's not unlike comparing – respectively – a work of Tolstoy with a Japanese haiku'. See Counter Balance, 'European Investment Bank and the economic crisis', op. cit., pp. 3–4.
205 Handbook, op. cit., p. 34.
206 Transparency Policy, op. cit., point 4.3.2, p. 16.
207 Handbook, op. cit., p. 56.
208 One World Trust, 'Submission to the European Investment Bank to contribute to the second round of public consultation on the review of EIB's Public Disclosure Policy', 18/11/2005, p. 3. Online. Available HTTP <http://www.eib.org/attachments/general/events/contribution2_oneworldtrust.pdf> (accessed 24 July 2012).
209 On this idea of accountability as 'responsiveness', see R. Mulgan, 'Accountability: An Ever-Expanding Concept', *Public Administration* 78, 2000, 566 ff.

prior to project approval precludes stakeholders from providing meaningful input on, or from opposing, a project.

The EIB also faces criticism for its reluctance to disclose finance *contracts*. Earlier transparency policies explicitly excluded disclosure of finance contracts, save the client's waiver.[210] Such a radical position was at odds with the Aarhus Convention, whose Compliance Committee found that environmental clauses of a finance contract could qualify as 'environmental information' to be disclosed under the Convention, notably when 'there is a significant public interest in disclosure . . . and a relatively small amount of harm to the [other] interests involved'.[211] The EU Ombudsman in turn found that confidentiality could justify refusing to disclose a loan contract, subject to the EIB's appreciation.[212] It now seems that the EIB has somewhat relaxed its position, and that it may stand fairly open to partial disclosures preserving confidential information where possible. The Transparency Policy also no longer embargoes finance contracts.[213] Such progress is arguably due in part to procedures regularly introduced by NGOs before the Aarhus Convention Compliance Committee, the European Ombudsman or the EIB Complaints Mechanism (see below). 'Framework Agreements', i.e. agreements between the EIB and a country setting a framework for cooperation, are disclosed upon request, unless the partner country opposes this.[214] The Aarhus Convention Compliance Committee found in this regard that a lack of consent from the other party was not as such a ground to refuse access to a financial contract.[215] One wonders whether the EIB will implement this provision, whereas the Transparency Policy gives precedence to the Convention in case of discrepancy. Finance contracts are the most relevant documents for properly overseeing the activities of the EIB on human rights, social and environmental counts. Barriers to accessing such documents therefore stymie the operation of the accountability mechanisms applicable to the EIB, and the practices of other MLIs are in some instances more liberal on these accounts.[216]

---

210 See Decision of the European Ombudsman on complaint 948/2006/BU against the EIB, op. cit.

211 See Aarhus Compliance Committee's findings with Regard to Communication ACCC/C/2007/21 Concerning Compliance by the European Community with Its Obligations under the Convention, as adopted by the Compliance Committee at its 23rd Meeting, Geneva, 31 March–3 April 2009, pp. 6–7, paras 30 (b) and (c). Online. Available HTTP <http://www.unece.org/fileadmin/DAM/env/pp/compliance/C2007-21/Findings/ece_mp.pp_c.1_2009_2_add.1_eng.pdf> (accessed 24 July 2012).

212 European Ombudsman, op. cit., para. 1.11.

213 Transparency policy, op. cit., point 5.2.6, p. 10.

214 Ibid., point 4.2.1, p. 16.

215 See Aarhus Compliance Committee, op. cit., para. 31(b), p. 7.

216 See Nelson, op. cit., especially the chart at p. 1840. Comp. with EBRD, 'Public Information Policy', July 2011, Online. Available HTTP <http://www.ebrd.com/downloads/policies/pip/pipe.pdf> (accessed 24 July 2012). For a comparison of transparency practices across MLI, not covering the EIB, see Carrasco et al., op. cit.

9.4.2.2 Participation

Accountability has a prospective and a retrospective dimension. Participation is instrumental for prospective accountability, i.e. 'taking account' of the public's interests and preferences.[217] Stakeholder participation in government is also the most essential building block of democracy broadly understood,[218] a value having constitutional standing in the EU.[219] Participation of 'citizens' in the decisions of a government body is essential, yet true accountability requires that participation be extended to all 'stakeholders', i.e. those affected by such decisions.[220] The EIB acknowledges the necessity and the usefulness of stakeholder participation in its Transparency Policy, and intends to foster 'flows of information', so that information disclosure leads to dialogue between the EIB and its stakeholders.[221]

Participation in MLI activities must take place at the policy level and at operational level. Participation at the *policy level* means that the public must be enabled to weigh in on the definition of policies governing the pursuit of their missions by MLIs. The NGOs have been instrumental in emphasizing the public character of MLIs, and in their adoption of more socially and environmentally sensible policies.[222] Second, participation of stakeholders at *operational level* supposes that the EIB must engage with the people or groups affected by its decisions on particular projects, and reflect their views and interests in those decisions.

At policy level, the EIB has established an ongoing 'partnership' with civil society organizations (CSOs), taking various forms: consultations in the design of new policies;[223] annual briefing; and organization of, and participation in,

---

217 On the accountability–participation relationship, see M. W. Dowdle, 'Public Accountability: Conceptual, Historical and Epistemic Mappings', in M. W. Dowdle (ed.), *Public Accountability – Designs, Dilemmas and Experiences*, Cambridge: Cambridge University Press, 2006, pp. 12 and 20 ff.

218 See R.A. Dahl, *On Democracy*, New Haven: Yale University Press, 1998, pp. 35 ff. and H. Kelsen, 'Foundations of Democracy', *Ethics* 66, 1955, 1. In a global context, see G. De Búrca, 'Developing Democracy beyond the State', *Columbia Journal of Transnational Law* 46, 2008, 221.

219 See Art. 2 TEU, and Title II TEU, particularly Art. 8(3): 'Every citizen shall have the right to participate in the democratic life of the Union.'

220 The EIB recognizes this extended view of accountability in its Transparency Policy (op. cit., point i.4, p. 4), and defines a stakeholder as 'a person, a group or organisation who affects or can be affected by EIB Group's actions' (ibid., fn. 1). This is particularly important in a global context, where the categories of 'stakeholders' and 'citizens' do not entirely overlap. In this regard, see J.A. Scholte, 'Reconceptualizing Contemporary Democracy', *Indiana Journal of Global Legal Studies* 15, 2008, 305.

221 Transparency Policy, op. cit., point 1.2.1, p. 7.

222 See D.B. Hunter, 'Civil Society Networks and the Development of Environmental Standards at International Financial Institutions', *Chicago Journal of International Law* 8, 2007–2008, 437.

223 See Transparency Policy, op. cit., point 7.1, p. 11. See also in general EIB, 'Consultations'. Online. Available HTTP <http://www.eib.org/about/partners/cso/consultations/index.

CSO events.[224] To manage relations with CSOs, the EIB added a Civil Society Unit to its communication department.[225] The Civil Society Unit also implements the Transparency Policy. In addition, CSOs are also to some extent involved in the EIB's evaluation by its 'Operations Evaluation' division. However, stakeholders' engagement on policies is *ad hoc*, and the Transparency Policy simply states that the EIB may engage in public consultation 'on a voluntary basis', and on 'selected' policies.[226] This indicates that the EIB does not necessarily seek consultation on every policy revision.[227] The EIB therefore announces consultations on its website as they are required, with a timetable for the process.[228] So, for example, CSOs were consulted on the EIB's new Transparency Policy, and received two rounds of opportunity to comment on drafts.[229] The process was led by a 'Review Panel' composed of members of all EIB directorates having an interest in the contemplated policies.[230] The Board of Directors finally adopted the policy, having access to all the materials that were contributed to the consultation process. A problem in this respect may concern the real representativeness of the CSOs participating in the process. The objective of the EIB's 'engagement with civil society [is] to ensure that stakeholders are heard, and that the organization will respond adequately to their concerns. In this context, the EIB will prioritize stakeholders appropriately', and in this regard favours 'dialogue and cooperation with reputable international CSOs'.[231] It should, however, be kept in mind that international CSOs may

htm> (accessed 24 July 2012), and EIB, 'EIB Complaints Mechanism Policy, Public Disclosure Policy and Transparency Policy Review 2009 – Draft Consultation Report', February 2010. Online. Available HTTP <http://www.eib.org/attachments/consultations/consultation-report.pdf > (accessed 24 July 2012).

224 See EIB, 'Civil Society Events'. Online. Available HTTP <http://www.eib.org/about/partners/cso/events/index.htm> (accessed 24 July 2012). For the first time in late 2011, dialogue with civil society representatives took place at the level of the Board of Directors. See EIB, 'EIB Board values dialogue with civil society. Online. Available HTTP <http://www.eib.org/infocentre/events/all/board-of-directors-seminar-with-civil-society.htm> (accessed 25 July 2012).

225 See EIB, 'Contacts'. Online. Available HTTP <http://www.eib.org/about/partners/cso/contacts/index.htm> (accessed 24 July 2012).

226 Transparency Policy, op. cit., point 7.1, p. 11.

227 For example, the EIB was not planning to consult the public regarding its new Transport Lending Policy, and CSOs complained before the Complaints Office (now renamed 'Complaints Mechanism', see below), which recommended that the EIB engaged in consultation about this policy (see EIB Complaints Office, Conclusions Report, 16/12/2008. Online. Available HTTP <http://www.eib.org/about/cr/complaints/reporting/complaints_office_conclusions_report.pdf>, accessed 24 July 2012), which it did (see EIB, 'Public consultation on EIB's Transport Lending Policy'. Online. Available HTTP <http://www.eib.org/about/partners/cso/consultations/item/public-consultation-on-eibs-transport-lending-policy.htm>, accessed 24 July 2012).

228 Transparency Policy, op. cit., point 6, p. 19.

229 EIB, 'EIB Complaints Mechanism Policy, Public Disclosure Policy and Transparency Policy Review 2009 – Draft Consultation Report', op. cit.

230 Ibid., p. 1.

231 Transparency Policy, op. cit., points 6.1 and 6.3, p. 11.

themselves suffer from an accountability deficit, as many are first world organizations whose authority in representing the populations of developing countries is not necessarily straightforward.[232] The EIB in this regard did not set guidelines as to representativeness in its consultations, and seems to welcome any contribution, without proactively seeking dialogue with CSOs as representative of its stakeholders as possible.[233]

At operational level, the EIB recognizes that consulting local CSOs and direct stakeholders allows it to better appraise and monitor projects and to enhance their sustainability.[234] Stakeholder consultation for the EIB is essential throughout the life of a project, starting with the appraisal. Participation is one of the 'Standards' listed in the Statement,[235] as is it part of the Aarhus Convention which the EIB pledged to apply and which is implemented in EU law, notably in the EIA directive.[236] Stakeholder consultation should be conducted early in project appraisal, to resolve issues in a timely manner. For projects requiring an EIA under EU law (even if located outside the EU, as the EIA directive is the benchmark also for those projects[237]), consultation must follow the standards set by the Aarhus Convention, the EIA directive, the Strategic Environmental Assessment (SEA) Directive,[238] and the best practices in project finance:[239] it must be 'meaningful, transparent, and culturally appropriate', disseminate all information in a form and language appropriate to the relevant public, provide sufficient time for effective participation and include evidence that stakeholders' input was taken into account.[240] The EIB staff must ensure that the consultation was up to standard.[241] For projects not requiring an EIA under EU law, meaningful consultation should be conducted as well. For projects carried out outside the EU, the Statement provides that 'national law sets the minimum disclosure, consultation and participation

---

232 See e.g. P. Spiro, 'New Global Potentates: Nongovernmental Organizations and the Unregulated Marketplace', *Cardozo Law Review* 18, 1996–1997, 957.

233 Reports on the Transparency and Complaints Policies consultations, held in 2010, reveal that participating CSOs or individuals were mostly from the developed world. See EIB, 'EIB Complaints Mechanism Policy, Public Disclosure Policy and Transparency Policy Review 2009 – Draft Consultation Report', op. cit. The list of participants to the consultation on the new transport lending policy was not available at the time of writing.

234 See Transparency Policy, op. cit., point 5.3, p. 18. See also Statement, op. cit., para. 62, p. 20.

235 Statement, op. cit., paras 62 ff., p. 20.

236 Directive No. 85/337/EEC of the Council of 27 June 1985 on the assessment of the effects of certain public and private projects on the environment *OJ* L 175/40, 5 July 1985.

237 Handbook, op. cit., p. 133.

238 Directive No. 2001/42/EC of the European Parliament and of the Council of 27 June 2001 on the assessment of the effects of certain plans and programmes on the environment, *OJ*L197/30, 21/7/2001.

239 The EIB is developing consultation standards going beyond EIA requirements (Handbook, op. cit., p. 56)

240 Statement, op. cit., paras 63–64, p. 20.

241 Handbook, op. cit., p. 55.

requirements of the Bank'.[242] However, the External Mandate now commands the EIB to 'require' the presence of 'appropriate' local public consultation on social and environmental aspects of projects covered by the guarantee.[243]

The EIB's participation procedures at operational level are currently under review and are difficult to appraise. According to some analysts, they compare quite favourably with those of other MLIs,[244] but issues can nonetheless be identified in the current practice. First, a double standard is applied when projects do or do not require an EIA under EU law and EIB policies. If consultation standards under EIA rules are legally prescribed, those applied without an EIA remain at the level of generalities.[245] Also, the reference to EIAs and other EU legal requirements for out-of-EU projects may not be very operative as the pledge to apply such standards is not 'unequivocal' and remains subject to feasibility in regard of 'local conditions'.[246] A double standard may also exist between EU and non-EU projects when no EIA is required (which is the rule rather than the exception[247]): participation in EU projects follows EU standards while for out-of-EU projects national requirements may suffice.

Second, EIAs and the associated consultations, even when legally mandated, are the responsibility of the project promoter, and subject to conflicts of interest.[248] The EIB has issued staff guidelines for examining EIAs and weighing stakeholder concerns in appraising projects.[249] In practice, it is argued that the EIB seldom contradicts the conclusions of EIAs, and has insufficient expertise to address the environmental and social issues they contain.[250] In addition, the point raised above that the EIB publishes little or no information on projects prior to Board decisions curtails participation; many stakeholders will consequently have no opportunity to provide input in time. It is therefore not guaranteed that stakeholders' views and concerns will be taken into consideration in all EIB finance decisions. More generally, where an EIA is not required (and actually even when it is[251]), there is uncertainty about when and how to engage with the public. Also, the standard of review applicable to consultations carried out by project promoters is underspecified, and a clear method for computing

---

242 Statement, op. cit., para. 63, p. 20

243 External Mandate, op. cit., Art. 7(1).

244 Wright, op. cit., p. 37.

245 Though in such cases legal rules may still be applicable, e.g. deriving from the Aarhus Convention.

246 Wright, op. cit., p. 37.

247 Handbook, op. cit., p. 39: 'Not all projects require a full EIA in the sense defined by the EU Directive; indeed the need for a full EIA is the exception rather than the rule . . .'

248 Wilks, op. cit., p. 20.

249 Transparency Policy, op. cit., point 5.5, p. 19 and Handbook, op. cit., para. 101 and pp. 55–56.

250 Wilks, op. cit., p. 20. See, however, the recent creation of the ESO (above note 31).

251 Wright, op. cit., pp. 35–37, arguing that the promoter enjoys flexibility to determine the intensity and modalities of consultation, notably as these depend on feasibility with regard to local conditions.

their results into the project appraisal is lacking.[252] The Mid-Term Review confirms that, despite recent efforts, improvements can be made in engaging stakeholders and civil society systematically at project level. A proposed solution is to make more extensive use of the Union's delegations and the EIB's local offices.[253]

Finally, the particular question of the participation rights of indigenous peoples should be addressed for projects supported by the EIB. Indigenous peoples enjoy particular rights under international law. As such, they must express 'free, prior and informed consent' (FPIC) for decisions and projects affecting them. The participation threshold is high, and means readiness to negotiate, and recognition of indigenous peoples' *'right to reject* developments that do not gain community acceptance, based on informed choice'.[254] The FPIC standard is recognized in international instruments, namely the ILO Convention No. 169 on Indigenous and Tribal Peoples[255] and the UN Declaration on the Rights of Indigenous Peoples.[256] It was also acknowledged by influential consultative organs of the project finance world, such as the World Commission on Dams[257] and the Extractive Industries Review (EIR).[258] The FPIC standard has also been endorsed by the EU, e.g. in its development policies.[259] Still, MLIs seem to struggle with the concept, as the formulation 'free, prior and informed *consultation*' (FPICon) is widely used instead of 'consent'.[260] Even if the FPICon process must lead to 'broad community support', it is doubtful that this amounts to 'consent'.[261] The Inter-American Court of Human Rights interpreted FPIC as requiring genuine

---

252 One World Trust, 'Accountability Profile', op. cit., p. 1.
253 Mid-Term Review, op. cit., p. 16.
254 J. Cariño, 'Indigenous Peoples' Right to Free, Prior, Informed Consent: Reflections on Concepts and Practice', *Arizona Journal of International and Comparative Law* 22, 2005, 20, emphasis added.
255 ILO Convention No. 169 concerning Indigenous and Tribal Peoples in Independent Countries, done in Geneva on 27/6/1989, effective 5/9/1991. See particularly Arts 6(2) and 16(2).
256 UN General Assembly, 'United Nations Declaration on the Rights of Indigenous Peoples', Resolution 61/295, 13/9/2007, UN Doc. No. A/61/L.67 and Add.1.
257 World Commission on Dams, *Dams and Development – A New Framework for Decision-Making*, London, Earthscan, November 2000, p. 112. Online. Available HTTP <http://hqweb.unep.org/dams/WCD/report/WCD_DAMS%20report.pdf> (accessed 24 July 2012).
258 See Extractive Industries Review, 'Striking a Better Balance – Volume I: The World Bank Group and Extractive Industries', December 2003, p. 18. Online. Available HTTP <http://irispublic.worldbank.org/85257559006C22E9/All+Documents/85257559006C22E985256FF6006843AB/$File/volume1english.pdf> (accessed 24 July 2012).
259 See notably the European Consensus on Development, op. cit., para. 103.
260 See World Bank, 'Operational Manual', op. cit., Operational Policy 4.10: Indigenous people, July 2005.
261 See F. Mac Kay, 'The Draft World Bank Operational Policy 4.10 on Indigenous Peoples: Progress or More of the Same?', *Arizona Journal of International and Comparative Law* 22, 2005, 86–90.

consent, and not simply consultations,[262] leaving project deciders free to proceed irrespective of the opinion of indigenous peoples involved.

The EIB's Statement says that '[w]here the customary rights to land and resources of indigenous peoples are affected by a project, the Bank requires the promoter to prepare an acceptable Indigenous Peoples Development Plan. The plan must reflect the principles of the UN Declaration on the Rights of Indigenous Peoples, including free, prior and informed consent to any relocation.' It is still unclear how FPIC will be made operational in the future, as the EIB is still revising its guidance note on the 'Rights and Interests of Vulnerable Groups'.[263] The prior version of the guidance note provides that the ILO Convention No. 169 'provides the framework' for protecting indigenous peoples in relation to EIB projects, along with the EIR and other MLIs' policies. These multiple sources, however, do not entirely correspond on the question of FPIC versus FPICon. Moreover, the EIB Guidance Note on Involuntary Resettlement[264] does not require FPIC for resettling indigenous peoples, but to 'assess [the] willingness of the population to move' and the 'consultation processes'[265] and to 'assure that the rights of project affected people are respected and protected'.[266] The import of the EU and international FPIC standard in EIB policies is unclear. The current revision of the guidance note on vulnerable peoples represents an opportunity to clarify this point.

9.4.2.3 Recourses and remedies

Access to remedies for dissatisfied stakeholders is central in the accountability of a governing body. This designates the 'retrospective' side of the EIB's accountability, i.e. those mechanisms which are activated after there has been an alleged failure. Many mechanisms may seek to remedy harm, from hard ones (e.g. judicial process) to soft ones (e.g. mediation and dialogue). To some extent, the EIB is subject to accountability mechanisms of all sorts. Here we discuss the mechanisms which are open to the general public given the EIB's position as a public entity and as a result of its operations' human rights, environmental and social implications. This excludes mechanisms aimed at financially controlling the EIB;[267] at detecting and sanctioning fraud;[268] at overseeing the

---

262 Inter-American Court of Human Rights, *Case of the Saramaka People v Suriname*, Judgment on Preliminary Objections, Merits, Reparations, and Costs, Series C, No. 172, 28/11/2007, paras 134 and 137. Online. Available HTTP <http://www.corteidh.or.cr/docs/casos/articulos/seriec_172_ing.pdf> (accessed 24 July 2012).

263 Guidance Note 2, Handbook, op. cit., p. 111, characterizing indigenous peoples as 'vulnerable peoples'.

264 Guidance Note 1, ibid., p. 104.

265 Ibid., p. 105.

266 Ibid., p. 106.

267 See Audit Committee (above) and the Court of Auditors' mandate for EIB accounts (Art. 287 TFEU).

268 See OLAF's competence in fraud-related matters (Art. 325 TFEU and ECJ, Case C-15/00, op. cit.).

functioning of the EIB administration;[269] at settling disputes among EIB shareholders or between the EIB and other EU institutions, or contractual disputes between the EIB and its clients.[270] Many MLIs have been establishing redress mechanisms internally dealing with external stakeholder complaints.[271] The EIB did put such a mechanism in place, but we also review the significance of the ECJ's jurisdiction on EIB activities in terms of accountability toward the general public.

THE COMPLAINTS MECHANISM

Many MLIs, and in particular regional development banks, have for some time put internal mechanisms in place to allow stakeholders to voice concerns and obtain redress for harm caused by their operations.[272] Until 2008, the EIB relied on the European Ombudsman and on certain *ad hoc* loops leading to its higher level administration, but it is now equipped with a Complaints Mechanism. A 'Complaints Mechanism Division' was established as part of the 'independent Inspectorate General' (IG/CM).[273] It acts as the lower tier of the mechanism and hears complaints in the first instance. The European Ombudsman acts as a second recourse failing a satisfactory IG/CM decision. The IG/CM is competent for complaints on cases of 'maladministration'[274] by

269 The EIB has an internal and independent 'Operations Evaluations' unit (EV) which reviews the quality and results of the EIB group's activities, and suggests improvements of operational performance, accountability and transparency. See generally EIB, 'Operations Evaluation (EV) Terms of Reference', 28/11/2009. Online. Available HTTP <http://www.eib.org/attachments/thematic/ev_terms_of_reference_2009_en.pdf> (accessed 24 July 2012).
270 See Arts 271, 272 and 273 TFEU, and Art. 27 Statute.
271 See generally M. van Putten, *Policing the Banks – Accountability Mechanisms for the Financial Sector*, Montreal and Kingston: McGill-Queen's University Press, 2008.
272 See ibid. and Carrasco et al., op. cit.
273 The IG/CM used to be called the 'Complaints Office'. See EIB, 'EIB Complaints Mechanism – Operating Procedures', 4/2012, p. 3 (hereinafter the 'Operating Procedures'). Online Available HTTP <http://www.eib.org/attachments/strategies/complaints_mechanism_operating_procedures_en.pdf> (accessed 23 July 2012). The IG/CM has several functions: 1. Complaints Investigation Office (investigations/compliance reviews regarding registered complaints); 2. Mediation Function (mediation between, on one side, the Complainants/Requestors and, on the other side, the Bank's Management/Services and/or Project Promoter and/or national authorities); 3. Advisory Function (advice to senior management on broader and systemic issues related to policies, standards, procedures, guidelines, resources, and systems, on the basis of lessons learned from the complaints handling); 4. Monitoring Function (follow-up on further developments and implementation of proposed corrective actions and recommendations, accepted by the Management Committee). Its independence is 'ensured' by its having final responsibility over the admissibility, mediation and/or investigation to be performed for a particular complaint and the Conclusions Report. *Id.*, pp. 3–4.
274 Maladministration is defined as 'poor or failed administration. This occurs when the EIB Group fails to act in accordance with the applicable legislation and/or established policies, standards and procedures, fails to respect the principles of good administration

the EIB, but not for '[d]ecisions concerning the investment mandate of the EIB, its credit policy guidelines or the EIB's participation in financing operations'.[275] The Complaints Mechanism is primarily 'compliance-focused' as it will check that the EIB abided by applicable laws, rules, principles and standards in conducting its activities, and provide recommendations to the EIB management in that regard.[276] It also acts as a mediator between the complainant and the EIB by suggesting solutions for redress.[277] Whereas the IG/CM must hear out every party and aim for a consensual outcome, its conclusions are not binding on the EIB organs: their addressee, the Management Committee, may choose to apply them or not.[278]

Any person (whether or not an EU citizen) may file a complaint with the IG/CM against virtually any type of maladministration (either project-related or not),[279] without having to show an interest, or to identify the norm relied upon. This is liberal compared to other MLIs' practices.[280] Once the complaint is filed, the IG/CM checks its admissibility[281] and then performs an investigation and compliance review.[282] The EIB insists that stakeholder engagement must be

or violates human rights. Some examples . . . are: administrative irregularities, unfairness, discrimination, abuse of power, failure to reply, refusal of information, unnecessary delay. [It] may also relate to the environmental or social impacts of the EIB Group activities and to project cycle related policies and other applicable policies of the EIB.' See EIB, 'The EIB Complaints Mechanism – Principles, Terms of Reference and Rules of Procedure', 2/2/2010, updated 4/2012, p. 5 (hereinafter the 'Complaints Mechanism Policy'). Online. Available HTTP <http://www.eib.org/attachments/strategies/complaints_mechanism_policy_en.pdf/> (accessed 24 July 2012).

275 Ibid., p. 6.
276 Ibid., point 3.2. Relevant rules are EU Law, EIB policies, and Court of Justice-identified rules of good administration (see in this regard European Ombudsman, 'The European Code of Good Administrative Behaviour', September 2005. Online. Available HTTP <http://www.ombudsman.europa.eu/resources/code.faces> (accessed 24 July 2012). See EIB, 'Complaints Office Activity Report 2008', 2009, p. 3 (hereinafter the 'Activity Report'). Online. Available HTTP <http://www.eib.org/attachments/general/reports/complaints_office_annual_report_2008> (accessed 24 July 2012).
277 Complaints Mechanism Policy, op. cit., p. 6.
278 Ibid., point 7.16, p. 13, and Operating Procedures, point 2, p. 4.
279 Ibid., point 4.1, p. 12.
280 Activity Report, op. cit., pp. 10–11. See e.g. Art. 12 of the World Bank Inspection Panel's mandate, excluding standing for 'single individuals'. See IBRD and IDA, "The World Bank Inspection Panel", 22/9/1993, Resolution No. IBRD 93-10 and IDA 93-6. Online. Available HTTP <http://siteresources.worldbank.org/EXTINSPECTIONPANEL/Resources/ResolutionMarch2005.pdf> (accessed 24 July 2012), and IBRD and IDA, 'Review of the Resolution Establishing the Inspection Panel 1996 Clarification of Certain Aspects of the Resolution', 17/10/1996. Online. Available HTTP <http://siteresources.worldbank.org/EXTINSPECTIONPANEL/Resources/1996ReviewResolution.pdf> (accessed 24 July 2012).
281 For example, complaints must be filed within one year after the complainant has had knowledge of the fact complained about. See Complaints Mechanism Policy, op. cit., point 5.1, p. 12.
282 For which the IG/CM has access to 'any and all information necessary for the performance of its duties'. EIB staff must collaborate. See EIB, 'Operations Evaluations (EV) Terms of Reference', op. cit., p. 4, and Operational Procedures, point 4, pp. 5–6.

central in complaints procedures.[283] Next to punctual remedies, the IG/CM may suggest improvements to procedures and policies to the Management Committee, and follows up on them.[284] Dissatisfied complainants may file a confirmatory application or seize the European Ombudsman directly.[285] This 'standard procedure' before the IG/CM must not exceed 40 working days, with possible extensions for complex cases, or for consultations and dialogue in problem-solving.[286] An 'extended procedure' has also recently been set up specifically to handle complaints regarding the environmental and social impacts or the governance aspects of a project. The extended procedure may last up to 140 days and was developed in order to account for the complexity of such issues, and for the 'sensitivity of the relations involving project promoter, national authorities, civil society organisations and project affected people'.[287] Most notably, this procedure takes into account the 'project lifecycle', that is, the environmental, social and governance screening stages which a project must go through before receiving financing. If the project complained about is under appraisal at the time of the complaint, the concerns of the complainants will be communicated to the operational services, so as to be taken into consideration during the appraisal itself. If a complaint on a project is filed after the proposal for financing has been approved by the Management Committee, it will be addressed as such by the IG/CM, which may undertake an investigation/ compliance review, or engage in mediation with the consent of the parties. It should be noted that in conducting an investigation, the IG/CM may seek the advice of independent experts, or perform on-site verification visits.[288]

The proceedings and conclusions of the IG/CM are published only with the consent of the complainant.[289] To date, only one complaint has been documented on the EIB's website.[290] An annual report must also be published by the IG/CM.[291] In 2008, with the reform of the procedure, the number of complaints more than doubled,[292] seven of which related to the environmental and social impacts of financed projects.[293]

---

283 Complaints Mechanism Policy, op. cit., point 7.15, 9, p. 14.
284 Ibid., point 7.8–7.9, p. 13.
285 Ibid., point 11, p. 14.
286 Ibid., point 10, p. 14, and Operational Procedures, point 4.11, p. 9.
287 Operating Procedures, point 5.1, p. 10.
288 Ibid., pp. 10 ff.
289 Complaints Mechanism Policy, op. cit., point 13, p. 15.
290 See EIB, 'The EIB Complaints Mechanism – Reporting'. Online. Available HTTP <http://www.eib.org/about/cr/complaints/reporting/index.htm> (accessed 24 July 2012) and above.
291 Complaints Mechanism Policy, op. cit., point 13.4, p. 15, and Operating Procedures, point 8.4, p. 15. A report has to date only been published for 2008.
292 Activity Report, op. cit., p. 3
293 Ibid., p. 6. A parallel accountability mechanism for transparency and participation issues in environmental matters covered by the Aarhus Convention is its 'Compliance Committee'. See Art. 15 Aarhus Convention, op. cit., and UNECE, 'Background'. Online. Available HTTP <http://www.unece.org/env/pp/ccBackground.htm> (accessed 24 July 2012).

After exhaustion of the IG/CM procedure, the European Ombudsman acts as the higher tier of the Complaints Mechanism,[294] as the TFEU makes him competent to hear cases of maladministration by EU 'institutions, bodies, offices or agencies'.[295] The Ombudsman therefore provides an external and independent recourse.[296] We shall not describe here the mandate of, and procedures followed by, the Ombudsman,[297] but will point to one major deficiency of the competence of the Ombudsman with regard to the EIB's activities. Only EU citizens or 'any natural or legal person residing or having its registered office in a Member State' are normally entitled to complain to the Ombudsman.[298] This may exclude most complaints regarding projects carried out outside the EU, raising the most concern.[299] The EIB and the Ombudsman have signed a Memorandum of Understanding (MoU)[300] in which they agree that, when the only reason not to investigate is the fact that the complainant is not an EU citizen, the latter shall act *proprio motu*.[301] Potential applicants from outside the EU may, however, still be excluded for reasons such as cost or distance. The MoU is also not binding on the Ombudsman or the EIB, and states that the Ombudsman shall not second-guess EIB substantive policies (notably in regard of environmental, social or development issues), and shall strictly focus on compliance review and problem-solving,[302] contrary to the IG/CM, which can recommend policy changes.

Generally, the Complaints Mechanism is very soft and has no enforcement power on EIB organs. If no mutually agreeable solution can be found, it may be difficult to curb the EIB's or project promoters' decisions.[303] Finally, concern also exists regarding the capacity of the IG/CM and of the Ombudsman to carry out local fact-finding missions,[304] as well as about the accessibility of the Complaints Mechanism to the populations of developing countries, and their real capacity to make use of their right to complain.

294 Complaints Mechanism Policy, op. cit., point 4.3, p. 17.

295 Art. 228 TFEU.

296 Activity Report, op. cit., p. 10.

297 See Statute of the European Ombudsman, in Decision of the European Parliament of 9 March 1994 on the regulations and general conditions governing the performance of the Ombudsman's duties, *OJ* L 113/15, 4/5/1994, and amended by European Parliament Decisions of 14/3/2002 (*OJ* L 92/13, 9/4/2002) and 18/6/2008 (*OJ* L 189/25, 17/7/2008).

298 Arts 24 and 228 TFEU and Art. 22. of the Statute of the Ombudsman (op. cit.).

299 See generally Wilks, op. cit.

300 See Memorandum of Understanding between the European Ombudsman and the EIB concerning information on the Bank's policies, standards and procedures and procedures and the handling of complaints, including complaints from non-citizens and non-residents of the European Union, done in Luxembourg, 9/7/2008. Online. Available HTTP <http://www.eib.org/attachments/strategies/complaints_mou_eo_eib_en.pdf> (accessed 24 July 2012).

301 Art. 3 Statute of the Ombudsman (op. cit.) and Memorandum of Understanding, op. cit., p. 2.

302 Ibid., pp. 2–3.

303 Agreements with promoters, however, do happen. See Activity Report, op. cit., p. 5.

304 Mid-Term Review, op. cit., p. 25.

THE EUROPEAN COURT OF JUSTICE

The EIB is part of the EU order, while other MLIs are generally self-standing international organizations. In this regard, the ECJ could play an important role in the external accountability of the EIB. In this section we study the extent of the jurisdiction of the Court on EIB activities and its role in the EIB's external accountability. Judicial review is a fundamental tool to check the legality of an institution's acts, and therefore a strong rule of law guarantee.[305] Judicial review of EIB decisions could ensure, for instance, that an EIB decision to finance a project is in line with its mandate, or that it complies with EU law, in particular the human rights enshrined in the Charter of Fundamental Rights. Judicial review is generally absent from MLI accountability schemes, and this is criticized as a democratic deficit.[306]

Article 271 seems to establish a *lex specialis* regime in respect of the EIB:

> The Court of Justice of the European Union shall, within the limits hereinafter laid down, have jurisdiction in disputes concerning:
> [...]
>
> (b) measures adopted by the Board of Governors of the European Investment Bank. In this connection, any Member State, the Commission or the Board of Directors of the Bank may institute proceedings under the conditions laid down in Article 263;
> (c) measures adopted by the Board of Directors of the European Investment Bank. Proceedings against such measures may be instituted only by Member States or by the Commission, under the conditions laid down in Article 263, and solely on the grounds of non-compliance with the procedure provided for in Article 19 (2), (5), (6) and (7) of the Statute of the Bank . . .

This Article only provides for the review of decisions of the Board of Governors and of the Board of Directors (in limited cases), and states that only Member States and the Commission (and the Board of Directors for review of Board of Governors decisions) may institute proceedings, and not individuals affected by a decision of one of the Boards. And indeed the Court of First Instance (CFI) dismissed an action for annulment lodged by French citizens against a decision of the EIB Board of Directors to extend a loan to the city of Lyon for building a ring road around the city.[307] The CFI refused to apply its *Les Verts* reasoning against the Board of Directors' decision, because such an interpretation would

---

305 See ECJ, Case 294/83, *Les Verts v Parliament* [1986] ECR 1986, p. 01339, para. 23. On the role of the judicial system in upholding the rule of law in the EU, see M. L. Fernandez Esteban, *The Rule of Law in the European Constitution*, London: Kluwer Law International, 1999. The rule of law is referred to in the TEU, e.g. in the preamble, Art. 2 (values), and Art. 21 (external action).

306 See Head, 'For Richer or for Poorer', op. cit., pp. 268 and 299.

307 CFI, Case T-460/93, *Etienne Tête et al. v EIB*, [1993], ECR 1993, p. II-01257.

overstep the boundaries of Article 271(c) TFEU and was not warranted by the increased impact of EIB activities on citizens, contrary to that of the European Parliament in *Les Verts*. The CFI also reasoned further that it doubted the capacity of the claimants to demonstrate that the decision of the Board was of direct and individual concern to them, as it considered that the decision did not affect their legal situation.[308] The claim was therefore declared inadmissible.

On a later action for annulment lodged by the Commission against a decision of the Management Committee allegedly infringing OLAF's investigative powers, the Court gave a more flexible interpretation of Article 271, which does not cover Management Committee decisions. The Court ruled that the challenged decision was of the competence of the Board of Governors, and that it was reviewable under Article 271 (b), irrespective of the fact that the decision had been made by the Management Committee.[309] The Court justified its position by restating the requirement of the rule of law, which entails that 'the EIB is subject to judicial review by the Court, in particular as provided for in Article [271](b) EC'.[310]

And *in general*, could individuals affected by a decision of the EIB seek its annulment under the general regime of Article 263 TFEU, which now provides for the review of acts of 'bodies'? Indications can be found in a recent judgment of the General Court, based on the EC Treaty, on an action for annulment and damages lodged by a Greek IT company whose bid to install software at the EIB was not retained by the Management Committee following a tender procedure.[311] The EIB did not challenge the admissibility of the action, but the Court still ruled that Article 271 TFEU (ex-237 EC) is limited in scope and 'supplementary' to the general regime of Article 263 TFEU. The Union being based on the rule of law, '[a]cts formally adopted within the EIB by bodies other than those referred to in [Articles 271 (b) and (c) TFEU] . . . must . . . be amenable to judicial review if they are final and produce legally binding effects *vis-à-vis* third parties.'[312] And indeed Article 263 TFEU now allows review of 'the legality of acts of bodies . . . of the Union intended to produce legal effects *vis-à-vis* third parties'. Yet, individual actions for annulment against EIB *finance decisions* seem barred in several ways.

First, finance decisions are made by the Board of Directors, whose decisions are covered by Article 271(c), which as *lex specialis* excludes individual

---

308 Ibid., paras 17–18, and 22–23.
309 ECJ, Case C-15/00, op. cit., para. 73.
310 Ibid., para. 75.
311 General Court, Case T-461/08, op. cit.
312 Ibid., para. 50. Analogically, concerning another EU body, the European Agency for Reconstruction, the CFI drew from Les Verts the general principle that 'any act of a Community body intended to produce legal effects *vis-à-vis* third parties must be open to judicial review'. See Court of First Instance, Case T-411/06, *Sogelma v EAR*, [2008], ECR 2008, p. II-02771, para. 37.

applications under Article 263(4).[313] Should the Commission or a Member State, as guarantors of the public interest, wish to take the matter into their own hands and challenge a finance decision of the Board of Directors to protect harmed stakeholders, they could only do so based on the violation of Article 19(2) and (5)–(7) Statute, i.e. the provisions establishing a system of semi-binding opinions from Member States, the Commission and the Management Committee.[314] Second, the Management Committee's decisions in financing matters are limited to 'preparing' decisions of the Board of Directors, and are also not reviewable under Article 263 TFEU, as they are not 'intended to produce legal effects *vis-à-vis* third parties'.[315] Third, the Court draws a distinction between EIB decisions partaking of 'Community administration' in the framework of its 'current business', which the Management Committee is in charge of, such as procurement decisions, and the operations of the EIB in financial domains and on financial markets, such as finance decisions. The ECJ had already judged that the EIB's status as a bank under the Treaties required that its independence, autonomy and reputation be preserved in financial activities, and used that reasoning to determine whether the applicability to the EIB of certain EU legislations was 'compatible' with its independence and autonomy.[316] The General Court now seems to use the compatibility criterion to determine its jurisdiction, by implying that review would be possible for acts of 'administration', but not for 'finance' decisions, thereby perhaps introducing an exception to the general principle that acts of bodies intended to produce legal effects vis-à-vis third parties are open to judicial review.[317] Fourth, should decisions of the Board of Directors or the Management Committee in financial matters ever be considered reviewable, the strict individual standing conditions of Article 263(4) TFEU may prove difficult to meet for external stakeholders affected by projects concerned by such decisions.[318] In conclusion, these four

313 General Court, Case T-461/08, op. cit., para. 47, and K. Lasok and T. Millett, *Judicial Control in the EU: Procedures and Principles*, Richmond: Richmond Law & Tax, p. 146.
314 See above note 56.
315 The CFI ruled in Case T-460/93 (op. cit., para. 18) that the EIB is mainly a credit institution and that it 'therefore does not adopt decisions having legal effects *vis-à-vis* third parties who are not in receipt of EIB loans or guarantees'. The General Court in Case T-461/08 (op. cit., para. 48) is not of that view and argues that the EIB, notably the Management Committee, is capable of taking such decisions.
316 ECJ, Case 85/86, op. cit., para. 28, and ECJ, Case C-15/00, op. cit., para. 101 ff.
317 General Court, Case T-461/08, op. cit., paras 51–52.
318 In this regard, a 'Communication' to the Aarhus Convention Compliance Committee alleged that this limited access of individuals and NGOs to annulment actions against general acts of the Institutions breached the EU's access to justice obligation under the Aarhus Convention. The Committee found that, should the ECJ's case law on the matter be maintained, the EU would *fail to comply* with Art. 9, paras 3 and 4 of the Aarhus Convention, unless the lack of standing is compensated by appropriate administrative review mechanisms. See the Findings and Recommendations of the Aarhus Compliance Committee with Regard to Communication ACCC/C/2008/32 (Part I) Concerning Compliance by the European Community with its Obligations under the Convention, as

limits arguably render it nearly impossible for individual stakeholders of EIB projects to seek annulment of finance decisions.

The action for damages under Article 268 TFEU is on the contrary open to individuals, and the Court found it, in light of the rule of law and effective judicial protection principles, to be a sufficient substitute for the individual action for annulment against acts of the EIB.[319] In one case,[320] the EIB had signed a loan contract with Mali for the laying of an electrical supply line. The EIB was, however, not convinced by the ability of Mali's contractor to successfully perform the work and conditioned its disbursements to the choice of a more suitable one. Mali hired a new contractor and the dismissed contractor filed an action for damages in order to recoup the losses caused by the EIB's interferences in Mali's selection of a contractor.

The Court declared the action admissible, notably on the following grounds:

> It would be contrary to the intention of the authors of the Treaty if, when it acts through a Community body established by the Treaty and authorized to act in its name and on its behalf,[321] the Community could escape the consequences of the provisions of Article [268] and the second paragraph of Article [340] of the Treaty, the intention of which is to reserve for the Court's jurisdiction cases involving the non-contractual liability of the Community as a whole towards third parties. . . . The term 'institution' employed in the second paragraph of Article [340] of the Treaty must therefore not be understood as referring only to the institutions of the Community listed in Article [13 TEU] but as also covering, with regard to the system of non-contractual liability established by the Treaty, Community bodies such as the Bank.[322]

The action for damages also leads the Court *de facto* to review the legality of the acts of the EIB. However, the threshold to engage the non-contractual liability of a Community body is high and requires a rule conferring rights on individuals, an illegal conduct, a damage, and a causal link between the two.[323] The General

adopted by the Compliance Committee at its 32nd Meeting, Geneva, 11-14/4/2011, p. 22, para. 94. Online. Available HTTP <http://live.unece.org/env/pp/compliance/Compliancecommittee/32TableEC.html> (accessed 24 July 2012).

319 CFI, Case T-460/93, op. cit., para. 21.

320 ECJ, Case C-370/89, op. cit.

321 The EIB was acting in pursuance of the Sixth European Development Fund. See ibid., para. 5.

322 ECJ, Case C-370/89, op. cit., paras 15–16.

323 See ECJ, Joined Cases C-46/93 and C-48/93, *Brasserie du Pêcheur SA v Bundesrepublik Deutschland and The Queen v Secretary of State for Transport, ex parte: Factortame Ltd and others*, [1996], ECR 1996, p. I-01029, para. 51: 'the rule of law infringed must be intended to confer rights on individuals; the breach must be sufficiently serious; and there must be a direct causal link between the breach of the obligation resting on the State and the damage sustained by the injured parties.'

Court in the case above also seems to imply that actions for damages are inadmissible to the EIB's finance activities, so as to protect its autonomy and independence on financial markets.[324] Moreover, the condition pertaining to illegal conduct is difficult to meet, as the illegality must be 'sufficiently serious'. Seriousness is appraised in regard of the margin of appreciation that the body enjoys in making its decision.[325] A wide margin of discretion entails a marginal review by the Court.[326] The EIB clearly enjoys a wide margin of appreciation in its finance decisions due to the independence required on financial markets,[327] and to the numerous and interrelated factors to be considered in making a finance decision.[328] Also, EIB decisions can be deemed illegal against the Treaties, the Charter, its Statute, an international instrument, or applicable EU legislation, but it is dubious whether illegality could result from the EIB's disregard for its own internal policies. The ECJ has already judged that EU institutions were somehow bound by their internal acts not having legal value, like the Commission guidelines on the application of competition rules. Acting, without justification, contrary to those self-imposed limits could indeed run afoul of, for example, equal treatment or citizens' legitimate expectations.[329] But would such an interpretation be applicable, *mutatis mutandis*, to the Statement of Environmental and Social Principles and Standards, the Corporate Social Responsibility Statement, or the Environmental and Social Practices Handbook?

For completeness, a preliminary ruling under Article 267 TFEU could probably also be filed on questions of EU law interpretation regarding EIB activities, for instance if a contractual dispute were pending before an EU national court. One author doubts whether an exception of illegality could be raised against EIB decisions under the same article, as Article 271 limits

---

324 General Court, Case T-461/08, op. cit., para. 57.
325 ECJ, Cases C-46/93 and C-48/93, op. cit., para. 55: the 'sufficiently serious' threshold is met when 'the Member State or the Community institution concerned manifestly and gravely disregarded the limits on its discretion'. See ECJ, Case C-352/98, *Bergaderm et al. v Commission* [2000], ECR 2000, p. I-5291, para. 40ff.
326 P. Gilliaux, 'L'intensité du contrôle de la légalité par les juridictions communautaires', *Journal de Droit européen*, 2009, 44.
327 General Court, Case T-461/08, op. cit., para. 57.
328 Such a margin of appreciation is, however, not unlimited, and the Court has already judged that the EIB had overstepped it, notably in Case No. C-15/00 (op. cit.), para. 186.
329 See ECJ, Joined cases C-189/02 P, C-202/02 P, C-205/02 P to C-208/02 P and C-213/02 P, *Dansk Rørindustri et al.*, [2005], ECR 2005, p. I-05425, para. 211: 'In adopting such rules of conduct and announcing by publishing them that they will henceforth apply to the cases to which they relate, the institution in question imposes a limit on the exercise of its discretion and cannot depart from those rules under pain of being found, where appropriate, to be in breach of the general principles of law, such as equal treatment or the protection of legitimate expectations. It cannot therefore be precluded that, on certain conditions and depending on their content, such rules of conduct, which are of general application, may produce legal effects.'

standing for actions for annulment.[330] True, admitting the exception would lessen the EIB's autonomy and independence on financial markets. Yet a blanket exclusion is debatable as the exception of illegality is not subject to this limitation in Article 267 indent 1 (b), which includes acts of bodies. Moreover, the *raison d'être* of the exception of illegality is to serve as a safety net for claimants not meeting the standing conditions of Article 263 TFEU.[331]

In conclusion, the EIB has repeatedly been characterized by the ECJ as a body which, despite its autonomous status, was bound to comply with applicable EU law. It is unfortunate that the consequences of such an interpretation were not drawn completely concerning the justiciability of EIB finance decisions. In light of the EIB's reach and impact on local living conditions, the ECJ is the most reliable and effective accountability mechanism.[332] It is regrettable that the drafters of the Treaties chose not to extend the jurisdiction of the ECJ to individual requests to annul finance decisions. Unlike other MLIs, the EIB is part of a strong legal order but this is not sufficiently operationalized in terms of accountability. At present the EIB's retrospective accountability toward external stakeholders chiefly relies on bland 'maladministration' grounds and mechanisms just like all other MLIs. One can argue that the banking activities of the EIB and their involving third parties prevent them from being suspended to review actions coming from the public. However, such actions are justified by the public nature and impact of EIB decisions. Also, the argument that ECJ jurisdiction would affect (and possibly scare away) third-party investors and financial actors is misplaced. Recourses by dismissed tenderers are open against procurement decisions even though they may affect third parties (selected tenderers). The acts of the European Central Bank (ECB) regarding monetary policy and price stability are also subject to Article 263 TFEU even though they influence financial markets, and despite the ECB's necessary independence in its activities.[333] Such remedies are, however, warranted under the rule of law.

9.5 Concluding remarks

This chapter has reviewed the EIB's external accountability principles and practices with regard to human rights, social and environmental issues. It has revealed that the EIB, despite being the world's major development lender and an EU body, has largely imitated the practices of other MLIs. With regard to substantive accountability principles, EIB-financed projects are bound by EU law when located within the EU. However, the status of EU law is unclear when

330 Dunnett, op. cit., p. 755.
331 M. Wathelet and J. Wildemeersch, *Contentieux européen*, Brussels: Larcier, 2010, pp. 238–240.
332 See Head, 'Law and Policy in International Financial Institutions', op. cit., p. 220.
333 On the ECB's independence, see ECJ, Case C-11/00, *Commission v ECB* [2003], ECR 2003, p. I-07147, paras 130–135.

the EIB operates in the framework of its External Mandate. The role of EU law in setting a 'benchmark' for human rights, social and environmental practices for operations outside the EU is unclear and insufficient. Also, the voluntary standards which the EIB commits to follow are vague and incomplete, and hardly form a basis for accountability.

Procedurally, the transparency and participation principles applied by the EIB are fairly progressive. However, they still display a number of shortcomings as regards the involvement of stakeholders in the appraisal of projects and in the making of concrete finance decisions. One may also regret that the EIB largely escapes the jurisdiction of the ECJ, as judicial review would be the most effective remedy available to external stakeholders. The Complaints Mechanism/ European Ombudsman construction is in this regard too weak an alternative to judicial review.

In conclusion, more advantage should be taken of the EIB's being part of the EU legal order so as to guarantee effective accountability to external stakeholders. Most notably, EU law should play a more pervasive role in setting the normative framework of the EIB's operations, notably outside the EU. Likewise, the EU judicial system should be used, where possible, as an independent, reliable and credible accountability mechanism in case harm is caused by the EIB to its external stakeholders.

Appendix A

List of countries and years covered in the dataset

Country	*Years*
Albania*	2002–2007
Bulgaria	1999–2009
Croatia	2000–2009
Czech Republic	1999–2001
Estonia	1998–2008
Hungary	1998–2008
Latvia	1997–2008
Lithuania**	1995–2008
Macedonia, FYR	2003–2007
Poland	1996–2008
Romania	2003–2008
Ukraine	2001–2009

* Year 2006 is missing
** Years 1999, 2001 and 2003 are missing

Appendix B

Details of the industries included in the economic sectors.

Agriculture and Fisheries:	agriculture, hunting, forestry and fishing
Banking:	financial intermediation, real estate, renting and business activities
Manufacturing:	manufacturing
Mining:	mining and quarrying
Services:	hotels, restaurants, transport, storage, communication, wholesale, retail trade, reparations of motor vehicles and similar
Utilities:	electricity, gas and water supply

Index

Supported Export Credits 202–8;
Principles and Guidelines to Promote
Sustainable Lending Practices in the
Provision of Official Export Credits to
Low-Income Countries 206;
Recommendation on Bribery and
Officially supported Export Credit 206;
Recommendation on Common
Approaches on the Environment and
Officially Supported Export Credits 205;
see also Multilateral Agreement on
Investment (MAI)
Overseas Association Decision 297
Overseas Private Investment Corporation
(OPIC) 225–6

participation 160, 183–7, 294, 317, 323–8
performance requirements 241, 281–4, 291
Philippines 260
policy space (host State) 3, 26, 31,
  36, 47–69
political stability 160
poverty: 2, 7–8, 25, 71, 91, 100–4,
  206, 239
Poverty Reduction Strategy Papers 206
Principles for Responsible Contracts to
  favour the integration of the
  management of human rights risks
  in the negotiations between
  governments and investors 12–13, 163
progressive realization of economic and
  social rights 168–70
Public interest 36, 48, 66; welfare
  objectives 58
public powers doctrine *see* expropriation

reciprocity 39, 67
Regional Integration Agreements 33;
  negotiation framework 233, 237, 255,
  265, 268
regulatory sovereignty *see* policy space (host
  State)
regulatory chill 6, 217
Republic of Korea 239, 260, 271, 289
resource curse 158
responsibility, international: aid and
  assistance 221–2; Articles on the
  Responsibility of States for
  Internationally Wrongful Acts 219, 221;
  attribution of conduct to States 192–3,
  195, 208–9, 219–21; elements of
  governmental authority 193, 195,
  219–21; due diligence 216, 219, 221,
  227–8; foreseeability of harm 216, 225;

intent 216, 221–2; international
  obligations: breach 208, 213, 221–2;
  extraterritorial 192, 216, 218, 222;
  standard of care 219, 227; territorial
  210, 216, 218; remoteness of harm
  228; strict liability 216
right to development 4, 168–70, 172
right to food 164
right to health 165
right to information 170–4, 317–22
right to self-determination 29,
  165–8
right to water 164, 177–8
risk: actuarial analysis 197;
  commercial 194, 196, 224;
  political 189, 194, 196–7, 224;
  uncertainty 195, 197, 197n23,
  216
Root, Elihu 27
Ruggie, John 13n34, 163; *see also* United
  Nations Guiding Principles on
  Business and Human Rights
Russia 272

Singapore 248, 249; Singapore
  issues 271, 276
Small and Medium Enterprises
  (SMEs) 297, 300, 315
Special Rapporteur on the right to food
  163; *see also* Guiding Principles on
  Human Rights Impact Assessments
  of Trade and Investment Agreements
Special Representative of the United
  Nations Secretary-General on the
  issue of human rights and transnational
  corporations and other business
  enterprises 162, 173; *see also*
  Guiding Principles on Business and
  Human Rights sole effect doctrine
  see expropriation
South–South investment agreements 237
sovereignty 31–2, 47–8, 50, 55, 64–8
spillovers (from FDI) 2, 85–100, 103–5,
  109, 139, 185–7
standard of treatment (international) 25,
  27–8, 31, 33–36, 51, 53, 63, 67–8;
  customary minimum standard of
  treatment of aliens 26, 51, 63;
  rejection of 32, investor protection
  47, 49–50, 67; protection of aliens'
  property 48
Suriname 166
sustainable development 234, 239, 258,
  262, 280, 290, 291